W9-BTR-570

THE WILLIAMS-SONOMA BAKING BOOK

GENERAL EDITOR
CHUCK WILLIAMS

Contents

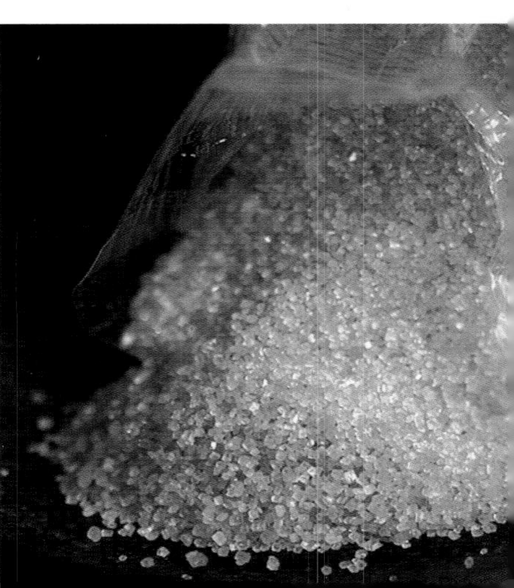

THE JOYS OF BAKING

Not so long ago, it was difficult to find the ingredients and tools for making crusty baguettes, dark chocolate cakes with molten interiors, or light, airy meringues. Nowadays, you can find nearly anything you need, from half a dozen different bread flours to chocolates of every taste and texture to high-speed machines that magically transform egg whites into puffy clouds. This inspired collection, packed with both everyday and special-occasion recipes, takes full advantage of the wealth of ingredients and tools available to home bakers today.

Over the years, customers and friends have often said to me, "I can cook, but I can't bake." I understand why baking is sometimes intimidating. It requires a level of precision that cooking doesn't. When you are making a stew, you can add a little more of this or a little less of that and still have a good dish. But baking is not nearly as forgiving. Too much liquid and your cake won't rise. Not enough liquid and your pie pastry will crack. The key is to start with simple recipes that rely on basic techniques, call for only a handful of ingredients, and don't take much time. As you make them, you will master new skills that will give you the confidence to try your hand at more complicated recipes.

A few simple rules will smooth the path as you bake your way through this book. First, use only the best ingredients. Even such pantry staples as flour yield better results when they have not sat on the shelf too long. Check the expiration date on all of your baking staples and purchase new supplies, if necessary. Buy fresh unsalted butter often, and take the time to find farm-fresh eggs, which will add a wonderful richness to many recipes, especially soufflés and custards. And when making fruit desserts, shop for the finest local seasonal produce possible.

Second, take the time to master the recipes—the batters and doughs, the fillings and frostings—that make up the building blocks of countless cakes, pies, and other baked desserts. They are all in the section titled Basic Recipes (pages 373–79), and once you have learned how to make Flaky Pastry Dough (page 373), Basic Tart Dough (page 373), Cookie Crumb Crust (page 374), Yellow Sponge Cake (page 374), Vanilla Buttercream (page 376), and more, you will be ready to build dozens of delicious desserts.

Third, use your eyes when you are baking. The recipes in this book usually give both visual and time guidelines for the various steps. But what you see often tells you more than a clock does. For example, many of the cookie recipes call for creaming butter until it is "fluffy and pale yellow." How long that step will take will depend on everything from the temperature of your kitchen and of your butter to the speed of your mixer. In other words, your eyes, not the minute hand, will tell you when the butter is ready. See the step-by-step text and photographs in the Baking Tips & Techniques section (pages 381–89) for more examples of how to judge several key baking tasks.

Finally, always be well organized. Take the time to ready everything, ingredients and equipment, before you begin to make a recipe. Start by reading the recipe all the way through so you know what you need and what steps are involved. Then, assemble your ingredients, measuring them carefully and making sure they are at the temperature the recipe specifies. Professional bakers often weigh ingredients for accuracy, which you can do as well because all of the recipes include equivalent weights. Check your equipment, too. Using the wrong-sized cake pan can produce a disappointing result. Next, read up on any key techniques that are new to you. When you are finally ready to begin baking, read the recipe through one more time to make sure everything you need is at hand.

The recipes in this book have been selected for all levels of bakers and all types of occasions. Quick and easy recipes, such as Scotch Shortbread (page 34) and Espresso Pound Cake (page 204), can be served at any time of the day. Seasonal fruit pies and tarts, like Ginger-Apricot Pie (page 222) and Strawberry Tart with Orange Cream (page 246), take advantage of the spring and summer markets. Recipes such as Fresh Coconut Cake with Fluffy Coconut Frosting (page 174) and Baguettes (page 284) are more challenging, but are always worth the effort. You'll find a big chapter devoted to cookies, brownies, and bars, among them such crowd-pleasers as Double Chocolate Chip Cookies (page 16), Lemon Curd Bars (page 31), Linzer Cookies (page 12), and Blondies (page 48). Finally, some savory baked items are included here, such as Leek & Goat Cheese Tart (page 370) and Cheese Soufflé (page 364)—perfect for brunch, lunch, or even dinner.

This extensive collection of baking recipes is guaranteed to inspire you to bake more often. And once you begin, you will quickly discover that there is no better gift to family and friends than a steady stream of homemade cookies, muffins, cakes, pies, and breads.

COOKIES & BARS

Linzer Cookies

MAKES ABOUT 1 DOZEN COOKIES

SIFTING

Sifting is a way of aerating ingredients to make light, evenly textured cookies. It is also a way of combining dry ingredients to evenly distribute a leavener such as baking powder. If you don't have a sifter, simply pass the ingredients through a fine-mesh sieve. (For small amounts of flour, whisking produces the same effect.) Always follow a recipe exactly when it comes to sifting. Unless the recipe says otherwise, sift the flour after measuring, since this will make a significant difference in the amount of flour used.

1 cup (5 oz/155 g) hazelnuts (filberts) or slivered almonds, toasted and skinned (page 60)

½ cup (4 oz/125 g) unsalted butter, at room temperature

½ cup (4 oz/125 g) granulated sugar

1 large egg yolk

1 tsp finely grated orange or lemon zest

¾ tsp pure vanilla extract

¼ tsp pure almond extract

1 cup (5 oz/155 g) all-purpose (plain) flour

½ tsp ground cinnamon

¼ tsp salt

About ¼ cup (2½ oz/75 g) seedless raspberry jam

Confectioners' (icing) sugar for dusting

IN A FOOD PROCESSOR, finely grind the toasted hazelnuts using short pulses (page 58). Set aside. In a large bowl, using an electric mixer on high speed, cream the butter until fluffy and pale yellow. Add the granulated sugar and continue beating until combined. Add the egg yolk, orange zest, vanilla, and almond extract and beat on low speed until well blended.

Sift the flour, cinnamon, and salt together into another bowl. Add the ground hazelnuts and stir to blend. Add the flour-nut mixture to the butter mixture and mix on low speed or stir with a wooden spoon until blended. The dough should be soft. Turn the dough out of the bowl, divide into 4 equal portions, and wrap each in plastic wrap. Refrigerate until chilled, about 1 hour.

Preheat the oven to 350°F (180°C). Lightly grease 2 baking sheets or line them with parchment (baking) paper. Remove 1 portion of the dough at a time from the refrigerator, place between 2 sheets of waxed paper, and roll out ¼ inch (6 mm) thick. Using a cookie cutter about 2½ inches (6 cm) in diameter, cut out the cookies. Cut a hole in the center of half of the cookies with a 1¼-inch (3-cm) cutter. Repeat to roll out the remaining dough portions, then reroll the dough scraps as needed to make 24 cutouts in all, cutting holes in half of them. If the dough becomes sticky, wrap it and chill in the freezer for about 10 minutes before rolling out.

Using a thin spatula, carefully transfer the cookies to the prepared pans. Bake until firm to the touch, about 12 minutes. Transfer the pans to wire racks. Loosen the cookies from the pans with the spatula, but leave in place on the pans until cooled.

To assemble, spread the solid cookies with about 1 teaspoon of the raspberry jam to within about ¼ inch (6 mm) of the edges. Using a fine-mesh sieve, dust the cutout cookies with confectioners' sugar. Top the solid cookies with the cutout cookies.

STORING COOKIES

Most cookies will keep well in a tightly sealed container for 3–5 days. First, be sure to let the cookies cool completely on wire racks. Then, place the cookies in an airtight container and separate with squares of waxed paper; this will keep the cookies fresh and crisp. Seal the container tightly and store at room temperature. Or, wrap the container in plastic wrap and freeze for up to 1 month.

Chocolate Chip Cookies

MAKES ABOUT 4 DOZEN COOKIES

1⅓ cups (7 oz/220 g) all-purpose (plain) flour

½ tsp baking powder

½ tsp baking soda (bicarbonate of soda)

½ tsp salt

½ cup (4 oz/125 g) unsalted butter, at room temperature

½ cup (4 oz/125 g) granulated sugar

½ cup (3½ oz/105 g) firmly packed light brown sugar

1 large egg

1 tsp pure vanilla extract

1 cup (6 oz/185 g) semisweet (plain) chocolate chips

1 cup (4 oz/125 g) walnuts, toasted (page 53), then coarsely chopped (optional)

PREHEAT THE OVEN TO 350°F (180°C). Have ready 2 ungreased baking sheets. Sift the flour, baking powder, baking soda, and salt onto a sheet of waxed paper; set aside.

In a large bowl, using an electric mixer on high speed, cream the butter until fluffy and pale yellow. Add the granulated sugar and brown sugar and continue beating until the mixture is no longer gritty when rubbed between your finger and thumb. Add the egg and vanilla and beat on low speed until blended, occasionally stopping the mixer and scraping down the sides of the bowl with a silicone spatula as needed.

Add the flour mixture to the butter mixture and mix on low speed or stir with a wooden spoon just until blended. Add the chocolate chips and the walnuts, if using, mixing or stirring just until blended.

With dampened hands, shape the dough into 1-inch (2.5-cm) balls and place on the baking sheets, spacing the cookies about 2 inches (5 cm) apart. Bake the cookies until golden brown around the edges, about 12 minutes. Let the cookies cool briefly on the pans on wire racks before transferring them to the racks to cool completely.

Black-and-White Cookies

MAKES ABOUT 5 DOZEN COOKIES

2 cups (10 oz/315 g) all-purpose (plain) flour

½ cup (4 oz/125 g) sugar

Pinch of salt

1 cup (8 oz/250 g) cold unsalted butter, cut into small pieces

1 large whole egg plus 1 large egg yolk

½ tsp pure vanilla extract

3 Tbsp unsweetened Dutch-process cocoa powder

LIGHTLY GREASE 2 BAKING SHEETS or line with parchment (baking) paper.

In a food processor, combine the flour, sugar, and salt. Add the butter pieces in 2 additions, pulsing after each addition, until the mixture has the consistency of coarse crumbs. Add the egg yolk and vanilla and pulse until the dough holds together. Divide the dough in half. Transfer one-half to a lightly floured work surface and knead in the cocoa until incorporated.

Lightly dust the work surface and a rolling pin with flour. Roll out each dough half into a 3-by-9-inch (7.5-by-23-cm) rectangle, ½–¾ inch (12 mm–2 cm) thick; trim the edges to even out. Place each rectangle on a large baking sheet and cover with plastic wrap. Refrigerate until well chilled, about 30 minutes. Meanwhile, in a small bowl, beat the whole egg until blended.

Preheat the oven to 350°F (180°C). Remove the 2 dough blocks from the refrigerator and assemble the checkerboard cookies (right).

Remove the dough blocks from the refrigerator, unwrap, and cut each crosswise into slices ¼ inch (6 mm) thick. Place the slices 1½ inches (4 cm) apart on the prepared pans and bake until firm when pressed, about 15 minutes. Let the cookies cool on the pans for about 2 minutes before transferring them to wire racks to cool completely.

CHECKERBOARD PATTERN

Using a sharp knife, cut each rectangle into 4 strips about ¾ inches (2 cm) wide (you should have 4 strips of each color). Arrange 2 chocolate strips and 2 plain strips in a checkerboard pattern, brushing the beaten egg between the strips and gently pressing together. Repeat with the remaining dough. Wrap in plastic and use a knife to square off the edges of each block. Refrigerate until well chilled, about 30 minutes.

Double Chocolate Chip Cookies

MAKES ABOUT 2 DOZEN COOKIES

VEGETABLE SHORTENING

These cookies, like many baked goods, call for using both butter and vegetable shortening. When cookie dough is made with butter alone, the cookies start to spread on the pan in the hot oven fairly quickly, because butter melts at a lower temperature than shortening. Cookies made with a combination of butter and shortening spread more slowly, resulting in a cookie with a thicker, puffier profile. Look for trans fat–free shortening, now widely available in supermarkets.

1 oz (30 g) unsweetened chocolate, coarsely chopped

1 cup (4½ oz/140 g) all-purpose (plain) flour

1½ tsp baking powder

¼ tsp salt

6 Tbsp (3 oz/90 g) unsalted butter, at room temperature

2 Tbsp vegetable shortening

⅔ cup (5⅓ oz/165 g) firmly packed light brown sugar

¼ cup (2 oz/60 g) granulated sugar

1 large egg, at room temperature

1 tsp pure vanilla extract

1 cup (6 oz/185 g) bittersweet or semisweet (plain) chocolate chips

½ cup (2 oz/60 g) coarsely chopped pecans or walnuts (optional)

PREHEAT THE OVEN TO 350°F (180°C) and line 2 baking sheets with parchment (baking) paper.

Put the chopped chocolate in the top of a double boiler and melt, stirring occasionally, over barely simmering water (see page 173). Set aside to cool.

In a bowl, whisk together the flour, baking powder, and salt until blended.

In another bowl, using an electric mixer on medium speed or a wooden spoon, beat together the butter, shortening, brown sugar, and granulated sugar until well blended and fluffy. Beat in the melted chocolate. Add the egg and vanilla and mix until blended. Add the flour mixture and stir until just blended. Add the chocolate chips and the nuts, if using, and continue stirring until just blended.

Drop the dough by heaping tablespoonfuls onto the prepared baking sheets, spacing the cookies about 1½ inches (4 cm) apart. Bake the cookies, 1 sheet at a time, until they are puffed but still look moist on top, about 15 minutes. Let the cookies cool briefly on the pans on wire racks before transferring them to the racks to cool completely.

Peanut Butter Cookies

MAKES ABOUT 3 DOZEN COOKIES

PIPING WITH CHOCOLATE

To give these cookies a decorative touch, pipe melted chocolate into the indentations made by the fork tines: Fit a pastry bag with a very small plain tip. Fold down the edge of the bag, creating a cuff, and fill the bag no more than halfway full with the chocolate. Unfold the top and twist it to squeeze the chocolate toward the tip. Holding the bag at a 45-degree angle with one hand, and leaving a small gap between the tip and the cookie, squeeze the bag to release the chocolate in a line.

½ cup (4 oz/125 g) unsalted butter, melted

½ cup (3½ oz/105 g) firmly packed light brown sugar

½ cup (4 oz/125 g) granulated sugar

1 cup (10 oz/315 g) creamy peanut butter

1 large egg

1 tsp pure vanilla extract

1⅓ cups (7 oz/220 g) all-purpose (plain) flour

½ tsp baking powder

½ tsp baking soda (bicarbonate of soda)

½ tsp salt

3 oz (90 g) semisweet (plain) chocolate, melted (optional; page 173)

IN A LARGE BOWL, using an electric mixture on medium speed or a wooden spoon, beat together the melted butter, brown sugar, granulated sugar, peanut butter, egg, and vanilla until well blended.

Sift the flour, baking powder, baking soda, and salt together onto a sheet of waxed paper. Add the flour mixture to the butter mixture and mix on low speed or stir with the wooden spoon just until combined. Cover and refrigerate until firm, about 2 hours.

Preheat the oven to 350°F (180°C). Generously grease 2 baking sheets. With dampened hands, shape the dough into 1-inch (2.5 cm) balls and place on the prepared baking sheets, spacing the cookies about 2 inches (5 cm) apart. Using the tines of a fork dipped in flour, lightly press on each dough ball to flatten slightly and make a pattern of parallel indentations.

Bake the cookies until the bottoms are golden brown, 12–15 minutes. Let the cookies cool briefly on the pans. Using a wide, flexible metal spatula, transfer the warm cookies to the racks to cool completely. If desired, use a pastry bag fitted with a narrow tip to pipe melted chocolate into the grooves of each cookie (left).

Chocolate–Peanut Butter Sandwiches

MAKES ABOUT 3 DOZEN COOKIES

FOR THE COOKIES:

¾ cup (6 oz/185 g) unsalted butter, at room temperature

¾ cup (6 oz/185 g) granulated sugar

2 large eggs

1 tsp pure vanilla extract

½ cup (2½ oz/75 g) all-purpose (plain) flour

½ cup (1½ oz/45 g) unsweetened Dutch-process cocoa powder

¼ tsp baking powder

¼ tsp baking soda (bicarbonate of soda)

⅛ tsp salt

FOR THE PEANUT BUTTER FILLING:

4 Tbsp (2 oz/60 g) unsalted butter, at room temperature

½ cup (2 oz/60 g) confectioners' (icing) sugar

½ cup (5 oz/155 g) creamy peanut butter

½ tsp pure vanilla extract

IN A LARGE BOWL, using an electric mixer on high speed or a wooden spoon, cream the butter until fluffy and pale yellow. Add the granulated sugar and continue beating until the mixture is no longer gritty when rubbed between your finger and thumb. Add the eggs and vanilla and stir or beat on low speed until blended.

Sift the flour, cocoa, baking powder, baking soda, and salt together onto a sheet of waxed paper. Add to the butter mixture and beat or stir just until blended. Cover and refrigerate until firm, about 2 hours.

Preheat the oven to 350°F (180°C). Lightly grease 2 baking sheets.

With dampened hands, shape the dough into ¾-inch (2-cm) balls and place on the prepared baking sheets, spacing the cookies about 2 inches (5 cm) apart. Using a spatula or the bottom of a glass that has been dusted with cocoa to prevent sticking, press down on each dough ball to flatten slightly. Bake the cookies until firm to the touch, 10–12 minutes. Transfer the cookies to wire racks to cool completely.

Meanwhile, make the peanut butter filling. In a large bowl, using a wooden spoon, combine the butter, confectioners' sugar, peanut butter, and vanilla. Beat with the spoon until blended and smooth. Cover and refrigerate until the cookies are cool.

Using a small offset spatula, spread the flat side of half the cookies with 1½ tsp of the peanut butter filling. Top each with a second cookie, flat side down. Press lightly to make a cookie sandwich.

STORAGE TIP: Store these cookies in an airtight container in a cool place, or refrigerate in warm weather.

PEANUT BUTTER

Made by grinding dry-roasted peanuts to a paste, peanut butter is a favorite food of young and old alike. It is available in two styles, creamy, or smooth, and chunky, that is, with finely chopped nuts mixed in for texture. Natural peanut butters are made without the additives that ease spreadability. They have a somewhat grainy consistency and a layer of oil on top that must be stirred in before using.

ICEBOX COOKIES

Also known as refrigerator cookies, icebox cookies are made by forming dough into a log or rectangular block and chilling it thoroughly. You can also press different types of dough together—vanilla and chocolate, peanut butter and chocolate—to make patterned cookies (see Black-and-White Cookies, page 15). Cookies are then sliced off the log or block and baked. When slicing the dough, give the block or log a quarter turn after every half dozen slices to keep the cookies perfectly square or round.

Pistachio-Spice Cookies

MAKES ABOUT 4 DOZEN COOKIES

1 cup (8 oz/250 g) unsalted butter, at room temperature

1¼ cups (9 oz/280 g) firmly packed light brown sugar

2 Tbsp dark molasses

2 large egg yolks

½ tsp pure almond extract

3 cups (15 oz/470 g) all-purpose (plain) flour

2 tsp ground cinnamon

1 tsp ground cardamom

1 tsp baking soda (bicarbonate of soda)

¼ tsp salt

1 cup (4 oz/125 g) finely chopped unsalted pistachios

IN A LARGE BOWL, using an electric mixer on high speed, cream the butter until fluffy and pale yellow. Add the brown sugar and continue beating until the mixture is no longer gritty when rubbed between your finger and thumb. Add the molasses, egg yolks, and almond extract and beat on medium speed or stir with a wooden spoon just until blended.

Sift the flour, cinnamon, cardamom, baking soda, and salt together onto a sheet of waxed paper. Add the flour mixture to the butter mixture in 4 additions, mixing on low speed or stirring until blended after each addition. Mix or stir in the pistachios until evenly distributed. The dough will appear dry and crumbly.

Turn the dough out onto a lightly floured work surface and press it into a round, smooth disk. Divide the dough in half, and roll each half into a log about 6 inches (15 cm) long. Flatten and square off each log, making a rectangular shape about 6 inches (15 cm) long, 3 inches (7.5 cm) wide, and 1½ inches (4 cm) thick. Wrap each rectangle in plastic wrap and refrigerate for at least 2 hours or preferably for 24 hours.

When ready to bake, preheat the oven to 325°F (165°C). Lightly grease 2 baking sheets or line them with parchment (baking) paper.

Using a sharp, thin knife, cut the chilled dough into slices ⅛ inch (3 mm) thick. Place the slices about 1 inch (2.5 cm) apart on the prepared sheets. Bake the cookies until the edges are golden, 10–12 minutes. Let the cookies cool on the pans on wire racks for about 2 minutes before transferring them to the racks to cool completely.

Bourbon Balls

MAKES ABOUT 4½ DOZEN COOKIES

1 box (12 oz/375 g) vanilla wafers, broken into pieces

6 oz (185 g) semisweet (plain) chocolate, finely chopped

½ cup (3½ oz/105 g) firmly packed light brown sugar

¼ cup (2½ fl oz/75 ml) light corn syrup

⅓ cup (3 fl oz/80 ml) bourbon

Pinch of salt

2 cups (8 oz/250 g) pecans, lightly toasted (page 53), then finely chopped

IN A FOOD PROCESSOR, working in batches, finely grind the vanilla wafer pieces using short pulses. Transfer to a large bowl and set aside. Alternatively, place the wafer pieces in a heavy-duty plastic bag and crush them with a rolling pin.

Put the chocolate in the top of a double boiler and melt, stirring occasionally, over barely simmering water (see page 173). Remove the melted chocolate from the heat and transfer to a bowl. Add the brown sugar, corn syrup, bourbon, and salt to the bowl and stir until completely blended. Stir in the crushed vanilla wafers and half of the chopped pecans.

Spread the remaining chopped pecans on a plate. With dampened hands, shape the dough into 1-inch (2.5-cm) balls. Roll the balls in the nuts to coat evenly.

Arrange the balls in layers, separated by waxed paper, in a tightly covered container. Refrigerate for 24 hours before serving, to blend the flavors.

MAKE-AHEAD TIP: These cookies will keep, refrigerated, for up to 2 weeks. Or, store in a tightly sealed container wrapped plastic wrap and freeze for up to 1 month. Bring to room temperature before serving.

PECANS

These nuts have smooth, brown, oval shells that break easily, making them good candidates for buying whole and shelling yourself. Raw, unshelled nuts have a longer shelf life than shelled nuts, and keep well for 6 months to 1 year if stored in a dark, dry place. Since nuts contain high amounts of oil, they will eventually turn rancid, so check them for freshness before adding to recipes.

Anise Biscotti

MAKES ABOUT 4 DOZEN BISCOTTI

½ cup (4 oz/125 g) unsalted butter, at room temperature

½ cup (4 oz/125 g) granulated sugar

2 large eggs

2 tsp pure vanilla extract

½ tsp pure anise extract

1 Tbsp aniseed, crushed

1¾ cups (9 oz/280 g) all-purpose (plain) flour

½ tsp baking powder

¼ tsp salt

1 egg white, lightly beaten

Coarse sugar crystals for sprinkling

PREHEAT THE OVEN TO 350°F (180°C). Lightly grease and flour 1 large baking sheet, or line it with parchment (baking) paper or a silicone baking mat (page 57), and have another ungreased baking sheet on hand.

In a large bowl, using an electric mixer on high speed, cream the butter until fluffy and pale yellow. Add the granulated sugar and continue beating until the mixture is no longer gritty when rubbed between your finger and thumb. Add the eggs one at a time, beating well on low speed after each addition. Beat in the vanilla, anise extract, and crushed aniseed on low speed until blended.

Sift the flour, baking powder, and salt together onto a sheet of waxed paper. Gradually add the flour mixture to the egg mixture and mix on low speed or stir with a wooden spoon just until blended. The dough should be very soft.

Turn the dough out onto a generously floured work surface and divide in half. With well-floured hands, transfer one-half onto the greased baking sheet and shape into a log about 12 inches (30 cm) long and 1½ inches (4 cm) in diameter. Place on one side of the sheet. Repeat with the remaining dough, leaving at least 4 inches (10 cm) between the logs. (They will spread as they bake.) Lightly brush the top of each log with some of the egg white and sprinkle with the coarse sugar crystals.

Bake the logs until the edges are golden, 25–30 minutes. Transfer the pan to a wire rack and let cool for 10 minutes. Using a serrated knife, cut the logs, still on the pan, on the diagonal into slices ½ inch (12 mm) thick. Carefully turn the slices on their sides and return them to the oven. When you run out of room on one baking sheet, start transferring slices to the other sheet. Bake until the edges are golden, about 10 minutes longer. Let cool completely on the pans on wire racks. Store in an airtight container.

ANISEED

The seed of the anise plant, a member of the parsley family, aniseed is used whole or ground and has a sweet aroma and taste reminiscent of licorice. It is a popular addition to many European baked goods, as these typical Italian biscotti demonstrate. Aniseed is also one of the flavorings used in anisette, a popular European licorice-flavored liqueur.

Double-Ginger Snaps

MAKES ABOUT 4 DOZEN COOKIES

2½ cups (12½ oz/390 g) all-purpose (plain) flour

1½ tsp ground ginger

1 tsp baking soda (bicarbonate of soda)

½ tsp ground cinnamon

¼ tsp ground cloves

¼ tsp salt

⅔ cup (5 fl oz/160 ml) canola oil

1 cup (7 oz/220 g) firmly packed light brown sugar

⅓ cup (3½ oz/105 g) dark molasses

1 large whole egg, lightly beaten, plus 1 large egg white

¾ cup (4½ oz/140 g) chopped homemade candied (crystallized) ginger (page 322), or purchased

½ cup (4 oz/125 g) coarse sugar crystals (far left)

PREHEAT THE OVEN TO 325°F (165°C). Lightly grease 2 baking sheets or line them with parchment (baking) paper.

Sift the flour, ground ginger, baking soda, cinnamon, cloves, and salt together onto a sheet of waxed paper.

In a large bowl, using a wooden spoon, stir together the oil, brown sugar, and molasses until well blended. Add the whole egg and beat until blended. Stir in the flour mixture and crystallized ginger.

Lightly beat the egg white in a small bowl. Spread the sugar crystals in a shallow bowl. With dampened hands, shape the dough into 1-inch (2.5-cm) balls. Brush each ball lightly with egg white and roll in the sugar to coat lightly. Place the cookies about 1 inch (2.5 cm) apart on the prepared pans.

Bake the cookies until the tops are set and crackled, 15–18 minutes. Let the cookies cool on the pans on wire racks for about 5 minutes before transferring them to the racks to cool completely. The cookies will firm as they cool.

COARSE SUGAR

Also called sanding sugar, this decorative sugar is appreciated for its large, pretty granules. In this recipe, dough balls are rolled in the coarse crystals giving the finished cookies a pleasant sweet, crunchy exterior. Coarse sugar can be found in a variety of colors at specialty food stores and kitchen stores.

Brown Sugar Tuiles

MAKES ABOUT 20 COOKIES

2 large egg whites

½ cup (3½ oz/105 g) firmly packed light brown sugar

1 tsp pure vanilla extract

Pinch of salt

6 Tbsp (3 oz/90 g) unsalted butter, melted and cooled

½ cup (2½ oz/75 g) all-purpose (plain) flour

½ cup (2 oz/60 g) sliced almonds or finely chopped pistachios (optional)

PREHEAT THE OVEN TO 350°F (180°C). Line a baking sheet with parchment (baking) paper.

In a large bowl, whisk together the egg whites, brown sugar, vanilla, and salt until smooth. Add the butter and flour and stir until blended.

Using 1 Tbsp of batter for each cookie and making no more than 5 cookies at a time, spread 4-inch (10-cm) circles on the baking sheet with an icing spatula or small offset spatula. Sprinkle each cookie with about 1 tsp of the nuts, if using.

Bake the cookies until the edges are browned and centers are golden, 6–8 minutes. Remove the baking sheet from the oven. Working quickly while the cookies are hot, lift them from the baking sheet with a wide spatula. Drape the cookies over a rolling pin and let cool for about 1 minute. Carefully transfer them to a wire rack and let cool completely. Form and bake the remaining cookies in batches.

SERVING TIP: For an elegant finale, serve the cookies with a scoop of vanilla ice cream.

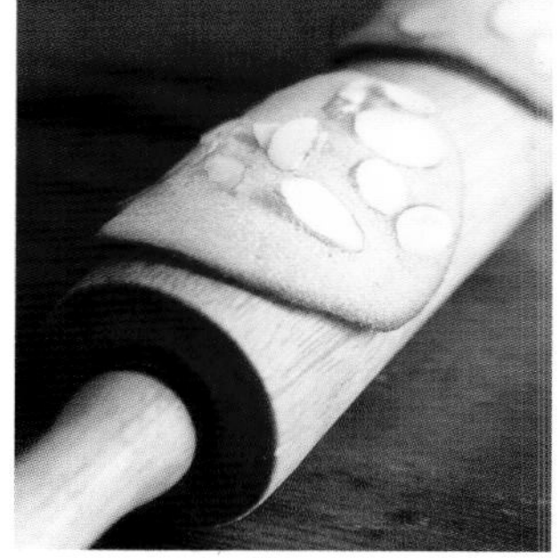

ABOUT TUILES

Tuile means "tile" in French, and these delicate cookies are named for the curved terra-cotta tiles traditionally found on roofs in the Mediterranean. They are made by spreading dollops of batter into large, thin, even circles on a baking sheet. Always bake tuiles in small batches, and be ready to shape them as soon as they come out of the oven: Using a flexible metal spatula, lift each hot cookie from the pan and drape it over a rolling pin or a similar object. As soon as the cookies are set, after no more than 1 minute, carefully transfer them to a wire rack to cool.

Neapolitan Cookies

MAKES ABOUT 6 DOZEN COOKIES

UNSALTED BUTTER

Good-quality unsalted butter is always fresher and more flavorful than salted butter. Do not be misled by the term *sweet cream butter;* all butter is made from sweet, not sour, cream. Therefore, a sweet-cream butter may be salted. Whipped butter has air whipped into it and should not be used in baking recipes. European-style butter generally has a higher fat content. It is perfect for spreading on warmed bread or for adding to sauces or buttercreams, but may throw off a recipe; avoid substituting it in cake and pastry recipes.

1 cup (8 oz/250 g) unsalted butter, at room temperature

1¼ cups (10 oz/315 g) sugar

1 large egg

1 tsp pure vanilla extract

¼ tsp salt

2¼ cups (11½ oz/360 g) all-purpose (plain) flour

1¼ tsp baking powder

1 oz (30 g) unsweetened chocolate, chopped, melted, and slightly cooled (page 173)

¼ cup (1 oz/30 g) finely chopped pecans

1 or 2 drops red food coloring

¼ tsp freshly grated nutmeg

IN A LARGE BOWL, using an electric mixer on high speed, cream the butter until fluffy and pale yellow. Add the sugar and continue beating until the mixture is no longer gritty when rubbed between your finger and thumb. Add the egg, vanilla, and salt and beat on low speed until well blended. Sift the flour and baking powder together onto a sheet of waxed paper and gradually beat or stir into the butter mixture just until blended.

Divide the dough evenly among 3 bowls. Knead the chocolate and pecans into the first bowl, the food coloring into the second bowl, and the nutmeg into the third bowl.

Line a 9-by-5-inch (23-by-13-cm) loaf pan with a sheet of waxed paper, overlapping the long sides by about 3 inches (7.5 cm). Scrape the nutmeg batter into the pan and, with a small offset spatula, press to the edges in an even layer. Smooth out the dough with your fingertips. Drop the pink-tinted batter by teaspoonfuls onto the nutmeg layer and press into an even layer. Smooth with your fingertips. Repeat with the chocolate batter. Fold the waxed paper over the top and press to smooth and compress the layers. Refrigerate until firm, at least 24 hours or up to 2 days.

Preheat the oven to 350°F (180°C). Lightly butter 2 baking sheets or line them with parchment (baking) paper. Use the waxed paper to lift the dough out of the pan. Invert onto a wooden board and remove the paper. Using a long, thin knife, cut the dough in half lengthwise. Cut crosswise into slices ¼ inch (6 mm) thick to make striped cookies.

Transfer the slices to the prepared sheets, placing the cookies at least 1½ inches (4 cm) apart. Bake the cookies until set and pale gold on the bottom, about 15 minutes. Let the cookies cool on the pans on wire racks for a few minutes before transferring them to the racks to cool completely.

Brandy Snaps

MAKES ABOUT 4 DOZEN COOKIES

½ cup (5½ oz/170 g) light molasses
½ cup (4 oz/125 g) unsalted butter
1¼ cups (4 oz/125 g) sifted cake (soft-wheat) flour
⅔ cup (5 oz/155 g) sugar
1 tsp ground cinnamon
¼ tsp salt
2 Tbsp brandy

PREHEAT THE OVEN TO 350°F (180°C). Generously grease 2 baking sheets or line with parchment (baking) paper. Have ready one or more slender rolling pins or wooden dowels ¾ inch (2 cm) in diameter.

In a small saucepan, bring the molasses to a boil over low heat. Add the butter and stir to melt. Remove from the heat.

Sift the sifted flour, sugar, cinnamon, and salt together onto a sheet of waxed paper. Stir the flour mixture into the butter mixture with a wooden spoon until blended. Stir in the brandy. The batter should be thick and syrupy.

Drop the batter by heaping teaspoonfuls onto the prepared pans, spacing the cookies about 3 inches (7.5 cm) apart and forming only 6 cookies. (The cookies must be baked in small batches, because, once baked, they must be shaped quickly before they cool and become brittle.)

Bake the cookies until they spread out and the surface is bubbly, 5–7 minutes. Let cool on the pan on a wire rack for just 1 minute, then, working quickly, use a thin, flexible metal spatula to remove 1 cookie at a time and wrap it around the rolling pin or dowel, placing the flat side of the cookie against the dowel, to make a hollow tube. Let the cookie set until it holds this shape. Use several dowels to shape as many cookies at one time as possible. If the cookies become too cool to shape easily, return them to the oven for a few moments; they will soften from the heat.

While the next batch bakes, slip the set cookies from the dowels to a wire rack. Let all the cookies cool to room temperature, then fill if desired (left) and serve.

MAKE-AHEAD TIP: These cookies can be stored for several days in an airtight container, then filled just before serving.

CREAM FILLING

If you are feeling indulgent, fill these cylindrical cookies with brandy–whipped cream filling. Chill 2 cups (16 fl oz/500 ml) heavy (double) cream, then stir in 2 Tbsp confectioners' (icing) sugar and 1 Tbsp brandy. Beat in a chilled, deep bowl with a whisk or an electric mixer just until soft peaks form. Do not overbeat, or the cream will turn into butter. Once whipped, the cream will hold for 30 minutes or so, covered, in the refrigerator. Use a pastry bag fitted with a large, plain tip to fill the cookies. Arrange on a platter and serve right away.

Brownies

MAKES 9 LARGE BROWNIES

½ cup (4 oz/125 g) unsalted butter, cut into 4 pieces

3 oz (90 g) unsweetened chocolate, finely chopped

1 cup (8 oz/250 g) sugar

Pinch of salt

2 large eggs, at room temperature

1 tsp pure vanilla extract

¾ cup (3 oz/90 g) cake (soft-wheat) flour, sifted

PREHEAT THE OVEN TO 350°F (180°C). Lightly grease an 8-inch (20-cm) square glass baking dish or metal pan.

In a saucepan over low heat, combine the butter and chopped chocolate. Heat, stirring often, until melted, about 4 minutes. Remove from the heat and, using a wooden spoon, stir in the sugar and salt.

Add the eggs and vanilla and stir until well blended. Sprinkle the sifted flour over the mixture and stir just until blended.

Pour the batter into the prepared dish and spread evenly, smoothing the top. Bake the brownies until a cake tester inserted into the center comes out almost completely clean, about 30 minutes, or 5 minutes longer if using a metal pan. Do not overbake.

Transfer the dish to a wire rack to cool completely before cutting the brownies into 2½-inch (6-cm) squares.

RECIPE VARIATION: For an even more decadent treat, stir ¾ cup (4½ oz/140 g) semisweet (plain) chocolate chips, peanut butter chips, or white chocolate chips into the brownie mixture after the flour is incorporated.

ABOUT CHOCOLATE

The chocolate-making process begins with cocoa beans that are fermented, roasted, shelled, and crushed into bits that are then ground and compressed to become chocolate liquor. Unsweetened chocolate is pure chocolate liquor with no sugar added. With more sugar added, the chocolate liquor becomes either semisweet or sweet chocolate. The addition of milk solids results in milk chocolate.

Lemon Curd Bars

MAKES 1 DOZEN BARS

FOR THE CRUST:

1 cup (4½ oz/140 g) all-purpose (plain) flour

⅓ cup (2⅓ oz/70 g) granulated sugar

½ tsp salt

⅛ tsp ground cinnamon

½ cup (4 oz/125 g) cold unsalted butter, cut into ½-inch (12-mm) pieces

FOR THE FILLING:

¾ cup (5¼ oz/160 g) granulated sugar

2 Tbsps all-purpose (plain) flour

Pinch of salt

1 tsp finely grated lemon zest (optional)

3 large eggs, at room temperature

½ cup (4 fl oz/125 ml) fresh lemon juice

3 Tbsp heavy (double) cream

Confectioners' (icing) sugar for dusting (optional)

TO MAKE THE CRUST, preheat the oven to 350°F (180°C). Lightly grease an 8-inch (20-cm) square baking dish, preferably heatproof glass (see right).

In a food processor, combine the flour, granulated sugar, salt, and cinnamon. Process briefly to blend. Add the butter pieces and pulse until the dough forms moist crumbs and sticks together when pinched, about 1 minute. There should be no trace of dryness. Press the dough into the bottom and 1 inch (2.5 cm) up the sides of the prepared baking dish, lightly flouring your fingertips if necessary to prevent them from sticking. Bake the crust until pale golden, 20–22 minutes. Let the crust cool completely on a wire rack. Reduce the oven temperature to 325°F (165°C).

To make the filling, whisk together the granulated sugar, flour, salt, and lemon zest, if using. Add the eggs, lemon juice, and cream and whisk until just blended. Carefully pour the mixture over the baked crust.

Bake until the filling is set but still jiggles slightly when the dish is gently shaken, about 20 minutes, or longer if using a metal pan. Let cool on the rack for about 30 minutes. Run the tip of a small knife along the inside of the dish to loosen the crust from the sides, then let cool completely.

Cut into 12 small rectangles and carefully remove from the dish with a spatula. Using a fine-mesh sieve, dust the rectangles with confectioners' sugar just before serving.

ABOUT COOKWARE

Acidic ingredients, such as citrus juice, tomatoes, vinegar, wine, and many vegetables, will react with cookware made from certain metals, including aluminum or cast iron. Although the reaction is harmless, it may turn a mixture gray or leave behind a metallic aftertaste. The same reaction occurs when eggs are cooked in aluminum or cast-iron pans. For these reasons, recipes that include ingredients such as lemon curd or pastry cream call for the use of nonaluminum pans. Stainless-steel and enamel-lined pans are excellent choices for cooking. Glass or enamel-lined baking dishes are good choices for baked dishes that use acidic ingredients.

PLUMPING DRIED FRUITS

Plumping raisins and other dried fruits softens them for eating and, if plumped in a spirit such as brandy or bourbon, adds flavor, too. Fruits are also sometimes plumped to make incorporating them into a batter easier, or, if they have become too hard, to regain their texture. the most common way to plump fruits is to immerse them in hot or warm water until they are rehydrated, and then drain them. When a spirit is used, its amount is usually specified, and then any remaining liquid is added to the batter as well.

Lizzies

MAKES ABOUT 5 DOZEN COOKIES

2½ cups (15 oz/470 g) raisins

½ cup (4 fl oz/125 ml) brandy

2 cups (8 oz/250 g) pecan halves

1 cup (4 oz/125 g) whole unblanched almonds

1 cup (4 oz/125 g) Brazil nuts

4 Tbsp (2 oz/60 g) unsalted butter, at room temperature

½ cup (3½ oz/105 g) firmly packed light brown sugar

2 large eggs

1½ cups (7½ oz/235 g) all-purpose (plain) flour

1½ tsp baking soda (bicarbonate of soda)

1½ tsp ground cinnamon

½ tsp ground nutmeg

½ tsp ground cloves

¼ tsp salt

3½ cups (1¼ lb/625 g) mixed dried fruits, snipped into ½-inch (12-mm) pieces

1 cup (6 oz/185 g) red candied cherries, halved

Candied Citrus Zest (page 378), diced

Confectioners' (icing) sugar for dusting

IN A BOWL, combine the raisins and brandy and stir to blend. Cover and let plump for 1 hour. Toast the pecans, almonds, and Brazil nuts (page 53). When cool, chop coarsely and set aside.

Preheat the oven to 325°F (165°C). Lightly grease 2 baking sheets or line them with parchment (baking) paper.

In a large bowl, using an electric mixer on high speed, cream the butter until fluffy and pale yellow. Add the brown sugar and continue beating until the mixture is no longer gritty when rubbed between your finger and thumb. Add the eggs one at a time, beating well on low speed after each addition.

Sift the flour, baking soda, cinnamon, nutmeg, cloves, and salt together onto a sheet of waxed paper. Combine the nuts and all of the dried fruits, the cherries, and candied orange zest in a large bowl. Add about ½ cup (2½ oz/75 g) of the flour mixture and toss to coat all of the fruit and nuts evenly.

Add the remaining flour mixture to the butter mixture and mix on low speed or stir with a wooden spoon just until blended. Add the raisins and brandy and the fruit mixture and stir until blended.

Drop the batter by mounded teaspoonfuls onto the prepared pans, spacing the cookies about 2 inches (5 cm) apart. Bake the cookies until set, about 15 minutes. Carefully transfer the cookies to wire racks to cool completely.

Using a fine-mesh sieve, dust the cookies with confectioners' sugar before serving.

NOTE: Lizzies are traditionally made only with candied fruit, but this version uses raisins and other dried fruits, such as apricots, prunes, pears, and figs, along with the typical candied orange zest.

Coconut Macadamia Triangles

MAKES 2 DOZEN COOKIES

1 cup (5 oz/155 g) plus 2 Tbsp all-purpose (plain) flour

¾ cup (6 oz/185 g) firmly packed light brown sugar, plus 1 Tbsp

¾ tsp salt

5 Tbsp (2½ oz/75 g) cold unsalted butter, cut into small pieces

2 Tbsp light corn syrup

1 tsp pure vanilla extract

1 large egg

1 cup (5 oz/155 g) unsalted macadamia nuts, lightly toasted (page 53) and coarsely chopped

½ cup (2 oz/60 g) shredded sweetened dried coconut

PREHEAT THE OVEN TO 375°F (190°C). Line the bottom and sides of a 9-inch (23-cm) square pan with aluminum foil and lightly grease the foil.

In a food processor, combine the 1 cup flour, the 1 Tbsp brown sugar, and ½ tsp of the salt. Process briefly to blend. With the machine running, add the butter a few pieces at a time until small crumbs form. Turn out into the prepared pan. Press the mixture into the pan in an even layer. Bake until the edges are golden, about 10 minutes.

Meanwhile, in a bowl, combine the 2 Tbsp flour, the ¾ cup brown sugar, the corn syrup, vanilla, egg, and the remaining ¼ tsp salt. Beat with a wooden spoon until thoroughly blended. Stir in the nuts and coconut until blended.

Spread the coconut topping over the warm baked bottom crust. Return to the oven and bake until the topping is lightly browned and the edges pull away from the pan sides, 15–20 minutes. Let cool completely in the pan on a wire rack. Use the foil to lift the cookie from the pan.

Cut the cookie into twelve 3-by-2¼-inch (7.5-by-5.5-cm) rectangles. Cut each rectangle in half on the diagonal to make triangles. Dip in chocolate, if desired (right).

DIPPING IN CHOCOLATE

Dipping cookies in chocolate adds an elegant touch to these treats. To achieve this look, melt 3 oz (90 g) semisweet (plain) chocolate in the top of a double boiler (see page 173). After cutting the cookies into triangles, dip 1 corner of each triangle in the melted chocolate and let cool on a sheet of waxed paper.

Scotch Shortbread

MAKES 27 BARS

CREAMING BUTTER

A first step in most cookie recipes, creaming aerates the butter, resulting in tender cookies. Cream the butter with an electric mixer or wooden spoon until it expands and lightens in color, and becomes soft and smooth, 3–4 minutes by mixer or longer by hand. Add the sugar and beat until the mixture is smooth when rubbed between your forefinger and thumb. Scrape down the sides of the bowl at least once during creaming.

1 cup (8 oz/250 g) unsalted butter, at room temperature

¼ cup (1 oz/30 g) confectioners' (icing) sugar

¼ cup (2 oz/60 g) granulated sugar, plus 1 Tbsp for sprinkling

2 tsp pure vanilla extract

1½ cups (7½ oz/235 g) all-purpose (plain) flour

¼ tsp salt

PREHEAT THE OVEN TO 300°F (150°C). Have ready an ungreased 9-inch (23-cm) square baking pan.

In a large bowl, using an electric mixer on high speed, cream the butter until fluffy and pale yellow. Add the confectioners' sugar and the ¼ cup granulated sugar and continue beating until the mixture is no longer gritty when rubbed between your finger and thumb. Beat in the vanilla.

Sift the flour and salt together onto a sheet of waxed paper. Gradually add the flour mixture to the butter mixture and mix on low speed or stir with a wooden spoon just until blended.

Using floured fingertips, press the dough evenly into the pan. Sprinkle evenly with the 1 Tbsp granulated sugar.

Bake the shortbread until the edges are golden, about 1 hour. Remove the pan from the oven and immediately use a thin, sharp knife to cut the shortbread into 3-by-1-inch (7.5 cm-by-2.5 cm) strips. Use a toothpick or the tines of a fork to decorate the shortbread with a pattern of dots. Let the strips cool in the pan on a wire rack for 30 minutes before transferring them to the rack to cool completely.

Sugar Cookies

MAKES ABOUT 3 DOZEN COOKIES

1¼ cups (12 oz/375 g) unsalted butter, at room temperature

¾ cup (6 oz/185 g) granulated sugar

1 large egg yolk

2 tsp pure vanilla extract

2 cups (10 oz/315 g) all-purpose (plain) flour

¼ tsp salt

Sugar for sprinkling, such as granulated, decorating, turbinado, maple, or confectioners' (icing)

IN A LARGE BOWL, using an electric mixer on high speed, cream the butter until fluffy and pale yellow. Add the granulated sugar in 3 additions, beating on low speed for 2 minutes after each addition. Add the egg yolk and vanilla and continue beating until well blended.

Sift the flour and salt together onto a sheet of waxed paper. Add the flour mixture to the butter mixture and mix on low speed or stir with a wooden spoon until blended.

Scrape the dough out onto a work surface and divide into 4 equal portions. Shape into disks, wrap in plastic wrap, and refrigerate for at least 2 hours or up to overnight.

Preheat the oven to 350°F (180°C). Lightly grease 2 baking sheets or line them with parchment (baking) paper.

Remove the dough disks from the refrigerator and let stand at room temperature for about 15 minutes. Working with 1 disk at a time, roll out the dough between 2 sheets of waxed paper to a thickness of ⅛–¼ inch (3–6 mm). Using cookie cutters, cut into circles or other shapes. Repeat with the remaining dough portions, then gather up the scraps and reroll them. If the scraps of dough have become sticky, refrigerate them for 10 minutes before rerolling. Try not to roll the same piece of dough more than twice.

Using an offset spatula, transfer the cookies to the prepared pans. Sprinkle with sugar. (If using maple or confectioners' sugar, bake the cookies, then sprinkle with sugar while still warm.) If using an intricately shaped cutter, refrigerate the cutout cookies for 15–30 minutes before baking.

Bake the cookies until they are lightly golden on the bottom, 10–12 minutes. Let the cookies cool briefly on the pans on wire racks before transferring them to the racks to cool completely.

SUGAR COOKIE VARIATIONS

For crisp sugar cookies with a smooth, dense chocolate taste, reduce the amount of flour in this recipe to 1¾ cups (9 oz/280 g) and add ½ cup (1½ oz/45 g) unsweetened Dutch-process cocoa powder. Sprinkle with granulated sugar or coarse sugar crystals, or decorate them with light-colored frosting, sprinkles, or shiny dragées. Or, after baking and cooling, dust the cookies with sifted confectioners' (icing) sugar (see page 46). For a subtle citrus flavor, substitute 1 tsp pure lemon extract in place of the vanilla.

Almond Crisps Drizzled with Chocolate

MAKES ABOUT 6 DOZEN COOKIES

SHINY CHOCOLATE DRIZZLE

One extra step makes the chocolate drizzled over these cookies stay shiny and fresh-looking after it cools. To achieve this look, add the vegetable shortening to the top of the double boiler with the chopped chocolate and melt, stirring until smooth and blended. The vegetable shortening will also prevent the glaze from cracking.

FOR THE ALMOND CRISPS:

½ cup (4 oz/125 g) unsalted butter, at room temperature

1 cup (7 oz/220 g) firmly packed light brown sugar

1 large egg

1 tsp pure vanilla extract

¾ cup (4 oz/125 g) all-purpose (plain) flour

1 tsp baking powder

½ tsp salt

½ cup (2 oz/60 g) finely chopped almonds

FOR THE CHOCOLATE GLAZE:

6 oz (185 g) semisweet (plain) chocolate, chopped

1 tsp solid vegetable shortening (optional; left)

IN A LARGE BOWL, using an electric mixer on high speed, cream the butter until it is fluffy and pale yellow. Add the brown sugar and continue to beat on high speed until the mixture is no longer gritty when rubbed between your finger and thumb. Add the egg and vanilla and beat on low speed until blended.

Sift the flour, baking powder, and salt together onto a sheet of waxed paper. Add to the butter mixture and mix on low speed or stir with a wooden spoon until well blended. Stir in the almonds.

Preheat the oven to 400°F (200°C). Have ready 2 ungreased baking sheets, preferably sheets with a nonstick finish.

Drop the batter by level teaspoonfuls onto the baking sheets, spacing the cookies at least 2 inches (5 cm) apart. Bake until the edges turn golden but the cookies are still soft, about 5 minutes. Let the cookies cool on the pans on wire racks for exactly 5 minutes, then carefully transfer them to the racks to cool completely.

To make the chocolate glaze, combine the chocolate and shortening, if using, in the top of a double boiler and melt, stirring occasionally, over barely simmering water (see page 173). Alternatively, combine the chocolate and shortening in a glass bowl and microwave on high for 1 minute, or until shiny and soft. Stir to even out the texture.

Using the tines of a fork, drizzle the chocolate on the top of a cooled cookie. Repeat with the remaining cookies. Set on wire racks and let cool until set, about 1 hour. To hasten cooling, refrigerate the cookies for about 15 minutes.

Coconut–Butterscotch Chip Cookies

MAKES ABOUT 4 DOZEN COOKIES

1⅓ cups (7 oz/220 g) all-purpose (plain) flour

½ tsp baking powder

½ tsp baking soda (bicarbonate of soda)

½ tsp salt

½ cup (4 oz/125 g) unsalted butter, at room temperature

½ cup (4 oz/125 g) granulated sugar

½ cup (3½ oz/105 g) firmly packed light brown sugar

1 large egg

½ tsp pure vanilla extract

1¾ cups (7 oz/220 g) sweetened shredded dried coconut

1½ cups (9 oz/280 g) butterscotch chips

PREHEAT THE OVEN TO 325°F (165°C). Have ready 2 baking sheets lined with parchment (baking) paper.

Sift the flour, baking powder, baking soda, and salt together onto a sheet of waxed paper; set aside.

In a large bowl, using an electric mixer on high speed, cream the butter until fluffy and pale yellow. Add the granulated sugar and brown sugar and continue beating until the mixture is no longer gritty when rubbed between your finger and thumb. Add the egg and vanilla and beat on low speed until blended, occasionally stopping the mixer and scraping down the sides of the bowl with a silicone spatula as needed.

Add the flour mixture to the butter mixture and mix on low speed or stir with a wooden spoon just until blended. Add the coconut and butterscotch chips, mixing or stirring just until blended.

With dampened hands, shape the dough into 1-inch (2.5-cm) balls or drop by rounded tablespoonfuls onto the prepared baking sheets, spacing the balls 2 inches (5 cm) apart.

Bake the cookies until golden brown around the edges, about 15 minutes. Let the cookies cool briefly on the pans on wire racks before transferring them to the racks to cool completely.

ABOUT CHIPS

Markets now carry chips made of milk chocolate, white chocolate, peanut butter, and old-fashioned butterscotch. You can also choose between standard-sized chips (or morsels) and mini chips that are about half the size. Store chips of any flavor in an airtight container in a cool, dry place to avoid bloom, a harmless dusting of white that forms on the surface of chocolate when it has been exposed to extreme temperatures.

Hazelnut & Dried Cherry Biscotti

MAKES ABOUT 4 DOZEN BISCOTTI

½ cup (4 oz/125 g) unsalted butter, at room temperature

¾ cup (6 oz/185 g) sugar

2 large eggs

2 tsp pure vanilla extract

1¾ cups (9 oz/280 g) all-purpose (plain) flour

½ tsp baking powder

½ tsp ground cinnamon

¼ tsp salt

1 cup (5 oz/155 g) hazelnuts (filberts), toasted and skinned (page 60), then coarsely chopped

½ cup (3 oz/90 g) dried tart cherries, coarsely chopped

1 tsp grated orange zest

PREHEAT THE OVEN TO 350°F (180°C). Lightly grease and flour 1 large baking sheet, or line it with parchment (baking) paper or a silicone baking mat (page 57), and have another ungreased baking sheet on hand.

In a large bowl, using an electric mixer on high speed, cream the butter until fluffy and pale yellow. Add the sugar and continue beating until the mixture is no longer gritty when rubbed between your finger and thumb. Add the eggs one at a time, beating well on low speed after each addition. Beat in the vanilla on low speed until blended.

Sift the flour, baking powder, cinnamon, and salt together onto a sheet of waxed paper. Gradually add the flour mixture to the egg mixture and mix on low speed or stir with a wooden spoon just until blended. Mix or stir in the hazelnuts, cherries, and orange zest until evenly distributed. The dough should be very soft.

Turn the dough out onto a generously floured work surface and divide in half. With well-floured hands, transfer one-half onto the greased baking sheet and shape into a log about 12 inches (30 cm) long and 1½ inches (4 cm) in diameter. Place on one side of the sheet. Repeat with the remaining dough, leaving at least 4 inches (10 cm) between the logs. (They will spread as they bake.)

Bake the logs until the edges are golden, 25–30 minutes. Transfer the pan to a wire rack and let the logs cool for 10 minutes. Using a serrated knife, cut the logs, still on the pan, on the diagonal into slices ½ inch (12 mm) thick. Carefully turn the slices on their sides and return them to the oven. When you run out of room on one baking sheet, start transferring slices to the other sheet. Bake until the edges are golden, about 10 minutes longer. Let cool completely on the pans on wire racks. Store in an airtight container.

ABOUT BISCOTTI

Biscotti means "twice baked" in Italian—and double baking is the secret to making these popular, crunchy cookies. To make biscotti, the dough is shaped into an oblong loaf and baked once. The baked loaf is then cut into slices that are baked again until they become dry and hard. As durable as they are tasty, these cookies keep extremely well and are a good choice to give as a gift. They are delicious served with fresh fruit, and are perfect for dunking in coffee or a sweet dessert wine.

ABOUT MORAVIAN COOKIES
These delicious, paper-thin spice cookies are a traditional treat at Christmastime in Moravia, a region that is today part of the Czech Republic. The cookies taste like a light, crisp version of gingerbread. They are the perfect accompaniment to a cup of tea or coffee during the cold winter months.

Moravian Molasses Cookies

MAKES ABOUT 6 DOZEN COOKIES

½ cup (4 oz/125 g) unsalted butter, at room temperature

½ cup (3½ oz/105 g) firmly packed dark brown sugar

⅔ cup (7½ oz/230 g) dark molasses

2½ cups (12½ oz/390 g) all-purpose (plain) flour

1 tsp baking soda (bicarbonate of soda)

½ tsp baking powder

1 tsp ground cinnamon

1 tsp ground ginger

¼ tsp ground allspice

2 tsp granulated sugar mixed with ¼ tsp ground cinnamon for sprinkling (optional)

IN A LARGE BOWL, using an electric mixer on high speed, cream the butter until fluffy and pale yellow. Beat in the brown sugar until no longer gritty when rubbed between your finger and thumb. Gradually beat in the molasses on low speed.

Sift the flour, baking soda, baking powder, cinnamon, ginger, and allspice together onto a sheet of waxed paper. Add the flour mixture to the butter mixture in 3 additions, mixing on low speed or stirring with a wooden spoon after each addition until blended.

Turn the dough out onto a lightly floured work surface and divide into 6 equal portions. Shape into disks, wrap in plastic wrap, and refrigerate for at least 2 hours or up to overnight.

Preheat the oven to 350°F (180°C). Lightly grease 2 baking sheets or line them with parchment (baking) paper.

Working with 1 disk at a time, roll out the dough on a floured surface to a thickness of about ⅛ inch (3 mm). Using a 2-inch (5-cm) fluted or plain cookie cutter, cut out shapes or rounds. Using a thin offset spatula, carefully transfer the cookies to the prepared pans, brushing off excess flour and placing them about 1 inch (2.5 cm) apart. Repeat with the remaining dough, then gather up the scraps, reroll them, and cut out additional cookies. If desired, sprinkle each cookie with some of the cinnamon-sugar mixture.

Bake the cookies until set, 6–8 minutes. Let the cookies cool on the pans on wire racks for about 2 minutes. Using a thin, flexible metal spatula, transfer them to the racks to cool completely.

NOTES: The dough for these delicate, full-flavored cookies is easy to handle, so don't be afraid to roll it out thinly.

Almond Sand Cookies

MAKES ABOUT 3½ DOZEN COOKIES

⅔ cup (5 oz/155 g) sugar

½ cup (2½ oz/75 g) chopped blanched almonds, plus ¾ cup (4 oz/125 g) whole almonds

¾ cup (6 fl oz/180 ml) browned butter (right), cooled slightly

¼ tsp pure almond extract

1¾ cups (9 oz/280 g) all-purpose (plain) flour

2 tsp baking powder

Pinch of salt

1 large egg white, lightly beaten

IN A FOOD PROCESSOR, combine the sugar and chopped almonds and finely grind using short pulses (page 58).

In a large bowl, combine the browned butter and almond mixture. Stir with a wooden spoon until evenly moistened. Stir in the almond extract.

Sift the flour, baking powder, and salt together onto a sheet of waxed paper. Stir the flour mixture into the butter mixture just until blended.

Preheat the oven to 300°F (150°C). Lightly grease 2 baking sheets or line them with parchment (baking) paper.

With lightly floured hands, shape the dough into ¾-inch (2-cm) balls and place on the prepared baking sheets, spacing them about 1 inch (2.5 cm) apart. Lightly brush the top of each ball with beaten egg white and press a whole almond down into the center. Pinch together any cracks that appear around the edges of the cookies. Bake the cookies until golden, about 20 minutes. Let the cookies cool completely on the pans on wire racks before carefully removing them with a thin spatula.

MAKE-AHEAD TIP: These cookies benefit from being made ahead of time, as their flavor improves after 2 or 3 days.

BROWNED BUTTER

Browned butter adds a deep flavor to these cookies. To brown the butter, melt 1 cup (8 oz/250 g) unsalted butter in a frying pan over medium heat until it foams. Reduce the heat to low and cook until the foam along the edges begins to turn golden, about 5 minutes. Remove from the heat and pour into a heatproof bowl. Let stand for 5 minutes. Spoon off the foam that rises to the top, and pour the clear liquid into a clean vessel, leaving the browned bits behind. You should have ¾ cup (6 fl oz/180 ml).

Chocolate Espresso Bars

MAKES 16 BARS

FOR THE BARS:

¾ cup (4 oz/125 g) all-purpose (plain) flour

½ cup (1½ oz/45 g) unsweetened Dutch-process cocoa powder

3 Tbsp instant espresso powder

¼ tsp baking powder

¼ tsp salt

½ cup (4 oz/125 g) unsalted butter, cut into pieces

2 oz (60 g) semisweet (plain) chocolate, coarsely chopped

2 large eggs

1 cup (7 oz/220 g) firmly packed light brown sugar

1 tsp pure vanilla extract

FOR THE GLAZE:

¼ cup (2 fl oz/60 ml) heavy (double) cream

1 tsp instant espresso powder

4 oz (125 g) semisweet (plain) chocolate, chopped

Pinch of salt

16 chocolate-covered espresso beans

PREHEAT THE OVEN TO 350°F (180°C). Generously grease an 8-inch (20-cm) square baking pan. Sift the flour, cocoa powder, espresso powder, baking powder, and salt together into a bowl; set aside.

In a small saucepan over low heat, combine the butter and chocolate. Heat, stirring often, until melted, about 2 minutes. Remove from the heat and let cool slightly.

In a bowl, whisk together the eggs and brown sugar until blended. Gradually stir in the melted chocolate mixture until blended. Stir in the vanilla, then add the flour mixture and stir until blended.

Pour the batter into the prepared pan. Bake until the edges pull away from the pan sides and the center is springy to the touch, about 25 minutes. Transfer the pan to a wire rack to cool.

Meanwhile, make the glaze. In a small saucepan over medium heat, combine the heavy cream and espresso powder. Heat, stirring, just until the powder is dissolved and bubbles start to appear around the pan edges. Add the chocolate and salt, remove from the heat, and stir just until the chocolate is melted. Let cool to room temperature.

Using a small offset spatula, spread the glaze in a thin layer over the espresso bars. Refrigerate until the glaze is set, about 30 minutes. Cut into 1½-by-2½-inch (4-by-6-cm) bars or 2-inch (5-cm) squares. Top each bar with a chocolate-covered espresso bean.

ESPRESSO POWDER

Instant espresso powder offers the most practical way to impart a good, rich coffee flavor to cookies, candies, and cakes. Sold in well-stocked food markets and specialty coffee stores, the fine powder dissolves quickly in hot liquid, to produce a bolder, more concentrated taste than regular instant coffee. This intense flavor comes with a solid dose of caffeine, however, so if you are sensitive to caffeine's effects, look for a brand of instant espresso powder labeled "decaffeinated."

CHOPPING CHOCOLATE
The teeth of a serrated knife work well to cut through all types of chocolate. With one hand gripping the handle of the knife and the other one on the top of the blade, push straight down to chop the chocolate block into small pieces. Aim for pieces that are about the same size to facilitate melting.

Crisp Chocolate Bites

MAKES ABOUT 3½ DOZEN COOKIES

6 Tbsp (3 oz/90 g) unsalted butter, cut into pieces

2 oz (60 g) unsweetened chocolate, chopped

1 cup (8 oz/250 g) granulated sugar

1 large egg

1 tsp pure vanilla extract

¾ cup (4 oz/125 g) all-purpose (plain) flour

¼ cup (¾ oz/20 g) unsweetened Dutch-process cocoa powder

½ tsp baking soda (bicarbonate of soda)

¼ tsp salt

½ cup (2 oz/60 g) confectioners' (icing) sugar

LIGHTLY GREASE 2 BAKING SHEETS or line with parchment (baking) paper. Set aside.

In a small saucepan over very low heat, combine the butter and chocolate. Heat, stirring occasionally, just until melted and smooth.

Pour the chocolate mixture into a large bowl and let cool slightly. Stir in the granulated sugar until evenly moistened. Add the egg and vanilla, beating until light and fluffy.

Sift the flour, cocoa, baking soda, and salt together onto a sheet of waxed paper. Gradually add the flour mixture to the chocolate mixture and stir to combine. Cover and refrigerate until firm, about 1 hour.

Preheat the oven to 375°F (190°C). Remove the cookie dough from the refrigerator. Shape the dough into ¾-inch (2-cm) balls and roll in the confectioners' sugar to coat completely. Place the balls about 1½ inches (4 cm) apart on the prepared pans. Bake the cookies until puffed and cracked on top, about 12 minutes. They may appear underdone in the center but will turn crisp as they cool. Let the cookies cool on the pans on wire racks for 2–3 minutes before transferring them to the racks to cool completely.

Hazelnut Meringues

MAKES ABOUT 5½ DOZEN MERINGUES

¾ cup (6 oz/185 g) superfine (caster) sugar

½ tsp cream of tartar

¼ tsp ground cinnamon

⅛ tsp ground ginger

Pinch of salt

4 large egg whites, at room temperature

1 tsp pure vanilla extract

1¼ cups (6½ oz/200 g) hazelnuts (filberts), toasted and skinned (page 60), then finely chopped

PREHEAT THE OVEN TO 275°F (135°C). Line 2 baking sheets with aluminum foil or parchment (baking) paper.

Sift the superfine sugar, cream of tartar, cinnamon, ginger, and salt together onto a sheet of waxed paper; set aside.

In a large bowl, combine the egg whites and vanilla. Using an electric mixer on medium speed (or a whisk), beat until soft and foamy. Increase the speed and, while continuing to beat, add the sugar mixture a little at a time, beating until stiff, glossy peaks form (see page 155), 3–4 minutes. Using a silicone spatula, fold in ¾ cup (3 oz/90 g) of the chopped hazelnuts.

Using a pastry bag with a large, plain tip, pipe the meringue onto the prepared pans, forming drops ¾–1 inch (2–2.5 cm) in diameter and spacing them about ½ inch (12 mm) apart. Alternatively, drop the meringue from the tip of a teaspoon to make bite-sized shapes. Sprinkle a few of the remaining nuts on top of each meringue.

Bake the meringues until lightly colored, 25–30 minutes. Turn off the oven and prop open the oven door about 1 inch (2.5 cm). Let cool completely, about 2 hours.

NOTE: This is a good recipe for using up leftover egg whites. Whites can be stored, tightly covered, in the refrigerator for up to 5 days or frozen for several months.

TROUBLESHOOTING EGG WHITES

For the best results when beating egg whites, do not let any egg yolk get into the whites as you separate the eggs. Cold eggs are the easiest to separate, as the yolks are less likely to break. Let the separated whites stand at room temperature for up to half an hour to warm slightly before beating. Use a spotlessly clean copper, stainless-steel, or glass bowl; any trace of grease will prevent the whites from whipping up to full volume.

Ruby Jewel Cookies

MAKES ABOUT 5 DOZEN COOKIES

DUSTING WITH SUGAR
Sifting delicate confectioners' sugar over cookies adds a pretty finishing touch. Confectioners' sugar, also called powdered sugar or icing sugar, is granulated sugar that has been finely crushed and mixed with a little cornstarch (cornflour). Always sift confectioners' sugar before using it for decorating or adding it to cookie dough as it has a tendency to form tiny lumps. To dust cookies, put the sugar in a fine-mesh sieve and tap the sieve gently as you move it over the cookies.

2 large egg yolks

1 tsp pure vanilla extract

2¼ cups (11½ oz/360 g) all-purpose (plain) flour

⅔ cup (5 oz/155 g) granulated sugar

1 cup (8 oz/250 g) cold unsalted butter, cut into small pieces

About ⅓ cup (3½ oz/105 g) seedless raspberry jam or other thick jam

Confectioners' (icing) sugar for dusting

PREHEAT THE OVEN TO 350°F (180°C). Have ready 2 ungreased baking sheets or miniature muffin pans and, if desired, about 5 dozen miniature paper muffin liners.

In a small bowl, whisk together the egg yolks and vanilla; set aside.

In a food processor, combine the flour and granulated sugar. Process briefly to blend. With the machine running, add the butter 2 or 3 pieces at a time and process until the mixture looks crumbly. With the machine still running, add the egg yolk mixture and process until blended and the dough begins to pull away from the sides of the bowl.

Turn the dough out onto a sheet of plastic wrap and shape it into a flat disk. Wrap and refrigerate until chilled, about 1 hour.

With lightly floured hands, shape the dough into ¾-inch (2-cm) balls. Place each ball in a paper liner, if using. Place the cookies 1 inch (2.5 cm) apart on the baking sheets or in the muffin pans.

Using the end of a wooden spoon handle dipped in flour to prevent sticking, make an indentation in the center of each cookie, but do not press all the way through the dough. Using a spoon or a pastry bag fitted with a plain tip (see page 383), fill each indentation with about ¼ tsp jam.

Bake the cookies until the edges are golden, 15–20 minutes. Let the cookies cool on the pans on wire racks. (If baking on sheets without paper liners, use a thin spatula to loosen the cookies carefully while they are still warm.) Transfer the cooled cookies to wire racks and, using a fine-mesh sieve, dust with confectioners' sugar (left).

Blondies

MAKES 16 BARS

1 cup (5 oz/155 g) plus 2 Tbsp all-purpose (plain) flour

¼ tsp salt

½ cup (4 oz/125 g) unsalted butter

1½ cups (10½ oz/330 g) firmly packed light brown sugar

1 large egg plus 1 large egg yolk, at room temperature

1½ tsp pure vanilla extract

PREHEAT THE OVEN TO 350°F (180°C). Grease an 8-inch (20-cm) square baking pan, line the bottom with parchment (baking) paper, and grease the parchment.

Sift the flour and salt together onto a sheet of waxed paper; set aside.

In a saucepan over medium heat, combine the butter and brown sugar. Heat, stirring often, until the sugar has dissolved. Continue to cook about 1 minute longer; the mixture will bubble but not boil. Set aside to cool, about 10 minutes.

Add the egg, egg yolk, and vanilla to the cooled sugar mixture and stir with a wooden spoon to combine. Sprinkle the sifted flour and salt over the sugar mixture and stir until just blended.

Pour the batter into the prepared pan, spreading it evenly with a spatula and smoothing the top. Bake until the center is springy to the touch and a cake tester inserted into the center comes out clean, 25–35 minutes. Do not overbake. Transfer the pan to a wire rack until cool enough to handle.

Run a small knife around the inside of the pan to loosen the blondies. Invert onto the rack, lift off the pan, and then carefully peel off the parchment paper. Let cool completely on the rack before cutting into 2-inch (5-cm) squares.

ABOUT EGGS

Eggs add structure, richness, moisture, and leavening to baked goods. Eggs come in a variety of sizes and grades. They are graded according to their age and the physical condition of their shell. Most baking recipes, including those in this book, use Grade A large eggs. Store eggs in the refrigerator in their original packaging away from strong odors and keep only until their sell-by date.

Almond Biscotti

MAKES ABOUT 2 DOZEN BISCOTTI

1½ cups (6 oz/185 g) cake (soft-wheat) flour

1½ cups (7½ oz/235 g) all-purpose (plain) flour

1 tsp baking powder

¾ tsp salt

1 cup (5½ oz/170 g) whole almonds, toasted (page 53)

4 large eggs

1 cup (8 oz/250 g) sugar

1½ tsp pure vanilla extract

½ tsp pure orange extract

1 Tbsp finely grated orange zest

PREHEAT THE OVEN TO 325°F (165°C). Line a baking sheet with parchment (baking) paper.

In a large bowl, combine the cake flour, all-purpose flour, baking powder, salt, and almonds. Stir to mix well.

In another bowl, using an electric mixer on medium speed, beat the eggs and sugar until pale yellow and light in texture, about 2 minutes. Add the vanilla, orange extract, and orange zest and mix well. Add the egg mixture to the flour mixture and stir just until blended. The dough will be soft and sticky.

Dust your hands with flour, transfer the dough to the prepared baking sheet, and form into a log 3–4 inches (7.5–10 cm) wide and about 12 inches (30 cm) long. Bake until a toothpick inserted into the center comes out clean, about 45 minutes. Use the parchment paper to lift the log and transfer it to a wire rack to cool for 15–20 minutes. Reduce the oven temperature to 275°F (135°C). Line the baking sheet with a new piece of parchment paper. Line a second baking sheet with paper.

Place the log on a cutting board and, using a long serrated knife, cut on the diagonal into slices ½ inch (12 mm) thick. Turn the slices on their sides and place on the prepared baking sheets, spacing them about ½ inch (12 mm) apart. Bake the biscotti for 15 minutes. Remove the baking sheets from the oven, turn the biscotti, and bake until pale golden brown, 10–15 minutes longer. Transfer the biscotti to wire racks to cool. If not serving right away, store them in an airtight container for up to 2 weeks.

VARIATION TIP: Use 1 cup (5 oz/155 g) hazelnuts (filberts) in place of the almonds. Toast them as directed on page 60.

VIN SANTO

This sweet, amber dessert wine has a slightly caramel flavor with hints of almond and fig, making it the perfect accompaniment to almond biscotti. White wine grapes selected for *vin santo* are left drying on the vine to allow the sugars to concentrate, and are further dried on rush mats in large, airy rooms. The wine is aged in small barrels for three or four years in a place where it is exposed to extreme temperature fluctuations, helping to impart the distinctive character for which the wine is known.

POLVORONES

Moorish in origin, *polvorones,* crumbly shortbreadlike cookies, were transplanted intact to Mexico by the Spanish, although they are similar to other short-crust cookies found throughout northern Europe. They were traditionally made with lard in Mexico, but nowadays solid vegetable shortening is often used to produce a lighter crumb and butter is added for flavor. For weddings, *polvorones* are wrapped individually in white tissue paper, the paper is twisted closed on opposite sides, and then the ends are shredded decoratively. For other celebrations, brightly colored tissue paper is used.

Polvorones

MAKES ABOUT 3 DOZEN COOKIES

½ cup (4 oz/125 g) unsalted butter, at room temperature

½ cup (4 oz/125 g) vegetable shortening

2½ cups (8 oz/250 g) sifted confectioners' (icing) sugar

1 tsp finely grated orange zest

1 Tbsp fresh orange juice

2 cups (10 oz/315 g) all-purpose (plain) flour

⅔ cup (2½ oz/75 g) ground walnuts (page 58)

¼ tsp sea salt

IN A BOWL, using an electric mixer on medium speed, beat together the butter and shortening until creamy. Add 1½ cups (5 oz/150 g) of the confectioners' sugar, the orange zest, and the orange juice and beat until blended.

In another bowl, stir together the flour, ground nuts, and sea salt. Add the flour mixture a tablespoonful at a time to the butter mixture, beating until thoroughly incorporated. The dough will be crumbly. Transfer the dough to a large sheet of plastic wrap and press the dough into a ball. Wrap and refrigerate for 1–2 hours.

Position a rack in the upper third of the oven and preheat the oven to 325°F (165°C). Line a baking sheet with parchment (baking) paper or a silicone baking mat (page 57).

Shape the dough into ¾-inch (2-cm) balls and place on the prepared baking sheet, spacing them about 1 inch (2.5 cm) apart and gently pressing them to flatten slightly. Bake the cookies until the edges turn pale gold, 10–15 minutes.

Meanwhile, place the remaining 1 cup (3 oz/90 g) confectioners' sugar in a shallow bowl. When the cookies are ready, remove the baking sheet from the oven. While they are still hot, using a spatula, remove the cookies one at a time and carefully roll them in the sugar. Set aside on a rack and let cool completely, then roll them again in the sugar, shaking off any excess.

Serve the cookies right away, or layer between sheets of parchment paper in an airtight container and store at room temperature for up to 3 days.

Spritz Cookies

MAKES ABOUT 5 DOZEN COOKIES

1 cup (8 oz/250 g) unsalted butter, at room temperature

¾ cup (6 oz/185 g) granulated sugar

2 large egg yolks

1 tsp pure vanilla extract

½ tsp pure almond extract

2¼ cups (11 oz/345 g) all-purpose (plain) flour

¼ tsp salt

1 egg white, lightly beaten

Granulated or colored sugar, sprinkles, or red or green glacéed cherries (optional)

PREHEAT THE OVEN TO 375°F (190°C). Have ready 2 ungreased baking sheets.

In a large bowl, using an electric mixer on high speed, cream the butter until fluffy and pale yellow. Add the granulated sugar and continue beating until the mixture is no longer gritty when rubbed between your finger and thumb. Beat in the egg yolks, vanilla, and almond extract on low speed just until blended.

Sift the flour and salt together onto a sheet of waxed paper. Add the flour mixture to the butter mixture and mix on low speed or stir with a wooden spoon until blended.

Fill a cookie press with dough following the manufacturer's instructions. Press the cookies out directly onto the pans. (Any dough that doesn't come out of the press neatly may be scraped off the baking sheet and put through the press again.) If the dough becomes too warm and sticky, refrigerate it for a few minutes to firm it up.

Lightly brush each cookie with egg white, and sprinkle with sugar or sprinkles or press a candied cherry in the center of each. Bake just until the edges are golden, 8–10 minutes. (If the shapes don't hold their definition after baking, refrigerate the dough for the next batch for 20 minutes to firm it up before pressing.) Let the cookies cool on the pans on wire racks for 1–2 minutes before transferring them to the racks to cool completely.

USING A COOKIE PRESS

Equipped with a selection of plates to create different shapes, a cookie press makes it easy to turn out batch after batch of beautiful cookies. Before using the press, roll the cookie dough inside a sheet of waxed paper into a log slightly smaller in size than the cylinder on the cookie press. Remove the paper and slip the dough into the cylinder. Screw the selected design plate securely into place. Holding the press upright, apply even pressure on the handle to press out the shaped cookies.

Ginger-Almond Sugar Cookies

MAKES ABOUT 3 DOZEN COOKIES

2 cups (10 oz/315 g) all-purpose (plain) flour

1 cup (5½ oz/170 g) unsalted almonds, toasted (right) and finely ground

½ tsp baking powder

¼ tsp salt

⅛ tsp ground ginger

1 cup (8 oz/250 g) unsalted butter, at room temperature

1½ cups (12 oz/375 g) granulated sugar

1 Tbsp firmly packed light brown sugar

1 large egg, plus 1 beaten egg

1 tsp pure vanilla extract

3½ Tbsp finely minced candied (crystallized) ginger, homemade (page 322), or purchased

36 unsalted blanched whole almonds

PREHEAT THE OVEN TO 375°F (190°C). Line 2 baking sheets with parchment (baking) paper.

In a bowl, whisk together the flour, ground almonds, baking powder, salt, and ground ginger; set aside.

In a bowl, using an electric mixer on medium speed, beat together the butter, 1 cup (8 oz/250 g) of the granulated sugar, and the brown sugar until light and fluffy, about 3 minutes. Add the 1 unbeaten egg, vanilla, and candied ginger and continue to beat on medium speed until combined, about 30 seconds. Reduce the speed to low, add the flour mixture, and beat just until combined.

Place the remaining ½ cup (4 oz/125 g) granulated sugar in a bowl. With dampened hands, shape the dough into 1½-inch (4-cm) balls and roll in the sugar to coat evenly. Place the balls about 2 inches (5 cm) apart on the prepared pans. Butter the bottom of a drinking glass, dip the bottom of the glass in the remaining sugar, and flatten the dough balls until they are ¾ inch (2 cm) thick. Brush the top of each flattened ball with the beaten egg and press a blanched almond down into the center.

Bake the cookies until golden brown around the edges and very lightly colored in the center, 15–20 minutes. Let the cookies cool on the pans on wire racks for about 3 minutes before transferring them to the racks to cool completely. The cookies should be crisp on the edges and chewy in the center. Store in an airtight container at room temperature for up to 1 week.

TOASTING ALMONDS AND OTHER NUTS

Almonds and other nuts are often toasted to intensify their flavor. To toast almonds, preheat the oven to 375°F (190°C) and spread the nuts on a baking sheet. Toast until they are fragrant and have begun to color, about 10 minutes, then remove from the pan and let cool completely. Sliced almonds will take less time, however. Check them after 4 minutes. For nuts with a higher oil content, such as pine nuts, cashews, and peanuts, reduce the toasting time to about 7 minutes. For tips on grinding nuts, see page 58.

Rugelach with Apricot-Pistachio Filling

MAKES ABOUT 2½ DOZEN COOKIES

FOR THE DOUGH:

¼ lb (125 g) cream cheese, cut into small pieces, at room temperature

½ cup (4 oz/125 g) unsalted butter, cut into small pieces, at room temperature

1 cup (5 oz/155 g) plus 2 Tbsp all-purpose (plain) flour

2 Tbsp granulated sugar

¼ tsp salt

FOR THE FILLING:

¾ cup (4 oz/125 g) dried apricots, halved

1 Tbsp granulated sugar

¼ tsp ground cinnamon

2 Tbsp finely chopped unsalted pistachios

Confectioners' (icing) sugar for dusting

IN A FOOD PROCESSOR, combine the cream cheese, butter, flour, granulated sugar, and salt. Pulse just until the dough begins to clump together. Turn the dough out onto a floured work surface and gather into a ball. Divide the dough into 4 equal portions, shape into disks, and wrap each disk in plastic wrap. Refrigerate the disks for at least 2 hours or up to 6 hours.

Meanwhile, make the filling. In a small saucepan over low heat, combine the apricots and ½ cup (4 fl oz/125 ml) water. Cover and cook, stirring occasionally, until the fruit absorbs the water, 10–15 minutes. Let cool slightly, then transfer to the food processor and process to a fairly smooth purée. Pour into a bowl and stir in the granulated sugar, cinnamon, and pistachios. Set aside.

Preheat the oven to 350°F (180°C). Line 2 baking sheets with parchment (baking) paper.

Lightly flour a work surface. Working with 1 disk at a time, roll out the dough into a 7-inch (18-cm) circle (left). Spread one-fourth of the filling evenly over the top. With a large knife, cut the dough into 6 wedges. Starting at the outside edge, gently roll up each wedge toward the point. (If needed, use a thin metal spatula to loosen the wedges from the work surface.) If the dough becomes too soft to roll, refrigerate for about 5 minutes to firm it up. As each piece is formed, place it at least 1 inch (2.5 cm) apart on the prepared baking sheets. Bend the ends of the dough a little toward the center to form a crescent shape. Repeat with the remaining dough and filling, flouring the work surface as needed.

Bake the rugelach until golden brown, about 20 minutes. Let cool on the pans on wire racks for about 5 minutes before transferring to the racks to cool completely. While still warm, use a fine-mesh sieve to dust the rugelach with confectioners' sugar.

ROLLING OUT DOUGH

To roll out dough, use a marble or wooden pin. Roll from the center toward the outside edge, using short, firm strokes and stopping just shy of the edge to keep it from becoming too thin. After each roll, rotate the dough a quarter turn to prevent it from sticking to the work surface. Lightly dust the surface and rolling pin with more flour as needed. Beginners may find it easier to roll out dough between 2 sheets of waxed paper, which prevents sticking and tearing.

Oatmeal Cookies

MAKES ABOUT 3 DOZEN COOKIES

½ cup (4 oz/125 g) unsalted butter

½ cup (4 oz/125 g) granulated sugar

½ cup (3½ oz/105 g) firmly packed dark brown sugar

1 large egg, lightly beaten

1 tsp pure vanilla extract

¾ cup (4 oz/125 g) all-purpose (plain) flour

¼ tsp baking soda (bicarbonate of soda)

¼ tsp ground cinnamon

¼ tsp ground nutmeg

¼ tsp salt

1½ cups (4½ oz/140 g) old-fashioned rolled oats

⅓ cup (1½ oz/45 g) finely chopped walnuts

IN A SAUCEPAN OVER LOW HEAT, melt the butter, then remove from the heat. Using a wooden spoon, beat in the granulated sugar and brown sugar until blended. Add the egg and vanilla and beat again until blended.

Sift the flour, baking soda, cinnamon, nutmeg, and salt together into a bowl. Stir the flour mixture into the egg mixture, then stir in the oats and walnuts. Cover and refrigerate for 1 hour.

Preheat the oven to 350°F (180°C). Generously grease 2 baking sheets.

Drop the batter by rounded tablespoonfuls onto the prepared pans, spacing the cookies at least 2 inches (5 cm) apart. Using a metal spatula, flatten each mound of batter into a disk about ⅓ inch (9 mm) thick.

Bake the cookies until golden brown, 12–15 minutes. Transfer the cookies to wire racks to cool completely.

SHAPING COOKIES

To shape drop cookies, fill one spoon, usually a tablespoon, with batter, and then use a second spoon to push the batter off onto the baking sheet. If you prefer perfectly round cookies, roll the batter into balls between dampened palms. Be sure to space the cookies about 2 inches (5 cm) apart on the pans, as the batter is typically buttery and the cookies will spread as they bake.

Cigarettes Russes

MAKES ABOUT 3 DOZEN COOKIES

FOR THE COOKIES:

6 Tbsp (3 oz/90 g) unsalted butter, at room temperature

1 cup (4 oz/125 g) confectioners' (icing) sugar

4 large egg whites, at room temperature

2 tsp pure vanilla extract

⅔ cup (3 oz/90 g) all-purpose (plain) flour

⅛ tsp salt

FOR THE CHOCOLATE DIP:

3 oz (90 g) semisweet (plain) chocolate, chopped

1½ tsp unsalted butter

1 tsp light corn syrup

PREHEAT THE OVEN TO 425°F (220°C). Grease 2 large baking sheets or line them with silicone baking mats (right).

In a large bowl, using an an electric mixer on high speed, cream the butter until fluffy and pale yellow. Gradually add the confectioners' sugar and continue beating until well blended. Add the egg whites, one-fourth at a time, beating well after each addition. Add the vanilla and beat until blended.

Sift the flour and salt together onto a sheet of waxed paper. Gradually stir the flour mixture into the butter mixture.

Drop the batter by level tablespoonfuls onto a prepared sheet, spacing them about 5 inches (13 cm) apart and forming only 4 cookies. (The cookies must be baked in small batches, because, once baked, they must be shaped quickly before they cool.) Using a lightly moistened offset spatula or the back of a spoon, spread the batter into thin ovals about 3 by 4 inches (7.5 by 10 cm).

Bake the cookies until they are just golden at the edges, about 3 minutes. Meanwhile, prepare a second batch on the remaining sheet. Remove the baked cookies from the oven. Working quickly, use a thin, flexible metal spatula to remove 1 baked cookie at a time and wrap it lengthwise around the handle of a wooden spoon to make a hollow tube. Transfer to a wire rack to cool and repeat with the remaining 3 cookies. If the cookies become too cool to shape easily, return them to the oven for 30 seconds to soften. Continue baking and rolling the remaining batter.

To make the chocolate dip, combine the chocolate, butter, and corn syrup in the top of a double boiler and melt, stirring occasionally, over barely simmering water (see page 173). Let cool slightly. Dip about 1 inch (2.5 cm) of each cookie into the chocolate. Place on a wire rack, with the dipped end not touching the rack, until set.

SILICONE BAKING MATS

Silicone-coated fiberglass baking mats are reusable nonstick liners that may be used any time a recipe calls for a greased or lined pan. They are especially handy for these very thin, delicate cookies, which are made from a liquidy batter that spreads on the baking sheet. The liners also promote uniform browning. They come in a range of sizes and can withstand oven temperatures of up to 500°F (260°C). To clean the mats, just wipe them with a soft cloth.

Nutty Butter Balls

MAKES ABOUT 5 DOZEN COOKIES

1 cup (8 oz/250 g) unsalted butter, at room temperature

¾ cup (6 oz/185 g) firmly packed light brown sugar

1 large egg, separated

1½ tsp pure vanilla extract

2 cups (10 oz/315 g) all-purpose (plain) flour

½ tsp salt

¼ tsp baking powder

2 cups (8 oz/250 g) pecans, finely ground (left)

½ cup (4 oz/125 g) multicolored coarse sugar crystals

IN A LARGE BOWL, using an electric mixer on high speed, cream the butter until fluffy and pale yellow. Add the brown sugar and continue beating until the mixture is no longer gritty when rubbed between your finger and thumb. Add the egg yolk and vanilla and beat on low speed until blended.

Sift the flour, salt, and baking powder together onto a sheet of waxed paper. Gradually add the flour mixture to the butter mixture, mixing on low speed until blended. Mix in ¾ cup (3 oz/90 g) of the ground pecans just until blended.

Preheat the oven to 350°F (180°C). Grease 2 baking sheets or line them with parchment (baking) paper. Alternatively, have ready 5 dozen miniature paper muffin liners.

Spread the remaining ground pecans in a shallow bowl. Lightly beat the egg white in a small bowl. With floured hands, shape the dough into ¾-inch (2-cm) balls. Brush the balls lightly with the egg white and roll in the pecans to coat lightly. Place the cookies about 1 inch (2.5 cm) apart on the prepared pans, or place each ball in a paper liner. Pour the sugar crystals into a shallow bowl.

Bake the cookies until the bottoms are lightly browned, 15–18 minutes. Let the cookies cool slightly on the pans on wire racks. Using a flexible metal spatula, remove the warm cookies from the pans and roll them in the sugar crystals to coat, or sprinkle the sugar on top if in paper liners. Let cool completely on wire racks.

GRINDING NUTS

To grind nuts, use a hand-cranked nut grinder or process in a food processor using short pulses to yield a coarse, crumbly texture. If using a food processor, beware of overprocessing the nuts into a smooth paste, which releases their oils and diminishes their flavor. For best results, combine the nuts with a little of the flour or sugar called for in the recipe and process for no longer than 5 to 10 seconds at a time.

Gingerbread People

MAKES 2–5 DOZEN COOKIES, DEPENDING ON SIZE

1 cup (8 oz/250 g) unsalted butter, at room temperature

½ cup (3½ oz/105 g) firmly packed light brown sugar

½ cup (4 oz/125 g) granulated sugar

1 cup (11 oz/345 g) light molasses

1 large egg

5 cups (25 oz/780 g) all-purpose (plain) flour

1 tsp baking soda (bicarbonate of soda)

1 Tbsp ground ginger

1 tsp ground cinnamon

½ tsp ground cloves

½ tsp salt

Royal Icing (page 376), for decorating

IN A LARGE BOWL, using an electric mixer on high speed, cream the butter until fluffy and pale yellow. Add the brown sugar and granulated sugar and beat until the mixture is no longer gritty when rubbed between your finger and thumb. Gradually beat in the molasses on low speed. Add the egg and beat until the mixture is blended.

Sift the flour, baking soda, ginger, cinnamon, cloves, and salt together onto a sheet of waxed paper. Gradually add the flour mixture to the butter mixture, mixing on low speed or stirring with a wooden spoon until well blended. Turn the dough out onto a floured work surface and, with floured hands, form into a large, smooth mound. Divide the dough into 4 equal portions, shape into disks, and wrap each disk in plastic wrap. Refrigerate for at least 2 hours or up to 2 days.

Preheat the oven to 400°F (200°C). Lightly grease 2 baking sheets or line them with parchment (baking) paper. Working with 1 disk at a time, roll out the dough between 2 sheets of waxed paper to a thickness of about ¼ inch (6 mm). Using gingerbread cookie cutters 3–5 inches (7.5–13 cm) tall, cut out figures. Use an offset spatula to transfer the cookies to a prepared pan. Repeat with the remaining dough portions, then gather up the scraps and reroll them. If the scraps of dough have become sticky, refrigerate them for 10 minutes before rerolling. For best results, do not roll the same piece of dough more than twice.

Bake the gingerbread figures until lightly browned on the bottom, about 6 minutes. Let cool on the sheets for 5 minutes before transferring to wire racks to cool completely. Dress up the cooled gingerbread figures with the royal icing, sugars, and other decorations (right).

GINGERBREAD DECORATIONS

Silvery or pearlescent dragées in a variety of sizes, small red or white candies, and colored sprinkles can dress up any gingerbread man (or woman). After the baked cookies have cooled, decorate with icing and use clean tweezers to place the desired decorations on the still-wet icing. For a more homey look, while the cookies are still warm, press dried currants, dried cranberries, or raisins down the center of each torso to make buttons. Or, before baking, use a clean garlic press to make gingerbread hair.

Hazelnut Dacquoises

MAKES 8 COOKIES

TOASTING & SKINNING HAZELNUTS

A light toasting heightens the flavor of nuts. Toasting hazelnuts also loosens their skins. Spread the nuts in a single layer on a baking sheet lined with parchment (baking) paper and toast in a preheated 350°F (180°C) oven until the skins start to darken and wrinkle, about 8 minutes. When the nuts are cool enough to handle, wrap them in a kitchen towel and rub vigorously to remove the skins. Not every speck will come off.

1¾ cups (9½ oz/270 g) hazelnuts (filberts), toasted (left)

2¼ cups (8 oz/225 g) confectioners' (icing) sugar, plus extra for dusting

3 large egg whites, at room temperature

¼ cup (2 oz/60 g) granulated sugar

⅔ cup (5 oz/140 g) plus 1 Tbsp unsalted butter, at room temperature

2 Tbsp Cognac

Pastry Cream (page 377), chilled

PREHEAT THE OVEN TO 300°F (150°C). On a piece of parchment (baking) paper, draw 16 circles, each 2½ inches (6 cm) in diameter and 1½ inches (4 cm) apart. Put the paper, marked side down, on a 12-by-18-by-1-inch (30-by-45-by-2.5-cm) baking sheet.

In a food processor, finely grind ⅔ cup (3½ oz/100 g) of the hazelnuts and 1 cup (3½ oz/100 g) of the confectioners' sugar using short pulses (see page 58).

Using a stand mixer fitted with the whisk attachment, beat the egg whites on medium speed until they start to foam. Add a third of the granulated sugar and beat until the whites are opaque, then add another third of the sugar. When the whites start to become firm, add the remaining sugar and increase the speed to high. Beat until the whites form stiff peaks but still look wet (see page 155). Carefully fold in the ground hazelnut mixture in 2 additions, making a hazelnut-meringue mixture.

Fill a pastry bag fitted with a ⅜-inch (1-cm) plain tip with the meringue mixture (see page 383). Starting in the center of each paper circle, pipe a continuous spiral, filling the circles. Using a fine-mesh sieve, dust the meringue disks with confectioners' sugar. Bake until the disks are browned and firm, 45–50 minutes. Transfer the disks, still on the paper, to a wire rack.

Using the stand mixer fitted with the paddle attachment, beat the butter on medium speed until creamy.

In the food processor, finely grind ¾ cup (4 oz/110 g) of the hazelnuts and the remaining 1¼ cups (4½ oz/125 g) confectioners' sugar using short pulses. Add the ground nut mixture to the butter and beat until thick. Add the Cognac. Reduce the speed to medium-low and beat in the pastry cream in 4 additions.

Put half of the filling in a pastry bag fitted with a ⅜-inch plain tip. Pipe the mixture on top of 8 of the meringues, dividing it evenly. Press the remaining meringues on top. Freeze for 30 minutes.

Using a spatula, cover the sides with the remaining filling. Chop the remaining ⅓ cup (2 oz/60 g) hazelnuts and spread them on waxed paper. Roll each pastry in the nuts to coat the sides. Refrigerate until ready to serve.

MUFFINS & QUICK BREADS

Blueberry Muffins

MAKES 12 MUFFINS

BLUEBERRIES

Plump blueberries, available from late spring through summer, are usually sold in pint boxes containing about 2 cups (8 oz/ 250 g) berries. The commercial berry is the North American high-bush variety, growing up to 15 feet high, primarily in Oregon, Washington, and Florida. Small, intensely flavored wild blueberries, native to New England and parts of Canada, can be used in this recipe as well. You can refrigerate berries for up to 2 days before using them. Do not wash them before storing, as the water will promote mold.

FOR THE TOPPING:

¼ cup (1½ oz/45 g) all-purpose (plain) flour

2 Tbsp granulated sugar

2 Tbsp firmly packed light brown sugar

¼ tsp ground cinnamon

2 Tbsp cold unsalted butter, cut into small pieces

FOR THE MUFFINS:

7 Tbsp (3½ oz/105 g) unsalted butter, at room temperature

¾ cup (6 oz/185 g) granulated sugar

2 large eggs

2¼ cups (11½ oz/360 g) all-purpose (plain) flour

4 tsp baking powder

½ tsp salt

1 cup (8 fl oz/250 ml) milk

1½ tsp pure vanilla extract

1½ cups (6 oz/185 g) fresh blueberries or frozen unsweetened blueberries, unthawed

Maple Butter (page 378) for serving

PREHEAT THE OVEN TO 375°F (190°C). Grease 12 standard muffin cups with butter or butter-flavored nonstick cooking spray.

To make the topping, in a small bowl, stir together the flour, granulated sugar, brown sugar, and cinnamon. Using a pastry blender or your fingers, cut or rub the butter into the flour mixture just until coarse crumbs form. Alternatively, combine the flour mixture and the butter in a food processor and pulse just until coarse crumbs form.

To make the muffins, in a bowl, using an electric mixer on medium speed, cream together the butter and sugar until light and fluffy. Add the eggs, one at a time, beating well after each addition until blended into the butter mixture.

In another bowl, stir together the flour, baking powder, and salt. Add the flour mixture to the butter mixture in 2 additions, alternating with the milk and vanilla. Stir just until evenly moistened. The batter will be slightly lumpy. Using a large silicone spatula, gently fold in the blueberries just until evenly distributed, no more than a few strokes. Take care not to break up the fruit. Do not overmix.

Spoon the batter into each muffin cup, filling it level with the rim. Sprinkle each muffin with some of the topping.

Bake the muffins until golden, dry, and springy to the touch, 20–25 minutes. A toothpick inserted into the center of a muffin should come out clean. Transfer the pan to a wire rack and let the muffins cool for 5 minutes. Unmold the muffins. Serve warm or at room temperature with the maple butter.

Banana-Nut Bread

MAKES ONE 9-BY-5-INCH (23-BY-13-CM) LOAF

BANANAS

The distinctive tropical flavor and fragrance of bananas and their meaty texture make them a satisfying addition to quick breads. For the most pronounced flavor, use very ripe, plump bananas that give when gently pressed, with a skin color that ranges from yellow with an abundance of brown and black freckles to almost completely blackened. If you have very ripe bananas but are unable to make banana bread right away, peel and freeze them until ready to use.

6 Tbsp (3 oz/90 g) unsalted butter, at room temperature

1 cup (8 oz/250 g) sugar

2 or 3 very ripe bananas, coarsely mashed (about 1½ cups/9 oz/280 g)

3 large eggs, lightly beaten

½ cup (4 fl oz/125 ml) buttermilk

2 cups (10 oz/315 g) all-purpose (plain) flour

1 tsp baking soda (bicarbonate of soda)

1 tsp baking powder

1 tsp ground nutmeg

½ tsp salt

¾ cup (3 oz/90 g) coarsely chopped walnuts, pecans, or hazelnuts (filberts)

PREHEAT THE OVEN TO 350°F (180°C). Grease and lightly flour a 9-by-5-inch (23-by-13-cm) loaf pan.

In a stand mixer fitted with the paddle attachment, beat together the butter and sugar on medium speed until creamy, about 1 minute. Add the bananas and eggs and beat until smooth. Add the buttermilk and beat just until combined.

In a bowl, stir together the flour, baking soda, baking powder, nutmeg, salt, and nuts. Add the flour mixture to the banana mixture and beat just until combined. The batter should be slightly lumpy. Scrape down the sides of the bowl.

Pour the batter into the prepared pan. It should be no more than two-thirds full. Bake until the top is dark golden brown and dry to the touch and the edges pull away from the pan sides, 55–60 minutes. A cake tester inserted into the center should come out clean. Let the bread cool in the pan for 5 minutes, then turn it out onto a wire rack and let cool completely. Cut into thick slices to serve.

STORAGE TIP: Wrap the bread tightly in plastic wrap and store at room temperature overnight or in the refrigerator for up to 5 days.

Lemon–Poppy Seed Muffins

MAKES 10 MUFFINS

½ cup (4 oz/125 g) unsalted butter, at room temperature

⅔ cup (5 oz/155 g) lemon sugar (right) or granulated sugar

2 large eggs, separated

1⅓ cups (7 oz/220 g) all-purpose (plain) flour

1 tsp baking powder

½ tsp baking soda (bicarbonate of soda)

2 Tbsp poppy seeds

Grated zest of 2 lemons

¼ tsp salt

½ cup (4 fl oz/125 ml) buttermilk

2 Tbsp strained fresh lemon juice

1 tsp pure vanilla extract

3 Tbsp coarse raw sugar for sprinkling

Lemon Curd (page 129) for serving

PREHEAT THE OVEN TO 350°F (180°C). Grease 10 standard muffin cups with butter or butter-flavored nonstick cooking spray or line with paper liners; fill the unused cups one-third full with water to prevent warping.

In a bowl, using an electric mixer on medium speed, cream together the butter and sugar until light and fluffy. Add the egg yolks, one at a time, beating well after each addition until blended.

In another bowl, stir together the flour, baking powder, baking soda, poppy seeds, lemon zest, and salt. Using the mixer on low speed, add the flour mixture to the butter mixture in 2 additions, alternating with the buttermilk, then the lemon juice and vanilla. Beat just until smooth.

In a large bowl, using the mixer with spotlessly clean beaters on high speed or a balloon whisk, beat the egg whites just until they form soft peaks (see page 155). Using a large silicone spatula, gently fold the egg whites into the batter until blended.

Spoon the batter into each muffin cup, filling it three-fourths full. Sprinkle each muffin with some of the raw sugar.

Bake the muffins until golden, dry, and springy to the touch, 20–25 minutes. A toothpick inserted into the center of a muffin should come out clean. Transfer the pan to a wire rack and let the muffins cool for 5 minutes. Unmold the muffins and let cool completely. Serve at room temperature with the lemon curd.

LEMON SUGAR

This simple recipe can be used to add lemon flavor to any recipe calling for sugar and lemon zest. Using a small paring knife or a vegetable peeler, remove the zest from 3 large lemons, leaving the bitter white pith behind; reserve the fruit and juice for another use. Place the zest in a food processor and add ½ cup (4 oz/120 g) granulated sugar. Pulse until the zest is evenly distributed. Add another ½ cup sugar and pulse until the zest is finely ground. Store in an airtight container in the refrigerator for up to 2 months. Makes about 1 cup (8 oz/250 g).

SESAME SEEDS
Used as a garnish, tiny, flat sesame seeds contribute a subtle nutty flavor and crunchy texture to baked goods such as muffins and breads and to many other dishes both savory and sweet. The seeds are an ingredient in cuisines of nearly every continent around the world. Of the several varieties available, the most common are pale tan in color. Black, red, and brown sesame seeds are also sold in some markets. Because sesame seeds have a high oil content, they are best stored in an airtight container in the refrigerator.

Cheddar Cheese Muffins

MAKES 7 MUFFINS

1¾ cups (9 oz/280 g) all-purpose (plain) flour

1¼ cups (5 oz/155 g) shredded sharp Cheddar cheese

2 Tbsp sugar

1 Tbsp baking powder

½ tsp salt

¼ tsp chili powder

1 large egg

3 Tbsp olive oil

1 cup (8 fl oz/250 ml) milk

1 Tbsp sesame seeds or 1½ tsp poppy seeds for sprinkling

PREHEAT THE OVEN TO 375°F (190°C). Grease 7 standard muffin cups with butter or butter-flavored nonstick cooking spray; fill the unused cups one-third full with water to prevent warping.

In a bowl, stir together the flour, cheese, sugar, baking powder, salt, and chili powder.

In another bowl, whisk together the egg, olive oil, and milk until blended. Make a well in the center of the flour mixture, add the milk mixture, and stir just until evenly moistened. The batter will be slightly lumpy.

Spoon the batter into each muffin cup, filling it level with the rim. Sprinkle each muffin with some of the sesame seeds.

Bake the muffins until golden, dry, and springy to the touch, 20–25 minutes. A toothpick inserted into the center of a muffin should come out clean. Transfer the pan to a wire rack and let the muffins cool for 5 minutes. Unmold the muffins. Serve warm or at room temperature.

Whole-Wheat Dinner Muffins

MAKES 9 MUFFINS

- **1¼ cups (6½ oz/200 g) whole-wheat or graham flour**
- **2 Tbsp yellow cornmeal**
- **3 Tbsp firmly packed light or dark brown sugar**
- **2 tsp baking powder**
- **½ tsp baking soda (bicarbonate of soda)**
- **½ tsp salt**
- **2 large eggs, separated**
- **3 Tbsp unsalted butter, melted, or sesame oil or olive oil**
- **1 cup (8 fl oz/250 ml) buttermilk**
- **2 Tbsp sour cream or plain yogurt**
- **1 tsp pure vanilla extract**
- **1½ Tbsp sesame seeds**

PREHEAT THE OVEN TO 375°F (190°C). Grease 9 standard muffin cups with butter or butter-flavored nonstick cooking spray; fill the unused cups one-third full with water to prevent warping.

In a bowl, stir together the flour, cornmeal, brown sugar, baking powder, baking soda, and salt.

In another bowl, whisk together the egg yolks, butter, buttermilk, sour cream, and vanilla until blended. Stir the buttermilk mixture into the flour mixture just until evenly moistened. The batter will be slightly lumpy.

In a large bowl, using an electric mixer with spotlessly clean beaters on medium speed or a balloon whisk, beat the egg whites just until they form soft peaks (page 155). Using a large silicone spatula, gently fold the egg whites into the batter until blended.

Spoon the batter into each muffin cup, filling it level with the rim. Sprinkle each muffin with some of the sesame seeds.

Bake the muffins until golden and springy to the touch, 20–25 minutes. A toothpick inserted into the center of a muffin should come out clean. Transfer the pan to a wire rack and let the muffins cool for 5 minutes. Serve warm or at room temperature.

WHOLE-WHEAT FLOUR

Known for its nutty, sweet flavor and aroma and its extra nutrition, whole-wheat flour is ground from the entire kernel of wheat. By contrast, all-purpose (plain) flour has had the bran and germ removed. Commercial whole-wheat flours vary from fine to more coarsely ground; the grinds may be used interchangeably in recipes. To produce fine grinds, all parts of the grain are equally ground. Medium and coarse grinds have varying amounts of bran dispersed throughout.

Apricot Bread with Hazelnuts

MAKES FOUR 6-BY-3½-INCH (15-BY-9-CM) LOAVES

ABOUT HAZELNUTS

Popular in French and Italian baking, and also known as filberts, these round nuts encased in a hard shell have a delightful crunch and rich, buttery flavor that shine in quick loaf breads, especially in combination with dried fruits. Hazelnuts have a thin inner skin that can be removed, if desired (see page 60).

22 dried apricot halves, coarsely chopped

½ cup (3 oz/90 g) dried currants

1 cup (8 fl oz/250 ml) boiling water

3 cups (15 oz/470 g) all-purpose (plain) flour

1 cup (7 oz/220 g) firmly packed light brown sugar

1 Tbsp baking powder

½ tsp baking soda (bicarbonate of soda)

1 tsp salt

3 Tbsp unsalted butter, melted, or hazelnut oil

2 large eggs, beaten

1⅓ cups (11 fl oz/345 ml) buttermilk

1 cup (4 oz/125 g) hazelnuts, chopped

PUT THE APRICOTS AND CURRANTS in a bowl. Add the boiling water. Set aside at room temperature and let cool to lukewarm, about 1 hour.

Preheat the oven to 350°F (180°C). Grease and flour four 6-by-3½-inch (15-by-9-cm) loaf pans or spray with nonstick cooking spray.

In a bowl, stir together the flour, brown sugar, baking powder, baking soda, and salt. Make a well in the center of the flour mixture and add the melted butter, eggs, and buttermilk. Beat until smooth, about 1 minute. Add the apricots and currants with their liquid and the hazelnuts to the batter. Beat just until blended and the fruit and nuts are evenly distributed. Pour the batter into the prepared pans.

Bake until the tops are browned and firm and the edges pull away from the pan sides, 45–50 minutes. A toothpick inserted into the center of a loaf should come out clean. Immediately unmold the loaves onto wire racks and let cool completely.

Wrap the loaves tightly in plastic wrap and refrigerate for at least 8 hours or up to 4 days. Cut into thick slices to serve.

Country Applesauce Muffins

MAKES 12 MUFFINS

2 cups (10 oz/315 g) all-purpose (plain) flour

1 cup (4 oz/125 g) walnuts, coarsely chopped, or 1 cup (6 oz/185 g) dark or golden (sultana) raisins

⅔ cup (5 oz/155 g) sugar

2 tsp baking powder

½ tsp baking soda (bicarbonate of soda)

½ tsp salt

1½ tsp ground cinnamon

1 tsp ground allspice

⅓ cup (3 fl oz/80 ml) almond oil, walnut oil, or canola oil

1 large egg

1 heaping cup (9 oz/280 g) applesauce, page 378 or purchased (see Notes)

PREHEAT THE OVEN TO 350°F (180°C). Grease 12 standard muffin cups with butter or butter-flavored nonstick cooking spray.

In a bowl, stir together the flour, walnuts, sugar, baking powder, baking soda, salt, cinnamon, and allspice.

In another bowl, whisk together the oil, egg, and applesauce until smooth. Make a well in the center of the flour mixture and stir in the applesauce mixture just until evenly moistened. The batter may seem dry at first, but it will loosen and smooth out as you beat the mixture.

Spoon the batter into each muffin cup, filling it level with the rim.

Bake the muffins until golden, dry, and springy to the touch, 25–30 minutes. A toothpick inserted into the center of a muffin should come out clean. Transfer the pan to a wire rack and let the muffins cool for 5 minutes. Unmold the muffins. Serve warm or at room temperature.

NOTES: When measuring the applesauce for this recipe, use a cup for measuring liquids, such as a glass measuring pitcher. This recipe can easily be doubled.

ALLSPICE

The berry of an evergreen tree, allspice tastes like a mixture of cinnamon, nutmeg, and cloves. It is often used around the holidays to add bold flavor to spiced cookies, cakes, and pies. Allspice can be used ground or whole. Buy it in the smallest amount you can from a store with high turnover, as it will begin to lose its flavor after 6 months. If possible, purchase allspice in bulk, buying only a little at a time. If you buy a can or jar, be sure to check it for a date to ensure freshness.

Cranberry-Orange Muffins

MAKES 10 MUFFINS

2 cups (10 oz/315 g) all-purpose (plain) flour

½ cup (4 oz/125 g) granulated sugar

½ cup (3½ oz/105 g) firmly packed light brown sugar

2 tsp baking powder

½ tsp salt

Grated zest of 1 orange

1 large egg

4 Tbsp (2 oz/60 g) unsalted butter, melted, or walnut oil

½ cup (4 fl oz/125 ml) milk

½ cup (4 fl oz/125 ml) strained fresh orange juice

1½ cups (6 oz/185 g) fresh cranberries or frozen cranberries, unthawed

½ cup (2 oz/60 g) pecans or walnuts, chopped

PREHEAT THE OVEN TO 375°F (190°C). Grease 10 standard muffin cups with butter or butter-flavored nonstick cooking spray; fill the unused cups one-third full with water to prevent warping.

In a bowl, stir together the flour, granulated sugar, brown sugar, baking powder, salt, and orange zest.

In another bowl, whisk together the egg, melted butter, milk, and orange juice until blended. Add to the flour mixture, stirring just until evenly moistened. The batter will be slightly lumpy. Using a large silicone spatula, fold in the cranberries and nuts just until evenly distributed, no more than a few strokes. Do not overmix. Spoon the batter into each muffin cup, filling it level with the rim.

Bake the muffins until golden, dry, and springy to the touch, 20–25 minutes. A toothpick inserted into the center of a muffin should come out clean. Transfer the pan to a wire rack and let the muffins cool for 5 minutes. Unmold the muffins. Serve warm or at room temperature.

CRANBERRIES

Harvested from bogs when cold weather arrives and available throughout the winter months, tart, fresh cranberries are a signature fresh fruit of autumn and early winter. They are packaged in 12-ounce (375-g) plastic bags that contain 3 cups of berries. Cranberries can be enjoyed throughout the year by freezing them in airtight freezer bags; they keep for up to 1 year in perfect condition. The combination of tart cranberries sweetened with oranges, another fruit of winter, is one of the classic flavor pairings in baking.

Pumpkin Bread with Dates

MAKES ONE 9-BY-5-INCH (23-BY-13-CM) LOAF

1½ cups (12 oz/375 g) sugar

1 cup (8 oz/250 g) canned pumpkin purée

2 large eggs

½ cup (4 fl oz/125 ml) nut oil, such as walnut or almond, or sunflower seed oil

1¾ cups (9 oz/280 g) all-purpose (plain) flour

1 tsp baking soda (bicarbonate of soda)

½ tsp baking powder

½ tsp salt

½ tsp ground cinnamon

½ tsp ground cloves

½ tsp freshly grated nutmeg

1 cup (6 oz/185 g) coarsely chopped pitted dates

PREHEAT THE OVEN TO 350°F (180°C). Grease a 9-by-5-inch (23-by-13-cm) loaf pan or spray with nonstick cooking spray.

In a bowl, whisk together the sugar, pumpkin purée, eggs, and oil until smooth.

In another bowl, stir together the flour, baking soda, baking powder, salt, cinnamon, cloves, and nutmeg.

Add the flour mixture to the pumpkin mixture and beat until smooth and well combined, 1–2 minutes. The batter will be thick. Using a large silicone spatula, fold in the dates just until evenly distributed, no more than a few strokes. Do not overmix. Scrape the batter into the prepared pan.

Bake until the top is browned and crusty and develops a long center crack, 60–70 minutes. A toothpick inserted into the center of the loaf should come out clean. Transfer the pan to a wire rack and let cool for 10 minutes. Unmold the loaf onto the rack and let cool completely. Cut into thick slices to serve.

ABOUT DATES

The handsome date palm flourishes in the desert climates of the Middle East and North Africa and in Southern California. The buttery rich fruits grow in large bunches containing up to a thousand dates. Varying from oval to elongated, they have a paper-thin skin and a long pit. Medjool, Khadrawy, and Halawy are the commonly marketed soft dates. Whole and pitted dates are available year-round.

ZESTING CITRUS

Citrus juice and zest are popular flavorings in baked goods. When a recipe calls for both, first remove the zest. Scrub the fruit, then pull a zester or a Microplane grater across the rind to yield thin strips of zest while leaving the pith behind. Wider and longer strips may be removed with a paring knife or vegetable peeler, then cut into smaller pieces.

Orange-Nut Bread

MAKES ONE 8½-BY-4½-INCH (21.5-BY-11.5-CM) LOAF

2 cups (10 oz/315 g) all-purpose (plain) flour

1 cup (8 oz/250 g) sugar

1 Tbsp baking powder

½ tsp salt

Grated zest of 1 orange

¾ cup (3 oz/90 g) walnuts, pecans, hazelnuts, or almonds, coarsely chopped

¼ cup (2 oz/60 g) unsalted butter, melted

2 large eggs, beaten

¾ cup (6 fl oz/180 ml) strained fresh orange juice

1 tsp pure vanilla extract

PREHEAT THE OVEN TO 325°F (165°C). Grease an 8½-by-4½-inch (21.5-by-11.5-cm) loaf pan or spray with nonstick cooking spray.

In a bowl, stir together the flour, sugar, baking powder, salt, and orange zest. Add the nuts and stir until evenly distributed. Make a well in the center and add the melted butter, eggs, orange juice, and vanilla. Stir until smooth.

Pour the batter into the prepared pan.

Bake until the top is browned and firm and the edges begin to pull away from the pan sides, 50–60 minutes. A toothpick inserted into the center of the loaf should come out clean. Transfer the pan to a wire rack and let cool for 10 minutes. Unmold the loaf onto the rack and let cool completely. Cut into thick slices to serve.

Peach Melba Muffins

MAKES 11 MUFFINS

1 cup (4 oz/125 g) fresh raspberries or frozen unsweetened raspberries, unthawed

½ cup (4 oz/125 g) sugar, plus 2 Tbsp

1 Tbsp berry liqueur, such as Chambord, or raspberry vinegar

2 cups (10 oz/315 g) all-purpose (plain) flour

2½ tsp baking powder

½ tsp salt

2 large eggs

6 Tbsp (3 oz/90 g) unsalted butter, melted

1 cup (8 fl oz/250 ml) milk

1 or 2 peaches, about 8 oz (250 g) each, peeled, pitted, and coarsely chopped (page 178)

¼ cup (1 oz/30 g) sliced (flaked) almonds for sprinkling

PREHEAT THE OVEN TO 375°F (190°C). Grease 11 standard muffin cups with butter or butter-flavored nonstick cooking spray; fill the unused cup one-third full with water to prevent warping.

In a small bowl, toss the raspberries with 1 Tbsp of the sugar and the liqueur. Let stand for 30 minutes. In a bowl, stir together the flour, ½ cup (4 oz/125 g) sugar, baking powder, and salt.

In another bowl, whisk together the eggs, melted butter, and milk until blended. Stir in the flour mixture just until evenly moistened, 15–20 strokes. The batter will be slightly lumpy. Using a large silicone spatula, gently fold in the peaches just until evenly distributed, no more than a few strokes. Take care not to break up the fruit.

Spoon the batter into each muffin cup, filling it half full. Divide the raspberries among the cups, using about 1 Tbsp per muffin, then cover with batter until level with the rim. Sprinkle with the remaining 1 Tbsp sugar and the almonds, dividing them evenly.

Bake the muffins until golden, dry, and springy to the touch, 25–30 minutes. Transfer the pan to a wire rack and let cool for 5 minutes. Serve warm or at room temperature.

ABOUT PEACH MELBA

This muffin recipe is based on Peach Melba, a classic dessert with fresh poached peach halves filled with vanilla ice cream and topped with raspberry sauce—called "Melba sauce"—and toasted almonds. The dish is the gustatory handiwork of the French chef Auguste Escoffier. He created the combination in the late 1800s to honor Dame Nellie Melba, the most popular opera star of the day, who often ate in his restaurant. The pairing of sweet peaches and tart raspberries is a delectable treat.

Cinnamon-Crunch Sweet Potato Muffins

MAKES 12 MUFFINS

SWEET POTATOES

These plump edible roots are available year-round but are most abundant in markets in autumn and winter. Some of these vegetables—members of the morning glory family—have tan skin and light yellow flesh; others have darker red-orange skin and flesh. The latter type is often called a yam in the United States, although it is not a true yam. Red-orange sweet potatoes are slightly moister and sweeter than the tan variety, which has the same texture as a russet potato when cooked and mashed.

FOR THE TOPPING:

3 Tbsp sugar

1 tsp ground cinnamon

FOR THE MUFFINS:

2 sweet potatoes or yams (orange-fleshed sweet potatoes), 14 oz (440 g) total weight, peeled and cut into chunks

1¾ cups (9 oz/280 g) all-purpose (plain) flour

½ tsp ground cinnamon

½ tsp freshly grated nutmeg

2 tsp baking powder

½ tsp salt

2 large eggs

½ cup (4 oz/125 g) sugar

½ cup (4 fl oz/125 ml) canola oil or walnut oil

½ cup (4 fl oz/125 ml) milk

½ tsp orange oil, or grated zest of 1 orange

¾ cup (3 oz/90 g) pecans, coarsely chopped

TO MAKE THE TOPPING, in a small bowl, stir together the sugar and cinnamon.

To make the muffins, bring a saucepan three-fourths full of water to a boil, add the sweet potatoes, and cook until tender, 15–20 minutes. Remove from the heat and drain thoroughly. Transfer to a food processor and pulse until slightly fluffy. Scrape into a bowl and let cool to room temperature.

Preheat the oven to 400°F (200°C). Grease 12 standard muffin cups with butter or butter-flavored nonstick cooking spray.

In a bowl, stir together the flour, cinnamon, nutmeg, baking powder, and salt.

In another bowl, combine the eggs, sugar, oil, milk, and orange oil. Whisk vigorously for 1 minute. Add the mashed sweet potatoes and beat until completely blended. Add the flour mixture and stir just until evenly moistened. The batter will be slightly lumpy. Using a large silicone spatula, fold in the pecans just until evenly distributed, no more than a few strokes. Do not overmix.

Spoon the batter into each muffin cup, filling it three-fourths full. Sprinkle each muffin with some of the topping, dividing it evenly.

Bake the muffins until golden, dry, and springy to the touch, 20–25 minutes. A toothpick inserted into the center of a muffin should come out clean. Transfer the pan to a wire rack and let the muffins cool for 5 minutes. Unmold the muffins. Serve warm.

NOTE: Canned sweet potatoes or yams can be substituted for fresh in this recipe. Drain them well before mashing.

Spinach-Pesto Muffins

MAKES 12 MUFFINS

FOR THE PESTO:

1 clove garlic

1/8 cup (2/3 oz/19 g) pine nuts

1/2 cup (1/2 oz/15 g) loosely packed fresh basil leaves

1/4 cup (1/4 oz/8 g) loosely packed fresh flat-leaf (Italian) parsley leaves

1/4 cup (2 fl oz/60 ml) olive oil

1/4 cup (1 oz/30 g) grated Parmesan cheese

Salt as needed

FOR THE BATTER:

3 cups (15 oz/470 g) all-purpose (plain) flour

1 Tbsp baking powder

1 1/4 tsp salt

3 large eggs, beaten

2/3 cup (5 fl oz/160 ml) olive oil

1 cup (8 fl oz/250 ml) milk

1 package (10 oz/315 g) frozen chopped spinach, thawed and squeezed dry

1 cup (4 oz/125 g) shredded mozzarella cheese

TO MAKE THE PESTO, in a food processor or blender, purée the garlic clove. Add the pine nuts, basil, and parsley and process until finely chopped. With the machine running, slowly pour in the olive oil and pulse briefly to make a coarse paste. Add the Parmesan and pulse to incorporate. Season with salt, if desired.

Preheat the oven to 375°F (190°C). Grease 12 standard muffin cups with butter.

In a bowl, stir together the flour, baking powder, and salt. In another bowl, whisk together the eggs, olive oil, and milk. Stir in the spinach until blended. Make a well in the center of the flour mixture and add the spinach mixture, stirring just until evenly moistened. The batter will be slightly lumpy. Using a large silicone spatula, fold in the pesto and mozzarella just until evenly distributed. Some streaks of pesto may remain. Do not overmix. Spoon the batter into each muffin cup, filling it level with the rim.

Bake the muffins until golden, dry, and springy to the touch, 20–25 minutes. A toothpick inserted into the center of a muffin should come out clean. Transfer the pan to a wire rack and let cool for 5 minutes. Unmold the muffins. Serve warm or at room temperature.

ABOUT PESTO

Made with fresh basil and pine nuts, Genoese pesto is the best-known pesto outside of Italy. It is hard to give exact measurements for the sauce, for although the ingredients are widely agreed upon, the proportions are a matter of taste. This pesto recipe results in a light, herbal pesto with just a hint of garlic. Some people may wish to add more garlic or more cheese, or substitute milder *pecorino romano* cheese for half of the Parmesan.

Beer Batter Bread

MAKES ONE 9-BY-5-INCH (23-BY-13-CM) LOAF

3 cups (15 oz/470 g) all-purpose (plain) flour

3 Tbsp firmly packed light brown sugar

1 Tbsp baking powder

1 tsp salt

1 bottle (12 fl oz/375 ml) beer, unopened and at room temperature

4 Tbsp (2 oz/60 g) unsalted butter, melted, plus extra for serving

PREHEAT THE OVEN TO 375°F (190°C). Grease a 9-by-5-inch (23-by-13-cm) loaf pan.

In a bowl, stir together the flour, brown sugar, baking powder, and salt. Open the beer and add it all at once; it will foam up. Stir briskly just until combined, about 20 strokes. The batter should be slightly lumpy. Pour into the prepared loaf pan and drizzle with the melted butter.

Bake until the top is crusty and a cake tester inserted into the center comes out clean, 35–40 minutes. Let rest in the pan for 5 minutes, then turn the loaf out onto a wire rack. Serve warm or at room temperature the day it is made. Cut into thick slices and accompany with plenty of butter.

SERVING TIP: Serve this bread with hearty soups, stews, and braises.

BEER FOR BREAD

A mixture of malted barley, hops, and cultured yeast brewed into a beverage by boiling, beer is considered to be as old as agriculture itself. It is favored in bread making because it adds its own good flavor and, as a product of fermentation, some of its own leavening power. This beer bread will take on the character of whatever beer you use, so the bread can taste different each time you make it.

Dark Chocolate Tea Bread

MAKES ONE 9-BY-5-INCH (23-BY-13-CM) LOAF

2 cups (10 oz/315 g) all-purpose (plain) flour

½ cup (2 oz/60 g) cake (soft-wheat) flour

¾ cup (2 oz/60 g) unsweetened Dutch-process cocoa powder

1 tsp baking soda (bicarbonate of soda)

1 tsp baking powder

½ tsp salt

5 Tbsp (2½ oz/75 g) unsalted butter, at room temperature

4 oz (125 g) cream cheese

1 cup (8 oz/250 g) granulated sugar

2 large eggs

1¼ cups (10 fl oz/310 ml) buttermilk

1½ tsp pure vanilla extract

⅔ cup (3½ oz/105 g) chopped toasted hazelnuts (filberts) (page 60)

1 Tbsp raw or coarse sugar

PREHEAT THE OVEN TO 350°F (180°C). Grease a 9-by-5-inch (23-by-13-cm) loaf pan.

In a bowl, stir together the all-purpose flour, cake flour, cocoa, baking soda, baking powder, and salt.

In another bowl, using an electric mixer on medium speed, cream together the butter and cream cheese until fluffy. Beat in the granulated sugar until combined. Add the eggs one at a time, beating well after each addition. The mixture should be fluffy.

Add the flour mixture to the creamed mixture in 2 additions, alternating with the buttermilk and vanilla, beginning with the flour mixture and beating until smooth after each addition. Fold in the hazelnuts just until evenly distributed. The batter should be very thick.

Scrape the batter into the prepared pan. It should be no more than two-thirds full. Smooth the surface and sprinkle with the raw sugar.

Bake until the top is firm to the touch and the edges pull away from the pan sides, about 1¼ hours. A cake tester inserted into the center of the top should come out clean. If necessary, cover loosely with aluminum foil for the last 10 minutes to prevent overbrowning. Immediately turn the loaf out of the pan onto a wire rack with a gentle motion, and let cool completely. Cut into thick slices to serve.

COCOA POWDER

Cocoa powder is made from cocoa beans, which are native to the tropics. The beans are roasted and then, over the course of several steps, transformed into a thick paste that is dried and ground into unsweetened cocoa powder. In the process, most of the cocoa butter is removed, making cocoa powder an excellent low-fat addition to breads. Unless a recipe specifies otherwise, use Dutch-process cocoa, which has been treated with an alkaline substance to smooth out the harsh acidic flavor elements.

MUFFIN PANS

A standard muffin pan contains 12 cups. Each is 2¾ to 3 inches (7 to 7.5 cm) wide by 1¾ inch (4.5 cm) deep, and has a capacity of about ½ cup (4 fl oz/125 ml). Some muffin pans have 6 cups. Restaurant supply stores carry professional muffin tins with 24 standard cups, suitable for large home ovens and recipes with high yields. Muffin pans can also be used for making cupcakes, rolls, and individual custards.

Vanilla-Pear Muffins

MAKES 14 MUFFINS

FOR THE TOPPING:

3 Tbsp sugar

2 Tbsp chopped walnuts, ground (page 58)

¼ tsp ground cinnamon

FOR THE MUFFINS:

2 cups (10 oz/315 g) all-purpose (plain) flour

½ cup (4 oz/125 g) sugar

2 tsp ground cinnamon

1 tsp freshly grated nutmeg

2 tsp baking powder

½ tsp baking soda (bicarbonate of soda)

½ tsp salt

2 large eggs

½ cup (4 fl oz/125 ml) canola oil or walnut oil

¾ cup (6 fl oz/180 ml) buttermilk

2 tsp pure vanilla extract

4 or 5 firm, ripe pears, 2 lb (1 kg) total weight, peeled, cored, and coarsely chopped

1 cup (4 oz/125 g) walnuts, coarsely chopped

PREHEAT THE OVEN TO 350°F (180°C). Grease 14 standard muffin cups with butter or butter-flavored nonstick cooking spray; fill the unused cups one-third full with water to prevent warping.

To make the topping, in a small bowl, stir together the sugar, walnuts, and cinnamon.

To make the muffins, in a bowl, stir together the flour, sugar, cinnamon, nutmeg, baking powder, baking soda, and salt.

In another bowl, whisk together the eggs, oil, buttermilk, and vanilla until blended. Add the flour mixture, stirring just until evenly moistened. The batter will be slightly lumpy. Using a large silicone spatula, gently fold in the pears and walnuts just until evenly distributed, no more than a few strokes. When mixing, take care not to break up the fruit. Do not overmix.

Spoon the batter into each muffin cup, filling it level with the rim. Sprinkle each muffin with some of the topping, dividing it evenly.

Bake the muffins until golden, dry, and springy to the touch, 20–25 minutes. A toothpick inserted into the center of a muffin should come out clean. Transfer the pan(s) to a wire rack and let the muffins cool for 5 minutes. Unmold the muffins. Serve warm or at room temperature.

Oatmeal–Golden Raisin Bread

MAKES ONE 9-BY-5-INCH (23-BY-13-CM) LOAF

1¼ cups (6½ oz/200 g) all-purpose (plain) flour

1 cup (3½ oz/105 g) quick-cooking rolled oats

⅔ cup (4 oz/125 g) golden raisins (sultanas), or a mixture of golden raisins and dried cherries

¾ cup (6 oz/185 g) firmly packed light brown sugar

1½ tsp baking powder

1 tsp baking soda (bicarbonate of soda)

½ tsp salt

1½ tsp ground cinnamon

½ tsp freshly grated nutmeg

¼ tsp ground allspice

2 large eggs, beaten

⅓ cup (3 fl oz/80 ml) almond oil or canola oil

¾ cup (7 oz/220 g) applesauce page 378, or purchased unsweetened applesauce

½ cup (4 fl oz/125 ml) buttermilk

1–2 Tbsp firmly packed light brown sugar (optional)

PREHEAT THE OVEN TO 350°F (180°C). Grease a 9-by-5-inch (23-by-13-cm) loaf pan or spray with nonstick cooking spray.

In a bowl, stir together the flour, oats, raisins, ¾ cup (6 oz/185 g) brown sugar, baking powder, baking soda, salt, cinnamon, nutmeg, and allspice. Make a well in the center and add the eggs, oil, applesauce, and buttermilk. Stir just until evenly moistened, 15–20 strokes. The batter will be slightly lumpy. Do not overmix.

Pour the batter into the prepared pan. If desired, sprinkle the batter evenly with the 1–2 Tbsp brown sugar.

Bake until the top is well browned and firm and the edges pull away from the pan sides, 40–50 minutes. A toothpick inserted into the center of the loaf should come out clean. Transfer the pan to a wire rack and let cool for 10 minutes. Unmold the loaf onto the rack and let cool completely. Cut into thick slices to serve. Alternatively, wrap the loaf tightly in plastic wrap and refrigerate for at least 8 hours, or up to 4 days. The loaf slices best when cold.

GOLDEN RAISINS

As the most common dried fruit used in baking, raisins provide intense bursts of flavor. Dark raisins are made by sun-drying grapes, most commonly seedless Thompson grapes. Golden raisins, also known as sultanas, are made with the same grapes as dark raisins, but instead of sun-dried, the grapes are bleached with sulfur dioxide and then mechanically dried in a dehydrator, which produces a plump result. Store both raisin types in covered containers at room temperature for up to a month or in the refrigerator for up to 6 months.

Blackberry Muffins

MAKES 12 MUFFINS

FOR THE TOPPING:

⅓ cup (3 oz/90 g) sugar

3 Tbsp all-purpose (plain) flour

Grated zest of ½ lemon

2 Tbsp unsalted butter, melted

⅓ cup (1½ oz/45 g) pecans, finely chopped

FOR THE MUFFINS:

2 cups (10 oz/315 g) all-purpose (plain) flour

¾ cup (6 oz/185 g) sugar

2 tsp baking powder

½ tsp baking soda (bicarbonate of soda)

½ tsp ground cinnamon

Grated zest of ½ lemon

¼ tsp salt

1 large egg, beaten

5 Tbsp (2½ oz/75 g) unsalted butter, melted

1 cup (8 fl oz/250 ml) buttermilk

2 cups (8 oz/250 g) fresh blackberries or 2½ cups (10 oz/315 g) frozen unsweetened blackberries, unthawed

PREHEAT THE OVEN TO 375°F (190°C). Grease 12 standard muffin cups with butter or butter-flavored nonstick cooking spray.

To make the topping, in a small bowl, stir together the sugar, flour, and lemon zest. Stir in the melted butter until the mixture is crumbly. Add the pecans and stir to combine.

To make the muffins, in a bowl, stir together the flour, sugar, baking powder, baking soda, cinnamon, lemon zest, and salt. Make a well in the center and add the egg, melted butter, and buttermilk. Stir just until evenly moistened. The batter will be slightly lumpy. Using a large silicone spatula, gently fold in the blackberries just until evenly distributed, no more than a few strokes. Take care not to break up or mash the fruit.

Spoon the batter into each muffin cup, filling it a little bit above the rim. Sprinkle each muffin with some of the topping, dividing it evenly (the sugar will melt and produce a glaze effect).

Bake the muffins until golden and springy to the touch, 25–30 minutes. A toothpick inserted into the center of a muffin should come out clean. Transfer the pan to a wire rack and let the muffins cool for 10 minutes. Unmold the muffins. Serve warm or at room temperature.

FREEZING BERRIES

Berries freeze well for up to 10 months, so you can make these muffins in seasons other than spring or summer, when berries can be found fresh from local growers. To freeze blueberries, raspberries, or blackberries, place the dried berries in a single layer on a baking sheet and freeze. When frozen, transfer the berries to freezer-proof containers. Thaw frozen berries at room temperature for about 1 hour. If necessary, transfer to a colander to drain.

DRIED PLUMS OR PRUNES

Plums, a stone fruit like peaches, are dried to produce prunes, resulting in dried fruits with a dark, firm flesh and a high sugar content. Dried plums, or prunes, are categorized by size, ranging from small to jumbo, with the larger grades having an appealing plumpness. Most of the prunes sold in the United States are produced in California. One of the common plums used is the d'Agen from France. For this recipe, look for prunes sold in airtight packages that help preserve their moisture content. Store at room temperature for up to a month or in the refrigerator for up to 6 months.

Dried Plum Bread

MAKES ONE 9-BY-5-INCH (23-BY-13-CM) LOAF

12 oz (375 g) moist-pack pitted prunes (dried plums), coarsely chopped

1 cup (8 fl oz/250 ml) boiling water

1 tsp pure vanilla extract

2 cups (10 oz/315 g) all-purpose (plain) flour

¾ cup (6 oz/185 g) sugar

¾ cup (3 oz/90 g) walnuts, chopped

2 tsp baking powder

1 tsp baking soda (bicarbonate of soda)

½ tsp salt

1 tsp ground cinnamon

½ tsp freshly grated nutmeg

1 large egg, beaten

4 Tbsp (2 oz/60 g) unsalted butter, melted

PREHEAT THE OVEN TO 350°F (180°C). Grease a 9-by-5-inch (23-by-13-cm) loaf pan or spray with nonstick cooking spray.

Put the prunes in a bowl and add the boiling water and vanilla. Let stand at room temperature until cool, 30–60 minutes.

In a bowl, stir together the flour, sugar, walnuts, baking powder, baking soda, salt, cinnamon, and nutmeg. Make a well in the center and add the egg, melted butter, and prune mixture with its liquid. Stir just until evenly moistened. Pour the batter into the prepared pan.

Bake until the top is browned and firm and the edges pull away from the pan sides, 55–60 minutes. A toothpick inserted into the center of the loaf should come out clean. Transfer the pan to a wire rack and let cool for 10 minutes. Unmold the loaf onto the rack and let cool completely. Wrap the loaf tightly in plastic wrap and store at room temperature overnight. Cut into thick slices to serve.

Dried Fig Muffins

MAKES 11 MUFFINS

1 cup (8 fl oz/250 ml) apple juice

6 Tbsp (3 oz/90 g) unsalted butter, cut into small pieces

12 oz (375 g) dried figs, stemmed and quartered

Grated zest of 1 large orange

2 cups (10 oz/315 g) all-purpose (plain) flour

½ cup (4 oz/125 g) granulated sugar

¼ cup (2 oz/60 g) firmly packed dark brown sugar

2½ tsp baking powder

½ tsp salt

2 large eggs, beaten

1½ tsp pure vanilla extract

IN A SMALL SAUCEPAN over medium-low heat, heat the apple juice and butter until the butter is melted, about 5 minutes. Remove from the heat and add the dried figs and orange zest. Set aside until the mixture comes to room temperature and the figs are softened, about 1 hour.

Preheat the oven to 375°F (190°C). Grease 11 standard muffin cups with butter or butter-flavored nonstick cooking spray or line with paper liners; fill the unused cup one-third full with water to prevent warping.

In a bowl, stir together the flour, granulated sugar, brown sugar, baking powder, and salt. Make a well in the center and add the cooled fig mixture, eggs, and vanilla. Stir just until evenly moistened. The batter will be slightly lumpy. Do not overmix.

Spoon the batter into each muffin cup, filling it level with the rim.

Bake the muffins until golden, dry, and springy to the touch, 20–25 minutes. A toothpick inserted into the center of a muffin should come out clean. Transfer the pan to a wire rack and let cool for 5 minutes. Unmold the muffins and let cool completely. Serve at room temperature.

DRIED FIGS

Sweet, chewy dried figs are delicious when added to baked goods. Choose either the pale Calimyrna, the most common variety found dried, or the dark Black Mission fig. Dried whole figs tend to be very stiff because the drying process needs to permeate the entire fruit; softening them first is important to the texture of the finished muffins. Here, the figs are macerated in hot apple juice so they turn a lovely mahogany color and give off an enticing perfume.

Onion & Shallot Muffins

MAKES 11 MUFFINS

SHALLOTS

Because of their delicate shape and color, shallots have a reputation for elegance. This diminutive member of the onion family grows in clusters of cloves like garlic and has a papery reddish or bronze skin. The white flesh lightly streaked with purple has a subdued onion flavor and cooks more quickly than the flesh of larger onions. To prepare a shallot, cut off both ends, then peel off the papery skin. Cut the bulb in half lengthwise and mince like you would a small onion.

5 Tbsp (3 fl oz/80 ml) olive oil

¼ cup (1½ oz/45 g) finely chopped red onion

1 medium to large shallot, minced

3 cups (15 oz/470 g) all-purpose (plain) flour

1⅓ cups (5½ oz/170 g) grated Jarlsberg or Swiss cheese

3 Tbsp minced fresh flat-leaf (Italian) parsley

4 tsp baking powder

1½ tsp salt

1 tsp crumbled dried oregano or marjoram

½ tsp celery seed

2 large eggs

1 cup (8 fl oz/250 ml) milk

PREHEAT THE OVEN TO 375°F (190°C). Grease 11 standard muffin cups with butter or butter-flavored nonstick cooking spray; fill the unused cup one-third full with water to prevent warping.

In a frying pan over medium heat, heat 3 Tbsp of the oil. Add the onion and shallot and sauté until translucent, 2–3 minutes. Remove from the heat and let cool.

In a bowl, stir together the flour, 1 cup (4 oz/125 g) of the cheese, the parsley, baking powder, salt, oregano, and celery seed.

In another bowl, whisk together the eggs, remaining 2 Tbsp oil, and milk until blended. Add the cooled onions, along with any oil left in the pan. Make a well in the center of the flour mixture and stir in the onion mixture just until evenly moistened. The batter will be slightly lumpy.

Spoon the batter into each muffin cup, filling it level with the rim. Sprinkle each muffin with some of the remaining ⅓ cup (1½ oz/45 g) cheese.

Bake the muffins until golden, dry, and springy to the touch, 25–30 minutes. A toothpick inserted into the center of a muffin should come out clean. Transfer the pan to a wire rack and let the muffins cool for 5 minutes. Unmold the muffins. Serve warm or at room temperature.

CORNMEAL

In a bread this simple, the quality of the ingredients shows. Stone-ground cornmeal is more perishable since it contains the germ of the corn, but its coarser texture and more intense corn flavor make it a good choice here. Look for it in well-stocked supermarkets and in natural-foods stores.

Sweet Potato Corn Bread

MAKES ONE 9-INCH (23-CM) CORN BREAD

2 sweet potatoes or yams (orange-fleshed sweet potatoes), 1 lb (500 g) total weight, peeled and cut into chunks

1 cup (5 oz/155 g) fine- or medium-grind yellow cornmeal, preferably stone-ground

1 cup (5 oz/155 g) all-purpose (plain) flour

1 Tbsp sugar

1 Tbsp baking powder

½ tsp baking soda (bicarbonate of soda)

1 tsp salt

Pinch of ground allspice

Pinch of ground cinnamon

1¼ cups (10 fl oz/310 ml) buttermilk

2 large eggs, lightly beaten

3 Tbsp unsalted butter, melted

BRING A SAUCEPAN three-fourths full of water to a boil, add the sweet potatoes, and cook until tender, 15–20 minutes. Remove from the heat and drain thoroughly. Transfer to a food processor and pulse until slightly fluffy. Scrape into a bowl and let cool to room temperature.

Preheat the oven to 400°F (200°C). Grease a 9-inch (23-cm) square baking pan.

In a small bowl, stir together the cornmeal, flour, sugar, baking powder, baking soda, salt, allspice, and cinnamon.

Add the buttermilk, eggs, and melted butter to the sweet potatoes and mix well. Add the cornmeal mixture and stir just until combined, taking care not to overmix. The batter should be slightly lumpy. Pour the batter into the prepared pan.

Bake until the top is golden brown and the edges pull away from the pan sides, about 30 minutes. Place the pan on a rack to cool slightly. Cut into squares to serve.

Polenta Muffins with Fresh Herbs

MAKES 14 MUFFINS

1½ cups (7½ oz/235 g) all-purpose (plain) flour

1¼ cups (6½ oz/200 g) regular or instant polenta

¾ cup (3 oz/90 g) cake (soft-wheat) flour

¼ cup (2 oz/60 g) sugar

1 Tbsp baking powder

1 tsp baking soda (bicarbonate of soda)

1½ tsp salt

½ cup (4 oz/125 g) cold unsalted butter, cut into small pieces

⅓ cup (3 fl oz/80 ml) olive oil

3 large eggs

1⅓ cups (11 fl oz/345 ml) buttermilk

¼ cup (½ oz/15 g) packed chopped fresh flat-leaf (Italian) parsley

2 Tbsp minced fresh chives

2 Tbsp minced fresh savory, marjoram, or basil

PREHEAT THE OVEN TO 375°F (190°C). Grease 14 standard muffin cups with butter or butter-flavored nonstick cooking spray; fill the unused cups one-third full with water to prevent warping.

In a bowl, stir together the all-purpose flour, polenta, cake flour, sugar, baking powder, baking soda, and salt. Using an electric mixer on low speed, add the butter and olive oil and beat until thick crumbs form. Add the eggs, buttermilk, parsley, chives, and savory. Beat just until the mixture is smooth and the herbs are evenly distributed. Take care not to overbeat or the muffins will lose their lightness.

Spoon the batter into each muffin cup, filling it level with the rim.

Bake the muffins until golden, dry, and springy to the touch, 20–25 minutes. A toothpick inserted into the center of a muffin should come out clean. Transfer the pan(s) to a wire rack and let the muffins cool for 5 minutes. Unmold the muffins. Serve warm or at room temperature.

POLENTA

These muffins are inspired by Italian polenta, a term that refers to cornmeal that is cooked in water or stock and eaten while soft for breakfast or as a side dish. The traditional preparation uses coarse-ground cornmeal. For these muffins, medium-ground cornmeal may be substituted for Italian polenta and will result in muffins with a slightly different, but equally appealing texture. Instant polenta is also available but lacks the hearty texture of the long-cooking variety.

Zucchini Bread

MAKES ONE 8½-BY-4½-INCH (21.5-BY-11.5-CM) LOAF OR THREE 6-BY-3-INCH (15-BY-7.5-CM) LOAVES

8 oz (125 g) zucchini (courgettes), trimmed

½ cup (4 fl oz/125 ml) canola oil

¾ cup (6 oz/185 g) sugar

2 large eggs

1 tsp pure vanilla extract

1½ cups (7½ oz/235 g) all-purpose (plain) flour

2 tsp baking powder

1½ tsp ground cinnamon

½ tsp salt

¼ tsp baking soda (bicarbonate of soda)

½ cup (3 oz/90 g) chopped pitted moist-pack prunes (dried plums)

⅓ cup (1½ oz/45 g) coarsely chopped walnuts

PREHEAT THE OVEN TO 350°F (180°C). Grease and lightly flour one 8½-by-4½-inch (21.5-by-11.5-cm) loaf pan or three 6-by-3-inch (15-by-7.5-cm) loaf pans.

Using the large holes of a box grater-shredder or the large-holed shredder blade of a food processor, shred the zucchini. You should have about 1 cup (5 oz/155 g). Set aside.

In a bowl, combine the oil, sugar, eggs, and vanilla. Beat vigorously with a whisk or with an electric mixer on medium speed until pale and creamy, about 1 minute. Stir in the shredded zucchini until blended.

In a bowl, stir together the flour, baking powder, cinnamon, salt, baking soda, prunes, and walnuts. Add the flour mixture to the zucchini mixture and stir just until combined. The batter will be stiff. Scrape the batter into the prepared pan(s).

Bake until the top is firm to the touch and the edges pull away from the pan sides, 50–60 minutes for a large loaf, 35–40 minutes for small ones. A cake tester inserted into the center of a loaf should come out clean. Let cool in the pan(s) on a rack for 10 minutes. Turn the bread out, place upright on the rack, and let cool completely.

LOAF PANS

Loaf pans give form to breads that are too moist to hold their own shape. They range in shape and size, but the standard size is 8½ by 4½ by 2¾ inches (21.5 by 11.5 by 7 cm), with a capacity of 5½ cups (44 fl oz/1.3 l). Be careful when trying to substitute a pan of a different size than what's called for in a recipe. For the best results, the batter should fill the pan about two-thirds full.

Spiced Carrot-Nut Muffins

MAKES 24 MUFFINS

4 large eggs

1 cup (8 fl oz/250 ml) canola oil or walnut oil

2 cups (1 lb/500 g) sugar

3 cups (15 oz/470 g) all-purpose (plain) flour

2 tsp baking powder

1 tsp baking soda (bicarbonate of soda)

½ tsp salt

2 tsp ground cinnamon

¼ tsp ground allspice

3 or 4 carrots, 12 oz (375 g) total weight, peeled and shredded

1½ cups (6 oz/185 g) walnuts, pecans, or hazelnuts, coarsely chopped

PREHEAT THE OVEN TO 350°F (180°C). Grease 24 standard muffin cups with butter or butter-flavored nonstick cooking spray.

In a large bowl, combine the eggs, oil, and sugar. Using a whisk or an electric mixer on medium speed, vigorously beat just until smooth and slightly thickened, 1 full minute.

In another bowl, stir together the flour, baking powder, baking soda, salt, cinnamon, and allspice. Add to the egg mixture and, using the mixer on low speed or a wooden spoon, beat until smooth. Using a large silicone spatula, fold in the carrots and nuts, about 20 strokes. Scrape down the sides of the bowl and stir again.

Spoon the batter into each muffin cup, filling it no more than three-fourths full.

Bake the muffins until golden, dry, and springy to the touch, 20–25 minutes. A toothpick inserted into the center of a muffin should come out clean. Transfer the pans to wire racks and let cool for 5 minutes. Unmold the muffins. Serve warm or at room temperature.

SHREDDING VS. GRATING

Shredding refers to the process of cutting food into thin, narrow strips. One of the easiest ways to do this is to use the largest holes of a box grater-shredder, which are ideal for shredding vegetables such as carrots as well as medium-soft cheeses such as Cheddar. Grating, on the other hand, is the process of reducing foods, such as lemon zest or hard Parmesan cheese, into tiny particles using the finest rasps of a grater-shredder. You may also shred and grate foods using a mandoline or food processor fitted with the appropriate disk.

Tomato & Goat Cheese Muffins

MAKES 10 MUFFINS

GARBANZO FLOUR

This flour, ground from dried chickpeas and therefore also known as chickpea flour, is a staple in the Mediterranean and Middle East, where it is used to make flatbreads, fritters, and savory pancakes. It is also an ingredient in the breads and pancakes made by Indian cooks. The flour has a distinctive and very appealing, naturally sweet flavor. It may be difficult to find on supermarket shelves. If this is the case, look for it in natural-foods stores or in Indian markets, where it is sometimes labeled *besan*.

6 Tbsp (3 oz/90 g) unsalted butter

4 small green (spring) onions, including 1 inch (2.5 cm) of the tender green parts, finely chopped

2½ Tbsp minced fresh basil

1½ cups (7½ oz/235 g) all-purpose (plain) flour

1 cup (4½ oz/140 g) garbanzo flour

3½ tsp baking powder

½ tsp salt

1¼ cups (10 fl oz/310 ml) milk

2 large eggs

3 oz (90 g) fresh white goat cheese, divided into 10 equal portions

2 plum (Roma) tomatoes, halved lengthwise, then each half cut into 3 chunks

PREHEAT THE OVEN TO 400°F (200°C). Grease 10 standard muffin cups with butter or butter-flavored nonstick cooking spray; fill the unused cups one-third full with water to prevent warping.

In a small frying pan over low heat, melt the butter. Add the green onions and sauté until almost translucent, 1–2 minutes. Stir in the basil. Remove from the heat.

In a bowl, stir together the all-purpose flour, garbanzo flour, baking powder, and salt.

In another bowl, whisk together the milk and eggs until well blended. Make a well in the center of the flour mixture, then pour in the milk mixture and green onion mixture. Stir just until evenly moistened, using no more than 15–20 strokes. The batter will be thick and lumpy.

Spoon the batter into each muffin cup, filling it half full. Shape each portion of goat cheese into a round and set it in the center of the muffin batter. Place 1 or 2 tomato chunks on top of the cheese and gently press into the batter. Cover the cheese and tomato with batter until level with the rim.

Bake the muffins until golden, dry, and springy to the touch, 18–22 minutes. Do not overbake. To check the muffins, carefully lift a muffin from the pan; the sides should be browned. Transfer the pan to a wire rack and let the muffins cool for 5 minutes. Unmold the muffins. Serve warm or at room temperature.

MUFFIN-BAKING TIPS

The muffins in this book should be baked on the middle rack of the oven. If you are using more than one muffin pan, allow at least 1 inch (5 cm) between each pan so heat can circulate. Also, if using more than one pan, arrange them side by side rather than on separate racks. Avoid opening the oven until near the end of baking, or it will not maintain the correct heat level, causing the muffins to rise unevenly. Muffins are done when golden brown around the edges and springy to the touch on top.

Cinnamon-Buttermilk Muffins

MAKES 9 MUFFINS

FOR THE MUFFINS:

7 Tbsp (3½ oz/105 g) unsalted butter, at room temperature

⅔ cup (5 oz/155 g) sugar

1 large egg

1½ cups (7½ oz/235 g) all-purpose (plain) flour

1½ tsp baking powder

½ tsp baking soda (bicarbonate of soda)

½ tsp salt

½ tsp freshly grated nutmeg

½ cup (4 fl oz/125 ml) buttermilk

1½ tsp pure vanilla extract

FOR THE TOPPING:

⅔ cup (5 oz/155 g) sugar

1 Tbsp ground cinnamon

6 Tbsp (3 oz/90 g) unsalted butter, melted

PREHEAT THE OVEN TO 350°F (180°C). Grease 9 standard muffin cups with butter or butter-flavored nonstick cooking spray; fill the unused cups one-third full with water to prevent warping.

To make the muffins, in a bowl, using an electric mixer on medium speed, cream together the butter and sugar until light and fluffy. Add the egg, beating well to incorporate until pale and smooth.

In another bowl, stir together the flour, baking powder, baking soda, salt, and nutmeg. Add to the butter mixture in 2 additions, alternating with the buttermilk and vanilla. Stir just until evenly moistened. The batter will be slightly lumpy.

Spoon the batter into each muffin cup, filling it three-fourths full.

Bake the muffins until golden, dry, and springy to the touch, 20–25 minutes. A toothpick inserted into the center of a muffin should come out clean. Transfer the pan to a wire rack and let the muffins cool for 5 minutes. Unmold the muffins and let stand until cool enough to handle.

To make the topping, in a small, shallow bowl, stir together the sugar and cinnamon. Have ready the melted butter in another small bowl. Holding the bottom of a muffin, dip the top into the melted butter, turning to coat it evenly. Immediately dip the top in the cinnamon-sugar mixture, coating it evenly, then tapping it to remove excess sugar. Transfer to the rack, right side up. Repeat with the remaining muffins. Let cool completely before serving.

NOTE: These cakelike muffins are made from a batter similar to that used for making donuts, but are baked instead of fried.

Sour Cherry–Coconut Streusel Muffins

MAKES 12 MUFFINS

FOR THE COCONUT STREUSEL:

1/3 cup (2 1/2 oz/75 g) firmly packed light brown sugar

1/3 cup (2 oz/60 g) all-purpose (plain) flour

1/4 cup (2 oz/60 g) cold unsalted butter, cut into small pieces

1/2 cup (1 1/2 oz/45 g) sweetened flaked coconut

FOR THE MUFFINS:

2 cups (10 oz/315 g) all-purpose (plain) flour

1/2 cup (4 oz/125 g) granulated sugar

4 tsp baking powder

1/2 tsp salt

1/4 cup (2 oz/60 g) unsalted butter, melted

2 large eggs, beaten

1 cup (8 fl oz/250 ml) half-and-half (half cream) or milk

16 oz (500 g) jarred or canned pitted sour red pie cherries, drained and dried on paper towels

PREHEAT THE OVEN TO 375°F (190°C). Grease 12 standard muffin cups with butter or butter-flavored nonstick cooking spray.

To make the coconut streusel, in a small bowl, stir together the brown sugar and flour. Using a pastry blender or your fingers, cut or rub in the butter until the mixture is crumbly. Stir in the coconut.

To make the muffins, in a bowl, stir together the flour, sugar, baking powder, and salt.

In another bowl, whisk together the melted butter, eggs, and half-and-half. Make a well in the center of the flour mixture and add the egg mixture. Beat until thick and creamy. The batter will be slightly lumpy. Do not overmix.

Spoon the batter into each muffin cup, filling it one-third full. Drop in a few cherries, add batter just to cover, and then drop in a few more cherries. Spoon on more batter until the cups are filled level with the rims. Sprinkle each with 1 heaping Tbsp of coconut streusel.

Bake the muffins until golden, dry, and springy to the touch, 20–25 minutes. Transfer the pan to a wire rack and let cool for 5 minutes. Unmold the muffins. Serve warm or at room temperature.

SOUR CHERRIES

Smaller in size than sweet cherries and more elusive to find, fresh, dark red sour cherries are too acidic to eat out of hand but are prized for baking. Also called tart cherries, they are a regional specialty grown in Michigan, the heart of cherry country. The main varieties are Early Richmond, Montmorency, and Morello. Sour cherries are available in jars and cans. Cherries packed in water, often labeled "pie cherries," retain a tangy flavor that is excellent in muffins and scones.

Corn Bread with Corn Kernels

MAKES ONE 10-INCH (25-CM) ROUND OR 9-BY-13-INCH (23-BY-33-CM) RECTANGULAR BREAD

¾ cup (6 oz/185 g) unsalted butter, at room temperature

1¼ cups (10 oz/315 g) sugar

3 large eggs

1½ cups (7½ oz/235 g) fine- or medium-grind yellow cornmeal, preferably stone-ground

1 cup (4 oz/125 g) cake (soft-wheat) flour

½ cup (2½ oz/75 g) all-purpose (plain) flour

⅓ cup (2 oz/60 g) whole-wheat (wholemeal) pastry flour or corn flour (see Notes)

1 Tbsp baking powder

1 tsp salt

2 cups (16 fl oz/500 ml) buttermilk

1½ cups (9 oz/280 g) fresh or thawed frozen corn kernels, or 1 can (8¾ oz/270 g) whole-kernel corn, drained

PREHEAT THE OVEN TO 400°F (200°C). Grease a 10-inch (25-cm) round springform pan or a 9-by-13-inch (23-by-33-cm) glass baking dish with butter or nonstick cooking spray. If using a glass baking dish, reduce the oven temperature to 375°F (190°C).

In a bowl, using an electric mixer on medium speed, cream together the butter and sugar until light and fluffy. Add the eggs, one at a time, beating well after each addition.

In another bowl, stir together the cornmeal, cake flour, all-purpose flour, whole-wheat pastry flour, baking powder, and salt. Using the mixer on low speed, add the flour mixture to the butter mixture in 2 additions, alternating with the buttermilk. Beat until smooth and well combined. Using a large silicone spatula, fold in the corn kernels just until evenly distributed, no more than a few strokes. Do not overmix. Pour the batter into the prepared pan.

Bake until the edges are golden brown and pull away from the pan sides, 35–40 minutes. A toothpick inserted into the center of the bread should come out clean. Transfer the pan to a wire rack and let cool for 15 minutes. Remove the sides of the springform pan, if using. Serve warm or at room temperature, cut into wedges or squares.

NOTES: This bread is best served the day it is made. If there are leftovers, store, wrapped in plastic, in the refrigerator. Look for whole-wheat pastry flour and corn flour in natural-foods stores.

CUTTING CORN KERNELS OFF THE COB

To cut corn kernels off the cob, hold an ear of corn by its pointed end and stand it upright and at a slight angle with its stem end resting in the bottom of a wide bowl. Using a sharp knife, cut down the length of the cob, taking off 3 or 4 rows of kernels at a time and rotating the ear slightly with each cut. Cut as close to the cob as possible. Continue until all the kernels have been removed.

Sour Cream–Blueberry Bread

MAKES ONE 9-BY-5-INCH (23-BY-13-CM) LOAF

2 medium-ripe bananas

2 cups (10 oz/315 g) all-purpose (plain) flour

¾ cup (6 oz/185 g) sugar

1½ tsp baking soda (bicarbonate of soda)

½ tsp salt

½ tsp ground cinnamon

½ cup (2 oz/60 g) chopped pecans

2 large eggs

½ cup (4 oz/125 g) sour cream

1 tsp pure vanilla extract

½ cup (4 oz/125 g) unsalted butter, melted

1 heaping cup (4 oz/125 g) fresh or frozen blueberries

PREHEAT THE OVEN TO 350°F (180°C). Grease a 9-by-5-inch (23-by-13-cm) loaf pan with butter or butter-flavored nonstick cooking spray.

Mash the bananas well with a fork or coarsely purée them in a food processor. Measure out 1 cup (6 oz/185 g) and set aside.

In a bowl, stir together the flour, sugar, baking soda, salt, cinnamon, and nuts. In another bowl, whisk together the eggs, sour cream, vanilla, butter, and the 1 cup mashed banana pulp. Make a well in the center of the flour mixture, add the banana mixture, and stir just until combined. The batter should be slightly lumpy. Gently fold in the blueberries, taking care not to break them up or mash them. Pour the batter into the prepared pan.

Bake the bread until the top is firm to the touch and a cake tester inserted into the center comes out clean, 50–60 minutes. Let cool in the pan on a wire rack for 30 minutes. Unmold the loaf onto the rack and let cool completely. Cut into thick slices to serve.

VANILLA EXTRACT

The evocative flavor of vanilla is a favorite in quick breads. Always buy pure vanilla extract, never imitation, for the best flavor and quality. Look for dusky Bourbon vanilla, bottled in Madagascar, or Tahitian vanilla, which has a lighter, more floral flavor and aroma.

Chocolate Chip Muffins

MAKES 12 MUFFINS

½ cup (4 oz/125 g) unsalted butter, melted

¾ cup (12 fl oz/375 ml) buttermilk

2 large eggs

1 Tbsp pure vanilla extract

2 cups (10 oz/315 g) all-purpose (plain) flour

¾ cup (6 oz/185 g) sugar

2 tsp baking powder

½ tsp baking soda (bicarbonate of soda)

½ tsp salt

2 cups (12 oz/375 g) semisweet (plain) chocolate chips

PREHEAT THE OVEN TO 350°F (180°C). Grease 12 standard muffin cups with butter or butter-flavored nonstick cooking spray or line with paper liners.

In a bowl, whisk together the melted butter, buttermilk, eggs, and vanilla until smooth.

In another bowl, stir together the flour, sugar, baking powder, baking soda, and salt. Make a well in the center of the flour mixture, add the buttermilk mixture, and beat until smooth and well mixed, 1–2 minutes. Using a large silicone spatula, fold in the chocolate chips just until evenly distributed. Do not overmix. Spoon the batter into each muffin cup, filling it level with the rim.

Bake the muffins until golden, dry, and springy to the touch, 20–25 minutes. A toothpick inserted into the center of a muffin should come out clean. Transfer the pan to a wire rack and let cool for 5 minutes. Unmold the muffins and let cool completely. Serve at room temperature.

SEMISWEET CHOCOLATE

Sweet and mellow semisweet chocolate is a combination of cocoa butter and chocolate liquor—the smooth brown paste that is ground from roasted cocoa beans—blended with sugar, vanilla, and lecithin, a fatty plant-based additive that contributes a smooth texture. The chocolate is sold in bar form and as chips ranging in size from ½ inch (12 mm) to ⅛ inch (3 mm). In most recipes, semisweet chocolate can be used interchangeably with bittersweet chocolate, which is similar.

WALNUT OIL

Excellent for baking, walnut oil was once a specialty item but is now commonly sold in well-stocked supermarkets. The subtly flavored oil is extracted from raw walnut meats and is very nutritious and high in unsaturated fat. For this recipe, do not use toasted walnut oil, a favorite in French cooking, as it is not the same as plain walnut oil. To prevent the oil from becoming rancid, store it in the refrigerator. It will keep for up to 3 months. Canola oil can be substituted in this recipe.

Banana-Walnut Muffins

MAKES 10 MUFFINS

1½ cups (7½ oz/235 g) all-purpose (plain) flour

¾ cup (6 oz/185 g) sugar

¾ cup (3 oz/90 g) walnuts, coarsely chopped

1½ tsp baking soda (bicarbonate of soda)

¼ tsp salt

½ cup (4 fl oz/125 ml) walnut oil or canola oil

1 large egg

2 or 3 medium to large very ripe bananas, slightly mashed to yield 1¼ cups (10 oz/315 g)

3 Tbsp buttermilk

PREHEAT THE OVEN TO 375°F (190°C). Grease 10 standard muffin cups with butter or butter-flavored nonstick cooking spray; fill the unused cups one-third full with water to prevent warping.

In a bowl, stir together the flour, sugar, chopped walnuts, baking soda, and salt.

In another bowl, whisk together the oil, egg, mashed bananas, and buttermilk until blended. Add the flour mixture and beat well until evenly combined and creamy.

Spoon the batter into each muffin cup, filling it level with the rim.

Bake the muffins until golden, dry, and springy to the touch, 20–25 minutes. A cake tester inserted into the center of a muffin should come out clean. Transfer the pan to a wire rack and let the muffins cool for 5 minutes. Unmold the muffins. Serve warm or at room temperature.

Zucchini Muffins

MAKES 10 MUFFINS

- **1½ cups (7½ oz/235 g) all-purpose (plain) flour**
- **¾ cup (6 oz/185 g) sugar**
- **2 tsp baking powder**
- **¼ tsp baking soda (bicarbonate of soda)**
- **¼ tsp salt**
- **½ tsp ground cinnamon**
- **2 large eggs**
- **⅓ cup (3 fl oz/80 ml) canola oil or almond oil**
- **¼ cup (2½ oz/75 g) orange marmalade**
- **1 tsp pure vanilla extract**
- **1 zucchini (courgette), 4 oz (125 g) total weight, shredded and drained on paper towels**
- **¾ cup (3 oz/90 g) dark raisins or dried sweet cherries**
- **¼ cup (1 oz/30 g) pecans or almonds, chopped**

PREHEAT THE OVEN TO 400°F (200°C). Grease 10 standard muffin cups with butter or butter-flavored nonstick cooking spray; fill the unused cups one-third full with water to prevent warping.

In a bowl, stir together the flour, sugar, baking powder, baking soda, salt, and cinnamon.

In another bowl, whisk together the eggs, oil, marmalade, vanilla, and zucchini until blended. Add the flour mixture to the zucchini mixture in 3 additions and beat just until evenly moistened and smooth. Stir in the raisins and nuts just until evenly distributed. The batter will be stiff.

Spoon the batter into each muffin cup, filling it no more than three-fourths full.

Bake the muffins until golden, dry, and springy to the touch, 17–20 minutes. A cake tester inserted into the center of a muffin should come out clean. Transfer the pan to a wire rack and let the muffins cool for 5 minutes. Unmold the muffins. Serve warm or at room temperature.

ZUCCHINI

The long, straight-necked zucchini (courgette) is by far the best known of the summer squashes. These dark green or bright gold squashes are actually gourds, just like winter squashes, but are harvested when they are immature and their seeds and skin are sweet and tender. Before using the zucchini in this recipe, rinse and dry, then cut off the stem end before shredding onto layers of paper towels to absorb some of the excess moisture.

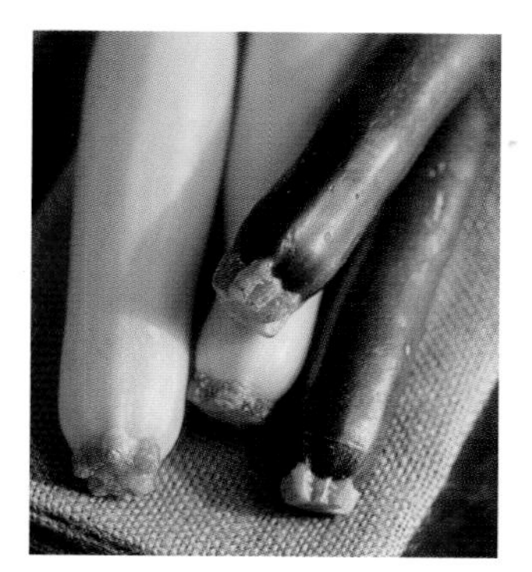

Honey-Raisin Bran Muffins

MAKES 18 MUFFINS

ABOUT BRAN

Wheat bran, the outer layer of grains of wheat, is a by-product of the flour-milling process. Although almost tasteless, fresh bran contributes a mild earthy flavor to muffins and other baked goods and is added to recipes along with flour to boost the fiber content and overall nutrition. Unprocessed wheat bran, which has not been toasted, is also packaged as miller's bran. Look for it in the cereal section of supermarkets or in natural-foods stores. Because bran is high in natural oils, it should be stored in the refrigerator to maintain freshness.

2 cups (10 oz/315 g) all-purpose (plain) flour

2 cups (8 oz/250 g) unprocessed bran flakes

1½ cups (9 oz/280 g) mixed dark and golden (sultana) raisins

⅓ cup (1 oz/30 g) toasted wheat germ

2 tsp baking soda (bicarbonate of soda)

1 tsp baking powder

1 tsp salt

½ cup (4 oz/125 g) unsalted butter, at room temperature

½ cup (3½ oz/105 g) firmly packed light or dark brown sugar

½ cup (6 oz/185 g) honey

1 cup (8 oz/250 g) plain yogurt

½ cup (4 fl oz/125 ml) buttermilk

2 tsp pure vanilla extract

3 large eggs, beaten

PREHEAT THE OVEN TO 400°F (200°C). Grease 18 standard muffin cups with butter or butter-flavored nonstick cooking spray; fill the unused cups one-third full with water to prevent warping.

In a bowl, stir together the flour, bran flakes, raisins, wheat germ, baking soda, baking powder, and salt.

In another bowl, using an electric mixer on medium speed or a wooden spoon, cream together the butter, brown sugar, and honey until fluffy. Beat in the yogurt, then the buttermilk and vanilla, until well blended and smooth.

Make a well in the center of the flour mixture and add the butter mixture and the eggs. Beat just until evenly moistened. The batter will be thick and slightly lumpy.

Spoon the batter into each muffin cup, filling it level with the rim.

Transfer the filled pan(s) to the oven and immediately reduce the oven temperature to 350°F (180°C). Bake the muffins until golden, dry, and springy to the touch, 18–22 minutes. A toothpick inserted into the center of a muffin should come out clean. Transfer the pan(s) to wire racks and let cool for at least 15 minutes. Unmold the muffins. Serve warm or at room temperature.

Maple-Pecan Bread

MAKES ONE 9-BY-5-INCH (23-BY-13-CM) LOAF

MAPLE SYRUP

Luxurious, pure maple syrup is a sumptuous treat. Maple syrup, produced by boiling the sap of the sugar maple tree, is characterized by grade. Grade A Light or Fancy is pale and delicate. Grade A Medium and Dark and Grade B syrups, both excellent for baking, are progressively a bit thicker, darker in color, and slightly stronger in flavor. Grade B syrup, robust in flavor, is the choice of discriminating bakers for its pronounced maple taste.

1½ cups (6 oz/185 g) pecans

2½ cups (13 oz/405 g) all-purpose (plain) flour

1 cup (8 oz/250 g) sugar

1 Tbsp baking powder

½ tsp salt

3 large eggs, beaten

4 Tbsp (2 oz/60 g) unsalted butter, melted

1 cup (8 fl oz/250 ml) buttermilk

¾ cup (6 fl oz/180 ml) pure maple syrup

PREHEAT THE OVEN TO 350°F (180°C). Grease a 9-by-5-inch (23-by-13-cm) loaf pan or spray with nonstick cooking spray.

In a food processor, combine half of the pecans and ¾ cup (4 oz/125 g) of the flour. Process until a finely ground nut flour forms. Coarsely chop the remaining pecans and set aside.

In a bowl, stir together the remaining 1¾ cups (9 oz/280 g) flour, the nut flour, sugar, baking powder, and salt. Make a well in the center and add the eggs, melted butter, buttermilk, and maple syrup. Stir just until evenly moistened, 15–20 strokes. The batter will be slightly lumpy. Using a large silicone spatula, fold in the chopped pecans just until evenly distributed, no more than a few strokes.

Pour the batter into the prepared pan.

Bake for 30 minutes, then rotate the pan and bake until the top is golden brown, about 30 minutes longer. Reduce the oven temperature to 325°F (165°C) and continue baking until the top is browned and firm and the edges begin to pull away from the pan sides, 10–15 minutes longer. A toothpick inserted into the center of the loaf should come out clean. Transfer the pan to a wire rack and let cool for 10 minutes. Unmold the loaf onto the rack and let cool completely. Wrap tightly in plastic wrap and store at room temperature overnight. Cut into thick slices to serve.

Sweet Carrot-Cranberry Muffins

MAKES 14 MUFFINS

4 large eggs

¾ cup (6 fl oz/180 ml) canola oil

1½ tsp pure vanilla extract

2 cups (10 oz/315 g) all-purpose (plain) flour

1¾ cups (14 oz/440 g) sugar

2 tsp ground cinnamon

2 tsp poppy seeds

1 tsp baking powder

1 tsp baking soda (bicarbonate of soda)

½ tsp salt

3 cups (15 oz/155 g) shredded carrots (3–4 carrots)

¾ cup (3 oz/90 g) dried cranberries or ¾ cup (4½ oz/140 g) golden raisins (sultanas)

PREHEAT THE OVEN TO 350°F (180°C). Grease 14 standard muffin cups with butter or butter-flavored nonstick cooking spray; fill the unused cups one-third full with water to prevent warping.

In a large bowl, combine the eggs, oil, and vanilla. Beat vigorously with a whisk until smooth and slightly thickened, about 1 minute. In another bowl, stir together the flour, sugar, cinnamon, poppy seeds, baking powder, baking soda, and salt. Gradually stir the flour mixture into the egg mixture and beat just until smooth, about 20 strokes. Scrape down the sides of the bowl. Fold in the carrots and cranberries just until combined.

Spoon the batter into each muffin cup, filling it three-fouths full.

Bake the muffins until golden, dry, and springy to the touch, 20–25 minutes. A cake tester inserted into the center of a muffin should come out clean. Transfer the pans to wire racks and let the muffins cool for 10 minutes. Unmold the muffins. Serve warm or at room temperature.

DELICATE BATTERS

To add the raisins and shredded carrots to the batter, first spoon them on top of the batter. Then, using a silicone spatula with the blade held vertically, cut straight down into the center of the two mixtures to the bottom of the bowl and pull the spatula toward you and then up the side of the bowl. Give the bowl a quarter turn and repeat the motion just until the two mixtures are combined. This technique is called "folding." If the batter is overmixed, it will lose air and the batter will not rise fully.

YOGURT

Yogurt, a thick, creamy, slighty sour fermented milk product, contains beneficial living bacterial cultures and is an easily digestible food. Made from whole, low-fat, or nonfat milk, yogurt may be used as the liquid ingredient in muffins and quick breads, bestowing a tart flavor and tender texture. It can also substitute for sour cream in many baking recipes, delivering the same pleasant dairy taste with far fewer calories. Before purchasing a carton of yogurt, always check the sell-by date to ensure that it is the freshest possible product.

Lemon-Yogurt Muffins

MAKES 12 MUFFINS

2 cups (10 oz/315 g) all-purpose (plain) flour

½ cup (4 oz/125 g) sugar

1¼ tsp baking powder

1 tsp baking soda (bicarbonate of soda)

¼ tsp salt

Grated zest and juice of 1 lemon, preferably organic

1¼ cups (10 oz/315 g) plain yogurt

2 large eggs, lightly beaten

5 Tbsp (2½ oz/75 g) unsalted butter, melted

¼ tsp pure lemon extract or lemon oil (optional)

FOR THE TOPPING:

⅓ cup (1½ oz/45 g) finely chopped walnuts or pecans

1½ Tbsp sugar

½ tsp ground mace

PREHEAT THE OVEN TO 375°F (190°C). Grease 12 standard muffin cups with butter or butter-flavored nonstick cooking spray.

In a bowl, stir together the flour, sugar, baking powder, baking soda, salt, and lemon zest. Make a well in the center and add the yogurt, eggs, melted butter, lemon juice, and lemon extract, if using. Vigorously whisk until thoroughly combined, about 20 strokes. The batter will be fluffy but slightly lumpy. Scrape down the sides of the bowl. Spoon the batter into each muffin cup, filling it three-fourths full.

To make the topping, in a small bowl, stir together the nuts, sugar, and mace. Sprinkle each muffin with about 2 tsp of the topping.

Bake the muffins until golden around the edges and dry and springy to the touch, 16–20 minutes. A toothpick inserted into the center of a muffin should come out clean. Transfer the pan to a wire rack and let the muffins cool for 5 minutes. Unmold the muffins. Serve warm or at room temperature.

Date-Walnut Loaf

ONE 8½-BY-4½-INCH (21.5-BY-11.5-CM) LOAF

- **1 cup (5 oz/140 g) pitted dates, roughly chopped**
- **3 Tbsp brandy or Grand Marnier**
- **1 cup (3½ oz/100 g) walnuts, lightly toasted (page 53) and coarsely chopped**
- **1½ tsp baking soda (bicarbonate of soda)**
- **¼ tsp salt**
- **3 Tbsp unsalted butter, melted and cooled to room temperature**
- **¾ cup (6 fl oz/170 ml) warm water**
- **¾ cup (5½ oz/155 g) sugar**
- **2 large eggs, lightly beaten**
- **1½ cups (7 oz/200 g) all-purpose (plain) flour**

PREHEAT THE OVEN TO 325°F (165°C). Grease an 8½-by-4½-inch (21.5-by-11.5-cm) loaf pan with butter.

In a small bowl, soak the dates in 1 Tbsp of the brandy for about 10 minutes.

In a large bowl, using a large silicone spatula, stir together the dates with the brandy, the walnuts, baking soda, salt, melted butter, and water until combined. Stir in the sugar and eggs, then stir in the flour until thoroughly combined.

Pour the batter into the prepared pan.

Bake until the bread is puffed and browned, 50–60 minutes. A toothpick inserted into the center of the loaf should come out clean. Transfer the pan to a wire rack and let the bread cool completely. Unmold the loaf onto a serving plate and turn it right side up. Spoon the remaining 2 Tbsp brandy, a little at a time, over the loaf so that the bread absorbs all of it. Cut into thick slices and serve.

NOTE: This sturdy cake is ideal for shipping as a gift. The brandy not only adds flavor but also helps preserve the cake.

SERVING TIP: Serve with afternoon coffee or tea or as a simple dessert.

WALNUTS

The furrowed, double-lobed nutmeat of the walnut has an assertive, rich flavor. The most common variety is the English walnut, also known as the Persian walnut, which has a light brown shell that cracks easily. Black walnuts have a stronger flavor and extremely hard shells but are a challenge to find.

Bacon & Gruyère Muffins

MAKES 9 MUFFINS

7 or 8 thin slices smoked bacon

2 cups (10 oz/315 g) all-purpose (plain) flour

2 Tbsp sugar

1 Tbsp baking powder

½ tsp salt

1 large egg

4 Tbsp (2 oz/60 g) unsalted butter, melted

1 cup (8 fl oz/250 ml) milk

2 Tbsp sour cream or plain yogurt

¾ cup (3 oz/90 g) finely diced Gruyère or Swiss cheese

PREHEAT THE OVEN TO 400°F (200°C). Grease 9 standard muffin cups with butter or butter-flavored nonstick cooking spray; fill the unused cups one-third full with water to prevent warping.

In a frying pan over medium-high heat, cook the bacon slices until crisp, 6–8 minutes, turning as needed. Using tongs, transfer to paper towels to drain. Let the bacon cool, then crumble. Set aside.

In a bowl, stir together the flour, sugar, baking powder, and salt.

In another bowl, whisk together the egg, melted butter, milk, and sour cream until blended. Add the egg mixture to the flour mixture and stir just until evenly moistened. The batter will be slightly lumpy. Using a large silicone spatula, fold in the bacon and cheese just until evenly distributed, no more than a few strokes. Do not overmix.

Spoon the batter into each muffin cup, filling it level with the rim.

Bake the muffins until golden, dry, and springy to the touch, 20–25 minutes. A toothpick inserted into the center of a muffin should come out clean. Transfer the pan to a wire rack and let the muffins cool for 5 minutes. Unmold the muffins. Serve warm or at room temperature.

SERVING TIP: These muffins make great accompaniments to soups, salads, and omelets.

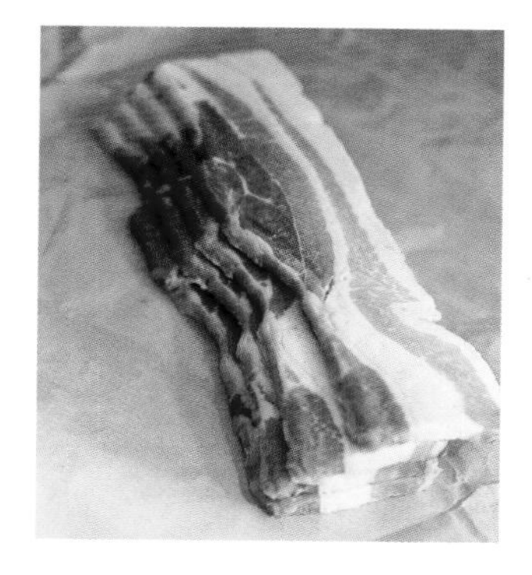

BACON

Look for bacon that has been smoked over apple wood, which gives it a sweet flavor. Purchase thick-sliced bacon for a more intense smoky taste. For added bacon flavor in this recipe, replace 2 Tbsp of the melted butter with 2 Tbsp of the rendered bacon fat.

Steamed Rye & Maple Brown Bread

MAKES ONE 1-LB (500-G) LOAF

½ cup (2½ oz/75 g) medium-grind yellow cornmeal, preferably stone-ground, or semolina flour

½ cup (2½ oz/75 g) whole-wheat (wholemeal) flour or graham flour

½ cup (2 oz/60 g) medium-grind rye flour

1 tsp baking soda (bicarbonate of soda)

½ tsp salt

¼ tsp baking powder

1 cup (8 fl oz/250 ml) buttermilk

⅓ cup (4 fl oz/125 ml) maple syrup or ⅓ cup (4 oz/125 g) light molasses

½ cup (2 oz/60 g) dried cranberries

ABOUT BROWN BREAD

Yellow cornmeal, whole-wheat (wholemeal) flour, and rye flour are the traditional grains used in Boston brown bread. Steamed breads such as this one were popular in colonial America, as they could be made in a kettle over an open fire in the days when an oven was a luxury. Even today, this steamed bread is the classic accompaniment to Boston baked beans, a favorite Sunday lunch in New England.

GENEROUSLY GREASE a 1-pound (500-g) cylindrical coffee can or a 6-cup (1.5-l) tin pudding mold with a clip-on lid.

In a bowl, stir together the cornmeal, whole-wheat flour, rye flour, baking soda, salt, and baking powder.

In a small bowl, stir together the buttermilk and maple syrup. Make a well in the center of the flour mixture, add the buttermilk mixture, and stir just until combined. The batter will be slightly lumpy. Stir in the cranberries.

Scrape the batter into the prepared can; it should be no more than two-thirds full. Cover tightly with a square of aluminum foil held in place by a thick rubber band or with the lid of the mold.

Set the can on a trivet or wire rack in the bottom of a stockpot, making sure it is centered and level. Add hot water to the stockpot to come halfway up the sides of the can. Cover the pot and bring the water to a gentle boil. Reduce the heat to a simmer. Steam, checking the water level occasionally and adding more hot water as needed, until the bread is puffed, slightly firm to the touch, and slightly moist, about 1¼ hours. A toothpick inserted into the center should come out clean.

Carefully remove the hot can from the water bath. Transfer to a wire rack and remove the cover. Let stand for a few minutes, then unmold the loaf, place it on its side, and let cool slightly or completely. Cut into thick rounds to serve.

SERVING TIP: Serve brown bread warm with roast chicken, pork, duck, or goose, or with baked beans. It is also delicious at room temperature, spread with cream cheese.

STORAGE TIP: Wrap the bread in plastic wrap and refrigerate for up to 3 days. Reheat in a 300°F (150°C) oven for 10 minutes.

Jam-Filled Muffins

MAKES 12 MUFFINS

- **2 cups (10 oz/315 g) all-purpose (plain) flour**
- **¾ cup (6 oz/185 g) sugar**
- **1 Tbsp baking powder**
- **½ tsp baking soda (bicarbonate of soda)**
- **½ tsp salt**
- **6 Tbsp (3 oz/90 g) unsalted butter, melted**
- **2 large eggs**
- **1 tsp pure vanilla extract**
- **¼ tsp pure almond extract**
- **1¼ cups (10 oz/315 g) sour cream**
- **⅓–½ cup (4–5 oz/125–155 g) jelly or seedless jam, such as red currant jelly or raspberry, blackberry, or strawberry jam**

PREHEAT THE OVEN TO 375°F (190°C). Grease 12 standard muffin cups with butter or butter-flavored nonstick cooking spray.

In a bowl, stir together the flour, sugar, baking powder, baking soda, and salt.

In another bowl, whisk together the melted butter, eggs, vanilla, almond extract, and sour cream until smooth. Add the egg mixture to the flour mixture and stir just until evenly moistened. The batter will be slightly lumpy. Do not overmix.

Spoon the batter into each muffin cup, filling it one-third full. Drop a heaping teaspoonful of jelly or jam into the center of the batter, then cover with batter until level with the rim.

Bake the muffins until golden, dry, and springy to the touch, 20–25 minutes. Transfer the pan to a wire rack and let the muffins cool for 5 minutes. Unmold the muffins. Serve warm or at room temperature.

JELLY VS. JAM

Sweet, spreadable fruit preserves baked inside these tender, rich, sour cream muffins offers a colorful, tasty surprise. Jelly and jam make equally delicious fillings. Jellies, such as red currant, have been strained to achieve a smooth, crystalline result. By contrast, raspberry, blackberry, and strawberry jams are made with whole berries and therefore have a chunky texture.

Corn Sticks

MAKES 20 CORN STICKS

1 cup (5 oz/155 g) fine- or medium-grind yellow cornmeal, preferably stone-ground

1 cup (5 oz/155 g) all-purpose (plain) flour or 1 cup (4 oz/125 g) whole-wheat (wholemeal) pastry flour

¼ cup (2 oz/60 g) sugar

1 Tbsp baking powder

1 tsp salt

3 large eggs

½ cup (4 fl oz/125 ml) milk

½ cup (4 fl oz/125 ml) heavy (double) cream

4 Tbsp (2 oz/60 g) unsalted butter, melted

1 cup (6 oz/185 g) fresh or thawed frozen corn kernels or 4 oz (125 g) bacon, cooked, drained, and crumbled

PREHEAT THE OVEN TO 425°F (220°C). Grease 2 cast-iron corn stick molds with butter. Place in the oven until hot, about 10 minutes.

In a bowl, stir together the cornmeal, flour, sugar, baking powder, and salt. In another bowl, whisk together the eggs, milk, and cream. Stir the milk mixture into the cornmeal mixture, then stir in the melted butter and corn kernels just until combined. The batter will be slightly lumpy.

Carefully remove the hot molds from the oven and place on a wire rack. Spoon the batter into each mold, filling it almost full and lightly smooth the surface. Return to the hot oven right away and bake until the tops are golden brown, 12–15 minutes. Carefully remove the hot molds from the oven and invert onto a rack. Regrease the pans, fill with the remaining batter, and bake. Serve the corn sticks warm or at room temperature. They are best when served on the same day they are made.

MAKE-AHEAD TIP: Corn sticks can be frozen in plastic freezer bags for up to 1 month and reheated just before serving. Warm the frozen breads in a preheated 400°F (200°C) oven for 5–7 minutes. Serve hot from the oven.

CORN STICK MOLDS

Corn sticks are old-fashioned dinner breads shaped to resemble an ear of native American maize. Once known as corn dodgers and shaped by hand, today corn sticks are baked in a rectangular cast-iron pan with individual corn-ear molds. The breads emerge crusty on the top and the bottom.

Jalapeño-Cornmeal Muffins

MAKES 11 MUFFINS

1¼ cups (7½ oz/235 g) fine- or medium-grind yellow cornmeal, preferably stone-ground

1¼ cups (6½ oz/200 g) all-purpose (plain) flour

3 Tbsp sugar

2½ tsp baking powder

1 tsp salt

2 jalapeño chiles, seeded and minced

1 zucchini (courgette), 4 oz (125 g), shredded

¼ cup (2 fl oz/60 ml) olive oil or sesame oil

2 large eggs, beaten

1½ cups (12 fl oz/375 ml) buttermilk

3 Tbsp grated Parmesan or Asiago cheese

PREHEAT THE OVEN TO 400°F (200°C). Grease 11 standard muffin cups with butter or butter-flavored nonstick cooking spray; fill the unused cup one-third full with water to prevent warping.

In a bowl, stir together the cornmeal, flour, sugar, baking powder, and salt. Stir in the jalapeño chiles and zucchini and toss to distribute evenly. Make a well in the center of the flour mixture and add the oil, eggs, and buttermilk. Stir just until evenly moistened, using no more than 15–20 strokes. The batter will be slightly lumpy.

Spoon the batter into each muffin cup, filling it level with the rim. Sprinkle each muffin with some of the cheese, dividing it evenly.

Bake the muffins until golden and springy to the touch, about 25 minutes. A toothpick inserted into the center of a muffin should come out clean. Remove from the oven and unmold the muffins onto a wire rack. Serve warm or at room temperature.

JALAPEÑO CHILES

The thumb-sized jalapeño chile has thick flesh that may be green or red and can range from mildly hot to fiery. When working with jalapeños or other hot chiles, it is advisable to wear rubber gloves to prevent burns. The heat from a chile, carried in the membranes, can linger for hours on your skin, so thoroughly wash your hands, the cutting board, and knife with hot, soapy water as soon as you finish working. To add more heat to the muffins, use 3 chiles; for milder-flavored muffins, use 1 chile.

Almond Stollen

MAKES 1 LARGE LOAF

¾ cup (3 oz/90 g) slivered blanched almonds

2½ cups (12½ oz/390 g) all-purpose (plain) flour, plus extra for sprinkling

⅔ cup (5 oz/155 g) granulated sugar

2 tsp baking powder

½ tsp baking soda (bicarbonate of soda)

½ tsp ground mace

½ tsp freshly grated nutmeg (see page 193)

½ tsp salt

½ cup (4 oz/125 g) unsalted butter, at room temperature, plus 2 Tbsp, melted

½ lb (250 g) cream cheese, at room temperature

1 large egg

2 Tbsp amaretto (left)

½ tsp pure vanilla extract

½ tsp pure almond extract

½ cup (3 oz/90 g) golden raisins (sultanas)

½ cup (3 oz/90 g) finely chopped dried apricots

½ cup (2 oz/60 g) dried tart cherries

Confectioners' (icing) sugar for dusting

PREHEAT THE OVEN TO 350°F (180°C). Line a baking sheet with parchment (baking) paper.

In a food processor, combine the almonds and 1 cup (5 oz/155 g) of the flour. Process to make a fine meal. In a bowl, combine the almond mixture with the remaining flour and the granulated sugar, baking powder, baking soda, mace, nutmeg, and salt.

In a stand mixer fitted with the paddle attachment, cream together the butter and cream cheese on medium speed until fluffy, about 2 minutes. Add the egg, amaretto, vanilla, and almond extract and beat until smooth. Reduce the speed to low and beat in the raisins, apricots, and cherries. Beat in the dry ingredients, ½ cup (2½ oz/75 g) at a time, until a stiff batter forms, about 2 minutes.

Turn the batter out onto a floured board and gently knead a few times to make a cohesive dough. Transfer the dough to the prepared sheet. Pat into a thick oval about 10 inches (25 cm) long and 8 inches (20 cm) wide. Make a crease down the center of the oval with a chopstick or the blunt edge of a knife and, without stretching, gently fold the long side over to within ¾ inch (2 cm) of the opposite edge, forming a long, narrow loaf with tapered ends. Press the top edge lightly to seal.

Bake until the stollen is lightly browned and a cake tester inserted into the center comes out clean, 40–45 minutes. Remove from the oven and brush lightly with the melted butter. Dust with confectioners' sugar. Let cool completely on the baking sheet. Dust with confectioners' sugar once more before serving.

AMARETTO

This almond-flavored liqueur originated in Saronno, Italy, in the sixteenth century. Its elusive almond flavor is derived from crushed apricot pits. Almonds and apricots are members of the same plant family, and apricot pits have a flavor reminiscent of almonds. Amaretto retains its character in the heat of the oven, making it a perfect flavoring ingredient for baking, especially when used to complement the flavor of almonds. Brandy can be substituted for the amaretto in this recipe.

Welsh Bara Brith

MAKES ONE 9-BY-5-INCH (23-BY-13-CM) LOAF

1¼ cups (10 fl oz/310 ml) boiling water

2 tea bags Darjeeling or English Breakfast tea, decaffeinated if desired

1 cup (6 oz/185 g) mixed dried fruits, chopped

1 cup (6 oz/185 g) dried currants

¼ cup (1½ oz/45 g) diced dried pineapple

1 cup (7 oz/220 g) firmly packed light brown sugar

2¾ cups (14 oz/440 g) all-purpose (plain) flour

2 tsp baking powder

½ tsp baking soda (bicarbonate of soda)

2 tsp ground cinnamon

¾ tsp salt

1 large egg, lightly beaten

½ cup (4 fl oz/125 ml) buttermilk

1 Tbsp unsalted butter, melted, plus extra for greasing

3 Tbsp orange marmalade

POUR THE BOILING WATER into a heatproof bowl. Add the tea bags and let steep for 10 minutes; remove the tea bags. Add the mixed dried fruits, currants, pineapple, and brown sugar and stir well. Cover with plastic wrap and let stand at room temperature for 1 hour to plump the fruit.

Preheat the oven to 325°F (165°C). Grease a 9-by-5-inch (23-by-13-cm) loaf pan. If using a glass baking dish, set the oven to 300°F (140°C).

In another bowl, stir together the flour, baking powder, baking soda, cinnamon, and salt. Add the soaked fruit and its liquid, the egg, buttermilk, melted butter, and marmalade. Stir until well blended. Spoon the batter into the prepared pan.

Bake until the loaf is brown and crusty and a cake tester inserted into the center comes out clean, 1¼–1½ hours. Let stand in the pan on a rack for 10 minutes, then turn the loaf out onto the rack. Serve warm or at room temperature.

HISTORY OF BARA BRITH

British baking has a long-standing tradition of fruit breads leavened with baking powder and destined for the tea table, and every region has its own recipe for currant bread. Bara brith originated in the Welsh countryside, *bara* being the local word for "bread" and *brith* meaning "spotted" or "freckled." The dried fruit is soaked in tea to plump it, and a sweet spice blend is typically ground fresh in a mortar for each batch of bread.

COFFEE CAKES, SCONES & BISCUITS

Macadamia Nut Coffee Cake

MAKES ONE 9-INCH (23-CM) CAKE

MACADAMIA NUTS

Buttery-rich macadamia nuts have a pleasurable melt-in-your-mouth consistency. Native to Australia, macadamia trees have been planted in Hawaii, where they flourish. Because the shells are very hard, the nuts are usually sold shelled in vacuum-packed jars or in bulk. Shelled nuts go rancid quickly and therefore should be used right away or stored in the refrigerator. The delicious oil extracted from macadamias is extremely low in saturated fats, cholesterol-free, and high in omega-3 fatty acids, making it healthier than olive oil. The oil should also be refrigerated.

FOR THE TOPPING:

2/3 cup (4 oz/125 g) all-purpose (plain) flour

1/3 cup (3 oz/90 g) granulated sugar

1 tsp ground cinnamon

1/2 tsp ground ginger

6 Tbsp (3 oz/90 g) cold unsalted butter, cut into small pieces

FOR THE CAKE:

1 cup (5 oz/155 g) all-purpose (plain) flour

1/2 cup (2 oz/60 g) cake (soft-wheat) flour

1/2 cup (4 oz/125 g) granulated sugar

1/2 cup (4 oz/125 g) firmly packed light brown sugar

1 1/2 tsp baking powder

1 tsp baking soda (bicarbonate of soda)

1/4 tsp salt

1 cup (8 oz/250 g) sour cream

2 large eggs

1/2 cup (4 fl oz/125 ml) macadamia nut oil

1 1/2 tsp pure vanilla extract

1 cup (5 oz/155 g) unsalted macadamia nuts, coarsely chopped

PREHEAT THE OVEN TO 350°F (180°C). Grease a 9-inch (23-cm) round springform pan. Line the bottom with a round of parchment (baking) paper and grease the paper.

To make the topping, in a small bowl, stir together the flour, sugar, cinnamon, and ginger. Using a pastry blender or your fingers, cut or rub in the butter until coarse crumbs form. Set aside.

To make the cake, in a bowl, stir together the all-purpose flour and cake flour, granulated sugar, brown sugar, baking powder, baking soda, and salt.

In another bowl, whisk together the sour cream, eggs, oil, and vanilla until well blended. Stir the sour cream mixture into the flour mixture. Using an electric mixer on medium speed or a wire whisk, beat until smooth and creamy, about 1 minute.

Pour half of the batter into the prepared pan and spread it evenly. Sprinkle evenly with half of the topping. Cover evenly with the remaining batter. Sprinkle evenly with the nuts, gently pressing them into the batter, then cover with the remaining topping.

Bake until the topping is golden brown, 40–45 minutes. A toothpick inserted into the center of the cake should come out clean. Transfer the pan to a wire rack and let cool for 20 minutes. Remove the sides of the springform pan. Serve warm or at room temperature, cut into wedges.

NOTE: Canola oil may be substituted for the macadamia nut oil.

KNEADING BISCUIT DOUGH

Recipes usually instruct the baker to knead biscuit dough briefly after mixing. The word "knead" is a misnomer, however, as the action of folding and pushing biscuit dough is a far more delicate technique: Pull the dough over itself from the far side, making a double layer, and then, with the palm of your hand, push the dough forward with only the lightest pressure, to smear some of the small butter pieces in the dough. Give the dough a quarter turn and repeat to make 6–12 brief strokes, no more, adding flour 1 Tbsp at a time if needed to prevent sticking.

Buttermilk Biscuits

MAKES SIXTEEN 2½-INCH (6-CM) BISCUITS

1½ cups (7½ oz/235 g) all-purpose (plain) flour

1½ cups (6 oz/185 g) cake (soft-wheat) flour or white pastry flour

1 Tbsp sugar

4 tsp baking powder

1¼ tsp salt

¼ tsp baking soda (bicarbonate of soda)

½ cup (4 oz/125 g) plus 2 Tbsp cold unsalted butter, cut into pieces

1 cup (8 fl oz/250 ml) well-chilled buttermilk

PREHEAT THE OVEN TO 425°F (220°C). Line a baking sheet with parchment (baking) paper.

In a food processor, combine the all-purpose flour, cake flour, sugar, baking powder, salt, and baking soda. Process briefly to mix. Add the butter and, using short pulses, mix the butter into the flour mixture until the mixture resembles coarse crumbs. Add the buttermilk all at once, and pulse just to moisten all the ingredients. The dough will stiffen during mixing. It should be slightly shaggy, but not overly sticky or wet. Do not overmix the dough.

Sprinkle a work surface with cake flour. Scrape the sides and bottom of the work bowl and turn out the dough; it will be very soft. Sprinkle the top with cake flour. With floured hands, gently knead the dough just a few times (left). Pat the dough into a loose rectangle about 1½ inches (4 cm) thick. With a plastic dough scraper or large silicone spatula, fold the rectangle like a letter, overlapping the short sides in the middle to make 3 layers. Roll or pat out the dough into a rectangle 1 inch (2.5 cm) thick, sprinkling a little flour beneath the dough as needed to prevent sticking. Using a 2½-inch (6-cm) biscuit cutter dipped in flour, cut out the biscuits by pushing the cutter straight down and lifting up without twisting. Cut as close together as possible for a minimum of scraps. Pack together and reroll the scraps to cut out additional biscuits.

Place the biscuits on the prepared baking sheet, spacing them about 1 inch (2.5 cm) apart. Bake the biscuits until firm to the touch and the tops and bottoms are golden brown, 15–18 minutes. Let cool for a few minutes, then serve hot.

NOTE: Biscuit flour, usually labeled simply "white flour," is milled from 100 percent soft winter wheat. It can be used in place of both of the flours in this recipe.

Almond-Currant Scones

MAKES 10 LARGE OR 16 MEDIUM SCONES

4 cups (1½ lb/625 g) all-purpose (plain) flour

3 Tbsp granulated sugar

2 tsp baking powder

1 tsp baking soda (bicarbonate of soda)

¼ tsp fine sea salt

1 cup (8 oz/250 g) cold unsalted butter, cut into 16 cubes

Grated zest of 1 orange

2 large eggs

1 cup (8 fl oz/250 ml) plus 2 Tbsp buttermilk

¾ cup (2½ oz/75 g) slivered blanched almonds

¾ cup (4½ oz/140 g) dried currants

2 Tbsp raw or turbinado sugar

IN A FOOD PROCESSOR, combine the flour, granulated sugar, baking powder, baking soda, and salt. Pulse twice to blend. Add the butter and orange zest and pulse 3 or 4 times until the mixture looks like large bread crumbs. Transfer to a large bowl.

In a large glass measuring pitcher, whisk together the eggs and buttermilk. Pour over the flour mixture and scatter with the almonds and currants. Stir only until the mixture is evenly blended and comes together into a soft dough. Using a light touch, form the dough into 10 large, flattened rounds (each about the size of a tennis ball) or 16 medium, flattened rounds (each about the size of a golfball). Place 1 inch (2.5 cm) apart on 1 large or 2 small ungreased baking sheets. Place the baking sheets in the refrigerator to chill for at least 15 minutes or for up to overnight (cover with plastic wrap if refrigerating overnight).

Preheat the oven to 375°F (190°C). Sprinkle a pinch of the raw sugar on top of each scone. Bake the scones until pale golden brown on top, about 20 minutes. Let cool briefly on a wire rack, then serve right away.

DRIED FRUITS

Currants are a traditional ingredient in scones, a classic British treat often served at breakfast and tea. Unlike the tart fresh currants used to make jellies and jams, tiny dried currants are actually dried Zante grapes, or raisins. You can use other dried fruits in place of the currants, including cherries, cranberries, blueberries, or finely chopped apricots. The chewiness of dried fruits are the perfect counterpoint to the crunchy almonds in these scones.

Popovers

MAKES 6 LARGE OR 12 SMALL POPOVERS

3 Tbsp unsalted butter, melted

3 large eggs

1 cup (8 fl oz/250 ml) whole milk

1 cup (5 oz/155 g) all-purpose (plain) flour

¼ tsp salt

Butter, jam, apple butter, and/or preserves for serving

HAVE READY A STANDARD 6-CUP or miniature 12-cup popover pan, a 12-cup muffin pan, or 12 individual 3½-inch (9-cm) soufflé dishes. Lightly grease the pan or dishes with 2 Tbsp of the melted butter. If using individual cups or dishes, place them, not touching, on a baking sheet.

In a deep bowl (preferably with a pouring spout), whisk together the eggs, milk, and the remaining 1 Tbsp melted butter until foamy. Beat in the flour and salt until smooth. Do not overmix. The batter will be thin. Pour the batter into each of the prepared cups, filling it two-thirds full.

Place the pan(s) on the center rack of a cold oven and immediately turn the temperature to 375°F (190°C). Bake the popovers until they are puffed high, deep golden brown, and dry to the touch, 35–45 minutes for standard-sized popovers and about 25 minutes for miniature popovers. Do not open the oven door for the first 30 minutes of baking, or the popovers may not rise fully.

Remove the pan(s) from the oven and immediately pierce the side of each popover with the tip of a sharp knife to allow steam to escape. Let cool for 5 minutes. Run the knife around the rim of each cup and unmold into a napkin-lined basket. Serve the popovers right away with the spread of your choice.

MAKE-AHEAD TIP: Popovers may be frozen and reheated. After baking, let cool completely on a wire rack and place in a zippered plastic freezer bag. Freeze for up to 1 month. To reheat, arrange the popovers on a baking sheet lined with parchment (baking) paper and place in a preheated 350°F (180°C) oven for 5–7 minutes.

POPOVER PANS

While you can use a muffin tin or ceramic dishes to make crusty, hollow popovers, deep nonstick popover cups give more room for the crown to expand properly into a dramatic dome. The dark-finish cups are available individually or connected in a frame-style pan with 6 standard or 12 miniature cups.

Chocolate Coffee Cake

MAKES ONE 9-BY-13-INCH (23-BY-33-CM) CAKE

FOR THE STREUSEL:

2/3 cup (4 oz/125 g) all-purpose (plain) flour

1/2 cup (3 1/2 oz/105 g) firmly packed light brown sugar

1/2 tsp ground cinnamon

6 Tbsp (3 oz/90 g) cold unsalted butter, cut into small pieces

3/4 cup (4 1/2 oz/140 g) chocolate chips (see Notes)

FOR THE CAKE:

1 1/2 cups (7 1/2 oz/235 g) all-purpose (plain) flour

1/2 cup (2 oz/60 g) cake (soft-wheat) flour

2/3 cup (2 oz/60 g) unsweetened Dutch-process cocoa powder

1 tsp baking soda (bicarbonate of soda)

1 tsp baking powder

1/2 tsp salt

1/2 cup (4 oz/125 g) unsalted butter

1 cup (8 oz/250 g) granulated sugar

3 large eggs

1 1/4 cups (10 oz/315 g) sour cream

1 1/2 tsp pure vanilla extract

PREHEAT THE OVEN TO 350°F (180°C). Grease and flour a 9-by-13-inch (23-by-33-cm) baking pan or dish. If using a glass baking dish, set the oven temperature to 325°F (165°C).

To make the streusel, in a small bowl, stir together the flour, brown sugar, and cinnamon. Using a pastry blender or your fingers, cut or rub in the butter until coarse crumbs form. Stir in the chocolate chips until evenly distributed.

To make the cake, in a bowl, stir together the all-purpose flour, cake flour, cocoa, baking soda, baking powder, and salt.

In another bowl, using an electric mixer on medium speed, cream together the butter and sugar until light and fluffy. Add the eggs, one at a time, beating thoroughly after each addition. Add the flour mixture in 2 or 3 additions, alternating with the sour cream and vanilla. Using the mixer on low speed, beat the batter until smooth and fluffy, about 2 minutes.

Pour the batter into the prepared pan and spread it evenly. Sprinkle the streusel mixture evenly over the batter.

Bake until the topping is golden brown, 40–45 minutes. A toothpick inserted into the center of the cake should come out clean. Transfer the pan to a wire rack and let cool completely. Cut into squares to serve.

NOTES: Semisweet (plain) or bittersweet chocolate chips can be used in this coffee cake recipe. To intensify the chocolate flavor, add 1 1/2 tsp pure chocolate extract when beating in the sour cream and vanilla.

STORING & REHEATING COFFEE CAKES

This coffee cake stores well after it is baked and completely cooled. Cover with plastic wrap and keep for 4 days in the refrigerator, or enclose in a freezer bag or wrap tightly in plastic wrap and foil and freeze for up to 2 months. To defrost, remove from the freezer, unwrap slightly, and allow to stand for a few hours or overnight. To reheat, unwrap completely and place on a baking sheet in a preheated 300°F (150°C) oven until heated through, 10–20 minutes. If heating up individual pieces, remove from the oven after 5–8 minutes. Or, heat in the microwave for about 1 minute, checking at 10-second intervals until warmed to your liking.

Cream Tea Scones with Currants

MAKES 8 SCONES

2 cups (10 oz/315 g) all-purpose (plain) flour, plus extra for sprinkling

1 Tbsp granulated sugar

2½ tsp baking powder

¼ tsp salt

4 Tbsp (2 oz/60 g) cold unsalted butter, cut into pieces

2 large eggs

⅔ cup (5 fl oz/160 ml) heavy (double) cream

½ cup (3 oz/90 g) dried currants

1 heaping Tbsp raw or coarse sugar

Butter and Lemon Curd (right) or jam for serving

PREHEAT THE OVEN TO 400°F (200°C). Line a baking sheet with parchment (baking) paper.

In a bowl, stir together the flour, granulated sugar, baking powder, and salt. Add the butter to the flour mixture. Using a pastry blender or 2 knives, cut in the butter until the mixture resembles coarse crumbs.

In a small bowl, whisk together the eggs and cream. Add all but 2 Tbsp of the egg mixture to the flour mixture all at once and stir until a sticky dough forms. Quickly stir in the currants, just until evenly distributed.

Turn the dough out onto a lightly floured work surface. Knead gently until the dough holds together, about 6 times. The dough should be soft; do not overknead. Divide into 2 equal portions and pat each portion into a round about 1 inch (2.5 cm) thick and 6 inches (15 cm) in diameter. Cut each round into 4 equal wedges.

Place the wedges, 2 inches (5 cm) apart, on the prepared sheet. Brush each wedge with the reserved egg mixture and sprinkle with the raw sugar. Bake the scones until golden brown, about 15 minutes. Serve right away with butter and lemon curd or jam.

LEMON CURD

In a heavy saucepan, combine 5 large egg yolks and ½ cup (4 oz/125 g) sugar. Whisk vigorously for 1 minute. Add the freshly grated zest of 2 lemons and ¼ cup (2 fl oz/60 ml) lemon juice and whisk for 1 minute longer. Cook gently over low heat, stirring, until slightly thickened, 10–15 minutes. Remove from the heat and stir in 6 Tbsp (3 oz/90 g) unsalted butter. Let cool, stirring occasionally. Cover tightly and chill before serving. Makes about 1 cup (11 oz/345 g).

Peach Streusel Coffee Cake

MAKES ONE 9-INCH (23-CM) CAKE

FOR THE STREUSEL:

¾ cup (4 oz/125 g) all-purpose (plain) flour

⅓ cup (2½ oz/75 g) firmly packed light brown sugar

¼ cup (2 oz/60 g) granulated sugar

1 tsp ground cinnamon

6 Tbsp (3 oz/90 g) cold unsalted butter, cut into small pieces

FOR THE CAKE:

1½ cups (7½ oz/235 g) all-purpose (plain) flour

¾ cup (6 oz/185 g) granulated sugar

2 tsp baking powder

½ tsp salt

1 large egg

4 Tbsp (2 oz/60 g) unsalted butter, melted

½ cup (4 fl oz/125 ml) milk

1½ tsp pure vanilla extract

1 tsp pure almond extract

2 firm, ripe peaches, 1 lb (500 g) total, peeled (page 178), pitted, and sliced 1 inch (2.5 cm) thick

PEACHES

Choose peaches that give slightly to gentle pressure, that emanate a flowery fragrance, and that are free of bruises or blemishes. The amount of red in a peach's skin depends on its variety and has little to do with ripeness. Avoid peaches with tinges of green, however; this means they were picked too early. Any peach variety is delicious in this coffee cake, from fruits that are bright yellow-orange with a rosy blush to those that are the palest white. Even ripe peaches, however, may be difficult to peel. For more on peeling peaches, see page 178.

PREHEAT THE OVEN TO 350°F (180°C). Grease and flour a 9-inch (23-cm) round springform pan or square baking pan or baking dish. If using a glass baking dish, set the oven temperature to 325°F (165°C).

To make the streusel, in a bowl, stir together the flour, brown sugar, granulated sugar, and cinnamon. Using a pastry blender or your fingers, cut or rub in the butter until coarse crumbs form.

To make the cake, in a bowl, stir together the flour, sugar, baking powder, and salt.

In another bowl, using an electric mixer on medium speed or a wire whisk, beat the egg, melted butter, milk, vanilla, and almond extract until creamy, about 1 minute. Add to the flour mixture and beat just until evenly moistened. There should be no lumps or dry spots. Do not overmix.

Pour the batter into the prepared pan and spread it evenly. If using a springform pan, arrange the peach slices in concentric circles from the pan sides to the center. If using a square pan, arrange the slices in rows. Gently press the slices into the batter. Sprinkle evenly with the streusel.

Bake until the topping is golden brown, 40–45 minutes. A toothpick inserted into the center of the cake should come out clean. Transfer the pan to a wire rack and let cool for 20 minutes. Remove the sides of the springform pan, if using. Serve warm or at room temperature, cut into wedges or squares.

Baking Soda Biscuits

MAKES ABOUT 12 BISCUITS

BISCUIT SAVVY

Biscuits are ubiquitous on tables in the American South. To approximate the type of soft-wheat, low-gluten flour that is widely available in the South but harder to find elsewhere, use a mixture of cake and all-purpose flours for this recipe. There are time-tested secrets to achieving the perfect texture in biscuits. Gentle handling is key: Knead the dough just until it holds together, and use a light touch when patting it out. When cutting out the biscuits, push straight down, and don't twist the cutter. This will help the biscuits to rise straight and tall and to retain their flaky layers during baking.

1 cup (5 oz/155 g) all-purpose (plain) flour

1 cup (4 oz/125 g) cake (soft-wheat) flour

1 Tbsp sugar

2 tsp cream of tartar

1 tsp baking soda (bicarbonate of soda)

½ tsp salt

4 Tbsp (2 oz/60 g) chilled vegetable shortening, cut into ½-inch (12-mm) pieces

2 Tbsp chilled unsalted butter, thinly sliced

¾ cup (6 fl oz/180 ml) whole milk, or as needed

PREHEAT THE OVEN TO 400°F (200°C). In a bowl, sift together the all-purpose flour, cake flour, sugar, cream of tartar, baking soda, and salt. Using a pastry blender or 2 knives, cut in the shortening and the butter until the mixture resembles coarse crumbs with some pea-sized pieces of fat. Using a wooden spoon, stir in just enough milk to make a soft, moist dough. You may not need all of the milk. Do not overmix.

Turn the dough out onto a lightly floured work surface. Knead 6–8 times, just until smooth; do not overknead. Pat the dough into a round about ½ inch (12 mm) thick. Using a 2¼-inch (5.5-cm) biscuit cutter dipped in flour, cut out biscuits as close together as possible for a minimum of scraps. Pack together and reroll the scraps to cut out additional biscuits. (For square biscuits, which have the advantage of not creating scraps, pat the dough into an 8-by-6-inch/20-by-15-cm rectangle about ½ inch/12 mm thick. Cut crosswise into 4 equal portions, then lengthwise into 3 equal portions to make 12 squares.)

Place the biscuits on an ungreased baking sheet. Bake the biscuits until golden brown, about 18 minutes. Let cool for a few minutes, then serve hot or warm.

VARIATION TIP: These biscuits pair well with a variety of accompaniments and can be served for breakfast, tea, or dessert. Slice the biscuits and serve with a pat of high-quality fresh butter or Maple Butter (page 378); Sweetened Whipped Cream (page 377) and mixed berries; Lemon Curd (page 129); or Tangerine Curd (page 142).

Spiced Apple Coffee Cake

MAKES ONE 9-INCH (23-CM) CAKE

1¾ cups (9 oz/280 g) all-purpose (plain) flour

1½ tsp baking powder

¼ tsp salt

⅓ cup (2½ oz/75 g) firmly packed light brown sugar

1½ tsp ground cardamom

1 tsp ground cinnamon

1 lb (500 g) tart cooking apples (page 244), peeled, cored, and coarsely chopped, then tossed in 2 Tbsp lemon juice

½ cup (4 oz/125 g) unsalted butter, at room temperature

8 oz (250 g) cream cheese, at room temperature

1½ cups (12 oz/375 g) granulated sugar

1 tsp pure vanilla extract

2 large eggs

Vanilla Glaze (left)

PREHEAT THE OVEN TO 350°F (180°C). Grease and flour a 9-inch (23-cm) round springform pan or square baking pan or baking dish. If using a glass baking dish, reduce the oven temperature to 325°F (165°C).

In a bowl, stir together the flour, baking powder, and salt. In a small bowl, stir together the brown sugar, cardamom, and cinnamon. Add to the apples and toss to coat.

In another bowl, using an electric mixer on medium speed, cream together the butter, cream cheese, granulated sugar, and vanilla until light and fluffy. Add the eggs, one at a time, beating well after each addition. Slowly add the flour mixture and beat well until smooth. Using a large spatula, gently fold in the apples just until incorporated.

Pour the batter into the prepared pan and spread it evenly. Bake until the top is golden brown, 60–70 minutes. A toothpick inserted into the center of the cake should come out clean. Transfer the pan to a wire rack and let cool for 5 minutes. Remove the sides of the springform pan, if using, and place the cake on a wire rack set over a piece of waxed paper to catch any drips. Drizzle with the glaze. Let the cake cool to room temperature. Cut into wedges or squares to serve.

VANILLA GLAZE

As a delicious final touch, a glaze adds a hint of extra flavor and an attractive sheen to a coffee cake. To make the glaze, in a small bowl, whisk together ¾ cup (3 oz/90 g) confectioners' (icing) sugar, sifted; 2 Tbsp condensed skim milk, warmed; and ½ tsp pure vanilla extract until smooth and pourable. Adjust the consistency of the glaze by adding more milk, a few drops at a time, if necessary.

Italian Almond Coffee Cake

MAKES ONE 10-INCH (25-CM) CAKE

FOR THE ALMOND CAKE:

⅔ cup (3 oz/90 g) slivered blanched almonds

3¼ cups (16½ oz/515 g) all-purpose (plain) flour

⅔ cup (5 oz/155 g) firmly packed light brown sugar

Grated zest of 2 lemons

1 Tbsp baking powder

Pinch of salt

¾ cup (6 oz/185 g) plus 2 Tbsp cold unsalted butter, cut into small pieces

1 large egg

2 tsp pure vanilla extract

FOR THE FILLING:

3½ cups (15 oz/470 g) whole-milk ricotta cheese

Grated zest of 1 orange

1 Tbsp golden rum

¾ cup (6 oz/185 g) granulated sugar

4 oz (125 g) semisweet (plain) chocolate, coarsely chopped

Almond Brittle (right)

Confectioners' (icing) sugar for dusting (optional)

TO MAKE THE ALMOND CAKE, preheat the oven to 325°F (165°C). Spread the almonds on a baking sheet and toast, stirring twice, until light brown, 8–10 minutes. Transfer to a plate and let cool slightly, then pour into a food processor. Add ¼ cup (1½ oz/45 g) of the flour and process until a finely ground nut flour forms.

In a stand mixer fitted with the paddle attachment, stir together the remaining 3 cups (15 oz/470 g) flour, nut flour, brown sugar, lemon zest, baking powder, and salt on low speed. Add the butter and continue to mix until fine crumbs form.

In a small bowl, whisk together the egg and vanilla until blended, then add to the flour mixture. Mix lightly, just until evenly moistened. The batter will be crumbly.

To make the filling, in a bowl, combine the ricotta, orange zest, rum, and sugar. Using the mixer on medium speed, beat until smooth and fluffy. Fold in the chocolate and almond brittle just until evenly distributed.

Grease a 10-inch (25-cm) round springform pan. Increase the oven temperature to 350°F (180°C). Pour half of the cake batter into the prepared pan and, using a large silicone spatula, mound it slightly higher around the edges than in the center. Gently and evenly tamp down with the spatula to flatten any bubbles (do not press firmly). Spread the ricotta filling over the batter in an even layer, leaving a 1-inch (2.5-cm) margin around the edge. Spread the remaining batter in an even layer over the cheese filling right up to the pan sides. Gently and evenly tamp to flatten the batter.

Bake until the top is golden brown, 40–45 minutes. Transfer the pan to a wire rack and let cool completely. Remove the sides of the springform pan. If desired, dust with confectioners' sugar. Serve at room temperature, cut into wedges.

ALMOND BRITTLE

This brittle adds texture to a coffee cake inspired by the Italian *crostata di ricotta*. To make the brittle, grease a baking sheet and a large metal spatula. In a large, heavy frying pan over medium heat, cook ⅓ cup (3 oz/90 g) granulated sugar, shaking gently, until it liquefies and turns golden. Take care not to splash; the sugar will be scalding hot. Remove from the heat and stir in ⅔ cup (3 oz/90 g) slivered blanched almonds. Pour onto the prepared sheet and press with the spatula into a single layer. Let cool to room temperature, then break into ½-inch (12-mm) pieces

Cranberry-Orange Scones

MAKES 12 SCONES

BUTTERMILK

Today buttermilk, originally the liquid residue that remained in the churn once cream was transformed into butter, is made by adding healthful bacteria to whole or low-fat milk. The bacteria convert the natural milk sugars into lactic acid, resulting in a creamy, tangy product that delivers a tender crumb to scones and biscuits. If you are ready to bake scones but have only dry buttermilk powder on hand, add ¼ cup (1 oz/30 g) of the powder to the dry ingredients and 1 cup (8 fl oz/250 ml) water to the wet ingredients for each cup of buttermilk called for in the recipe.

FOR THE SCONES:

3 cups (15 oz/470 g) all-purpose (plain) flour

3 Tbsp granulated sugar

2½ tsp baking powder

½ tsp baking soda (bicarbonate of soda)

½ tsp salt

Grated zest of 1 orange, preferably organic, or 1 tsp orange oil

10 Tbsp (5 oz/155 g) cold unsalted butter, cut into pieces, plus extra for serving

1 cup (8 fl oz/250 ml) cold buttermilk

¾ cup (4½ oz/140 g) dried cranberries

¼ cup (1½ oz/45 g) chopped dried apricots

FOR THE GLAZE (OPTIONAL):

¾ cup (3 oz/90 g) confectioners' (icing) sugar, sifted

1 Tbsp fresh orange juice, or as needed

PREHEAT THE OVEN TO 425°F (220°C). Line a baking sheet with parchment (baking) paper.

In a bowl, stir together the flour, granulated sugar, baking powder, baking soda, salt, and orange zest. Add the butter to the flour mixture. Using a pastry blender or 2 knives, cut in the butter until the mixture resembles coarse crumbs.

Add the buttermilk to the flour mixture all at once and stir until a sticky dough forms. Stir in the cranberries and apricots just until evenly distributed.

Scrape the sides and bottom of the bowl and turn the dough out onto a lightly floured work surface. With floured hands, gently knead the dough 8–10 strokes; the dough will be very soft. Press the dough into a loose rectangle about 1½ inches (4 cm) thick. Fold the rectangle like a letter, overlapping the short sides in the middle. Pat out the dough into a thick rectangle. Divide in half. Pat each portion into a round ¾ inch (2 cm) thick and 8 inches (20 cm) in diameter. Cut each round into 6 wedges.

Place the wedges, 2 inches (5 cm) apart, on the prepared sheet. Bake the scones until golden brown, 14–18 minutes. Transfer to wire racks.

If desired, in a small bowl, stir together the confectioners' sugar with the orange juice until smooth. Adjust the consistency with a little more juice, if needed; it should be thick but pourable. Using a pastry brush, brush the glaze over the hot scones. Let stand for at least 10 minutes to set the glaze. Serve the scones warm with butter.

Cheddar Drop Biscuits

MAKES 20 BISCUITS

4 cups (20 oz/625 g) all-purpose (plain) flour

4 tsp baking powder

1 tsp baking soda (bicarbonate of soda)

1½ tsp salt

¾ cup (6 oz/185 g) cold unsalted butter, cut into pieces

2 cups (8 oz/250 g) coarsely shredded medium-sharp Cheddar cheese

1 large egg

1¾ cups (14 fl oz/430 ml) cold buttermilk

3 Tbsp sesame seeds

PREHEAT THE OVEN TO 350°F (180°C). Grease 20 standard muffin cups with butter or butter-flavored nonstick cooking spray; fill the unused cups one-third full with water to prevent warping.

In a large bowl or in the bowl of a stand mixer fitted with the paddle attachment, stir together the flour, baking powder, baking soda, and salt. Add the butter to the flour mixture. Using a pastry blender or 2 knives, or with the mixer on low speed, cut the butter into the flour mixture until the mixture resembles coarse crumbs, about 2 minutes. Add the cheese and stir just to combine.

Turn off the machine and add the egg and all but 2 Tbsp of the buttermilk. Mix gently by hand or on low speed just until the dough forms a sticky mass. Stir a little harder or increase the speed to medium for about 10 seconds; the mass will form a moist, sticky clump on the spoon or paddle and will start to pull away from the bowl sides. Drizzle the remaining buttermilk into the bottom of the mixing bowl to moisten the dry mixture that collects at the bottom; mix just to combine this into the dough. The dough will be very soft.

Using a silicone spatula, scrape the dough from the paddle and the sides and bottom of the bowl onto a lightly floured work surface. With floured hands, gently knead the dough 6–8 times, leaving it very soft and as sticky as possible. Cut the dough in half, then divide each half into 10 equal portions; don't worry if they are lumpy and uneven. Place each portion in one of the prepared muffin cups and sprinkle lightly with some of the sesame seeds.

Bake the biscuits until golden brown and firm to the touch, 25–30 minutes. Turn out onto wire racks and let cool slightly. Serve warm.

CHEDDAR CHEESE

Cheddar, first made in the village of Cheddar in England, is appreciated for its tangy, salty flavor, which ranges from mild to sharp, depending on age. Farmhouse Cheddars are stronger than other varieties. Although naturally a creamy white, Cheddar is often dyed orange with annatto, a paste made from achiote seeds.

Raspberry–Sour Cream Coffee Cake

MAKES ONE 10-INCH (25-CM) CAKE

CRUMB TOPPINGS

Crumbly sweet toppings are sprinkled on top of coffee cakes or muffins before baking or are sometimes used as a filling. Another term for this common topping is streusel. Such toppings consist of flour; sugar; sometimes spices, nuts, or citrus zest; and butter. The butter, either melted or cut into pieces, is worked into the flour and other ingredients to form coarse crumbs. The topping bakes into a crumbly or crusty texture, depending on the ingredients used.

FOR THE TOPPING:

1 cup (5 oz/155 g) all-purpose (plain) flour

2/3 cup (5 oz/155 g) granulated sugar

Grated zest of 1 lemon

1/2 cup (4 oz/125 g) unsalted butter, melted

FOR THE CAKE:

1 3/4 cups (9 oz/280 g) all-purpose (plain) flour

1 cup (8 oz/250 g) granulated sugar

2 tsp baking powder

1/4 tsp baking soda (bicarbonate of soda)

1/4 tsp salt

3 large eggs

1 cup (8 oz/250 g) sour cream

1 tsp pure vanilla extract

2 cups (8 oz/250 g) fresh raspberries

2 Tbsp confectioners' (icing) sugar

PREHEAT THE OVEN TO 350°F (180°C). Grease and flour a 10-inch (25-cm) round springform pan. To make the topping, in a small bowl, stir together the flour, sugar, and zest. Add the melted butter and stir with a fork until the mixture is crumbly.

To make the cake, in a bowl, stir together the flour, sugar, baking powder, baking soda, and salt. In another bowl, whisk together the eggs, sour cream, and vanilla until well blended. Make a well in the center of the flour mixture and add the sour cream mixture. Beat until smooth and fluffy, about 2 minutes.

Pour the batter into the prepared pan and spread it evenly. Cover evenly with the raspberries. Sprinkle the crumb topping evenly over the berries.

Bake until the topping is golden brown, 38–42 minutes. A toothpick inserted into the center of the cake should come out clean. Transfer the pan to a wire rack and let cool for 20 minutes. Remove the sides of the springform pan. Using a fine-mesh sieve, dust with the confectioners' sugar and serve warm or at room temperature, cut into wedges.

Strawberry-Rhubarb Breakfast Cake

MAKES ONE 9-INCH (23-CM) TUBE CAKE

FOR THE TOPPING:

2 Tbsp sugar

½ tsp ground cinnamon

FOR THE CAKE:

4 large eggs

1⅓ cups (11 oz/345 g) sugar

¾ cup (6 fl oz/180 ml) canola oil or walnut oil

3 cups (15 oz/470 g) all-purpose (plain) flour

2 tsp baking soda (bicarbonate of soda)

1 tsp baking powder

2 tsp ground cinnamon

1 tsp ground mace

1 tsp salt

4 cups (1 lb/500 g) fresh strawberries, hulled and coarsely chopped

1 or 2 stalks fresh rhubarb, 4 oz (125 g) total weight, cut crosswise into ½-inch (12-mm) slices, or 1 cup (8 oz/250 g) thawed frozen sliced rhubarb

PREHEAT THE OVEN TO 350°F (180°C). Grease a 9-inch (23-cm) angel food cake pan with a removable bottom.

To make the topping, in a small bowl, stir together the sugar and cinnamon.

To make the cake, in a large bowl, using an electric mixer on medium-high speed, beat together the eggs and sugar for about 1 minute. Add the oil and beat on high speed until thick and pale, about 2 minutes.

In another bowl, stir together the flour, baking soda, baking powder, cinnamon, mace, and salt. Add the egg mixture and, using the mixer on low speed or a wooden spoon, beat until thoroughly blended, about 1 minute. Add the strawberries (and their juice, if any) and the rhubarb and, using a large silicone spatula, gently fold in just until evenly distributed. Take care not to break up the fruit. Do not overmix.

Pour the batter into the prepared pan and spread it evenly. Sprinkle the topping evenly over the batter.

Bake until the topping is golden brown, 60–70 minutes. A toothpick inserted into the center of the cake should come out clean. Run a knife between the cake and the sides of the pan, and lift up the center tube to separate the cake from the pan sides. Place on a wire rack to cool completely. Run a knife under the bottom and around the sides of the tube, invert the cake to remove the tube, then place the cake upright on a serving plate.

PREPARING PANS

Many recipes call for greasing the sides and bottoms of pans with butter or oil. The best oil is the one called for in the recipe or a mild oil that will not clash with the other flavors, such as canola oil. Butter-flavored nonstick cooking spray is indispensable for evenly greasing baking pans and muffin cups. Lightly greasing even nonstick pans guarantees that baked goods can be effortlessly unmolded.

Almond Scones with Tangerine Curd

MAKES 12 SCONES AND 1½ CUPS (12 FL OZ/375 ML) CURD

MAKING CITRUS CURDS

An English delicacy, citrus curds are traditionally spread on warm scones and tea breads or used as a pastry filling. Curds are simple to make: Egg yolks and sugar are beaten with citrus juice over hot water until thickened, then the mixture is stabilized by adding butter, which allows it to remain thick when chilled. Although curds can be made in a double boiler, they are easier to make in a stainless-steel bowl set over a pan of simmering water. The larger, wider bowl facilitates whisking. Citrus curd will keep for 1 week in the refrigerator.

FOR THE CURD:

1 large whole egg, plus 4 large egg yolks

⅓ cup (3 oz/90 g) sugar

Pinch of kosher salt

Grated zest of 1 tangerine

¾ cup (6 fl oz/180 ml) fresh tangerine juice

6 Tbsp (3 oz/90 g) cold unsalted butter

FOR THE SCONES:

2½ cups (12½ oz/390 g) unbleached all-purpose (plain) flour

½ cup (2 oz/60 g) blanched almonds, finely ground (see page 58)

2 Tbsp sugar

1 Tbsp baking powder

¾ tsp fine sea salt

6 Tbsp (3 oz/90 g) cold unsalted butter, cut into small pieces

2 large eggs, beaten

½ cup (4 fl oz/125 ml) heavy (double) cream

¼ tsp pure almond extract

1 large egg yolk mixed with 1 Tbsp half-and-half (half cream)

¼ cup (1 oz/30 g) sliced (flaked) almonds

TO MAKE THE CURD, in a saucepan over medium-low heat, bring 1 inch (2.5 cm) of water to a low simmer. In a stainless-steel bowl, combine the whole egg, egg yolks, sugar, and kosher salt and whisk to combine. Whisk in the tangerine zest and juice. Place the bowl over the pan of simmering water and whisk until the eggs are warm and begin to thicken, about 3 minutes. Whisk in the butter 1 Tbsp at a time and continue to whisk constantly until the mixture is thick enough to form a thick, nondissolving ribbon on the surface when dropped from the whisk, at least 10 minutes total. Remove from the heat and strain through a fine-mesh sieve into a bowl. Cover with plastic wrap, pressing it directly on the surface to prevent a skin from forming, and let cool. Refrigerate for at least 2 hours or up to 1 week.

Preheat the oven to 425°F (220°C). Line a baking sheet with parchment (baking) paper. To make the scones, in a large bowl, combine the flour, ground almonds, sugar, baking powder, and sea salt and whisk until well blended. Add the butter to the flour mixture. Using a pastry blender or 2 knives, cut in the butter until the mixture resembles coarse crumbs. In another bowl, whisk together the eggs, cream, and almond extract. Stir into the dry ingredients just until evenly moistened.

Turn the dough out onto a floured work surface, form it into a ball, and gently knead a few times until smooth. Pat into a disk about 1 inch (2.5 cm) thick and cut into 12 equal wedges. Place the wedges on the prepared pan, spacing them 2 inches (5 cm) apart. Brush the tops lightly with the yolk mixture. Sprinkle each wedge with about 1 tsp of the sliced almonds.

Bake the scones until golden brown on the bottoms and lightly golden on the tops, about 15 minutes. Transfer to a wire rack and let cool for a few minutes. Serve warm, with the tangerine curd.

Tiny Roquefort Popovers

MAKES 24 MINIATURE POPOVERS

POPOVER SAVVY

Most recipes call for pricking popovers as soon as they come out of the oven, to prevent them from becoming soggy. These light and lacy popovers won't need it. You will need 1 or 2 miniature popover or muffin pans with a nonstick finish, however, to be sure the popovers are easily freed from the cups. As noted in the recipe, you can reheat them, but do not refrigerate, or they will become irreversibly soggy.

1 cup (5 oz/155 g) all-purpose (plain) flour

½ tsp salt

¼ tsp freshly ground white pepper

1 Tbsp finely chopped fresh flat-leaf (Italian) parsley

1¼ cups (10 fl oz/310 ml) milk, at room temperature

2 eggs, at room temperature

1 Tbsp unsalted butter, melted

3 oz (90 g) Roquefort, crumbled

POSITION AN OVEN RACK in the bottom third of the oven and preheat to 450°F (220°C). Generously grease two 12-cup nonstick miniature popover or muffin pans.

In a large bowl, whisk together the flour, salt, white pepper, and parsley. In a large measuring pitcher, whisk together the milk, eggs, and melted butter. Pour the milk mixture over the flour mixture and whisk together just until combined (don't worry if a few lumps remain). Pour the batter into each of the prepared popover cups, filling it to within about ¼ inch (6 mm) of the rim (about 1½ Tbsp each). Place a scant 1 tsp of crumbled cheese in the center of each filled cup.

Bake the popovers for 10 minutes. Do not open the oven door during this time. Reduce the heat to 350°F (180°C) and continue to bake until brown, crusty. and fully puffed, 8–10 minutes longer.

Remove the pan from the oven and immediately unmold the popovers into a warmed platter or napkin-lined bowl. Serve at once. Or, let cool on wire racks for up to 2 hours, then reheat in a 350°F (180°C) oven for 10 minutes.

Sweet Potato Biscuits

MAKES 12 BISCUITS

FOR THE BISCUITS:

1 orange-fleshed sweet potato (about 8 oz/250 g)

1¼ cups (10 fl oz/310 ml) buttermilk

2½ cups (12½ oz/390 g) all-purpose (plain) flour

1 cup (4 oz/125 g) cake (soft-wheat) flour

5 tsp baking powder

4 tsp sugar

¾ tsp salt

⅔ cup (6 oz/185 g) cold solid vegetable shortening, cut into small pieces

¼ cup (2 oz/60 g) cold unsalted butter, cut into small pieces

FOR THE HONEY BUTTER:

¾ cup (6 oz/185 g) unsalted butter, at room temperature

⅓ cup (4 oz/125 g) honey

PREHEAT THE OVEN TO 400°F (200°C). Prick the sweet potato several times with a fork. Place it directly on the oven rack and bake until very tender, about 1¼ hours. Let cool completely.

Position a rack in the upper third of the oven and raise the oven temperature to 450°F (230°C). Peel the sweet potato and force it through the medium disk of a food mill or a large-mesh sieve into a bowl. Add the buttermilk and whisk until smooth.

In a large bowl, sift together the all-purpose flour, cake flour, baking powder, sugar, and salt. Add the shortening and butter. Using a pastry blender, cut the fat into the flour mixture until the pieces of fat resemble corn kernels. Add the buttermilk mixture and stir until a soft, crumbly dough forms.

Turn the dough out onto a well-floured surface and gently knead 8–10 times, just until the dough holds together. Roll or pat out the dough into a 6-by-12 inches (15-by 30-cm) rectangle. Using a knife, cut the dough into 12 rectangular biscuits.

Place the biscuits on an ungreased insulated baking sheet or doubled regular baking sheet. Bake the biscuits until they have risen and their edges and bottoms are lightly browned, 12–14 minutes.

Meanwhile, make the honey butter. In a small bowl, cream together the butter and honey until light and fluffy. Serve the biscuits hot, accompanied with the honey butter.

MAKE-AHEAD TIPS: The sweet potato can be baked 1 day ahead and kept at room temperature. The dry and wet mixtures can be prepared several hours in advance, but do not combine them until you are ready to bake. The honey butter can be prepared several days ahead and refrigerated.

HONEY VARIETIES

Clover honey is the variety most people are familiar with, but it is not the only type of honey available. Depending on the source of the nectar, honey ranges from almost white to deep, rich brown. In general, the lighter the color, the more delicate the flavor. The flavor also varies according to the plants that surround the hive. Possible varieties include light, mild alfalfa, lavender, raspberry, or orange blossom, as well as stronger buckwheat, eucalyptus, or tupelo.

Cranberry–Sour Cream Coffee Cake

MAKES ONE 9-BY-13-INCH (23-BY-33-CM) CAKE

STREUSEL

Made from butter, flour, sugar, and sometimes nuts, streusel cooks into a topping similar to the American crisp and the British crumble, terms that are often used interchangeably. Streusel can be sprinkled over muffins, cupcakes, pies, or fresh, soft fruit before baking. In the oven, the butter melts and causes the dry mixture to cook into a crisp, crumbly topping. Without the butter, the mixture would simply scorch.

FOR THE STREUSEL:

¾ cup (4 oz/125 g) plus 2 Tbsp all-purpose (plain) flour

¼ cup (2 oz/60 g) sugar

½ cup (4 oz/125 g) cold unsalted butter, cut into 8 pieces

FOR THE CAKE:

1¼ cups (10 oz/310 g) sour cream

1¼ tsp baking soda (bicarbonate of soda)

⅛ tsp fine sea salt

½ cup (4 oz/125 g) unsalted butter, at room temperature

1¼ cups (10 oz/315 g) sugar

2 large eggs, lightly beaten

1¾ cups (9 oz/280 g) all-purpose (plain) flour

1¾ tsp baking powder

½ cup (3 oz/90 g) semisweet (plain) chocolate chips

½ cup (2 oz/60 g) dried cranberries, soaked in warm water for 15 minutes, drained, and squeezed dry

TO MAKE THE STREUSEL, in a chilled bowl, stir together the flour and sugar. Using a pastry blender or 2 knives, cut in the butter until coarse crumbs form. Work the mixture with your hands until it will hold together when compressed, then squeeze it between your hands into several firm pieces. Cover and refrigerate.

Preheat the oven to 350°F (180°C). Grease a 9-by-13-inch (23-by-33-cm) baking dish.

Place the sour cream in a bowl and sift the baking soda and salt over the top. Stir to blend evenly and set aside.

In a large bowl, using an electric mixer on medium speed or a wooden spoon, beat together the butter, sugar, and eggs until fluffy, 3–5 minutes. Sift the flour and baking powder over the top and mix in, then beat in the sour cream mixture. Using a silicone spatula, stir in the chocolate chips and drained cranberries just until evenly distributed. Scrape the batter into the prepared dish and smooth the surface. Scatter the streusel mixture evenly over the top, breaking it up into large crouton-sized pieces (some of the streusel mixture may be small crumbs).

Bake until a toothpick inserted into the center of the cake comes out almost completely clean, 40–45 minutes. Transfer to a wire rack to cool. Serve warm or at room temperature, cut into squares.

Gougères

MAKES ABOUT 3 DOZEN GOUGÈRES

6 Tbsp (3 oz/90 g) unsalted butter, cut into small pieces

1 tsp fine sea salt

1/8 tsp cayenne pepper

1/4 tsp sweet Hungarian paprika

1 cup (5 oz/155 g) all-purpose (plain) flour

5 large eggs

3/4 cup (3 oz/90 g) shredded Gruyère cheese

3/4 cup (3 oz/90 g) grated Parmesan cheese

1 tsp milk

PLACE RACKS in the top and bottom thirds of the oven and preheat to 425°F (220°C). Line 2 baking sheets with parchment (baking) paper.

In a heavy saucepan, combine 1 cup (8 fl oz/250 ml) water, butter, sea salt, cayenne, and paprika. Bring to a boil over medium heat and cook until the butter melts. Remove from the heat and quickly add the flour all at once, beating vigorously with a wooden spoon, until completely blended. Place the pan over medium-high heat and beat until the mixture forms a mass in the center of the pan and the pan bottom begins to be coated with the cooked mixture, 1–2 minutes; do not heat the mixture above lukewarm.

Remove from the heat and use the spoon to make a well in the center of the mixture. Immediately add 1 of the eggs and beat with the spoon until completely blended, then beat in 3 more of the eggs, one at a time. Beat in the Gruyère and one-third of the Parmesan cheese until melted and thoroughly blended.

To form the gougères, spoon the paste into a pastry (piping) bag fitted with a 1/2-inch (12-mm) plain tip. (If you don't have a pastry bag and tip, use a teaspoon.) Pipe mounds of the paste about 1 inch (2.5 cm) in diameter and 1/2 inch (12 mm) high onto the prepared sheets, spacing them 2 inches (5 cm) apart.

In a small bowl, beat the remaining egg with the milk. Brush the gougères with the egg mixture, taking care not to mash them down, and sprinkle the remaining Parmesan cheese over the tops. Place the sheets on the racks in the oven and bake until the gougères are lightly browned and doubled in size, about 20 minutes. Remove from the oven, but leave the oven on. Using a small, sharp knife, cut a small slit in the side of each gougère. Return the sheets to the oven for 5 minutes to dry out the inside of the gougères. Transfer the gougères to wire racks to cool. Serve warm or at room temperature, piled into a large bowl or passed on trays.

GRUYÈRE

Produced in both France and Switzerland, Gruyère is a cow's milk cheese with a subtle, nutty flavor. It shreds easily and melts beautifully, making it excellent for cooking, and is a superlative table cheese. Swiss Gruyère is one of the traditional cheeses used in fondue. The French version of this cheese, also called Gruyère de Comté, or simply Comté, is aged longer than Swiss Gruyère. Hence, it has a deeper flavor that is preferred for gougères and other French dishes.

CAKES & TORTES

Devil's Food Cake with Fudge Frosting

MAKES 10–12 SERVINGS

FROSTING SAVVY

If the crust of a cake layer seems tough, or if the layer has an uneven top, trim it away with a serrated knife before frosting. To prevent the cut surface from shedding crumbs and spoiling the frosting, spread it with a thin layer of frosting (called the crumb layer) before applying the final frosting. To keep a serving plate clean while frosting a cake, place strips of waxed paper 4 inches (10 cm) wide in a square to cover the edges of the plate. Center the cake on the plate, making sure the strips are positioned to cover the plate on all sides. Frost the cake and then carefully pull away the strips.

2⅓ cups (10½ oz/330 g) all-purpose (plain) flour

1 cup (3 oz/90 g) unsweetened cocoa powder, sifted

1½ tsp baking powder

½ tsp baking soda (bicarbonate of soda)

½ tsp salt

¾ cup (6 oz/185 g) unsalted butter, at room temperature

2 cups (1 lb/500 g) firmly packed light brown sugar

2 tsp pure vanilla extract

4 large eggs, at room temperature

1½ cups (12 fl oz/375 ml) buttermilk, at room temperature

FOR THE FROSTING:

12 oz (375 g) bittersweet chocolate, finely chopped

1¾ cups (14 fl oz/430 ml) heavy (double) cream

½ cup (4 oz/125 g) sour cream

Pinch of salt

PREHEAT THE OVEN TO 350°F (180°C). Lightly grease the bottoms of two 9-by-2-inch (23-by-5-cm) round cake pans and line with parchment (baking) paper. Grease the paper and the sides of the pans and dust with flour. In a large bowl, sift together the flour, cocoa, baking powder, baking soda, and salt. In another large bowl, using an electric mixer on medium speed, beat the butter until smooth. Gradually add the brown sugar and continue beating until fluffy. Beat in the vanilla. Add the eggs one at a time, beating well after each addition. Add the flour mixture in 3 additions, alternating with the buttermilk in 2 additions, mixing on low speed after each addition. Divide the batter between the prepared pans and spread it out evenly. Tap the pans gently on the counter to dispel air pockets.

Bake until a cake tester inserted in the center of a cake comes out clean, 25–30 minutes. Let cool on a wire rack for 15 minutes. Run a table knife around the inside edges of the pans to loosen the layers. Invert onto the rack and lift off the pans, then carefully peel off the parchment paper. Let the layers cool completely before frosting.

To make the frosting, in the top of a double boiler, combine the chocolate and heavy cream and melt, stirring occasionally, over barely simmering water (see page 173). Whisk until well blended and let cool slightly. Add the sour cream and salt and stir just until blended. Set aside, stirring occasionally, until room temperature. Whisk the frosting briefly until lighter in color and thick enough to spread.

To assemble the cake, brush away any loose crumbs from both layers. Place one layer, top side down, on a flat serving plate. Using an icing spatula, spread about a third of the frosting on top. Place the other layer, top side down, on the first layer and press gently. Spread a thin layer of frosting over the entire cake to seal in any crumbs, then thickly coat the cake with the remaining frosting (see page 382). Serve right away or keep covered at room temperature until ready to serve.

Almond & Cherry Cheesecake

MAKES 12–14 SERVINGS

FOR THE CHEESECAKE:

2 Tbsp unsalted butter

3 cups (18 oz/500 g) fresh, frozen, or drained jarred Bing or other dark sweet cherries

2 Tbsp fresh lemon juice

1¼ cups (9 oz/250 g) plus ¼ cup (2 oz/60 g) sugar

2 Tbsp amaretto

Biscotti Crust (left)

1½ lb (670 g) cream cheese

1 Tbsp cornstarch (cornflour)

4 large eggs, at room temperature

1 cup (8 oz/225 g) sour cream

1 tsp pure vanilla extract

1 tsp pure almond extract

¼ tsp salt

FOR THE TOPPING:

1 cup (8 oz/225 g) sour cream

¼ cup (2 oz/60 g) sugar

1 tsp pure vanilla extract

1 tsp pure almond extract

¼ cup (1½ oz/45 g) sliced (flaked) almonds, toasted (see page 53)

TO MAKE THE CHEESECAKE, in a large frying pan over medium-high heat, melt the butter. Add the cherries and 1 Tbsp of the lemon juice and cook for about 1 minute. Sprinkle with the ¼ cup sugar and cook, stirring, for 3–5 minutes. Stir in the amaretto and cook for 1 minute. Refrigerate until completely cool.

Preheat the oven to 300°F (150°C). Completely wrap the outside of a 9-inch (23-cm) springform pan with a double thickness of wide aluminum foil. Spread the biscotti crust in the bottom of the pan (left).

Using a stand mixer, beat together the cream cheese and 1¼ cups sugar with the paddle on medium-high speed until smooth. Beat in the cornstarch. Add the eggs one at a time, beating well after each addition. Beat in the sour cream, remaining 1 Tbsp lemon juice, vanilla, almond extract, and salt. Pour the cherry mixture into the pan with the prepared crust and spread it evenly, without marring the crumb layer. Pour in the filling and spread it to the pan edges.

Set the pan inside a large roasting pan and fill with about 1 inch (2.5 cm) of very hot tap water. Bake for 1 hour. Turn off the oven and let the cheesecake remain in the warm oven, without opening the door, for 1 hour longer to cool slowly (this will help prevent it from cracking). Remove from the water bath and place on a wire rack.

To make the topping, preheat the oven to 300°F (150°C). In a bowl, whisk together the sour cream, sugar, vanilla, and almond extract. Spread the topping over the warm cheesecake. Sprinkle with the almonds. Bake until the topping looks slightly set, about 8 minutes. Let cool for about 1 hour. Refrigerate for at least 8 hours or up to overnight. Carefully unclasp and remove the pan sides. Place the cake, on the pan bottom, on a serving plate and refrigerate until serving.

BISCOTTI CRUST

The Italian cookies known as biscotti, meaning "twice baked," have a crunchy texture perfect for creating a thin crumb crust. The almond-flavored variety called for here boosts the flavor of the almond extract and liqueur used in the cheesecake filling. Before making the crust, butter the bottom and sides of the pan. Add 4 almond biscotti (about 4 oz/110 g) to a food processor and process to a fine powder. Transfer to a bowl. Add 2 Tbsps melted unsalted butter and mix until evenly combined. Place in the prepared pan and spread in an even layer over the bottom.

Lemon Pudding Cakes

MAKES 8 SERVINGS

½ cup (2½ oz/75 g) all-purpose (plain) flour

¼ tsp salt

3 large eggs, separated

1 cup (8 oz/250 g) sugar

1 tsp finely grated lemon zest

⅓ cup (3 fl oz/80 ml) fresh lemon juice (about 2 large lemons)

1⅓ cups (11 fl oz/330 ml) whole milk

PREHEAT THE OVEN TO 350°F (180°C). Place eight ½-cup (4–fl oz/125-ml) ramekins in a large baking dish and pour in water to reach halfway up the sides of the ramekins.

In a small bowl, stir together the flour and salt. In a separate nonreactive bowl, using an electric mixer on medium speed, beat the egg yolks with ¾ cup (6 oz/180 g) of the sugar until pale and thick, about 3 minutes. Stir in the flour mixture and beat until very thick, 2 minutes more. Stir in the lemon zest, juice, and milk.

Using an electric mixer on high speed, whip the egg whites until foamy. Sprinkle in the remaining ¼ cup (2 oz/60 g) sugar and whip until soft peaks form when the beaters are lifted. Using a silicone spatula, stir one-fourth of the egg whites into the lemon mixture. Gently fold in the rest just until no streaks of egg white are visible. Divide the mixture evenly among the ramekins.

Bake until the centers are firm to the touch and the edges pull away slightly from the sides of the ramekins, 40–45 minutes. Remove from the oven but leave in the water bath for 15–20 minutes. Serve warm or at room temperature straight from the ramekins.

SOFT VS. STIFF PEAKS

For this recipe, the egg whites should be whipped just until they form soft peaks that slump to one side when the beaters are lifted. To make a meringue, the egg whites need to be whipped longer, until they form stiff peaks that will stand upright. The eggs should still appear moist and satiny and not grainy—that is a sign of overwhipping.

Chocolate-Almond Cake with Caramel Sauce

MAKES 8–10 SERVINGS

7 oz (200 g) 70-percent bittersweet chocolate, finely chopped

¾ cup (6 oz/170 g) unsalted butter, cut into chunks

1 cup (7 oz/200 g) superfine (caster) sugar

4 large eggs, separated, at room temperature

½ tsp pure almond extract

¼ cup (1 oz/30 g) plus 1 Tbsp cake (soft-wheat) flour

¼ tsp salt

½ cup (3 oz/85 g) blanched whole almonds, lightly toasted (page 53)

Confectioners' (icing) sugar for dusting

Caramel Sauce (page 377), chilled, for serving

PREHEAT THE OVEN TO 325°F (165°C). Grease and flour a 9½-inch (24-cm) savarin mold (see page 396).

In a stainless-steel bowl, combine the chocolate and butter and melt, stirring occasionally, over barely simmering water (see page 173). Remove from the heat and whisk to combine. Whisk in ¾ cup (5 oz/140 g) of the superfine sugar, the egg yolks, and the almond extract. In a food processor, process the flour, salt, and almonds until finely ground; do not overprocess. Whisk the flour mixture into the chocolate mixture.

Using a stand mixer, beat the egg whites with the whisk on medium speed until they start to foam. Add a third of the remaining ¼ cup (2 oz/60 g) superfine sugar and beat until the whites are opaque, then add another third of the sugar. When the whites start to increase in volume and become firm, add the remaining sugar and increase the speed to high. Beat until the whites form soft peaks but still look wet (see page 155). Using a large silicone spatula, carefully fold a third of the whites into the chocolate mixture, then fold in the remaining whites (right). Pour the batter into the prepared mold and smooth the top.

Bake until the cake is puffed and a cake tester inserted into the center comes out clean or with only a few crumbs clinging to it, 40–45 minutes. Let cool on a wire rack to room temperature. Run a table knife around the edges of the mold and tap the bottom on a countertop to release the cake. Invert the cake onto a serving plate.

Just before serving, using a fine-mesh sieve, dust the cake with confectioners' sugar and drizzle with caramel sauce.

FOLDING IN EGG WHITES

This process is used to combine two mixtures or ingredients of different densities, such as a heavy batter and whipped egg whites: Scoop a third of the whites onto the center of the batter. Using a large silicone spatula, sweep it down through the whites to the bottom of the bowl, then draw the spatula back up in a circular motion, bringing some batter with it. Rotate the bowl a quarter turn. Repeat, rotating the bowl after each fold, just until the whites are incorporated. Now that the batter is lightened, fold in the remaining egg whites.

Mango Layer Cake with Coconut & Buttercream

MAKES 8–10 SERVINGS

PREPARING MANGOES

Ripe mangoes give slightly when pressed and are highly fragrant. To remove the fruit in cubes, use a sharp knife to cut down the length of the fruit, just grazing the large, flat pit. Repeat on the other side. Score the cut side of the mango in a grid pattern; don't cut through the skin. Push against the skin side to pop the cubes out, then cut across the base of the cubes to free them.

Génoise (page 375)
1 tsp dark rum
Sugar Syrup (page 186)
Vanilla Buttercream (page 376)
1 large ripe mango, cubed and coarsely chopped (left) (about 1½ cups/9 oz/250 g)
⅔ cup (2 oz/60 g) unsweetened shredded coconut, lightly toasted (page 212)

MAKE THE GÉNOISE AS DIRECTED, let cool completely, and place right side up on a work surface. Carefully cut the cake into 2 equal layers (see page 205). Put the top layer, cut side up, on a serving plate.

In a small bowl, stir together the rum and sugar syrup. Brush the cake with about half of the syrup.

Spoon about a fourth of the buttercream into a pastry bag fitted with a ½-inch (12-mm) plain tip (see page 383). Pipe a ring of buttercream around the outside edge of the cake. Evenly arrange the chopped mango inside the middle of the buttercream ring. Position the remaining layer, cut side down, on top. Peel off the parchment paper. Brush with the remaining syrup. Refrigerate the cake for 30 minutes to firm the filling; keep the remaining buttercream at room temperature.

Using a straight frosting spatula, spread the top and sides of the cake with the buttercream, making it as smooth as possible (see page 382). Gently press some of the coconut onto the sides of the cake and sprinkle the rest on top.

Refrigerate the cake until 30 minutes before serving to set the frosting.

Ginger Cake

MAKES 8–10 SERVINGS

½ cup (4 fl oz/125 ml) buttermilk, at room temperature

1 Tbsp peeled and grated fresh ginger

1½ cups (7½ oz/235 g) all-purpose (plain) flour

½ tsp baking soda (bicarbonate of soda)

2 tsp ground ginger

1 tsp ground cinnamon

½ tsp fine sea salt

¼ tsp ground cloves

¼ tsp ground allspice

Pinch of freshly ground pepper

½ cup (4 oz/125 g) unsalted butter, at room temperature

½ cup (3½ oz/105 g) firmly packed light brown sugar

½ cup (5½ oz/170 g) light molasses

2 large eggs, at room temperature

1 Tbsp dark rum

1 tsp pure vanilla extract

Orange Zabaglione (right), made just before serving

Minced candied (crystallized) ginger, page 322 or purchased, for garnish

PREHEAT THE OVEN TO 350°F (180°C). Grease the bottom of an 8-inch (20-cm) springform pan and line the bottom with a round of parchment (baking) paper. Grease the paper and the sides of the pan and dust with flour. In a small bowl, combine the buttermilk and fresh ginger.

Sift the flour, baking soda, ground ginger, cinnamon, sea salt, cloves, allspice, and pepper together onto a sheet of waxed paper. In a large bowl, using a whisk or an electric mixer on medium speed, beat together the butter and brown sugar until light and fluffy. Stir in the molasses. Beat in the eggs, then the rum and vanilla, until smooth. Gradually stir the flour mixture into the butter mixture until smooth. Stir in the buttermilk mixture until blended. Pour the batter into the prepared pan and smooth the top.

Bake until a cake tester inserted into the center comes out clean, 25–30 minutes. Transfer the pan to a wire rack and let the cake cool for 10 minutes. Remove the sides of the pan. Invert the cake onto the wire rack and remove the pan bottom and the paper. Turn the cake right side up and let it cool slightly or completely.

Just before serving, make the zabaglione (right).

Cut the cake into slices and top each with a spoonful of the warm zabaglione. Sprinkle with candied ginger. Serve the remaining zabaglione in a sauceboat alongside.

MAKE-AHEAD TIP: The cake may be made up to 1 day ahead and served at room temperature.

ORANGE ZABAGLIONE

To make the zabaglione, a well-loved Italian dessert sauce, for this recipe, in a saucepan over high heat, bring 1 inch (2.5 cm) of water to a boil, then reduce the heat so only a few bubbles rise from the pan bottom. In a stainless-steel or unlined copper bowl, whisk 1 whole large egg, 3 large egg yolks, and ¼ cup (2 oz/60 g) granulated sugar until frothy. Place the bowl over the simmering water and add the grated zest of 1 orange, ¼ cup (2 fl oz/60 ml) fresh orange juice, and 2 Tbsp *each* dry Marsala and Cointreau. Whisk constantly until thick enough to mound when dropped from the whisk, 6–8 minutes.

Rolled Blackberry Cake

MAKES 4–6 SERVINGS

ROLLED CAKES

This recipe calls for a thin rectangular sponge cake that is rolled into a cylinder while still warm from the oven, then cooled, unrolled, spread with a filling, and then rolled again. The cake is sliced crosswise when served, revealing a spiral design. These cakes are sometimes called jelly rolls—especially when they are spread with jelly as the first (or only) layer—or Swiss rolls.

One 12-by-9-inch (30-by-23-cm) Yellow Sponge Cake (page 374), still warm from the oven

½ cup (4 fl oz/125 ml) heavy (double) cream, preferably not ultra-pasteurized

½ tsp pure vanilla extract

1 Tbsp confectioners' (icing) sugar, plus extra for dusting

1 cup (4 oz/125 g) blackberries

BAKE THE SPONGE CAKE as directed and let cool in the pan on a wire rack for 5–10 minutes.

When the sponge cake is still warm to the touch, use a thin metal spatula or knife to loosen the edges from the pan. With a long side toward you, gently roll the cake into a cylinder with the parchment (baking) paper still attached to the bottom. Allow the cake to cool completely, about 45 minutes, then gently unroll it on a work surface and remove the parchment paper.

In a large bowl, combine the cream, vanilla, and confectioners' sugar. Using a wire whisk, beat until soft peaks form when the whisk is lifted, 5–7 minutes.

To assemble, spread the center of the cooled cake with whipped cream and scatter the berries on top of the cream. With a long side of the cake toward you, roll it into a log. Transfer the log, seam side down, to a long serving platter. Cover with plastic wrap and refrigerate until well chilled, at least 1 hour or up to 8 hours.

To serve, using a fine-mesh sieve, dust the top of the cake with a generous coating of confectioners' sugar. Cut the cake crosswise into slices.

Almond Pound Cake with Orange–Dried Apricot Sauce

MAKES 8 SERVINGS

ORANGE-DRIED APRICOT SAUCE

In a saucepan over medium-high heat, combine 7 oz (220 g) dried apricots and 2½ cups (20 fl oz/ 625 ml) orange juice. Bring to a boil, then reduce the heat to medium-low and simmer, stirring occasionally, for 1 hour. Cool for 10 minutes. Transfer half of the mixture to a blender and purée until smooth. Return to the pan and stir in ½ tsp pure vanilla extract and 3 Tbsp Grand Marnier.

1 cup (8 oz/250 g) unsalted butter, at room temperature

¾ cup (5½ oz/170 g) superfine (caster) sugar

¼ tsp salt

1 tsp pure vanilla extract

3 large whole eggs plus 3 egg yolks, at room temperature

1¼ cups (6½ oz/200 g) all-purpose (plain) flour

¾ cup (3 oz/90 g) ground almonds (page 58)

1 tsp baking powder

2 Tbsp slivered almonds

Orange-Dried Apricot Sauce (left)

PREHEAT THE OVEN TO 350°F (180°C). Grease the bottom of a 9-by-5-inch (23-by-13-cm) nonstick loaf pan and line the bottom with parchment (baking) paper. Grease the paper and sides of the pan.

In a bowl, using an electric mixer on medium speed, beat together the butter, sugar, and salt until pale and fluffy, 8–10 minutes. Add the vanilla, then add the eggs and egg yolks one at a time, beating well after each addition (don't worry if the batter looks curdled). Using a wide-mesh sieve, sift in the flour, ground almonds, and baking powder and beat until smooth, scraping down the sides of the bowl as necessary. Pour the batter into the prepared pan.

Bake for 25 minutes, then sprinkle the almonds over the top. Continue to bake until a cake tester inserted into the center comes out clean, about 25 minutes longer. Remove from the oven and let cool in the pan on a wire rack for 10 minutes. Run a table knife around the inside edges of the pan to loosen the cake. Invert onto your hand, peel off the paper, and place right side up on the rack to cool completely. Cut the cake into thick slices and serve each with a large spoonful of the sauce.

Chocolate Mousse Cake

MAKES 10–12 SERVINGS

6 oz (185 g) bittersweet chocolate, coarsely chopped

½ cup (4 oz/125 g) unsalted butter

2 whole large eggs, plus 4 large eggs, separated, at room temperature

¾ cup (6 oz/185 g) granulated sugar

2 Tbsp Kahlúa

1 tsp pure vanilla extract

Pinch of kosher salt

¼ tsp cream of tartar

FOR THE CRÈME CHANTILLY:

½ cup (4 fl oz/125 ml) heavy (double) cream

½ cup (4 oz/125 g) crème fraîche, homemade (page 378), or purchased

2 Tbsp confectioners' (icing) sugar

½ tsp pure vanilla extract

Unsweetened cocoa powder for dusting

PREHEAT THE OVEN TO 350°F (180°C). Line the bottom of a 9-inch (23-cm) springform pan with parchment (baking) paper. In the top of a double boiler, combine the chocolate and butter and melt, stirring occasionally, over barely simmering water (see page 173). Remove from the heat and set aside to cool for about 10 minutes.

In a large bowl, whisk together the whole eggs and egg yolks until blended. Add ½ cup (4 oz/125 g) of the granulated sugar and whisk until blended. Stir in the chocolate mixture, then the Kahlúa, vanilla, and kosher salt. In a large bowl, using a balloon whisk, beat the egg whites with the cream of tartar until soft peaks form (see page 155). Gradually beat in the remaining ¼ cup (2 oz/60 g) granulated sugar and beat until stiff, glossy peaks form. Stir a large spoonful of the egg whites into the chocolate mixture to lighten it. Using a silicone spatula, gently fold in the remaining whites just until blended. Pour the batter into the prepared pan and smooth the top. Bake until the cake is puffed and set and the top is cracked, about 35 minutes. Transfer the pan to a wire rack and let the cake cool completely, about 3 hours. The center will sink as it cools.

Just before serving, make the crème Chantilly: In a deep bowl, combine the cream and crème fraîche. Whisk just until thick enough for the whisk to leave a path when pulled across the surface. Stir in the confectioners' sugar and vanilla.

To serve, unclasp and remove the pan sides, then run a long, thin icing spatula between the cake and the paper. Carefully slide the cake onto a serving plate. Cut the cake into slices and spoon a large dollop of the cream over each slice. Using a fine-mesh sieve, dust the cream and cake with cocoa powder and serve.

CRÈME CHANTILLY

This French dessert sauce is simply cream beaten until lightly thickened, then sweetened and flavored. Unlike cream that is beaten until peaks form, it is used to gently spoon over foods or to pool onto dessert plates. Combining half heavy (double) cream and half crème fraîche gives the sauce the lightness of whipped cream and the tangy flavor of crème fraîche.

Black Forest Cake

MAKES 8–10 SERVINGS

POACHED CHERRIES

A filling of cherries and kirsch-flavored whipped cream is standard in this classic German cake. To poach the cherries, in a small saucepan over medium heat, bring 1¾ cups (14 fl oz/390 ml) water and ⅓ cup (2½ oz/70 g) granulated sugar to a boil, stirring occasionally. Add 1 cup (6 oz/170 g) fresh pitted Bing or other dark sweet cherries, reduce the heat to low, and cook until soft, about 10 minutes. Let the cherries cool, then drain; discard the syrup. Frozen or jarred cherries may also be used. Cook the frozen cherries as directed above. Jarred cherries have already been poached.

FOR THE CAKE:

½ cup (2 oz/60 g) cake (soft-wheat) flour

½ cup (2 oz/60 g) Dutch-process cocoa powder

6 large eggs, at room temperature

1 tsp pure vanilla extract

¾ cup (5½ oz/155 g) sugar

½ cup (4 oz/110 g) unsalted butter, melted and cooled to room temperature

FOR THE FILLING AND FROSTING:

2½ cups (20 fl oz/560 ml) heavy (double) cream

2 Tbsp confectioners' (icing) sugar

1 tsp kirsch

Sugar Syrup (page 186)

Poached cherries (left)

Semisweet (plain) chocolate curls (page 248)

PREHEAT THE OVEN TO 350°F (180°C). Line the bottom of a 9-by-3-inch (23-by-7.5-cm) round cake pan with parchment (baking) paper.

Sift the flour and cocoa powder together onto a sheet of waxed paper; set aside. Using a stand mixer, beat the eggs, vanilla, and sugar with the whisk on high speed until tripled in volume, about 5 minutes. Remove the bowl from the mixer. Sift the flour mixture over the egg mixture in 2 additions and carefully fold in with a large silicone spatula. Fold a large dollop into the melted butter, then fold back into the egg mixture. Pour into the prepared pan and smooth the top. Bake until the cake is puffed, 30–35 minutes. Let cool completely on a wire rack.

Meanwhile, make the filling and frosting: Whip the cream and confectioners' sugar to medium-stiff peaks. In a small bowl, combine the kirsch and sugar syrup.

Run a table knife around the inside edges of the pan and unmold the cake onto a work surface. Turn right side up, leaving the parchment paper in place. Cut the cake into 3 equal layers (see page 205). Put the top layer, cut side up, on a serving plate. Brush with some of the syrup, then spread with about a fourth of the whipped cream. Strew the cherries over the cream (reserve one for garnish), leaving a ½-inch (12-mm) border of cream around the edge. Position the middle layer on the cream. Brush with some of the syrup and spread with another fourth of the cream. Position the third layer, cut side down, on the cream and peel off the paper. Brush with the remaining syrup. Spread the remaining whipped cream on the top and sides of the cake (see page 382).

Scatter the chocolate curls on the top of the cake. Put the reserved cherry in the middle. Refrigerate until ready to serve.

RAMEKINS
These small, round porcelain baking dishes, most often found in 3–4 inch (7.5–10 cm) diameters, are used for cooking or serving individual portions of sweet or savory foods. They are especially useful when cooking soft custards or cakes with soft centers, as in this recipe. Ramekins can be found at specialty kitchen stores and some supermarkets.

Molten Chocolate Cakes

MAKES 6 SERVINGS

8 oz (250 g) bittersweet chocolate, finely chopped

¼ cup (2 oz/60 g) unsalted butter, cut into pieces

1 tsp pure vanilla extract

Pinch of salt

4 large egg yolks

6 Tbsp (2½ oz/75 g) sugar

2 Tbsp Dutch-process cocoa powder, sifted, plus extra for dusting

1 tsp finely grated orange zest (optional)

3 large egg whites, at room temperature

Raspberry Coulis (page 377) or Crème Anglaise (page 377) for serving (optional)

PREHEAT THE OVEN TO 400°F (200°C). Lightly grease six ¾-cup (6–fl oz/ 180-ml) ramekins and dust with cocoa. Set the ramekins on a small baking sheet.

In the top of a double boiler, combine the chocolate and butter and melt, stirring occasionally, over barely simmering water (see page 173). Whisk until the mixture is glossy and smooth. Remove from the heat and stir in the vanilla and salt. Cool slightly.

In a large bowl, using an electric mixer on medium-high speed, beat together the egg yolks, half of the sugar, the cocoa, and the zest, if using, until thick. Spoon the chocolate mixture into the yolk mixture and whisk just until blended.

In a bowl, using clean beaters, beat the egg whites on medium-high speed until very foamy and thick. Sprinkle in the remaining sugar and increase the speed to high. Continue beating until stiff, glossy peaks form (see page 155). Spoon half of the beaten whites onto the chocolate mixture and whisk just until blended. Add the remaining whites and stir gently just until blended. Divide evenly among the ramekins.

Bake until the cakes are puffed and the tops are cracked, about 13 minutes. Remove from the oven and serve right away in the ramekins, with a drizzle of raspberry coulis or crème anglaise, if desired.

Vanilla Cheesecake

MAKES 16 SERVINGS

Graham Cracker Crust (page 374)

4 packages (8 oz/250 g each) cream cheese, at room temperature

2 Tbsp all-purpose (plain) flour

¼ tsp salt

1¼ cups (8¾ oz/270 g) sugar

½ cup (4 oz/125 g) sour cream

1 Tbsp pure vanilla extract

3 large eggs, at room temperature

PREHEAT THE OVEN TO 400°F (200°C). Lightly grease a 9-inch (23-cm) springform pan. Make the graham cracker crust, then pour it into the prepared pan and press it evenly onto the bottom and about 1½ inches (4 cm) up the sides (right). Bake until lightly golden and set, about 10 minutes. Let cool on a wire rack. Reduce the oven temperature to 300°F (150°C).

To make the filling, in a large bowl, combine the cream cheese, flour, and salt. Using an electric mixer on medium-high speed, beat until very smooth and fluffy, stopping and scraping down the sides frequently. Add the sugar, sour cream, and vanilla. Beat until well blended, again scraping down the sides frequently. Add the eggs one at a time, beating well after each addition. Pour into the crust.

Bake until the filling is set but the center still jiggles slightly when the pan is gently shaken and the edges are slightly puffed, 60–70 minutes. The filling will firm as it cools. Let cool on a wire rack to room temperature. Cover and refrigerate until well chilled (overnight is best).

To serve, unclasp and remove the pan sides, then run a long, thin icing spatula between the pan bottom and the crust. Carefully slide the cake onto a flat serving plate. Using a thin-bladed knife, cut the cake into slices, dipping the knife into hot water and wiping it dry before each cut.

FORMING THE CRUST

A crumb crust is classic for cheesecake. After creating the crumb mixture, pour it into the prepared pan. Spread the crumbs around the bottom of the pan, leaving any crumbs that stick to the sides of the pan where they are. Using a straight-sided, flat-bottomed coffee mug, press against the crumbs from the center outward to form an even layer on the bottom and up the sides of the pan. You can also use your hand, wrapping it in a plastic bag to keep crumbs from sticking to your fingers.

Madeleines

MAKES ABOUT 2 DOZEN MADELEINES

1¼ cups (5 oz/155 g) cake (soft-wheat) flour

¼ tsp baking powder

¼ tsp salt

2 large whole eggs plus 2 large egg yolks, at room temperature

¾ cup (6 oz/185 g) sugar

1 tsp pure vanilla extract

Grated zest of ½ lemon

½ cup (4 oz/125 g) unsalted butter, melted and cooled

PREHEAT THE OVEN TO 375°F (190°C). Generously brush a standard 12-mold madeleine pan with melted butter and lightly dust with flour, tapping out any excess. (If using a nonstick pan, there is no need to dust it with flour, but brushing with butter will add flavor.)

Sift the flour, baking powder, and salt together into a bowl.

In a large bowl, using an electric mixer on medium-high speed, beat the whole eggs, egg yolks, and sugar until light and fluffy. Add the vanilla and lemon zest and beat until well combined.

Using a silicone spatula, fold the flour mixture into the egg mixture until blended. Add the melted butter and fold until well combined.

Drop the batter by heaping tablespoonfuls into the madeleine molds, filling each mold three-fourths full. Bake until golden brown and springy to the touch, about 15 minutes.

Immediately invert the pan onto a wire rack. If necessary, use a knife to pry the cakes gently from the pan. Let the cakes cool completely on the rack. Wipe out the pan, let cool, brush with melted butter, and dust with flour; repeat with the remaining batter.

MADELEINES

Madeleines are often classified as cookies, but with their light, airy texture, they are more like small, shell-shaped sponge cakes than crisp buttery cookies. Madeleines were made famous by the French author, Marcel Proust, who wrote about madeleines in his book, *Remembrance of Things Past*. The little cakes are baked in a lightweight tinned steel pan of the same name. A standard madeleine pan has 12 molds.

Lemon Sponge Cake

MAKES 10–12 SERVINGS

5 large eggs, at room temperature

3/4 cup (5 1/2 oz/155 g) sugar

3/4 tsp pure lemon extract

1 cup (4 oz/110 g) cake (soft-wheat) flour, sifted

1/4 cup (2 oz/60 g) unsalted butter, melted and cooled to room temperature

FOR THE FILLING AND FROSTING:

1/2 cup (4 fl oz/110 ml) heavy (double) cream

Lemon Curd (page 129)

Sugar Syrup (page 186)

Lemon Buttercream (page 376)

PREHEAT THE OVEN TO 375°F (190°C). Line the bottom of a 9-by-3-inch (23-by-7.5-cm) round cake pan with parchment (baking) paper.

Using a stand mixer, beat the eggs and sugar with the whisk on high speed until tripled in volume, about 5 minutes. Beat in the lemon extract. Remove the bowl from the mixer. Sift the flour over the egg mixture in 2 additions and carefully fold in with a large silicone spatula. Fold a large dollop into the melted butter, then fold back into the egg mixture. Pour into the prepared pan and smooth the top. Bake until the cake is puffed, 20–25 minutes. Let cool completely on a wire rack.

Meanwhile, make the filling and frosting: Whip the cream to soft peaks. Put the lemon curd in a bowl and carefully fold in the whipped cream in 2 additions.

Run a table knife around the inside edges of the pan and unmold the cake onto a work surface. Turn right side up, leaving the parchment paper in place. Cut the cake into 2 equal layers (see page 205). Put the top layer, cut side up, on a serving plate. Brush with some of the sugar syrup. Reserve a third of the buttercream for decorating the frosted cake. Fill a pastry bag fitted with a 1/2-inch (12-mm) plain tip with about 3/4 cup (6 fl oz/170 ml) of the buttercream, and pipe a ring around the outside edge of the cake (see page 383). Evenly spread the whipped cream mixture inside the buttercream ring. Position the second layer, cut side down, on the cream and peel off the paper. Brush with the remaining syrup. Refrigerate for 30 minutes; keep the remaining buttercream at room temperature.

Spread buttercream on the top and sides of the cake (see page 382). Spoon the reserved buttercream into the pastry bag fitted with a 1/2-inch (12-mm) star tip and pipe shells around the top edge (see page 383). Refrigerate until 30 minutes before serving.

CAKE FLOUR

Cake flour is milled from soft wheat and, as a result, contains less gluten and more starch than all-purpose (plain) flour. Because cake flour is milled finer than other flours, its particles are small, allowing it to blend into a batter easily. Cake flour is also bleached, which enables it to tolerate the high proportion of sugar and fat in cake batters. All these characteristics produce a tender cake with a fine crumb, making cake flour appropriate for this lemon sponge and other delicate cakes.

Strawberries-and-Cream Cake

MAKES 10–12 SERVINGS

One 8-inch (20-cm) Yellow Sponge Cake round (page 374)

About 6 cups (1½ lb/750 g) strawberries

Fluffy Whipped Cream Topping (page 378)

PREPARE THE CAKE AND ALLOW TO COOL COMPLETELY. Using a serrated knife, cut the cake into 3 equal layers (see page 205).

Reserve 8 attractive strawberries of uniform size for garnishing. Hull the remaining berries (right) and slice lengthwise. You should have about 2 cups.

Spoon about a fourth of the whipped cream topping on top of the bottom cake layer and spread evenly. Cover with half of the sliced strawberries. Place the second cake layer on top of the berries and spread with a third of the remaining whipped cream topping and all of the remaining sliced strawberries. Place the third cake layer on top.

Using a wire whisk, continue to beat the remaining whipped cream topping until medium peaks form when the whisk is lifted. Use the topping to frost the top and sides of the cake (see page 382). Decorate the top of the cake with the reserved berries.

MAKE-AHEAD TIP: It's best to bake the sponge cake a couple of hours ahead, then refrigerate it (away from strong odors) before assembling. Once assembled, let the cake come to room temperature for 20 minutes before serving.

HULLING STRAWBERRIES

To prepare the berries for use, remove the leaves, rinse the fruit gently, and pat dry with a paper towel. With a small, sharp knife, remove the stem and the white core, if there is one, in the center of the berry (this process is called "hulling"). Then cut as directed.

Chocolate-Orange Cupcakes

MAKES 12 CUPCAKES

3 Tbsp Dutch-process cocoa powder

¼ cup (2 fl oz/60 ml) hot water

1¼ cups (6 oz/170 g) all-purpose (plain) flour

½ tsp baking powder

½ tsp baking soda (bicarbonate of soda)

¼ tsp salt

1 orange

2 large eggs, at room temperature

¾ cup (5½ oz/155 g) granulated sugar

½ cup (4 fl oz/110 ml) buttermilk, at room temperature

½ tsp pure vanilla extract

¼ cup (2 oz/60 g) unsalted butter, melted and cooled to room temperature

FOR THE FROSTING:

6 oz (170 g) bittersweet chocolate

1 cup (8 oz/225 g) unsalted butter, at room temperature

2 cups (7 oz/200 g) confectioners' (icing) sugar

PREHEAT THE OVEN TO 350°F (180°C). Line 12 standard muffin cups with paper liners.

In a small bowl, stir the cocoa into the hot water until it dissolves; set aside. Sift the flour, baking powder, baking soda, and salt together into a bowl. Using the finest rasps of a handheld grater, grate the zest from the orange into the bowl. Set aside.

In a large bowl, whisk together the eggs and granulated sugar until well combined. Whisk in the buttermilk and vanilla, then the dissolved cocoa. Whisk in the melted butter, then the flour mixture.

Spoon the batter into each muffin cup, filling it about half full. Bake the cupcakes until puffed and a cake tester inserted into the center of a cupcake comes out clean, 15–20 minutes. Let cool completely on a wire rack. Remove the cupcakes from the pan.

To make the frosting, put the chocolate in the top of a double boiler and melt, stirring occasionally, over barely simmering water (right). Let cool to room temperature. Meanwhile, using a stand mixer, beat the butter and confectioners' sugar with the paddle on medium speed until creamy and smooth, about 3 minutes. Beat in the melted chocolate until combined. Fill a pastry bag fitted with a ½-inch (12-mm) star tip with the frosting and pipe a spiral on top of each cupcake (see page 383). Refrigerate the cupcakes until 30 minutes before serving to set the frosting.

MELTING CHOCOLATE

To melt chocolate, chop it into small pieces and put it in the top part of a double boiler set over barely simmering water. Heat until the chocolate melts, stirring occasionally. Do not allow any water or steam to come in contact with the chocolate, or it will become stiff and grainy. You can also melt chocolate in a heatproof bowl set over a saucepan of simmering water (see page 257) or in a microwave (see page 224).

Fresh Coconut Layer Cake with Fluffy Coconut Frosting

MAKES 8–10 SERVINGS

FRESH COCONUT

Sweetened dried coconut flakes can be purchased at any supermarket, but for the best coconut flavor, use a fresh coconut. Before buying a coconut, shake it to be sure it's full of coconut water, and pass up coconuts with any sign of mold around the "eyes." Coconut milk, which differs from coconut water, is extracted from grated coconut meat and is a labor of love to make at home. Canned unsweetened coconut milk is a fine convenience product; be sure to shake the can well before using.

FOR THE CAKE:

All-purpose (plain) flour for dusting

3 cups (9 oz/280 g) sifted cake (soft-wheat) flour

2 tsp baking powder

1 tsp salt

1 cup (8 oz/250 g) unsalted butter, at room temperature

2 cups (1 lb/500 g) granulated sugar

4 large eggs, separated

1 cup (8 fl oz/250 ml) canned unsweetened coconut milk

1 tsp pure vanilla extract

½ tsp pure coconut extract

FOR THE COCONUT SYRUP AND SHREDDED COCONUT:

1 fresh coconut

¼ cup (2 oz/60 g) granulated sugar

2 Tbsp confectioners' (icing) sugar

FOR THE FROSTING:

2 large egg whites, at room temperature

1½ cups (12 oz/375 g) granulated sugar

2 tsp corn syrup

¼ tsp cream of tartar

1 tsp pure vanilla extract

½ tsp pure coconut extract

TO MAKE THE CAKE, PREHEAT THE OVEN TO 350°F (180°C). Grease the bottoms of two 9-inch (23-cm) round cake pans and line with parchment (baking) paper. Grease the paper and sides of the pans and dust with flour.

Sift the cake flour, baking powder, and salt together onto a piece of waxed paper. In a large bowl, using an electric mixer on high speed, beat together the butter and granulated sugar until very light in color, 3–5 minutes. One at a time, beat in the egg yolks. On low speed, add the flour mixture in 3 additions, alternating with the coconut milk in 2 additions, and beating well after each addition. Beat in the vanilla and coconut extract.

In a clean bowl, using clean beaters, beat the egg whites on low speed until foamy. Increase the speed to high and beat until the whites form stiff peaks (page 155). Using a silicone spatula, stir about a fourth of the whites into the batter to lighten it, then fold in the remaining whites. Divide the batter between the prepared pans and spread it evenly in the pans.

Bake until the cakes are golden brown and the tops spring back when pressed gently in the center, about 30 minutes. Let the cakes cool for 5 minutes, then invert onto wire racks, lift off the pans, and peel off the paper. Turn the cakes right side up on the racks and let cool completely. Leave the oven on.

To make the coconut syrup, hold the coconut in one hand over a large bowl. Using a hammer, firmly rap the coconut around its equator until it cracks open, then catch the coconut water in the bowl. Strain the coconut water through a fine-mesh sieve. Measure out ½ cup (4 fl oz/125 ml) of the coconut water into a small saucepan (reserve the remainder for another use), add the granulated sugar, and bring to a boil over high heat, stirring often. Set aside to cool.

Using a small, sturdy knife such as an oyster knife or paring knife, pry out the coconut meat from the shell. Using a swivel-blade vegetable peeler, peel the inner skin from the coconut meat. Using a food processor fitted with the fine shredding disk or a rotary cheese grater, finely shred the coconut. Spread the shredded coconut on a baking sheet and toss with the confectioners' sugar. Bake, stirring often, until the coconut is dried and lightly toasted, 10–15 minutes. Set aside and let cool.

To make the frosting, in the top of a 2-qt (2-l) double boiler, combine the egg whites, granulated sugar, ⅓ cup (3 fl oz/ 80 ml) water, the corn syrup, and cream of tartar. Bring 1 inch (2.5 cm) water to a simmer over medium heat in the bottom pan. Place the top pan over (not touching) the simmering water. Using an electric mixer on high speed, beat until the frosting forms stiff, shiny peaks when the beaters are lifted, 5–7 minutes. Remove from the heat, add the vanilla and coconut extract, and beat for 1 more minute to cool slightly.

To assemble the cake, place a dab of frosting in the center of a serving plate. Place 1 cake layer, flat side up, on the plate. Brush the top with 2 Tbsp of the coconut syrup. Spread with ⅔ cup (1½ oz/45 g) of the frosting and sprinkle with ⅓ cup (1 oz/30 g) of the toasted coconut. Top with the second layer, flat side down, and brush with 2 more Tbsp coconut syrup; discard the remaining syrup. Generously frost the top and sides of the cake with the remaining frosting (see page 382). Press the remaining coconut on the top and sides of the cake.

Nesselrode Cake

MAKES 10–12 SERVINGS

THE ORIGINS OF NESSELRODE CAKE

The inspiration for this cake comes from Nesselrode pudding, a Russian dessert based on chestnuts, egg custard, dried fruits and candied zest, and cream. It was created in the early nineteenth century to honor Count Nesselrode, a leading figure in the drafting of the Holy Alliance of 1815, an agreement among the monarchs of Austria, Prussia, and Russia. Here, cake layers are filled with a rich mixture that recalls the legendary Russian dessert.

5 large eggs, at room temperature

¾ cup (5½ oz/155 g) sugar

1 cup (4 oz/110 g) cake (soft-wheat) flour, sifted

¼ cup (2 oz/60 g) unsalted butter, melted and cooled to room temperature

FOR THE FILLING AND FROSTING:

1 cup (8 fl oz/250 ml) heavy (double) cream

Pastry Cream (page 377), chilled

½ cup (3 oz/85 g) plus 2 Tbsp mixed dried fruit, such as dried currants, cranberries, and cherries, and chopped Candied Citrus Zest (page 378)

½ cup (2½ oz/70 g) plus 2 Tbsp sliced (flaked) almonds, lightly toasted (page 53)

1 tsp Grand Marnier

Sugar Syrup (page 186)

Vanilla Buttercream (page 376)

6 candied chestnuts, thinly sliced (optional)

PREHEAT THE OVEN TO 375°F (190°C). Line the bottom of a 9-by-3-inch (23-by-7.5-cm) round cake pan with parchment (baking) paper.

Using a stand mixer fitted with the the whisk attachment, beat the eggs and sugar on high speed until the mixture is tripled in volume, about 5 minutes. Remove the bowl from the mixer. Sift the flour over the egg mixture in 2 additions and carefully fold in with a large silicone spatula. Fold a large dollop into the melted butter, then fold back into the egg mixture. Pour into the prepared pan and smooth the top. Bake until the cake is puffed, 20–25 minutes. Let cool completely on a wire rack.

Meanwhile, make the filling and frosting: Whip the cream to soft peaks. Put the pastry cream in a bowl and then fold in the whipped cream in 2 additions. Fold in the ½ cup dried fruit and candied zest and the 2 Tbsp almonds. In a small bowl, stir together the Grand Marnier and sugar syrup.

Run a table knife around the inside edges of the pan and unmold the cake onto a work surface. Turn right side up, leaving the parchment paper in place. Cut the cake into 3 equal layers (see page 205). Put the top layer, cut side up, on a serving plate. Brush with some of the syrup. Spread half of the whipped cream mixture on top. Position the middle layer on the cream. Brush with some of the syrup and spread the remaining cream mixture on top. Position the third layer, cut side down, on the cream and peel off the paper. Brush with the remaining syrup. Refrigerate for 30 minutes.

Evenly spread the buttercream on the top and sides of the cake (see page 382). Press the ½ cup almonds onto the sides. Arrange the 2 Tbsp dried fruit and candied zest and the chestnut slices (if using) in a ring around the top edge. Refrigerate until 30 minutes before serving to set the frosting.

Yogurt Cake with Peach Purée

MAKES 8–10 SERVINGS

PEELING PEACHES

Before puréeing peaches, remove their skins by blanching. Bring a large saucepan three-fourths full of water to a boil; have ready a bowl of ice water. Cut a shallow X in the blossom end of each peach. Immerse the peaches, two at a time, in the boiling water until their skins start to pull away from the Xs, 5–10 seconds. Using tongs or a slotted spoon, lift them out and immediately plunge them into the ice water, then slip off the skins. Use a paring knife if needed.

FOR THE PEACH PURÉE:

6 ripe peaches, about 1½ lb (670 g) total weight, peeled (left)

About ¼ cup (2 oz/60 g) sugar

FOR THE YOGURT CAKE:

2 cups (9 oz/250 g) all-purpose (plain) flour

1½ tsp baking powder

¼ tsp salt

2 large eggs, at room temperature

1 cup (7 oz/200 g) sugar

1 cup (8 oz/225 g) whole-milk plain yogurt, at room temperature

½ tsp pure almond extract

¼ cup (2 oz/60 g) unsalted butter, melted and cooled to room temperature

TO MAKE THE PEACH PURÉE, cut the peeled peaches from the pits. In a food processor or blender, purée the peaches until smooth. Add the sugar to taste. Set aside (see Notes).

To make the cake, preheat the oven to 350°F (180°C). Line the bottom of a 9-by-3-inch (23-by-7.5-cm) round cake pan with parchment (baking) paper.

Sift the flour, baking powder, and salt together onto a sheet of waxed paper; set aside.

In a large bowl, whisk together the eggs and sugar until well combined. Whisk in the yogurt and almond extract, then the melted butter. Whisk in the flour mixture.

Pour the batter into the prepared pan and smooth the top. Bake until the cake is puffed and browned and a cake tester inserted into the center comes out clean, 30–40 minutes. Let cool completely on a wire rack. Run a table knife around the inside edges of the pan and invert the cake onto a serving plate. Peel off the parchment paper and place the cake right side up. Drizzle each serving with peach purée.

NOTES: If not serving the cake right away, refrigerate the peach purée. Bring to room temperature before using. Nectarines with their peels left on can be used in place of peaches.

Raspberry Charlotte

MAKES 4–6 SERVINGS

Unsalted butter for greasing

About 20 ladyfingers, each about 4 inches (10 cm) long and ¾ inch (2 cm) wide

½ cup (4 fl oz/125 ml) framboise

3 cups (12 oz/375 g) raspberries

2 cups (8 oz/250 g) strawberries, hulled

½ cup (4 oz/60 g) plus 3 Tbsp granulated sugar

2¼ tsp (1 package) unflavored powdered gelatin (page 226)

¼ cup (2 fl oz/60 ml) boiling water

3 egg yolks, lightly beaten

1 cup (8 fl oz/250 ml) heavy (double) cream

½ teaspoon pure vanilla extract

2 tsp confectioners' (icing) sugar

LIGHTLY BUTTER A 1½-QT (1.5-L) CHARLOTTE MOLD or soufflé dish with 4-inch (10-cm) sides. Cut a round of parchment (baking) paper to fit the bottom of the mold. Cut another piece about 4 inches wide and long enough to fit around the mold. Press the parchment paper around the inside of the mold; it should be flush with the top.

Place the ladyfingers flat side up on a work surface and brush with some of the framboise. Line the sides of the mold with the most attractive ladyfingers, with the round sides facing the mold. Reserve any remaining ladyfingers for another use.

In a food processor, combine 2¼ cups (18 oz/454 g) of the raspberries with all of the strawberries and purée until smooth. Strain through a fine mesh sieve into a large bowl, pressing on the berries with the back of a spoon. Stir in the ½ cup granulated sugar and the remaining framboise. Measure 1 cup (8 fl oz/250 ml) of the purée and refrigerate. In a small bowl, sprinkle the gelatin over the boiling water and stir to dissolve. Let cool to room temperature, then stir into the remaining purée. Set aside.

Place the egg yolks in a heatproof bowl. In a small saucepan over high heat, combine the 3 Tbsp granulated sugar and ⅓ cup (3 fl oz/80 ml) cold water. Bring to a boil and cook until the sugar dissolves and becomes a syrup, 1–2 minutes. Whisking constantly, slowly drizzle the syrup into the egg yolks. Set the bowl over a pan of barely simmering water and cook, whisking constantly, until the mixture is thick and pale yellow, 3–5 minutes; do not let it boil. Place the bowl in a larger bowl partially filled with ice water and whisk until the mixture is cool and falls back on itself in a ribbon.

In a large bowl, using an electric mixer on medium-high speed, whip the cream until medium-stiff peaks form. Add the egg yolk mixture and the vanilla to the berry-gelatin mixture and stir until well blended. Pour the resulting mixture along the sides of the bowl containing the whipped cream. Using a silicone spatula, fold the mixtures together just until mixed. Carefully spoon the mixture into the ladyfinger-lined mold. Cover with plastic wrap and refrigerate for at least 5 hours or for up to overnight.

Remove the plastic wrap, carefully invert the mold onto a chilled serving plate, and lift off. Peel off the parchment paper. Dust the ladyfingers with confectioners' sugar and spoon the reserved chilled purée around the edges of the charlotte. Garnish with the remaining raspberries. Cut the charlotte into wedges and serve.

LADYFINGERS

Ladyfingers—light, flat cookies that are as long as a finger—are available in many food stores and bakeries. *Savoiardi*, the Italian version of these delicate cookies, are sold in specialty-foods stores and by mail order. To make homemade ladyfingers, see page 375.

Flourless Chocolate Torte

MAKES 10 SERVINGS

CHOCOLATE GLAZE

To make the glaze, combine ½ cup unsalted butter (4 oz/125 g), cut into 4 pieces, and 8 oz (250 g) chopped bittersweet chocolate in the top of a double boiler and melt, stirring occasionally, over barely simmering water (see page 173). Whisk until blended. Remove from the heat and whisk in 2 Tbsp light corn syrup until smooth and glossy. Set the cold cake on a wire rack over a large plate or baking sheet. Slowly pour the warm glaze over the center of the cake. The glaze should cover the surface evenly, spilling over the edges and running down the sides.

Unsweetened cocoa powder for dusting

10 oz (315 g) bittersweet chocolate, finely chopped

¾ cup (6 oz/185 g) unsalted butter, cut into 6 pieces

5 large egg yolks

¼ cup (1¾ oz/50 g) plus 2 Tbsp sugar

1 Tbsp dark rum or brewed espresso (optional)

1 tsp pure vanilla extract

Pinch of salt

3 large egg whites, at room temperature

Chocolate Glaze (left)

PREHEAT THE OVEN TO 300°F (150°C). Grease the bottom of an 8-inch (20-cm) round cake pan and line with parchment (baking) paper. Grease the paper and the sides of the pan and dust with cocoa.

In the top of a double boiler, combine the chocolate and butter and melt over barely simmering water (see page 173). Whisk until blended and set aside to cool slightly.

In a large bowl, using an electric mixer on medium-high speed, beat together the egg yolks, ¼ cup sugar, dark rum (if using), vanilla, and salt until pale and very thick. Gradually pour in the chocolate mixture and continue beating until well blended.

In a deep, clean bowl, using clean beaters, beat the egg whites on medium-high speed until foamy. Gradually add the remaining 2 Tbsp sugar and continue to beat until medium-stiff peaks form (see page 155). Using a large silicone spatula, scoop half of the egg whites onto the chocolate mixture and fold them in gently. Fold in the remaining whites just until no streaks remain.

Pour the batter into the prepared pan and spread it evenly. Bake until the cake puffs slightly and a cake tester inserted into the center comes out very moist but not liquid, about 35 minutes. Do not overcook. Let cool on a wire rack for 30 minutes.

Run a table knife around the inside edges of the pan to loosen the cake, then invert onto a flat plate. Lift off the pan and carefully peel off the parchment paper. Let cool completely. Cover and refrigerate until very cold, at least 4 hours or up to overnight.

Glaze the cake with the chocolate glaze (left), then refrigerate again until firm, at least 2 hours. Transfer to a flat serving plate. Using a thin-bladed knife, cut the cake into small slices, dipping the knife into hot water and wiping it dry before each cut.

Spice Cake with Golden Raisins

MAKES 8–10 SERVINGS

SAVORY SPICES
Coriander and cayenne are seasonings not commonly found in recipes for sweets, but in this cake they add an intriguing earthiness, and in the case of the cayenne, a subtle spark that is nicely counterbalanced by the honey glaze. Because ground spices lose their potency over time, buy them in small quantities. Better yet, invest in an inexpensive coffee grinder and use it exclusively to grind whole spices, including all of those for this cake, just before use. A mortar and pestle and a steady effort will also reduce whole spices to a powder.

2 cups (9 oz/250 g) all-purpose (plain) flour

2 tsp baking powder

¾ tsp ground coriander

¾ tsp ground allspice

½ tsp salt

½ tsp ground cinnamon

¼ tsp ground cayenne pepper

¾ cup (6 fl oz/170 ml) whole milk, at room temperature

1 tsp pure vanilla extract

¾ cup (6 oz/170 g) plus 1 Tbsp unsalted butter, at room temperature

1 cup (6 oz/170 g) firmly packed dark brown sugar

½ cup (3½ oz/100 g) plus 2 Tbsp granulated sugar

2 large eggs, at room temperature, lightly beaten

½ cup (2 oz/60 g) golden raisins (sultanas)

¼ cup (2 oz/60 g) honey

PREHEAT THE OVEN TO 350°F (180°C). Line the bottom of a 9-by-3-inch (23-by-7.5-cm) round cake pan with parchment (baking) paper.

Sift the flour, baking powder, coriander, allspice, salt, cinnamon, and cayenne together onto a sheet of waxed paper; set aside. In a small bowl, combine the milk and vanilla; set aside.

Using a stand mixer fitted with the paddle attachment, beat the ¾ cup butter on medium speed until creamy. Add the brown sugar and the ½ cup granulated sugar and beat until the mixture is pale and fluffy. Slowly drizzle in the eggs, beating well after each addition. Reduce the speed to medium-low and add the flour mixture in 3 additions, alternating with the milk mixture in 2 additions, starting and ending with the flour mixture. Beat just until combined. Fold in the raisins.

Pour the batter into the prepared pan and smooth the top. Bake until the cake is browned and a cake tester inserted into the center comes out clean, 35–40 minutes. Let cool completely on a wire rack placed over a sheet of waxed paper. Run a table knife around the inside edges of the pan and invert the cake onto the rack. Peel off the parchment paper and turn the cake right side up.

In a small saucepan, combine the 2 Tbsp granulated sugar, the honey, and the 1 Tbsp butter. Bring to a boil over medium heat, stirring constantly, and cook for about 3 minutes to make a glaze. Pour over the cake. With a small offset frosting spatula, smooth the glaze on the top and sides. Transfer the cake to a serving plate.

VARIATION TIP: Other dried fruits, such as currants, cranberries, or cherries, may be used in place of the raisins.

Angel Food Cake

MAKES 10–12 SERVINGS

1 cup (4 oz/110 g) cake (soft-wheat) flour

1 cup (3½ oz/100 g) confectioners' (icing) sugar

¼ tsp salt

12 large egg whites, at room temperature

¾ cup (5 oz/140 g) superfine (caster) sugar

1½ tsp cream of tartar

1½ tsp pure vanilla extract

Strawberry Topping (page 377) for serving

PREHEAT THE OVEN TO 350°F (180°C). Have ready an ungreased angel food cake pan 10 inches (25 cm) in diameter and 4 inches (10 cm) deep. Sift the flour, confectioners' sugar, and salt together twice onto a sheet of waxed paper.

Using a stand mixer fitted with the whisk attachment, beat the egg whites on medium speed until they start to foam. Add a third of the superfine sugar and beat until the whites are opaque, then add another third of the sugar and the cream of tartar and continue beating. When the whites start to increase in volume and become firm, add the remaining sugar and the vanilla and increase the speed to high. Beat just until the whites form very soft peaks (see page 155). Do not overbeat. Remove the bowl from the mixer. Sift a third of the flour mixture over the egg whites and carefully fold in with a large silicone spatula. Sift and fold in the remaining flour mixture in 2 more additions.

Pour the batter into the pan and smooth the top. Bake until the top of the cake is lightly browned and feels springy to the touch, and a cake tester inserted into the center comes out clean, 40–45 minutes. Invert the cake (right). Using a very thin serrated knife, cut the cake into slices and serve with the strawberry topping.

COOLING ANGEL FOOD CAKE

Angel food cakes must be cooled upside down so that they stay tall. To do this, immediately invert the cake onto a countertop, if the pan has feet, or, over the neck of a wine bottle. Let cool completely. Tap the pan on a counter to release the cake, then invert it onto a serving plate (below). If necessary, run a thin-bladed knife around the outer edges of the pan and around the inside of the tube.

Rolled Chestnut Cream Cake

MAKES 14–16 SERVINGS

¼ cup (1 oz/30 g) cake (soft-wheat) flour

2 Tbsp Dutch-process cocoa powder

2 large eggs, separated, plus 2 whole large eggs, at room temperature

⅓ cup (2½ oz/70 g) plus 1 Tbsp sugar

2 cups (16 fl oz/450 ml) heavy (double) cream

¾ cup (9 oz/250 g) sweetened chestnut purée (right)

3 oz (85 g) bittersweet chocolate, finely chopped

Chocolate curls for decorating (page 248)

PREHEAT THE OVEN TO 475°F (245°C). Line a 12-by-18-by-1-inch (30-by-45-by-2.5-cm) baking sheet with parchment (baking) paper and grease the sides. Sift the flour and cocoa together onto a sheet of waxed paper; set aside. Put the egg yolks and the whole eggs in the bowl of a stand mixer. Beat with the whisk on medium speed while adding the ⅓ cup sugar in a steady stream. Increase the speed to high and beat until the eggs are almost doubled in volume, about 5 minutes. Transfer to a large bowl.

Thoroughly wash and dry the mixer bowl and whisk. Use the stand mixer to beat the egg whites with the whisk on medium speed until they start to foam. Add a third of the 1 Tbsp sugar and beat until opaque, then add another third of the sugar. When the whites start to increase in volume, add the remaining sugar and increase the speed to high. Beat until the whites form soft peaks but still look wet. Fold the whites into the egg yolk mixture. Sift the dry ingredients over the egg mixture and fold in.

Pour the batter onto the prepared sheet and spread it evenly. Bake until the cake is springy to the touch, 5–8 minutes, rotating the sheet halfway through. Run a table knife around the inside edges and slide the cake, still on the paper, onto a wire rack. Let cool completely.

Whip the cream to soft peaks. Carefully fold in the chestnut purée. Place the cake, paper side up, on another piece of parchment paper. Peel off the top piece of paper. Spread with about a third of the whipped cream mixture. Sprinkle with the chopped chocolate. With a long side of the cake toward you, roll it into a log. Transfer the log, seam side down, to a serving plate. Put the remaining whipped cream mixture into a pastry bag fitted with a ¾-inch (2-cm) star tip (see page 383). Starting where the log meets the plate, pipe lines of cream onto the log from end to end. Decorate with chocolate curls. Refrigerate until ready to serve.

CHESTNUT PURÉE

Canned chestnut purée comes in a variety of guises. It can be plain, seasoned with a little salt for use in savory preparations, or sweetened. For this cake, look for sweetened purée laced with crumbled bits of candied chestnuts. It is often labeled "chestnut spread." The spread is regularly used in the making of tortes, as a topping for ice cream, and as filling for pastries. It is also passed through a ricer and topped with whipped cream to make the classic French dessert known as Mont Blanc. Chestnut spread is carried in well-stocked grocery stores.

Hazelnut Cake with Chocolate Glaze

MAKES 12–14 SERVINGS

SUGAR SYRUP

Dense cakes like this one, as well as génoise cakes (page 375), are made with a small amount of butter, which can produce a somewhat dry cake. Brushing a sugar syrup onto the layers as they are assembled helps keep them moist. To make the sugar syrup, combine 1/4 cup (2 oz/60 g) sugar and 1/4 cup (2 fl oz/60 ml) water in a small saucepan over medium heat. Bring to a boil, stirring occasionally, until the sugar dissolves. Remove the pan from the heat and let cool to room temperature. If a flavoring is called for in the recipe, stir it into the cooled syrup.

FOR THE CAKE:

1 cup (4 1/2 oz/125 g) all-purpose (plain) flour

1/2 cup (2 oz/60 g) Dutch-process cocoa powder

1/4 tsp salt

2/3 cup (3 1/2 oz/100 g) hazelnuts (filberts), lightly toasted (page 60) and finely chopped

9 large eggs, separated, at room temperature

1 1/4 cups (9 oz/250 g) sugar

1/2 cup (4 oz/110 g) unsalted butter, melted and cooled to room temperature

12 oz (335 g) bittersweet chocolate, finely chopped

1 1/2 cups (12 fl oz/335 ml) heavy (double) cream

1 tsp dark rum

Sugar syrup (left)

2 oz (60 g) semisweet (plain) or bittersweet chocolate

8–12 candied flowers (page 379)

PREHEAT THE OVEN TO 325°F (165°C). Line the bottom of a 12-by-18-by-1-inch (30-by-45-by-2.5-cm) baking sheet with parchment (baking) paper.

Sift the flour, cocoa, and salt together onto a sheet of waxed paper. Stir in the hazelnuts. Set aside.

Using a stand mixer fitted with the whisk attachment, beat the egg yolks and 1 cup (7 oz/200 g) of the sugar on medium-high speed until the mixture is pale and thick, 3–5 minutes. Transfer to a large bowl.

Thoroughly wash and dry the mixer bowl and whisk. Beat the egg whites with the whisk on medium speed until they start to foam. Add a third of the remaining 1/4 cup (2 oz/50 g) sugar and beat until the whites are opaque, then add another third of the sugar. When the whites start to increase in volume and become firm, add the remaining sugar and increase the speed to high. Beat until the whites form soft peaks but still look wet (see page 155).

Using a large silicone spatula, carefully fold the dry ingredients into the yolk mixture. The batter will be very thick. Fold in the melted butter in 2 additions. Using the spatula, fold a third of the whites into the batter, then fold in the remaining whites.

Pour the batter onto the prepared sheet and, using an offset frosting spatula, spread it as evenly as possible. Bake until the cake is puffed and springy to the touch, 10–15 minutes. Let cool completely on a wire rack.

Meanwhile, make the glaze and finish: Transfer the bittersweet chocolate to a bowl. In a small saucepan over medium heat, heat the cream until small bubbles appear along the edges of the pan, then pour it over the chocolate. Gently whisk together by hand until the chocolate is melted, to make a ganache (page 393). Let cool to the consistency of stiff mayonnaise.

Put a piece of parchment paper on a work surface. Run a table knife around the inside edges of the pan. Holding a long side of the cake, invert the pan onto the paper. Remove the pan and peel off the top paper. Cut the cake crosswise into three equal rectangles measuring about 12-by-6 inches and put one of the rectangles on a serving platter.

In a small bowl, combine the rum and sugar syrup. Brush the cake with some of the syrup. Spread with about one fourth of the ganache. Position another piece of cake on the ganache. Brush with some of the syrup. Spread another fourth of the ganache on top. Position the third piece of cake on the ganache and brush with the remaining syrup. Refrigerate the cake for 30 minutes to firm the filling.

Using a serrated knife, trim the edges of the cake (see page 382) to make them even.

Place the remaining ganache in a bowl and place over a saucepan of simmering water, stirring occasionally, until the ganache is soft enough to spread. Using a small offset frosting spatula, spread the ganache on the top and sides of the cake, making it as smooth as possible.

Using parchment (baking) paper, cut a triangle with two sides about 7½ inches (19 cm) and one about 10½ inches (26.5 cm) and make a cone (right).

Place the semisweet chocolate in the top of a double boiler. Set over barely simmering water and stir occasionally until melted (see page 173). Using a teaspoon, fill the paper cone half full with the melted chocolate. Fold down the top to close the cone. With sharp scissors, cut a small hole in the tip of the filled cone. When piping, squeeze the cone with one hand and steady that hand with the other. Pipe a decorative lace pattern on the top of the cake. Decorate the cake with the candied flowers. Refrigerate until ready to serve. To serve, cut into slices with a thin, sharp knife.

MAKING A PAPER CONE

Using your thumb and forefinger, hold the middle of the long side of the triangle so it is toward you. With your right hand, grasp the right tip of the triangle and curl it upward to meet the tip pointing away from you. You will have created a conical shape using half of the triangle. Hold the two tips with your right thumb and forefinger, wrap the remaining half of the triangle around the conical shape to make a cone with a sharp point, adjusting the paper as necessary. Fold the tips inside. Secure the cone with a piece of tape.

Pecan Torte with Bourbon Whipped Cream

MAKES 10–12 SERVINGS

1¾ cups (7 oz/200 g) pecans
2 Tbsp all-purpose (plain) flour
¼ tsp salt
6 large eggs, separated, at room temperature
⅔ cup (4½ oz/130 g) sugar
Bourbon Whipped Cream (page 378)

PREHEAT THE OVEN TO 325°F (165°C). Line the bottom of a 9-by-3-inch (23-by-7.5-cm) round cake pan with parchment (baking) paper. In a food processor, process the pecans, flour, and salt until finely ground; do not overprocess. Set aside.

Using a stand mixer, beat the egg yolks and ⅓ cup (2¼ oz/65 g) of the sugar with the whisk on medium-high speed until pale and thick, 3–5 minutes. Using a large silicone spatula, fold in the pecan mixture. Transfer to a large bowl.

Thoroughly wash and dry the mixer bowl and whisk. Beat the egg whites with the whisk on medium speed until they start to foam. Add a third of the remaining ⅓ cup (2¼ oz/65 g) granulated sugar and beat until the whites are opaque, then add another third of the sugar. When the whites start to increase in volume and become firm, add the remaining sugar and increase the speed to high. Beat until the whites form soft peaks but still look wet (see page 155). Using the spatula, carefully fold a third of the whites into the pecan mixture, then fold in the remaining whites.

Pour the batter into the prepared pan and smooth the top. Bake until the cake is lightly browned and a cake tester inserted into the center comes out clean, 35–40 minutes. Let cool completely on a wire rack. Run a table knife around the inside edges of the pan and invert the cake onto a serving plate. Peel off the parchment paper. Turn the cake right side up on the serving plate.

Just before serving, make the whipped cream. Cut the torte into wedges and place a dollop of whipped cream alongside each serving.

TROUBLESHOOTING WHIPPED CREAM

Beating air into cream stiffens it for use as a filling, frosting, or garnish. Always take cream for whipping straight from the refrigerator; cream allowed to stand at room temperature is more likely to separate as it is being whipped. Also chill the bowl and beaters (or whisk) on warm days or in a warm kitchen. If you have overwhipped the cream, and it is too stiff, try folding in a few tablespoons of cream, one at a time, from the carton. Keep in mind that cream labeled "ultrapasteurized" will not rise to the same billowing heights as regular pasteurized cream.

Christmas Cake with Marzipan

MAKES 18 SERVINGS

ZESTING CITRUS

Choose organic fruit if possible and scrub it well. To make strips of zest like those used for the candied citrus zest in this recipe, shave off the colored part of the peel with a vegetable peeler or paring knife; don't include white pith, as it is bitter. To grate zest, use the next-to-smallest rasps on a box grater-shredder or a long, narrow grater designed especially for zesting citrus. You can also mince zest strips with a large chef's knife.

FOR THE CAKE:

Candied Citrus Zest (page 378)

½ cup (2½ oz/75 g) dried black Mission figs

½ cup (2½ oz/75 g) dried Calimyrna figs

1 cup (6 oz/185 g) dried pears

1 cup (6 oz/185 g) dried apricots

1 cup (5 oz/155 g) dried cherries

¾ cup (4½ oz/140 g) golden raisins (sultanas)

¾ cup (3½ oz/105 g) slivered blanched almonds

¾ cup (3 oz/90 g) pistachios

½ cup (4 fl oz/125 ml) Cointreau or light rum

½ cup (4 fl oz/125 ml) fresh orange juice

1 Tbsp fresh lemon juice

6 Tbsp (3 oz/90 g) unsalted butter, at room temperature

1½ cups (10½ oz/330 g) firmly packed light brown sugar

2 large eggs

1 tsp pure almond extract

½ tsp pure orange extract or oil

1 cup (5 oz/155 g) all-purpose (plain) flour

1 tsp baking powder

½ tsp fine sea salt

½ tsp ground allspice

½ tsp freshly grated nutmeg

¼ tsp ground cinnamon

¼ tsp ground mace

½ cup (4 fl oz/125 ml) brandy or light rum, plus more as needed

FOR THE TOPPING:

7 oz (220 g) marzipan

Slivered almonds and pistachios for garnish

TO MAKE THE CAKE, using a large chef's knife, finely chop the candied citrus zest, dried fruits, and nuts; dip the knife in hot water so it cuts cleanly. Reserve a few pieces of candied citrus zest for garnish. In a large bowl, combine all of the chopped ingredients. Add the Cointreau, orange juice, and lemon juice. Stir, cover, and let stand overnight at room temperature.

Preheat the oven to 300°F (150°C). Cut down one fold of a large, clean double-strength brown-paper bag. Cut out and discard the bottom. Draw a circle 17 inches (43 cm) in diameter on the paper and cut it out. Place a 9-inch (23-cm) tube pan in the center of the circle, and draw around the base of the pan and the inside of the tube. Fold the circle in half three times, keeping the pencil lines on the outside, and cut off the tip following the inside pencil line. Unfold the paper and cut along the folds about 4 inches (10 cm) toward the inner circle, stopping at the line. Grease the pan, fit the paper into the pan, and grease the paper.

In a large bowl, using a whisk or an electric mixer on medium speed, cream together the butter and brown sugar until light and fluffy. Beat in the eggs, almond extract, and orange extract.

In another bowl, combine the flour, baking powder, sea salt, allspice, nutmeg, cinnamon, and mace and stir to blend. Gradually stir the flour mixture into the butter mixture. Stir in the dried-fruit mixture and its liquid.

Pour the batter into the prepared pan and smooth the top evenly. Bake until the cake is just beginning to pull away from the sides of the pan, about 2 hours and 20–30 minutes. Transfer the pan to a wire rack and let the cake cool completely. (Because the cake is dense, it will take 3–4 hours to cool completely.)

Unmold the cake onto a wire rack and lift off the pan. Remove the paper from the cake and brush the top and sides with some of the ½ cup brandy. Soak a large piece of rinsed and wrung cheesecloth (muslin) in the remaining brandy, lightly wring it out, and wrap it around the cake to cover it completely.

Wrap the cake with aluminum foil and place it in a zippered plastic bag. Set in a cool, dark place and let age for 6–8 weeks.

Halfway through the aging time, unwrap the cake down to the cheesecloth, sprinkle it well with brandy on all sides, and rewrap.

To add the topping, unwrap the cake completely. Form the marzipan into a disk. On a cool surface, roll the marzipan out into a 9-inch (23-cm) round. Trim the edges. Place the round on top of the cake, pressing it gently, and trim a hole for the center. Place the almonds, pistachios, and candied citrus zest on top of the marzipan in a decorative pattern and press them into the marzipan. To serve, cut the cake into very thin slices and serve 2 or 3 slices per person.

NOTE: Plan to make this cake 6–8 weeks before you want to serve it.

MARZIPAN

A traditional holiday sweet, marzipan is a fine-textured blend of almond paste, sugar, and frequently egg whites. It is used as a filling or icing for sweet breads and cakes and for making candies in a variety of fanciful shapes. Marzipan is available in 7-oz (220-g) cylinders in specialty-foods shops. Seek out fresh marzipan; it should be soft and pliable in the package.

GINGERSNAP CRUST

The gingersnaps in this crust add a zesty contrast to the rich cheesecake. To make the crust, in a bowl, stir together 1½ cups (4½ oz/140 g) finely crushed gingersnaps (about 36) and 4 Tbsp (2 oz/60 g) melted unsalted butter until the crumbs are evenly moistened. Transfer the crumbs to a 9-by-2½-inch (23-by-6-cm) springform pan and press evenly onto the bottom and 1 inch (2.5 cm) up the sides to form a thin, even crust. Refrigerate for 30 minutes before filling.

Rum-Raisin Cheesecake

MAKES 12 SERVINGS

½ cup (3 oz/90 g) raisins

¼ cup (2 fl oz/60 ml) dark rum

1½ lb (750 g) cream cheese, at room temperature

1 cup (8 oz/250 g) sugar

3 tsp pure vanilla extract

3 large eggs

1 tsp finely grated orange zest

Gingersnap Crust (left)

2 cups (16 oz/500 g) sour cream

PREHEAT THE OVEN TO 350°F (180°C). In a saucepan, combine the raisins and rum and heat over medium heat until the raisins are plump, about 10 minutes. Set aside.

In a bowl, using an electric mixer on medium speed, beat the cream cheese until smooth. Add ¾ cup (6 oz/185 g) of the sugar and 1 tsp of the vanilla and beat until blended. Add the eggs one at a time, beating just until smooth after each addition and stopping to scrape down the sides and bottom of the bowl. Add the raisins and rum and the orange zest and beat just until well mixed. Pour the filling into the prepared crust. Bake until firm, 50–60 minutes. Remove the cheesecake from the oven and place in the refrigerator on a kitchen towel to chill for 15 minutes. Raise the oven temperature to 450°F (230°C).

In a bowl, stir together the sour cream, the remaining ¼ cup (2 oz/ 65 g) sugar, and the remaining 2 tsp vanilla. Remove the cheesecake from the refrigerator, pour the sour cream mixture over the top, and return the cheesecake to the oven to bake for 10 minutes. Transfer to a wire rack and let cool completely, then cover and refrigerate until chilled, at least 24 hours or up to 3 days. To serve, unclasp and remove the pan sides. Transfer the cake to a serving plate and serve cold or at room temperature.

Carrot Cake

MAKES 9 SERVINGS

¾ lb (335 g) carrots, peeled and cut into ½-inch (12-mm) slices

1¼ cups (6 oz/170 g) all-purpose (plain) flour

2 tsp baking powder

½ tsp baking soda (bicarbonate of soda)

½ tsp salt

1 tsp ground cinnamon

½ tsp freshly grated nutmeg (right)

2 large eggs

1⅓ cups (8 oz/225 g) firmly packed light brown sugar

½ cup (4 fl oz/110 ml) whole milk

½ cup (4 oz/110 g) unsalted butter, melted and cooled to room temperature

¾ cup (3 oz/85 g) walnuts, lightly toasted (page 53) and chopped

½ cup (2½ oz/70 g) dried currants

Cream Cheese Frosting (page 376)

BRING A LARGE SAUCEPAN three-fourths full of water to a boil. Add the carrots and cook until tender, 10–15 minutes. Drain and let cool. In a food processor, purée the cooked carrots. You should have about 1 cup (8 fl oz/225 ml) purée.

Preheat the oven to 350°F (180°C). Line the bottom of an 8-inch (20-cm) square baking pan with parchment (baking) paper. Sift the flour, baking powder, baking soda, salt, cinnamon, and nutmeg together onto a sheet of waxed paper.

In a large bowl, whisk together the eggs and brown sugar until well combined. Whisk in the milk and melted butter. Whisk in the flour mixture and then the carrot purée. Using a large silicone spatula, stir in the walnuts and currants. Pour the batter into the prepared pan and smooth the top. Bake until the cake is lightly browned and a cake tester inserted into the center comes out clean, 45–50 minutes.

Let cool on a wire rack. Run a knife around the inside edges of the pan, invert the cake onto a serving plate, and peel off the parchment paper. Using a straight frosting spatula, spread the frosting on the top and sides of the cake. Refrigerate if not serving right away. Remove from the refrigerator 30 minutes before serving.

GRATING NUTMEG

Native to the East Indies, highly aromatic nutmeg is one of the oldest cultivated spices. It is the hard stone of the fruit of the nutmeg tree and is covered with a lacy, red webbing that is harvested as a separate spice, mace. Once nutmeg is grated, its oils quickly begin to evaporate and its flavor diminishes, so buy whole nutmegs, rather than preground, and grate as needed. Use a nutmeg grater, a tool with fine, sharp rasps and a small compartment for storing one or two nutmegs, or the finest rasps on a shredder-grater.

Mexican Chocolate Cake with Ancho Whipped Cream

MAKES 10–12 SERVINGS

MEXICAN CHOCOLATE

Deep, rich Mexican chocolate, often used for making hot chocolate, has a grainier texture than common baking or eating chocolate and contains cinnamon and sometimes almonds. If Mexican chocolate is not available, substitute 1 ounce (30 g) dark, semisweet (plain) chocolate, ½ teaspoon ground cinnamon, and a drop of pure almond extract.

Nonstick vegetable-oil cooking spray

1 tablet (3 oz/90 g) Mexican chocolate (left), coarsely chopped

1 cup (5½ oz/170 g) blanched almonds, toasted (page 53)

⅓ cup (1½ oz/45 g) all-purpose (plain) flour, sifted

¼ cup (¾ oz/20 g) Dutch-process cocoa powder, sifted

1 Tbsp ground ancho chile powder

½ cup (4 oz/125 g) unsalted butter, at room temperature

1 cup (8 oz/250 g) sugar

6 large eggs, separated, at room temperature

1 Tbsp Kahlúa or crème de cacao liqueur

¼ tsp pure almond extract

Pinch of sea salt

Ancho Whipped Cream (page 378)

Finely grated bittersweet chocolate for topping

PREHEAT THE OVEN TO 350°F (180°C). Line the bottom of a 9-by-2½-inch (23-by-6-cm) springform pan with parchment (baking) paper. Lightly grease the pan sides with the cooking spray. In a food processor, combine the chocolate and almonds and pulse to grind finely. Transfer to a small bowl. Add the flour, cocoa, and chile powder and whisk to mix. In a large bowl, using an electric mixer on medium speed, beat the butter until pale, about 2 minutes. Reduce the speed to low and gradually add ½ cup (4 oz/125 g) of the sugar, stopping the mixer at times to scrape down the bowl sides. Increase the speed to medium and beat until the mixture is light and fluffy, 3–5 minutes. Add the egg yolks one at a time, beating until the mixture is smooth, stopping to scrape down the bowl sides. With the mixer on low speed, add the ground chocolate mixture, Kahlúa, and almond extract and beat just until blended.

In a large bowl, combine the egg whites and sea salt. Using clean beaters, beat on low speed until frothy. Gradually add the remaining granulated sugar, beating constantly. Increase the speed to medium-high and beat until the whites form stiff, glossy peaks, about 2 minutes (see page 155). Using a large silicone spatula, gently fold a third of the whites into the batter. Fold in the remaining whites in 2 additions just until combined. Pour the batter into the prepared pan and smooth the top. Place the pan on a baking sheet to catch any drips. Bake the cake until a cake tester inserted into the center comes out clean, 40–45 minutes. Transfer the cake to a wire rack and let cool for 15 minutes. Unclasp and remove the pan sides. Place a wire rack on top of the cake and invert the cake and the rack together. Lift off the pan bottom and paper and let cool completely.

Whisk the ancho whipped cream until thick enough to hold its shape. Place the cake, bottom side up, on a serving plate and coat with a thick layer of the cream. Top with grated chocolate and serve.

Cinnamon-Applesauce Cake

MAKES 8 SERVINGS

1½ cups (7 oz/200 g) all-purpose (plain) flour

¼ tsp salt

1½ tsp ground cinnamon

½ tsp freshly grated nutmeg

1½ tsp baking powder

½ cup (4 oz/110 g) unsalted butter, at room temperature

1¼ cups (7½ oz/210 g) firmly packed light brown sugar

2 large eggs, at room temperature, lightly beaten

¾ cup (7 oz/200 g) Applesauce (page 378), or smooth unsweetened applesauce

½ cup (2 oz/60 g) walnuts, lightly toasted (page 53) and coarsely chopped

FOR THE SOUR CREAM TOPPING:

1 cup (8 oz/225 g) sour cream

1 Tbsp confectioners' (icing) sugar

¼ tsp ground cinnamon

PREHEAT THE OVEN TO 325°F (165°C). Generously grease a 5-cup (40–fl oz/1.1-l) brioche mold. Sift the flour, salt, cinnamon, nutmeg, and baking powder together onto a sheet of waxed paper.

Using a stand mixer fitted with the paddle attachment, beat the butter on medium speed until smooth and creamy. Add the brown sugar and beat until the mixture is pale and fluffy. Slowly drizzle in the eggs, beating well after each addition. Reduce the mixer speed to medium-low and add the flour mixture in 3 additions, alternating with the applesauce in 2 additions. Beat just until combined. Using a large silicone spatula, fold in the walnuts.

Pour the batter into the prepared mold and smooth the top. Bake for 40 minutes, then cover with aluminum foil. Continue to bake until the cake is puffed and a cake tester inserted into the center comes out clean, 20–25 minutes longer. Let the cake cool on a wire rack until the mold is cool to the touch. Tap the mold on a counter to release the cake, then invert it onto a serving plate.

Meanwhile, to make the topping, in a bowl, stir together the sour cream, confectioners' sugar, and cinnamon. Serve each slice with a spoonful of sour cream topping.

BRIOCHE MOLD

Baking this spiced applesauce cake in a traditional brioche mold, which is round and fluted and wider at the top than at the bottom, gives the cake the same distinctive shape as the popular, yeast-risen French breakfast bread that shares the mold's name. Available in a wide range of sizes, the molds were introduced in the nineteenth century (although the brioche dough enriched with egg and butter has existed much longer).

Babas au Rhum

MAKES 12 SERVINGS

FOR THE BABAS:

¼ cup (2 oz/60 g) unsalted butter, at room temperature

6 Tbsp (3 fl oz/85 ml) whole milk, warmed to 100°F (38°C)

2¼ tsp active dry yeast

2 large eggs, at room temperature, lightly beaten

1¾ cups (8 oz/225 g) all-purpose (plain) flour, plus flour as needed

1 tsp salt

2 Tbsp sugar

FOR THE SYRUP:

½ cup (3½ oz/100 g) sugar

¼ cup (2 fl oz/60 ml) dark rum

Vanilla ice cream or Sweetened Whipped Cream (page 377) for serving

ABOUT BABAS AU RHUM

Although theories about their history abound, these tall, cylindrical yeast-raised cakes probably originated in Russia and Poland, with the notion of a rum-based syrup added later by a Parisian pâtisserie. The baba's height is the result of using yeast in the dough. One of the most convenient forms of yeast to use in baking, active dry yeast must first be dissolved in warm liquid before mixing with the other dough ingredients, causing both the natural sugars in the flour and the sugar in the dough to ferment. This action produces carbon dioxide, which makes the dough rise.

IN A BOWL, whisk the butter until creamy. Set aside.

Put the warm milk in the bowl of a stand mixer, sprinkle the yeast on top, and stir a few times. Let stand until the yeast dissolves. Add the eggs. Add the 1¾ cups flour, salt, and sugar and beat with the paddle on medium-low speed for 1 minute. Let the dough rest for 10 minutes. Switch to the dough hook and knead on medium speed for 3 minutes. Continuing to knead with the dough hook, add the whisked butter in 2 additions along with a scant 1 Tbsp flour to help the butter blend into the dough. Make sure the butter is incorporated before mixing in the second addition. Cover and let stand in a warm place until the dough doubles in bulk, 1½–2 hours.

Lightly grease 12 small 2-by-1¼-by-1¾-inch (5-by-3-by-4.5-cm) popover molds. Divide the dough among the molds, filling each about one-third full. Place on a baking sheet, then in a large plastic bag. Gently shake the bag a few times to incorporate air and tie the opening shut. Put the molds in a warm place until the dough rises enough to reach the top of the molds, 30–45 minutes. When the dough is almost ready, preheat the oven to 375°F (190°C).

Bake until the babas are browned and puffed, and pull away from the edges of the molds, 15–20 minutes. Let stand on a wire rack. The babas should be warm when soaked in the syrup.

Meanwhile, make the syrup: In a saucepan over medium heat, bring 1 cup (8 fl oz/225 ml) water and the sugar to a boil, stirring to dissolve the sugar. Let cool to lukewarm and add the rum. Pour into a shallow pan.

Soak the babas in the syrup, turning them frequently, until spongy but not falling apart, about 30 minutes. Transfer to dessert plates and serve with ice cream.

Mixed Berry Cheesecake

MAKES 10 SERVINGS

SPRINGFORM PANS

A springform pan has removable sides that are secured with a clasp, a design that allows cakes baked in it to be removed easily. After the cake is baked, the clasp is opened and the pan sides are released, freeing the cake. You can serve the cake directly from the bottom of the pan, or you can run a long, thin spatula under the cake to loosen it and then slide it onto a flat serving platter.

1 lb (500 g) cream cheese (see Note)

⅔ cup (5 oz/155 g) sugar

2 large eggs

1 cup (8 fl oz/250 ml) sour cream

½ tsp pure vanilla extract

Graham Cracker Crust (page 374)

FOR THE TOPPING:

1 cup (4 oz/125 g) raspberries

1 cup (4 oz/125 g) blueberries

¼ cup (3 oz/90 g) red currant jelly (optional)

TO MAKE THE FILLING, IN A BOWL, using an electric mixer on medium speed, beat the cream cheese until smooth. Add the sugar and continue beating until combined. Add the eggs one at a time and mix well; do not overbeat. Add the sour cream and vanilla, then beat until smooth. Pour the mixture into the prepared crust.

Bake the cheesecake for 1 hour. Turn off the oven and let the cheesecake remain in the warm oven, without opening the door, for 1 hour longer to cool slowly (this will help prevent it from cracking). Let the cake cool completely on a wire rack before refrigerating, then chill for at least 3 hours or up to overnight.

Remove the cheesecake from the refrigerator and unclasp and release the pan sides. If necessary, run a table knife around the inside edge of the pan to release the cake before lifting the pan sides away.

Arrange the berries in a circular pattern (or as you wish) on top of the cheesecake. Up to an hour before serving, in a small saucepan over low heat, heat the currant jelly until it liquefies. Using a pastry brush, gently brush the jelly on the berries, giving the cake a glossy finish. (The jelly will soften and drip if the cheesecake is stored too long.) Serve the cheesecake at room temperature, cut into neat wedges.

NOTE: Do not use nonfat or low-fat cream cheese for this recipe.

Pound Cake

MAKES 8–10 SERVINGS

1½ cups (6¾ oz/205 g) all-purpose (plain) flour

¼ tsp baking soda (bicarbonate of soda)

¼ tsp salt

¾ cup (6 oz/185 g) unsalted butter, at room temperature

1 cup (7 oz/220 g) sugar

1½ tsp pure vanilla extract

¼ tsp pure almond extract (optional)

2 large eggs, at room temperature

½ cup (4 oz/125 g) sour cream, at room temperature

PREHEAT THE OVEN TO 325°F (165°C). Lightly grease an 8½-by-4½-inch (21.5-by-11.5-cm) loaf pan, preferably glass, and dust with flour.

In a bowl, whisk together the flour, baking soda, and salt until blended. In another bowl, using a mixer on medium to medium-high speed, beat together the butter, sugar, vanilla, and almond extract (if using) until light and fluffy. Add the eggs one at a time, beating well after each addition, just until blended. Sprinkle half of the flour mixture over the egg mixture and stir until both are just incorporated. Stir in the sour cream, then sprinkle with the remaining flour mixture and stir until evenly distributed.

Pour the batter into the prepared pan and tap gently on the counter to even out and settle the ingredients. Bake until a cake tester inserted into the center comes out clean, about 70 minutes, or longer if using a metal pan. Let cool on a wire rack for 15 minutes.

Run a table knife around the inside edges of the pan, invert the cake onto the rack, and lift off the pan. Place the cake on one of its sides and continue cooling. Serve warm or at room temperature.

POUND CAKE VARIATIONS

A slice of pound cake is buttery, rich, and delicious all by itself, but it takes well to additions, too. Vary this cake's flavor by omitting the almond extract and stirring in 1 tsp finely grated lemon zest, 2 Tbsp fresh lemon juice, and 1 Tbsp poppy seeds, or 2 Tbsp minced candied (crystallized) ginger. If you like almond, add the optional almond extract and sprinkle sliced (flaked) almonds on top before baking. You can also layer pound cake slices with fresh fruit.

Caramelized Pear Upside-Down Gingerbread

MAKES 9 SERVINGS

8 Tbsp (4 oz/110 g) unsalted butter, at room temperature

½ cup (3½ oz/100 g) granulated sugar

2 firm but ripe, large pears, such as Comice or Anjou, peeled, cored, and cut lengthwise into ⅛-inch (3-mm) slices

1¾ cups (8 oz/225 g) all-purpose (plain) flour

1½ tsps baking soda (bicarbonate of soda)

2 tsp ground ginger

½ tsp ground cardamom

½ tsp ground cinnamon

¼ tsp salt

1 Tbsp peeled and finely chopped fresh ginger

⅓ cup (2 oz/60 g) firmly packed dark brown sugar

1 large egg, at room temperature, lightly beaten

¾ cup (8 oz/225 g) light molasses

¾ cup (6 fl oz/170 ml) whole milk, at room temperature

IN AN 8-INCH (20-CM) SQUARE, heavy aluminum cake pan placed over medium heat, melt 2 Tbsp of the butter. Add the granulated sugar and cook, stirring occasionally, until the sugar melts and turns light brown, 5–7 minutes. Arrange the pear slices in the pan in 4 overlapping rows. Set aside.

Preheat the oven to 350°F (180°C). Sift the flour, baking soda, ground ginger, cardamom, cinnamon, and salt together onto a sheet of waxed paper. Stir in the fresh chopped ginger. Set aside.

Using a stand mixer fitted with the paddle attachment, beat the remaining 6 Tbsp (3 oz/85 g) butter on medium speed until creamy. Add the brown sugar and beat until the mixture is pale and fluffy. Slowly drizzle in the egg, beating well. Beat in the molasses. Reduce the speed to medium-low and add the flour mixture in 3 additions, alternating with the milk in 2 additions, starting and ending with the flour mixture. Beat just until combined. Pour the batter on top of the pears and spread it evenly to the edges of the pan. Bake until the top of the cake is puffed, 35–40 minutes. Let cool on a wire rack for 10 minutes.

Run a table knife around the inside edges of the pan and shake it to make sure the cake is not sticking. (If it sticks, set the pan over low heat and warm for 1–2 minutes, gently shaking it until the cake is free.) Place a serving plate upside down on the pan. Wearing oven mitts, invert the plate and pan together. Lift off the pan. Dislodge any pear slices that stick to the pan and place on top of the cake. Serve at room temperature.

CAKE-BAKING TIPS

A few tips will ensure perfectly baked cakes every time: First, the temperature inside the oven often does not always agree with the thermostat settting. Put an oven thermometer on the rack where the cake is baking to determine your oven's accuracy, then adjust the thermostat accordingly. Also, no oven bakes evenly, so learn your oven's hot spots. Always rotate pans 180 degrees halfway through baking, whether or not a recipe instructs you to do so, to ensure an even bake, especially when using large rectangular pans.

Gâteau Basque

MAKES 8–10 SERVINGS

2 cups (9 oz/250 g) all-purpose (plain) flour

2 tsp baking powder

¼ tsp salt

1 medium orange

4 large eggs, at room temperature

1¼ cups (9 oz/250 g) sugar

2 tsp pure vanilla extract

¾ cup (6 oz/170 g) unsalted butter, melted and cooled to room temperature

Pastry Cream (page 377), chilled

¼ cup (2½ oz/70 g) cherry, raspberry, or strawberry preserves

PREHEAT THE OVEN TO 325°F (165°C). Line the bottom of a 9-by-3-inch (23-by-7.5-cm) round cake pan with parchment (baking) paper. Sift the flour, baking powder, and salt together onto a sheet of waxed paper; set aside. Remove the zest from the orange, then juice the orange (right). You should have ⅓ cup (3 fl oz/80 ml) juice.

Using a stand mixer fitted with the whisk attachment, beat 3 of the eggs and the sugar on high speed until pale, thick, and almost doubled in volume, 4–5 minutes. Reduce the speed to low. Beat in the orange zest, orange juice, and vanilla. Increase the speed to medium-low and add the flour mixture in 3 additions, alternating with the melted butter in 2 additions, drizzling the butter in slowly. Beat just until combined.

Pour half of the batter into the prepared pan, spreading it to the edges with a small offset frosting spatula. Spread the pastry cream on top, to within 1 inch (2.5 cm) of the sides of the pan. Spread the preserves over the pastry cream to within 1 inch (2.5 cm) of the pan sides. Pour the remaining batter on top and spread it to the edges of the pan.

In a small bowl, whisk together the remaining egg with 1 Tbsp water. Brush the mixture on top of the cake. Bake until the cake is puffed and browned, 50–55 minutes. Let cool completely on a wire rack. Run a table knife around the edges of the pan and invert the cake onto a serving plate. Peel off the parchment paper and turn the cake right side up.

JUICING CITRUS

A variety of tools are available for removing the zest, the colored portion of the peel, from citrus fruits. They include old-fashioned handheld graters with fine rasps, Microplane graters with razor-edged holes, zesters that remove fine strips in a single stroke, and paring knives or vegetable peelers for cutting away zest in long strips. When juicing only a few fruits, a simple hand device, such as a wooden reamer or a shallow bowl with a fluted, inverted cone at its center, will suffice. When you need both zest and juice, remove the zest first.

Espresso Pound Cake

MAKES 8–10 SERVINGS

COFFEE IN CAKES

Many cake batters flavored with coffee call for brewed coffee, but this pound cake uses ground roasted beans, for a more robust coffee taste. Choose dark-roasted beans, such as French, Italian, or espresso roast, and buy them from a shop that roasts frequently and has a steady turnover of inventory. For the best flavor, grind the beans to as fine a powder as possible. If you do not have a coffee grinder, buy coffee beans within a day of baking the cake and ask the shop to grind them for you.

1½ cups (7 oz/200 g) all-purpose (plain) flour

1 tsp baking powder

¼ tsp salt

1 Tbsp finely ground dark-roast coffee beans (left)

1 lemon

⅔ cup (5 oz/140 g) unsalted butter, at room temperature

1 cup (7 oz/200 g) sugar

2 large eggs, at room temperature, lightly beaten

⅓ cup (3 fl oz/80 ml) buttermilk, at room temperature

PREHEAT THE OVEN TO 350°F (180°C). Generously grease an 8½-by-4½-inch (21.5-by-11.5-cm) loaf pan.

Sift the flour, baking powder, and salt together into a bowl. Stir in the ground coffee. Using the finest rasps of a handheld grater, grate the zest from the lemon into the bowl. Set aside.

Using a stand mixer, beat the butter with the paddle on medium speed until creamy. Add the sugar and beat until the mixture is pale and fluffy. Slowly drizzle in the eggs, beating well after each addition. Reduce the speed to medium-low and add the flour mixture in 3 additions, alternating with the buttermilk in 2 additions, starting and ending with the flour mixture. Beat just until combined.

Pour the batter into the prepared pan and smooth the top. Bake until the cake is browned and a cake tester inserted into the center comes out clean, 50–60 minutes. Let the cake cool completely on a wire rack. Run a table knife around the inside edges of the pan and turn the cake out onto a serving plate. Place the cake right side up.

SERVING TIP: Try this pound cake for breakfast or with a cup of tea in the afternoon.

Cloche Café

MAKES 6–8 SERVINGS

5 large eggs, separated, plus 1 large egg yolk, at room temperature

⅔ cup (4½ oz/125 g) granulated sugar

1 cup (4½ oz/125 g) all-purpose (plain) flour

Coffee Sugar Syrup (see Note)

Coffee Meringue Buttercream (page 376)

Confectioners' (icing) sugar for dusting

Candied coffee beans for decorating

PREHEAT THE OVEN TO 350°F (180°C). Generously grease a 6-cup (48–fl oz/1.5-l) charlotte mold. Using a stand mixer fitted with the whisk attachment, beat the egg whites on medium speed until they start to foam. Add a third of the granulated sugar and beat until the whites are opaque, then add another third of the sugar. When the whites start to become firm and increase in volume, add the remaining sugar and increase the speed to high. Beat until the whites form soft peaks but still look wet (see page 155). In another bowl, whisk the yolks by hand until blended. Using a large silicone spatula, carefully fold the yolks into the whites. Sift the flour over the egg mixture in 2 additions and carefully fold in.

Pour the batter into the prepared mold and smooth the top. Bake until the cake is browned and puffed, and a cake tester inserted into the center comes out clean, 20–25 minutes. Let cool on a wire rack for 10 minutes, then unmold. If necessary, tap the pan on a counter to release the cake.

Cut the cake into 4 equal layers (right). Put the widest layer, cut side up, on a serving plate. Brush with some of the coffee sugar syrup. Reserve about half of the buttercream for the outside of the cake. Spread a thin layer of the remaining buttercream on the layer. Continue to alternate layers of cake brushed with syrup and spread with buttercream. You will have 4 layers of cake and 3 layers of buttercream. The shape of the assembled cake will resemble that of the mold (and original whole baked cake). Refrigerate for 30 minutes. Spread the buttercream over the top and sides (see page 382). Using a fine-mesh sieve, dust the cake with confectioners' sugar and decorate with candied coffee beans. Refrigerate until ready to serve.

NOTE: To make the coffee sugar syrup, follow the instructions for making Sugar Syrup (page 186), but add 1 tsp instant espresso powder to the sugar before dissolving in the water.

CUTTING CAKE LAYERS

Toothpicks make excellent guides for cutting a cake into layers. Using a ruler, insert toothpicks at regular intervals around the side of the cake, dividing it into 2, 3, or even 4 horizontal layers. Placing one hand on top of the cake, and using a long, serrated knife positioned just above the line of toothpicks marking the layer, cut the cake with an even sawing motion. Lift off the top layer and carefully set it aside, then remove the row of toothpicks you used as a guide. If the cake has more than 2 layers, repeat to cut the additional layers.

Classic Birthday Cake

MAKES 10–12 SERVINGS

VANILLA FROSTING

Not everyone likes chocolate, and we should all get what we like on our birthdays. To make vanilla frosting, in a bowl, using an electric mixer on medium speed, beat together 1 cup (8 oz/250 g) room-temperature unsalted butter, 4 cups (1 lb/500 g) confectioners' (icing) sugar, ⅓ cup (3 fl oz/80 ml) heavy (double) cream, 2¼ tsp pure vanilla extract, and ¼ tsp salt until smooth. Use right away. Makes about 3 cups (24 oz/750 g). If desired, sprinkle 2 cups (6 oz/185 g) lightly toasted shredded coconut (see page 212) over the top and sides of the frosted cake and press gently.

2¾ cups (12⅓ oz/385 g) all-purpose (plain) flour

1 Tbsp baking powder

¼ tsp salt

¾ cup (6 oz/185 g) unsalted butter, at room temperature

1¾ cups (12¼ oz/380 g) sugar

3 large eggs, at room temperature

2 tsp pure vanilla extract

1¼ cups (10 fl oz/310 ml) buttermilk

Chocolate Frosting (page 375)

PREHEAT THE OVEN TO 350°F (180°C). Lightly grease the bottoms of two 9-by-2-inch (23-by-5-cm) round cake pans and line with parchment (baking) paper. Grease the paper and the sides of the pans and dust with flour. In a bowl, whisk together the flour, baking powder, and salt until well blended. In another bowl, using an electric mixer on medium speed, beat the butter until smooth. Slowly add the sugar and continue beating until well blended and fluffy. Add the eggs one at a time, beating well after each addition, until just blended. Beat in the vanilla. Add the flour mixture in 3 additions, alternating with the buttermilk in 2 additions, beating on low speed after each addition.

Divide the batter between the prepared pans and spread it evenly. Bake until a cake tester inserted into the center of a cake comes out clean, 25–30 minutes. Let cool on a wire rack for 15 minutes. Run a table knife around the inside edges of the pans to loosen the layers. Invert onto the rack and lift off the pans, then carefully peel off the parchment paper. Let the layers cool completely before frosting.

To assemble the cake, brush away any loose crumbs from both layers. Place one layer, top side down, on a flat serving plate. Using an icing spatula, spread about a third of the frosting on top. Place the other layer, top side down, on the first layer and press gently. Spread a thin layer of frosting over the entire cake to seal in any crumbs, then coat the cake with the remaining frosting (see page 382). Serve right away or keep covered at room temperature until ready to serve.

Gingerbread with Maple Whipped Cream

MAKES 9 SERVINGS

GINGERBREAD SPICES

Among the earliest-known baked sweets, gingerbread is most recognizable as a soft, dark, moist cake flavored with dark molasses, ground dried gingerroot, and other spices such as cinnamon. It is related to firm, dry-textured cookies or breads, such as the French *pain d'épices* and the English parkin. For the best gingerbread, use fresh ground ginger that is gently spicy-hot. Keep in mind that spices lose potency after long storage, so before preparing gingerbread, replace any spices that are more than 6 months old.

1½ cups (7½ oz/235 g) all-purpose (plain) flour

½ tsp baking soda (bicarbonate of soda)

¼ tsp salt

4 tsp ground ginger

1¼ tsp ground cinnamon

¼ tsp ground allspice

¼ tsp ground cloves

½ cup (4 oz/125 g) unsalted butter, at room temperature

½ cup (3½ oz/105 g) firmly packed light or dark brown sugar

2 large eggs

⅔ cup (4 oz/125 g) light or dark molasses

⅔ cup (5 fl oz/160 ml) buttermilk

1½ tsp pure vanilla extract

Maple Whipped Cream (page 378)

PREHEAT THE OVEN TO 350°F (180°C). Grease an 8- or 9-inch (20- or 23-cm) square baking pan or dish and dust with flour, tapping out the excess. If using a glass baking dish, set the oven temperature to 325°F (165°C).

In a bowl, stir together the flour, baking soda, salt, ginger, cinnamon, allspice, and cloves.

In another bowl, using an electric mixer on medium speed, cream together the butter and brown sugar until fluffy. Add the eggs, one at a time, beating well after each addition. Beat in the molasses. Add the flour mixture in 2 additions, alternating with the buttermilk and vanilla. Beat well until fluffy and smooth yet thick.

Pour the batter into the prepared pan and spread it evenly.

Bake until the top is dry to the touch and the edges pull away from the pan sides, 35–40 minutes. A cake tester inserted into the center of the cake should come out clean. Transfer the pan to a wire rack and let cool for 30 minutes.

Serve the gingerbread warm or at room temperature, cut into squares and accompanied by the maple whipped cream.

Pumpkin Mousse Cake

MAKES 10–12 SERVINGS

Génoise (page 375)

2¼ tsp (1 package) unflavored powdered gelatin (page 226)

1¾ cups (15 oz/420 g) fresh pumpkin purée (page 255) or canned pumpkin purée

½ cup (3½ oz/100 g) granulated sugar

¼ tsp salt

¼ tsp ground cinnamon

¼ tsp ground cloves

¼ tsp freshly grated nutmeg

1 Tbsp dark rum

1⅔ cups (13 fl oz/360 ml) plus ½ cup (4 fl oz/110 ml) heavy (double) cream

1 tsp confectioners' (icing) sugar

MAKE THE GÉNOISE AS DIRECTED, let cool completely, and place right side up on a work surface. Cut the cake into 2 equal layers (see page 205).

In a small bowl, sprinkle the gelatin over 2 Tbsp cold water, stir, and let soften until opaque, about 3 minutes. In a saucepan over medium heat, combine about ½ cup (4 oz/110 g) of the pumpkin purée, the granulated sugar, and the salt and heat, stirring, until the sugar dissolves. Stir in the softened gelatin and let cool to room temperature. In a bowl, stir the pumpkin mixture into the remaining pumpkin purée. Whisk in the cinnamon, cloves, nutmeg, and rum. Using a stand mixer or by hand, whip the 1⅔ cups cream to soft peaks. Using a large silicone spatula, gently fold a third of the cream into the purée, then fold in the remaining cream, making a mousse.

Peel off the paper from the bottom cake layer. Put the layer, cut side up, into the bottom of a 9-inch (23-cm) round springform pan. Spread half of the mousse evenly over the cake. Trim ½ inch (12 mm) from the outside edge of the remaining layer. Center it, cut side down, on top of the mousse. Top with the remaining mousse, pushing it between the cake and the pan and smoothing the top. Refrigerate until set, at least 4 hours or up to overnight.

Warm the sides of the pan with a kitchen towel soaked in hot water and wrung out. Unclasp and remove the pan sides and smooth the sides of the mousse with a frosting spatula. Whip the ½ cup cream and the confectioners' sugar to medium peaks. Spoon into a pastry bag fitted with a ½-inch (12-mm) star tip. Pipe shells around the top edge and a few in the center of the cake (right). Run a thin knife under the cake to free it from the bottom of the springform pan and transfer to a serving plate. Refrigerate the cake until ready to serve.

PIPING FROSTING SHELLS

To pipe decorative shells, hold the pastry bag perpendicular to the top edge of the cake and with the tip just touching the cake. As you squeeze the bag, lift the tip and then return it alongside the starting point, to form a loop of frosting. Make connecting loops around the cake. For more information, see page 383.

Chiffon Cake with Summer Fruit Compote

MAKES 10–12 SERVINGS

CHIFFON CAKE

Light and moist, chiffon cakes are an American invention of the late 1940s. The most noteworthy characteristic is the use of a flavorless oil, rather than the typical butter. The oil, along with egg yolks, ensures a tender crumb, and whipped egg whites, aided by baking powder, deliver the height. Because the oil is bland (grapeseed, shown above, and canola are good choices), other flavorings, such as citrus and vanilla, are always added. The batter is fairly liquid, so the egg whites must be whipped a little stiffer than for most baking recipes.

FOR THE CAKE:

2 cups (8 oz/225 g) cake (soft-wheat) flour

2½ tsp baking powder

¾ tsp salt

1½ cups (10½ oz/300 g) granulated sugar

6 large eggs, separated, plus 2 large egg whites, at room temperature

½ cup (4 fl oz/110 ml) canola oil

1 Tbsp grated orange zest

1 Tbsp pure vanilla extract

FOR THE GLAZE:

3 Tbsp fresh orange juice

2 cups (7 oz/200 g) confectioners' (icing) sugar, sifted

FOR THE FRUIT COMPOTE:

2 cups (8 oz/225 g) mixed ripe fruit (see Note)

¼–½ cup (2–3½ oz/60–100 g) granulated sugar

PREHEAT THE OVEN TO 325°F (165°C). Have ready an ungreased angel food cake pan 10 inches (25 cm) in diameter and 4 inches (10 cm) deep. Sift the flour, baking powder, and salt together into a large bowl. Add 1 cup (7 oz/200 g) of the granulated sugar. Add the egg yolks, ¾ cup (6 fl oz/170 ml) water, oil, orange zest, and vanilla and whisk until smooth.

Using a stand mixer, beat the egg whites with the whisk on medium speed until they start to foam. Add a third of the remaining ½ cup (3½ oz/100 g) granulated sugar and beat until the whites are opaque, then add another third of the sugar. When the whites start to increase in volume, add the remaining sugar and increase the speed to high. Beat until the whites form stiff peaks but still look wet (see page 155). Using a large silicone spatula, carefully fold a third of the beaten whites into the batter, then fold in the remaining whites.

Pour the batter into the pan. Bake until the cake is puffed and lightly browned, 55–65 minutes. Immediately invert the cake onto a countertop if the pan has feet or, if it does not, over the neck of a wine bottle. Let cool completely. Run a thin-bladed knife around the outer edges of the pan and around the inside of the tube. Invert the cake onto a large serving plate.

To make the glaze, in a bowl, whisk together the orange juice and confectioners' sugar. Pour over the cake and let run down the sides. Let the glaze set.

To make the compote, put the fruit into a bowl, sprinkle with granulated sugar to taste, and gently stir.

To serve, spoon some of the compote alongside each slice.

NOTE: For the compote, use a combination of fruits in season: blueberries and/or halved strawberries with sliced nectarines, or sliced peeled peaches, or sliced plums.

Coconut Cake with Mango Topping

MAKES 8 SERVINGS

FOR THE CAKE:

Nonstick vegetable-oil cooking spray

1½ cups (7½ oz/235 g) all-purpose (plain) flour

1½ tsp baking powder

½ tsp salt

½ cup (4 oz/125 g) unsalted butter, at room temperature

¾ cups (6 oz/185 g) sugar

2 large eggs

1½ tsp coconut extract

½ tsp pure vanilla extract

½ cup (4 fl oz/125 ml) whole milk

1 cup (4 oz/125 g) sweetened shredded coconut, lightly toasted (left)

FOR THE MANGO TOPPING:

2 large ripe mangoes, peeled, pitted, and cut into ¼-inch (6-mm) cubes (page 158)

2 tsp fresh lime juice

1–2 Tbsp sugar

POSITION A RACK IN THE LOWER THIRD OF THE OVEN and preheat to 325°F (165°C). Grease a 9-by-5-inch (23-by-13-cm) loaf pan with the cooking spray. Dust the pan with flour, then tap out any excess.

To make the cake, sift the flour, baking powder, and salt together into a bowl; set aside. Using a stand mixer fitted with the paddle attachment, beat the butter on medium speed until pale and fluffy. Add the sugar and beat well. Add the eggs one at a time, beating well after each addition. Add the coconut extract and vanilla. Add the flour mixture in 2 additions, alternating with the milk, beating on low speed after each addition. Reserve 1 Tbsp of the shredded coconut for garnish and stir in the remainder.

Pour the batter into the prepared pan. Bake until the top is golden and the cake is firm, 55–60 minutes. Let cool in the pan on a wire rack for 30 minutes. Turn out of the pan.

In a large bowl, toss together the mango cubes with the lime juice and sugar to taste. Place a slice of warm coconut cake on each dessert plate. Spoon the mango mixture over each slice of cake and garnish with the reserved coconut. Serve right away.

TOASTING COCONUT

Toasting coconut enhances and concentrates the flavor of the fruit. In this dish, the buttery richness of the toasted coconut complements the pound cake and adds texture to the fresh mango topping. To toast, spread the coconut on a baking sheet and toast in a preheated 350°F (180°C) oven until the edges are lightly golden brown, 8–10 minutes. Cool completly before using.

Pineapple Upside-Down Cake

MAKES 8 SERVINGS

Nonstick vegetable-oil cooking spray

½ fresh pineapple, peeled and trimmed (page 234)

4 Tbsp (2 oz/60 g) unsalted butter

¾ cup (6 oz/185 g) firmly packed brown sugar

FOR THE CAKE:

1¾ cups (9 oz/280 g) all-purpose (plain) flour

1 tsp baking powder

¼ tsp salt

⅛ tsp freshly grated nutmeg

2 large eggs

2 tsp pure vanilla extract

¾ cup (6 oz/185 g) unsalted butter, at room temperature

1 cup (8 oz/250 g) granulated sugar

½ cup (4 fl oz/125 ml) whole milk

PREHEAT THE OVEN TO 350°F (180°C). Lightly grease a 9-inch (23-cm) round cake pan with the cooking spray.

Cut the pineapple crosswise into slices ½ inch (12 mm) thick. With a paring knife or small cookie cutter, remove the core from each slice. Cut the pineapple rounds into half-moons and set aside.

In a small saucepan over medium heat, melt the butter. Add the brown sugar and stir until small bubbles appear, 2–3 minutes. Remove the mixture from the heat and pour into the prepared pan. Arrange 7–8 pineapple half-circles in the pan in a circular pattern. Set aside.

To make the cake, in a bowl, mix together the flour, baking powder, salt, and nutmeg; set aside. In another bowl, whisk together the eggs and vanilla; set aside.

In a stand mixer fitted with the paddle attachment, beat the butter until pale and fluffy. Gradually add the granulated sugar and beat for 2–3 minutes longer. Slowly add the egg mixture, beating well after each addition. Add the flour mixture in 2 additions, alternating with the milk, beating on low speed after each addition. Continue beating, scraping down the sides of the bowl as needed, until the batter is completely smooth. Do not overmix the batter.

Pour the batter on top of the pineapple slices in the prepared pan, spreading it evenly. Bake until the top of the cake is lightly golden and the center springs back when touched, 35–45 minutes. Let the cake cool in the pan on a wire rack for 5–10 minutes, then turn out onto a platter and scrape the remaining juices over the top of cake. Let cool slightly and serve warm.

UPSIDE-DOWN CAKE VARIATION

If desired, leave the pineapple rounds whole, making sure to still cut out the hard core of each round. Lay the rounds in the cake pan, overlapping them in a decorative fashion. Place a poached cherry (see page 164) in the center of each round.

Eggnog Bavarian Cream Cake

MAKES 8 SERVINGS

Chocolate Ladyfingers (page 375)

2¼ tsp (1 package) unflavored powdered gelatin (page 226)

1 cup (8 fl oz/225 ml) whole milk

½ cup (4 oz/110 g) sugar

3 large egg yolks

2 tsp brandy or Cognac

1 tsp pure vanilla extract

⅛ tsp freshly grated nutmeg

1 cup (8 fl oz/225 ml) heavy (double) cream

Chocolate curls for decorating (page 248)

MAKE THE LADYFINGERS AS DIRECTED. Line a 5-cup (40–fl oz/1.1-l) brioche mold with the most attractive ladyfingers, trimming them to fit if needed and placing the rounded sides facing the mold.

In a small bowl, sprinkle the gelatin over 2 Tbsp cold water, stir, and let soften until opaque, about 3 minutes. In a small saucepan over medium heat, heat the milk and ¼ cup (2 oz/55 g) of the sugar, stirring occasionally, until small bubbles appear along the edges of the pan.

Meanwhile, in a bowl, whisk together the egg yolks and the remaining ¼ cup (2 oz/55 g) sugar until well combined. Pour the hot milk mixture into the yolk mixture in a slow, steady stream, whisking constantly, then return the mixture to the pan. Cook over medium heat, whisking constantly, until the mixture thickens and registers 170°F (77°C) on an instant-read thermometer, 5–7 minutes. Remove from the heat and whisk in the softened gelatin. Using a fine-mesh sieve, strain the custard into a bowl. Stir in the brandy, vanilla, and nutmeg. Set the bowl in a larger bowl partially filled with ice water and whisk occasionally until the mixture cools and is just starting to set, about 10 minutes.

Meanwhile, whip the cream to soft peaks. Using a large silicone spatula, gently fold a third of the cream into the custard, then fold in the remaining cream. Pour the custard into the lined mold. Refrigerate until set, at least 4 hours.

Invert the mold onto a serving plate and warm the sides of the mold with a kitchen towel soaked in hot water and wrung out. Lift off the mold. Decorate the top with chocolate curls. Refrigerate until serving.

TEMPERING EGGS

If egg yolks are heated too quickly, they will curdle. To prevent this from happening when making the custard base for this Bavarian cream and similar recipes, you must "temper" the eggs, or heat them gently. First, pour hot milk in a thin stream into the yolks and sugar, whisking constantly. After returning this mixture to the saucepan over medium heat, whisk constantly to warm the eggs gradually and thicken the custard. Use an instant-read thermometer to test the temperature; it should not rise above 170°F (77°C) or the eggs will harden.

Bûche de Noël

MAKES 12–16 SERVINGS

ICING SPATULAS

Also called frosting spatulas, these long, flat, metal utensils have slender 6- to 12-inch (15- to 30-cm) blades that resemble round tipped knives. They are very flexible to facilitate the smooth spreading of icing or frosting onto cakes, pastries, and other baked items, particularly on rounded surfaces. Icing spatulas come in a range of widths: a wide spatula is useful when covering a large area, such as frosting a sheet cake; a thin spatula is helpful when doing precise work on pastries or cakes, as in this recipe.

FOR THE CAKE:

1 cup (4½ oz/140 g) all-purpose (plain) flour

¾ tsp baking powder

¼ tsp salt

4 large eggs, at room temperature

⅔ cup (4⅔ oz/145 g) granulated sugar

1¼ tsp pure vanilla extract

Confectioners' (icing) sugar for dusting

FOR THE FROSTING:

10 oz (315 g) bittersweet chocolate, finely chopped

2¼ cups (18 fl oz/560 ml) heavy (double) cream

1 tsp pure vanilla extract

Pinch of salt

Sugar Syrup (page 186), with 2–3 Tbsp coffee-flavored liqueur stirred into the syrup, cooled

Chocolate curls for garnish (page 248)

PREHEAT THE OVEN TO 350°F (180°C). Grease a 15½-by-10½-inch rimmed baking sheet and line the bottom with parchment (baking) paper. Grease the paper and the sides of the pan with butter and dust with flour.

To make the cake, in a bowl, whisk together the flour, baking powder, and salt. In a large bowl, using an electric mixer on medium-high speed, beat the eggs until pale and thick, about 3 minutes. Add the sugar and vanilla and continue beating until tripled in volume, about 3 minutes more. Sprinkle the flour mixture over the eggs and, using a silicone spatula, fold gently just until blended. Pour the batter into the prepared pan and spread it evenly. Bake until the cake springs back when touched, 13–15 minutes.

While the cake is baking, lay a clean kitchen towel on the counter and sift confectioners' sugar generously onto it, covering it evenly. When the cake is ready, remove it from the oven and immediately run a table knife around the inside edges of the pan to loosen the cake. Holding the cake in place, invert the pan onto the prepared towel. Lift off the pan and carefully peel off the paper. Beginning with a long side, roll up the cake and towel together. Set on a rack and let cool.

To make the frosting, in a stainless steel bowl, combine the chocolate and cream and melt, stirring occasionally, over barely simmering water (see page 173). Remove the bowl from the heat and refrigerate, stirring occasionally, until cold, about 2 hours. When the mixture is cold, add the vanilla and salt. Using a mixer on medium-high speed, beat the chocolate mixture briefly until firm enough to hold a soft dollop.

To assemble the *bûche*, unroll the cake and brush it liberally with the cooled syrup. Using an icing spatula, spread a third of the frosting over the cake. Gently reroll the cake and place, seam side down, on a cutting board. Frost the top and sides of the roll with the remaining frosting, using long strokes. Using a serrated knife, trim each end on a sharp angle. Transfer to a serving plate and garnish with the chocolate curls.

PIES & TARTS

Lattice-Topped Sweet Cherry Pie

MAKES ONE 9-INCH (23-CM) PIE, OR 8 SERVINGS

FRESH SWEET CHERRIES

Cherries come in two primary types: sweet and sour (or tart). Cherry pies are often made with jarred or canned sour cherries, but this pie uses fresh sweet cherries. (See the recipe variation if you wish to use sour cherries.) Fresh cherries have a short summer season. Look for large, plump, smooth cherries that are darkly colored for their variety and preferably still have their stems attached.

Flaky Pastry Dough, Lattice-Top Variation (page 373)

¾ cup (6 oz/185 g) sugar

3 Tbsp cornstarch (cornflour)

¼ tsp salt

4 cups (24 oz/750 g) fresh sweet cherries, pitted

1 tsp pure vanilla extract

½ tsp pure almond extract

2 Tbsp cold unsalted butter, cut into small pieces

ROLL OUT THE DOUGH DISK into a 12-inch (30-cm) round (see page 385). Transfer the dough round to a 9-inch (23-cm) pie pan or dish. Trim the edge, leaving ½ inch (1 cm) of overhang. Refrigerate or freeze the pie shell until firm, about 30 minutes.

In a small bowl, stir together the sugar, cornstarch, and salt. Place the cherries in a large bowl, sprinkle with the sugar mixture, and toss to distribute evenly. Add the vanilla and almond extract and mix well. Immediately transfer the cherry mixture to the dough-lined pan and dot with the butter.

Roll out the second portion of dough to make a rectangular shape about ⅛ inch (3 mm) thick. Trim to cut out a 14-by-11-inch (35-by-28-cm) rectangle. Use the dough rectangle to make a lattice top as directed on page 386. Refrigerate the pie until the dough is firm, 20–30 minutes.

Meanwhile, place an oven rack in the middle of the oven and preheat to 425°F (220°C). Bake the pie for 15 minutes. Reduce the oven temperature to 350°F (180°C) and continue to bake until the crust is golden and the filling is thick and bubbling, 40–50 minutes. Transfer the pie to a wire rack and let cool completely. Serve at room temperature.

SERVING TIPS: You can reheat the pie in a 350°F (180°C) oven for 10–12 minutes. If desired, accompany each serving with a scoop of vanilla ice cream.

RECIPE VARIATION: You can also make this pie with sour cherries. Replace the fresh sweet cherries with 4 cups (24 oz/750 g) drained jarred or canned pitted sour cherries, reserving ⅓ cup (3 fl oz/80 ml) cherry liquid. Stir together 1 cup (8 oz/250 g) sugar with the cornstach (cornflour) and salt. Add the reserved cherry liquid to the cherries with the vanilla; omit the almond extract.

Ginger-Apricot Pie

MAKES ONE 9-INCH (23-CM) PIE, OR 8 SERVINGS

APRICOTS

Apricots, small cousins of the peach, are native to northern China, where they still grow wild today. They are cultivated in many warm climates worldwide, from California to the south of France, but have only a brief season, from late spring to mid-summer. Look for apricots that are fragrant and have rich orange skin with a pink blush. If fully ripe, they give slightly when gently pressed. To hasten ripening, put the apricots in a paper bag along with a banana and close the bag.

Flaky Pastry Dough, Double Crust Variation (page 373)

¾ cup (6 oz/185 g) sugar

2 Tbsp cornstarch (cornflour)

2 Tbsp quick-cooking tapioca

1½ tsp ground ginger

1 tsp ground cinnamon

⅛ tsp salt

2 lb (1 kg) apricots, pitted and sliced ½ inch (12 mm) thick (about 5 cups)

1 tsp finely grated orange or lemon zest

1 Tbsp cold unsalted butter, cut into small pieces

ROLL OUT THE DOUGH DISKS into two 12-inch (30-cm) rounds (see page 385). Transfer 1 dough round to a 9-inch (23-cm) pie pan or dish. Trim the edge, leaving ¾ inch (2 cm) of overhang. Refrigerate or freeze the pie shell and the second dough round until firm, about 30 minutes.

In a bowl, stir together the sugar, cornstarch, tapioca, ginger, cinnamon, and salt. Place the apricots in a large bowl, sprinkle with the orange zest and the sugar mixture, and toss to distribute evenly. Transfer to the dough-lined pan and dot with the butter.

Position the second dough round over the filled pie and trim the edge to leave 1 inch (2.5 cm) of overhang. Fold the edge of the top round under the edge of the bottom round and crimp or flute the edges to seal (see page 386). Using a small, round cookie cutter or a small, sharp knife, cut 4 or 5 holes or slits in the top to allow steam to escape during baking. Refrigerate the pie until the dough is firm, 20–30 minutes.

Meanwhile, place an oven rack in the lower third of the oven and preheat to 375°F (190°C). Bake the pie until the crust is golden and the filling is thick and bubbling, 50–60 minutes. Transfer to a wire rack and let cool completely to set. Serve at room temperature or rewarm in a 350°F (180°C) oven for 10–15 minutes just before serving.

Sweet Potato Pie with Spiced Pecans

MAKES ONE 9-INCH (23-CM) PIE, OR 8 SERVINGS

Flaky Pastry Dough (page 373)

FOR THE FILLING:

1 large Garnet yam (orange-fleshed sweet potato), 12–14 oz (375–440 g)

¾ cup (6 oz/185 g) firmly packed light brown sugar

½ tsp salt

2 large eggs

1 tsp ground cinnamon

1 tsp ground ginger

¼ tsp ground allspice

1¼ cups (10 fl oz/310 ml) heavy (double) cream

Spiced Pecans (right)

Sweetened Whipped Cream (page 377) for serving

ROLL OUT THE DOUGH DISK into a 12-inch (30-cm) round (see page 385). Transfer the dough round to a 9-inch (23-cm) pie pan or dish. Trim the edge of the dough round, leaving ¾ inch (2 cm) of overhang. Fold the overhang under itself and pinch it together to create a high edge on the pan's rim. Flute the edge decoratively (see page 386). Refrigerate or freeze the pie shell until firm, about 30 minutes.

Meanwhile, place an oven rack in the lower third of the oven and preheat to 375°F (190°C). Partially bake the pie shell as directed on page 385. Transfer to a wire rack. Leaving the oven rack in place, reduce the oven temperature to 350°F (180°C).

To make the filling, prick the yam several times with a fork, put directly on the oven rack, and bake until tender when pierced with a knife, about 55 minutes. Alternatively, cook the yam in the microwave on high heat until tender, about 6 minutes on each side. Set aside to cool.

Peel the cooled yam and mash the pulp with a fork, or purée in a food processor, until smooth. Measure out 1 cup (8 oz/250 g) of the purée for the filling. (Reserve any remaining yam for another use.)

In a large bowl, stir together the brown sugar, salt, and eggs. Add the cinnamon, ginger, and allspice and mix well. Stir in the yam purée and cream and beat until smooth. Pour into the partially baked pie shell.

Bake until the filling is firm, about 20 minutes. Remove the pie from the oven, quickly sprinkle the spiced pecans evenly over the surface, and then continue to bake until the filling is slightly risen and firm in the middle, 20–25 minutes longer. Slice into wedges and serve with whipped cream.

SPICED PECANS

This pie topping, made with crunchy, rich pecans tossed with brown sugar and cinnamon, is a wonderful complement to the smooth creaminess of the pie. The pecans get toasted during baking, adding an extra buttery taste. To make the topping, in a small bowl, stir together 1 Tbsp firmly packed light brown sugar, ¼ cup (1 oz/30 g) coarsely chopped pecans, and ¼ tsp ground cinnamon. Set aside until ready to use.

Raspberry & Chocolate Tartlets

MAKES TWELVE 2-INCH TARTLETS, OR 6 SERVINGS

MELTING CHOCOLATE IN A MICROWAVE

You can melt chocolate in a double boiler (see page 173) or in a microwave. If microwaving the chocolate, check it every 30 seconds to avoid scorching. When the chocolate is shiny and soft, remove it and stir until smooth.

Basic Tart Dough (page 373)

8 oz (250 g) semisweet (plain) chocolate, chopped into small slivers

6 Tbsp (3 oz/90 g) unsalted butter

2 Tbsp light corn syrup

¼ cup (2½ oz/75 g) raspberry jam

4 cups (1 lb/500 g) raspberries

ROLL OUT THE DOUGH DISK into a 12-inch (30-cm) round (see page 385). Using a 2½- to 3-inch (6- to 7.5-cm) round cookie cutter or a cardboard circle and a small, sharp knife, cut out as many rounds as possible from the rolled-out tart dough. Press the dough scraps together and reroll to cut out additional rounds; you should have a total of 12. Transfer the rounds to twelve 2-inch (5-cm) tartlet pans. Ease into the pans and pat firmly into the bottoms and up the sides. Trim off any excess dough by gently running a rolling pin across the tops of the pans. Press the dough into the sides to extend it slightly above the rims. Refrigerate or freeze the tartlet shells until firm, about 30 minutes.

Meanwhile, place an oven rack in the lower third of the oven and preheat to 375°F (190°C). Place the tartlet shells on a baking sheet for easy removal from the oven. Fully bake the shells as directed on page 385. Transfer to wire racks and let cool completely.

In the top of a double boiler, combine the chocolate, butter, and corn syrup, and melt, stirring occasionally, over barely simmering water (see page 173). (Alternatively, in a microwaveproof bowl, combine the chocolate, butter, and corn syrup and melt in the microwave (left). Remove from the stove top or microwave oven and stir until smooth.)

Pass the raspberry jam through a medium-mesh sieve to remove the seeds. Spread 1 tsp of the jam in the bottom of each shell and fill as full as possible with the chocolate mixture. Let the filled tartlets stand at room temperature until set, 1–2 hours.

Before serving the tartlets, place 1 raspberry, stem end down, on top of the chocolate in the middle of each tartlet and surround with additional raspberries. (You will need 7 or 8 raspberries for each tartlet.) Remove the tartlets from the pans and serve.

Citrus Chiffon Pie

MAKES ONE 9-INCH (23-CM) PIE, OR 8 SERVINGS

GELATIN

Gelatin is an odorless, colorless, tasteless thickener derived from collagen, a protein extracted from the bones, cartilage, and tendons of animals. There are two forms of gelatin available: powdered gelatin, popular with American cooks, and sheet or leaf gelatin, which is commonly used in Europe. Both need to be hydrated and melted before they can be added to a recipe. Do not confuse powdered gelatin with the sweetened, fruit-flavored gelatin desserts sold in boxes.

¼ cup (2 fl oz/60 ml) cold water

2¼ tsp (1 package) unflavored powdered gelatin (page 226)

¾ cup (6 oz/185 g) granulated sugar

⅛ tsp salt

¾ cup (6 fl oz/180 ml) fresh lemon juice, strained

1 Tbsp finely grated orange zest

4 large egg yolks, lightly beaten

1¼ cups (10 fl oz/310 ml) heavy (double) cream

¼ cup (1 oz/30 g) confectioners' (icing) sugar

1 Cookie Crumb Crust (page 374), made with gingersnaps

HAVE READY AN ICE BATH made by partially filling a bowl with water and ice cubes.

Pour the cold water into a saucepan and sprinkle with the gelatin. Let sit until the gelatin softens and swells, 5–10 minutes. Stir in the granulated sugar, salt, lemon juice, orange zest, and egg yolks; the gelatin will be lumpy. Place the gelatin mixture over medium heat and cook, stirring constantly, until the gelatin melts and the mixture thickens, 6–8 minutes. Do not let the mixture boil. Set the saucepan in the ice bath and let cool until the mixture is cold to the touch.

In a large bowl, using an electric mixer on medium-high speed or a whisk, beat together the cream and confectioners' sugar until thick, soft peaks form. Spoon the whipped cream into the gelatin mixture and fold together with a silicone spatula until smooth. Pour into the prepared crumb crust and smooth the top. Refrigerate the pie until it is cold and firm, 3–4 hours.

Let the pie stand at room temperature for about 20 minutes before serving.

NOTE: This recipe contains eggs that may be only partially cooked; for more information, see page 392.

Pear & Frangipane Tart

MAKES ONE 9½-INCH (24-CM) TART, OR 8 SERVINGS

Basic Tart Dough (page 373)
2 Tbsp unsalted butter
1½ cups (8 oz/250 g) raw unblanched, whole almonds, finely ground (page 344)
⅔ cup (5 oz/155 g) sugar
2 large eggs, lightly beaten
½ tsp pure almond extract
1 tsp pure vanilla extract
2 Tbsp dark rum
¼ tsp salt
1 tsp finely grated fresh lemon zest
2 Anjou or Bartlett (Williams') pears, peeled, quartered, and cored
⅓ cup (3½ oz/105 g) apricot jam

ROLL OUT THE DOUGH DISK into a 12-inch (30-cm) round (see page 385). Transfer the dough round to a 9½-inch (24-cm) tart pan, preferably with a removable bottom. Trim off any excess dough by gently running a rolling pin across the top of the pan. Press the dough into the sides of the pan so that it extends slightly above the rim. Refrigerate or freeze the tart shell until firm, about 30 minutes.

Meanwhile, place an oven rack in the lower third of the oven and preheat to 375°F (190°C). Partially blind bake the tart shell as directed on page 385. Transfer the tart shell to a wire rack. Leaving the oven temperature at 375°F (190°C), place an oven rack in the middle of the oven.

In a small saucepan over medium heat, melt the butter and cook until golden brown, about 5 minutes. Remove from the heat and let cool to the touch. In a bowl, stir together the ground almonds, sugar, eggs, almond extract, vanilla, rum, salt, lemon zest, and melted butter. Spread evenly in the partially baked tart shell. Slice each pear quarter crosswise into slices ⅛ inch (3 mm) thick, keeping each one together. Arrange each quarter core side down and stem end toward the center in the pan. Use your hand to flatten and fan each quarter slightly and press the slices into the filling.

Bake the tart until the filling is firm to the touch in the center and slightly golden, 40–45 minutes. Transfer to a wire rack to cool. In a saucepan over low heat, heat the jam until it liquefies. Pour through a fine-mesh sieve set over a small bowl. Using a pastry brush, gently brush the top of the tart with a thin coating of jam. If using a tart pan with a removable bottom, let the sides fall away, then slide the tart onto a serving plate. Serve warm or at room temperature.

FRANGIPANE
This almond-flavored custard is made with finely ground almonds and/or pure almond extract, sugar, and eggs. It is often used to fill tarts and pastries. The rich, nutty flavoring of the frangipane is the perfect complement to fall fruits, such as pears or apples.

Fresh Fig Galette with Ricotta & Honey

MAKES ONE 9½-INCH (24-CM) GALETTE, OR 8 SERVINGS

ABOUT FIGS

Fresh figs come in many shapes, colors, and sizes. Well-known varieties include the deep purple, sweet-tasting Mission fig, the amber-skinned Kadota, the green-skinned Adriatic, and the golden Calimyrna, or Smyrna, figs. Black Mission figs are the best choice for this recipe. Figs have two seasons; the first begins in early summer and lasts until midsummer, and the second runs from late summer into autumn. Figs do not ripen off the tree so they must be picked ripe. Choose plump fruits that are soft to the touch but not wrinkled or bruised, and that have firm stems.

Flaky Pastry Dough (page 373)

1 cup (8 oz/250 g) ricotta cheese

4 Tbsp (3 oz/90 g) honey

¼ cup (2 fl oz/60 ml) heavy (double) cream

2 large egg yolks

2 tsp finely grated orange zest

¼ tsp ground cardamom

Pinch of salt

10–12 ripe black Mission figs (8 oz/250 g), stemmed and quartered lengthwise

ROLL OUT THE DOUGH DISK into a 12-inch (30-cm) round (see page 385). Place the dough round on a baking sheet lined with parchment (baking) paper. Fold in 1 inch (2.5 cm) of the outer edge of the dough and pleat to form a rim for the galette. Refrigerate the dough until firm, 15–20 minutes. Meanwhile, place an oven rack in the lower third of the oven and preheat to 375°F (190°C).

Remove the galette shell from the refrigerator. Line with a sheet of aluminum foil large enough to cover the edges. Cover the center of the galette with a generous layer of pie weights. Partially bake the shell for 20 minutes, then lift an edge of the foil to check the dough. If it looks wet, continue to bake, checking every 5 minutes, until the dough is pale gold. Remove the weights and foil. The total baking time will be 25–30 minutes.

In a bowl, combine the ricotta, 2 Tbsp of the honey, the cream, and the egg yolks and stir to combine thoroughly. Mix in the orange zest, cardamom, and salt. Spread the mixture evenly over the partially baked galette crust.

Return the galette to the oven and bake until the filling is firm in the center, 15–18 minutes. Transfer the galette, still on the baking sheet, to a wire rack and let cool completely, about 30 minutes.

Arrange the figs, cut sides up and stem ends toward the middle, decoratively over the ricotta filling. Drizzle evenly with the remaining 2 Tbsp honey. Serve at once.

Rustic Nectarine Galette

MAKES ONE 10-INCH (25-CM) GALETTE, OR 6–8 SERVINGS

Flaky Pastry Dough (page 373)

¾ cup plus 1 Tbsp (4 oz/125 g) whole raw almonds, finely ground (page 344)

¼ cup (2 oz/60 g) plus 3 Tbsp sugar

½ tsp finely grated lemon zest

1 large egg yolk

4 large nectarines, 1–1½ lb (500–750 g) total weight

1 Tbsp unsalted butter, cut into small pieces

ROLL OUT THE DOUGH DISK into a 12-inch (30-cm) round (see page 385). Place the dough round on a baking sheet lined with parchment (baking) paper.

In a small bowl, stir together the ground almonds, the ¼ cup sugar, lemon zest, and egg yolk. Spread the mixture into an 8-inch (20-cm) circle in the center of the dough.

Cut each nectarine in half and remove the pit. Thinly slice each nectarine half lengthwise, holding the half together as you cut. Use your fingers to fan out the slices slightly, and place them rounded (skin) side up, in the center of the almond mixture. Repeat with the remaining nectarine halves, arranging them around the first nectarine half and leaving a 1½-inch (4-cm) border of dough uncovered along the edge. Fold the edge of the dough over the nectarines, pleating the dough loosely all around the edge and leaving the galette uncovered in the center. Sprinkle the nectarines with the remaining 3 Tbsp sugar and dot with the butter. Refrigerate the galette until the dough is firm, at least 30 minutes.

Meanwhile, preheat the oven to 375°F (190°C). Bake the galette until the crust is golden brown and the nectarines are tender when pierced with a skewer or small knife, 45–50 minutes. Let cool for 20 minutes before serving.

NECTARINES

Nectarines, a firmer cousin to the peach, have smooth yellow skin with red highlights. Select nectarines that are firm but not hard, fragrant, and free of blemishes. Nectarines continue to ripen when left at room temperature. If the nectarines give slightly when pressed, they are ready to eat. Use ripe fruit right away or refrigerate and use within 5 days.

Harvest Fruit Pandowdy

MAKES ONE 9-INCH (23-CM) PANDOWDY, OR 8 SERVINGS

Flaky Pastry Dough, Double-Crust Variation (page 373)

5 medium apples, peeled, halved, cored, and sliced ½ inch (12 mm) thick (about 5 cups/1¼ lb/625 g)

1½ cups (14 oz/440 g) mixed dried fruits such as apricots, peaches, currants, golden raisins (sultanas), and cherries, chopped if large

¾ cup (6 oz/185 g) firmly packed brown sugar

1 tsp ground cinnamon

½ tsp freshly grated nutmeg

¼ tsp salt

2 Tbsp cold unsalted butter, cut into ¼-inch (6-mm) cubes

1 Tbsp granulated sugar

ROLL OUT THE DOUGH DISKS into two 12-inch (30-cm) rounds (see page 385). Transfer 1 dough round to a 9-inch (23-cm) pie pan or dish. Refrigerate or freeze the pie shell and the second dough round until firm, about 30 minutes.

Meanwhile, place an oven rack in the lower third of the oven and preheat to 375°F (190°C). In a large bowl, stir together the apples, dried fruits, brown sugar, cinnamon, nutmeg, and salt. Pile the fruit mixture into the dough-lined pan. Dot with the butter. Position the second dough round on top of the fruit filling. Cut the top circle to fit inside the rim of the pan, about a 9-inch circle. Fold in the edge of the bottom round, overlapping the edge of the top round. Sprinkle the top with the granulated sugar.

Bake the pandowdy for 30 minutes, then reduce the oven temperature to 350°F (180°C) and remove from the oven. With a small, sharp knife, cut a crosshatch of 1-inch (2.5-cm) squares into the top crust. Using the edge of a spatula, press the top crust down into the apples. Continue baking the pie, pressing the crust into the apples twice more during the remaining baking time, until the apples are tender when pierced with a skewer or small knife and the crust is golden brown, about 30 minutes longer.

Let cool to room temperature to set the filling. When ready to serve, heat in a 350°F (180°C) oven until warmed through, about 10 minutes.

ABOUT PANDOWDIES

Typically, a pandowdy refers to a kind of deep-dish cobbler—sweetened sliced apples or other fruit topped with dough and baked. This variation uses a full pie crust, which is pushed down into the filling during baking so that it absorbs the delicious fruit juices.

Maple-Nut Pie

MAKES ONE 9-INCH (23-CM) PIE, OR 8 SERVINGS

REDUCING LIQUIDS

You can reduce any liquid simply by simmering it briskly. Doing this will decrease the volume through evaporation, concentrate the flavor, and thicken the consistency. The more you reduce a liquid, the deeper the flavor and the thicker the consistency. The resulting sauce is commonly called a reduction. Because flavors will be magnified by this process, it is best to use high-quality ingredients.

Flaky Pastry Dough (page 373)

2 cups (22 oz/690 g) maple syrup

2 large eggs, lightly beaten

¼ cup (2 oz/60 g) firmly packed light or dark brown sugar

⅛ tsp salt

2 Tbsp unsalted butter, melted

1 tsp pure vanilla extract

1½ cups (6 oz/185 g) pecans, coarsely chopped

Sweetened Whipped Cream (page 377) or Bourbon Whipped Cream (page 378), for serving

ROLL OUT THE DOUGH DISK into a 12-inch (30-cm) round (see page 385). Transfer the dough round to a 9-inch (23-cm) pie pan or dish. Trim the edge of the dough round, leaving ¾ inch (2 cm) of overhang. Fold the overhang under itself and pinch it together to create a high edge on the pan's rim. Flute the edge decoratively (see page 386). Refrigerate or freeze the pie shell until firm, about 30 minutes.

Meanwhile, place an oven rack in the lower third of the oven and preheat to 375°F (190°C). Partially bake the pie shell as directed on page 385. Transfer to a wire rack. Reduce the oven temperature to 350°F (180°C).

In a saucepan over medium-high heat, bring the maple syrup to a boil and boil for 8–10 minutes to reduce by about one-fourth. Remove from the heat and pour into a heatproof measuring pitcher. The syrup should be reduced to 1½ cups (12 oz/375 g). If necessary, return the syrup to the saucepan and continue to boil until sufficiently reduced. Let cool to room temperature before proceeding.

In a bowl, stir together the eggs, brown sugar, reduced maple syrup, salt, melted butter, and vanilla until well mixed. Add the pecans and stir well. Pour into the partially baked pie shell, making sure the pecans are evenly distributed.

Bake the pie until the center is slightly puffed and firm to the touch, 30–35 minutes. Transfer to a wire rack and let cool until just slightly warm, about 45 minutes. Slice into wedges and serve with the whipped cream.

TRIMMING PINEAPPLE

Pineapple has skin with a bumpy spiral pattern that must be removed before eating. Using a sharp knife, cut off the leaves at the top and slice off the bottom end. Holding the pineapple upright, slice off the skin just below the surface in long vertical strips, following the contour of the fruit and leaving the small brown eyes. Lay the pineapple on its side. Align the knife blade with the diagonal rows of eyes and cut shallow furrows, following a spiral pattern, to remove all of the eyes.

Pineapple–Brown Sugar Galette

MAKES ONE 9-INCH (23-CM) GALETTE, OR 8 SERVINGS

1 pineapple, trimmed (left)
Flaky Pastry Dough (page 373)
3–4 Tbsp firmly packed light brown sugar
1 Tbsp cold unsalted butter, cut into small pieces

CUT THE PINEAPPLE INTO SLICES ¼ inch (6 mm) thick; you should have 8–10 slices. Using a small knife or cookie cutter, remove the core from each slice to make a ring.

Roll out the dough into a 12-inch (30-cm) round. Place the dough round on a baking sheet lined with parchment (baking) paper. Overlap the pineapple rings in a spiral on the round, leaving a 1½-inch (4-cm) border of dough uncovered along the edge. Fold the edge of the dough over the pineapple, pleating the dough loosely around all the edge. Sprinkle the pineapple evenly with the brown sugar, using all of it if the pineapple is tart, and dot with the butter.

Measure the circumference of the galette and cut a strip of aluminum foil about 2 inches (5 cm) longer and 3–4 inches (7.5–10 cm) wide. Fold the foil strip in half lengthwise, and then wrap the strip around the edge of the galette. Secure the ends of the foil by twisting them together. Refrigerate the galette for at least 30 minutes.

Meanwhile, place an oven rack in the lower third of the oven and preheat to 400°F (200°C). Bake the galette until the crust is golden brown and the pineapple is tender when pierced with a fork, about 50 minutes. Transfer the baking sheet to a wire rack and let the galette cool slightly. Cut the galette into wedges and serve warm.

Deep-Dish Plum Pie

MAKES ONE 10-INCH (25-CM) PIE, OR 8 SERVINGS

1¼ cups (10 oz/315 g) sugar

3 Tbsp cornstarch (cornflour) or quick-cooking tapioca

½ tsp ground cinnamon

Pinch of salt

2½ lb (1.25 kg) plums, pitted and sliced ¼ inch (6 mm) thick (about 5 cups)

1 Tbsp cold unsalted butter, cut into small pieces

Flaky Pastry Dough (page 373)

Vanilla ice cream for serving (optional)

IN A SMALL BOWL, stir together the sugar, cornstarch, cinnamon, and salt. Set aside. Place the plums in a large bowl, sprinkle with the sugar mixture, and toss to distribute evenly. Immediately transfer to a 10-inch (25-cm) ceramic or glass deep-dish pie dish. Dot with the butter.

Roll out the dough disk into a 12-inch (30-cm) round (see page 385). Carefully position the dough round over the plums. Trim the edge neatly, leaving 1 inch (2.5 cm) of overhang, then place over the fruit, folding the overhang under and pressing against the sides of the dish to seal. Using a small, sharp knife, cut 5 or 6 slits in the top crust to allow steam to escape during baking. Refrigerate the pie until the dough is firm, about 30 minutes.

Meanwhile, place an oven rack in the lower third of the oven and preheat to 375°F (190°C). Bake the pie for 15 minutes. Reduce the oven temperature to 350°F (180°C) and continue to bake until the crust is golden and the filling is thick and bubbling, 50–60 minutes longer. Transfer to a wire rack and let cool completely. Serve at room temperature or rewarm in a 350°F (180°C) oven for 10–15 minutes just before serving. To serve, cut into wedges and spoon into individual serving bowls. If desired, accompany each serving with a scoop of vanilla ice cream.

PLUM TYPES

Fresh plums are available from late spring through summer. You will find these juicy fruits in an assortment of colors, from yellow and green to deep pink, purple, and scarlet. Check out the varieties at your local farmers' market, and choose a firm, fragrant fruit with sweet, tangy flesh (such as Simka, Santa Rosa, Seneca, or Satsuma). The small, oval, purple-skinned, golden-fleshed plums known as Italian, French, or prune plums will also make a delicious pie.

Chocolate Silk Pie with White Chocolate Drizzle

MAKES ONE 9-INCH (23-CM) PIE, OR 8 SERVINGS

Flaky Pastry Dough (page 373)

5 large eggs

1 cup (8 oz/250 g) sugar

5 oz (155 g) semisweet (plain) chocolate, chopped into thin slivers

2 tsp pure vanilla extract

1 Tbsp dark rum

1 cup (8 oz/250 g) unsalted butter, cut into pieces, at room temperature

1 chunk (1 oz/30 g) white chocolate

ROLL OUT THE DOUGH DISK into a 12-inch (30-cm) round (see page 385). Transfer the dough round to a 9-inch (23-cm) pie pan or dish. Trim the edge of the dough round, leaving ¾ inch (2 cm) of overhang. Fold the overhang under itself and pinch it together to create a high edge on the pan's rim. Flute the edge decoratively (see page 386). Refrigerate or freeze the pie shell until firm, about 30 minutes.

Meanwhile, place an oven rack in the lower third of the oven and preheat to 375°F (190°C). Fully bake the pie shell as directed on page 385. Transfer the pie shell to a wire rack and let cool completely.

In the top of a double boiler, whisk together the eggs and sugar until pale. Attach a candy thermometer (right) to the side of the top pan and set over, but not touching, barely simmering water in the bottom pan. Cook, stirring constantly, until the mixture reaches 140°F (60°C). Keep the mixture at 140°–150°F (60°–65°C) for 5 minutes. (If the mixture climbs above 150°F/ 65°C, remove it from the heat.) After 5 minutes, add the slivered chocolate and stir until the chocolate is melted. Remove from the heat and stir in the vanilla and rum. Let cool until warm but not hot, about 10 minutes. Stir the butter pieces into the warm chocolate mixture and mix until smooth. Pour into the fully baked pie shell. Refrigerate until firm, 3–4 hours.

Put the white chocolate in the top of the double boiler, and melt, stirring occasionally, over barely simmering water (see page 173). Alternatively, in a bowl, melt the white chocolate in the microwave for 30-second intervals. Using a fork, drizzle the white chocolate in a crosshatch pattern over the chilled pie.

Refrigerate the pie until ready to serve, but let stand at room temperature for about 20 minutes before serving.

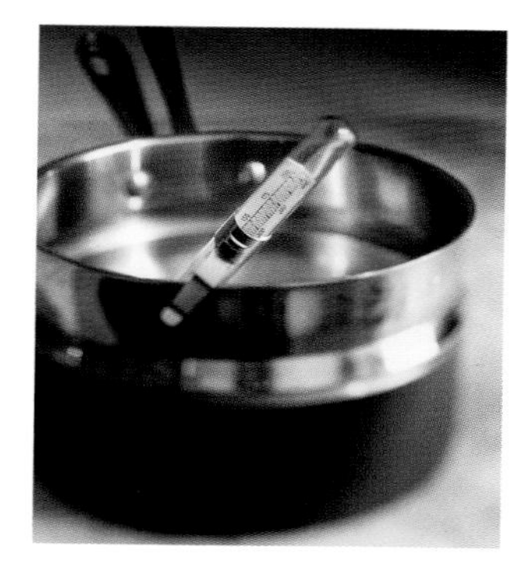

CANDY THERMOMETERS

The best candy thermometers have a mercury bulb and column mounted on a metal casing fitted with a clip that attaches to the side of a pan. Using a candy thermometer is important in this recipe to ensure that the eggs reach a temperature high enough to kill any bacteria but not so high as to overheat and curdle them. For an accurate reading, submerge the tip of the thermometer in the liquid, but do not let it touch the bottom of the pan. Do not use a digital thermometer for this recipe, which needs to be inserted 1–2 inches (2.5–5 cm) into a mixture to read correctly.

FRUIT GLAZE

A simple glaze made from jelly diluted with water gives fresh fruit tart fillings a lovely sheen and a finished look. In a small saucepan, combine 1/4 cup (2 1/2 oz/75 g) apple jelly or seedless raspberry jelly with 2 Tbsp water. Set the pan over low heat and cook, stirring the mixture constantly, until melted and smooth. Remove from the heat and let cool slightly. Using a small pastry brush, dab the glaze onto the fruit.

Raspberry Tart

MAKES ONE 9 1/2-INCH (24-CM) TART, OR 10–12 SERVINGS

Basic Tart Dough (page 373)

FOR THE CREAM FILLING:

1 cup (8 fl oz/250 ml) whole milk

2 large eggs, at room temperature

1/4 cup (1 3/4 oz/50 g) sugar

4 tsp cornstarch (cornflour)

Pinch of salt

1 tsp pure vanilla extract

1/4 cup (2 fl oz/60 ml) heavy (double) cream

3–4 cups (3/4–1 lb/375–500 g) raspberries

Fruit Glaze (left)

ROLL OUT THE DOUGH DISK into a 12-inch (30-cm) round (see page 385). Transfer the dough round to a 9 1/2-inch (24-cm) tart pan, preferably with a removable bottom. Trim off any excess dough by gently running a rolling pin across the top of the pan. Press the dough into the sides of the pan so that it extends slightly above the rim. Refrigerate or freeze the tart shell until firm, about 30 minutes.

Meanwhile, place an oven rack in the lower third of the oven and preheat to 375°F (190°C). Fully bake the tart shell as directed on page 385. Transfer to a wire rack and let cool completely.

To make the cream filling, in a saucepan over medium heat, warm the milk until small bubbles appear along the edges of the pan. Remove from the heat. In a bowl, whisk together the eggs, sugar, cornstarch, and salt. Slowly add the hot milk while whisking. Pour the mixture back into the pan and place over medium-low heat. Cook, whisking constantly, until the mixture comes to a boil and thickens. Continue to cook, whisking constantly, for 20 seconds. Pour into a clean bowl and gently press a piece of plastic wrap directly onto the surface to prevent a skin from forming. Refrigerate until cold, for at least 2 hours or up to 24 hours.

Whisk the vanilla into the chilled pastry cream until blended and smooth. In another bowl, using an electric mixer on medium-high speed, whip the cream until stiff peaks form. Fold the whipped cream into the pastry cream just until blended.

To assemble the tart, spoon the pastry cream into the cooled tart shell and spread it evenly. Arrange the raspberries randomly on top of the cream. Brush the berries with the fruit glaze. If using a tart pan with a removable bottom, let the sides fall away, then slide the tart onto a serving platter.

Raspberry Cream Pie

MAKES ONE 9-INCH (23-CM) PIE, OR 8 SERVINGS

FOR THE FILLING:

¼ cup (2 fl oz/60 ml) cold water

1½ tsp unflavored powdered gelatin (page 226)

⅔ cup (5 fl oz/160 ml) fresh raspberry purée (right), at room temperature

2 large eggs

½ cup (4 oz/125 g) sugar

Pinch of salt

¾ cup (6 fl oz/180 ml) heavy (double) cream

Cookie Crumb Crust (page 374), made with chocolate wafers or gingersnaps

Sweetened Whipped Cream (page 377) for serving

Whole fresh raspberries for serving

TO MAKE THE FILLING, pour the cold water into a saucepan and sprinkle with the gelatin. Let sit until the gelatin softens and swells, 5–10 minutes. Heat the gelatin over medium heat until clear and fluid, stirring as needed to dissolve, 3–4 minutes. Stir the gelatin mixture into the raspberry purée.

In a bowl, using an electric mixer on medium-high speed or a whisk, beat together the eggs, sugar, and salt until pale yellow. In a large bowl, using the mixer on medium-high speed or a whisk, whip the cream until thick, soft peaks form. Add the egg mixture and raspberry purée to the whipped cream and whip until smooth. Pour into the crumb crust, smoothing the top with a silicone spatula. Refrigerate until the filling is cold and firm, 4–6 hours.

Let the pie stand at room temperature for about 20 minutes before serving. Slice into wedges and serve with dollops of whipped cream and fresh raspberries.

NOTE: This recipe contains raw eggs; for more information, see page 392.

FRESH RASPBERRY PURÉE

Gently rinse and dry 4 cups (1 lb/500 g) raspberries. Place the berries in a food processor or blender and purée until smooth. Pour the purée through a medium-mesh sieve placed over a bowl to remove the seeds. You can also use another berry for this purée; other varieties that would work include blackberry, boysenberry, olallieberry, and loganberry.

Cream Cheese Pie with Oranges

MAKES ONE 9-INCH (23-CM) PIE, OR 8 SERVINGS

PEELING CITRUS

To peel a citrus fruit so that it can be sliced, start by cutting a thick slice off both the bottom and top, exposing the flesh beneath the peel. Then, holding the fruit upright on a cutting board, slice off the peel in thick strips, following the contour of the fruit and cutting off the white pith and membrane with the peel to reveal the flesh.

4 or 5 navel oranges, 2–2½ lb (1–1.25 kg) total weight

½ lb (250 g) cream cheese, at room temperature (see Note)

1 can (14 fl oz/430 ml) sweetened condensed milk

1 tsp pure vanilla extract

⅓ cup (3 fl oz/80 ml) fresh lemon juice, strained

Cookie Crumb Crust (page 374), made with graham crackers, gingersnaps, or chocolate wafers

USE A FINE MICROPLANE GRATER to finely zest 1 of the oranges; be sure to remove just the thin, colored portion of the rind, not the bitter white pith underneath. Measure 1 tsp zest and set aside. Using a sharp knife, peel all of the oranges (left). Slice the oranges crosswise into thin rounds and set aside on a paper towel–lined plate to drain.

In a bowl, using an electric mixer on medium speed, beat the cream cheese until smooth. Add the condensed milk, reserved orange zest, and vanilla and beat until smooth. Stir in the lemon juice. Pour the mixture into the prepared crumb crust and smooth the top. Arrange the orange slices on top of the pie, overlapping them in a decorative pattern, to cover the filling completely. Refrigerate the pie until well chilled, about 1 hour.

Let the pie stand at room temperature for 20 minutes before serving.

NOTE: Do not use nonfat cream cheese for this recipe. Cream cheese with one-third less fat will work, but traditional full-fat cream cheese will yield the best results.

Key Lime Pie

MAKES ONE 9-INCH (23-CM) PIE, OR 8 SERVINGS

FOR THE FILLING:

7 large egg yolks

4 tsp finely grated Key lime zest

2 cans (14 fl oz/430 ml each) sweetened condensed milk

1 cup (8 fl oz/250 ml) fresh Key lime juice, strained (about 24 limes)

Cookie Crumb Crust (page 374), made with graham crackers

Sweetened Whipped Cream (page 377)

PLACE AN OVEN RACK in the lower third of the oven and preheat to 350°F (180°C).

To make the filling, in a bowl, whisk together the egg yolks and lime zest until well mixed, about 1 minute. Add the condensed milk and then the lime juice, whisking well after each addition. Pour the filling into the graham cracker crust.

Bake until the filling is firm in the center, 20–24 minutes. Transfer to a wire rack and let cool completely. Refrigerate until cold and firm, 2–3 hours.

Using a pastry bag, pipe 8 large rosettes or a zigzag of whipped cream evenly around the edge of the pie (see page 383). Refrigerate until ready to serve, but let stand at room temperature for about 20 minutes before serving.

VARIATION TIP: Try adding 2 Tbsp tequila to the filling along with the lime juice.

KEY LIMES

Key limes are small, round, and pale green to yellow, with mild juice, thin skin, and many seeds. Some are grown in the Florida Keys, Texas, and California, but they are more widely produced in Mexico and Central America. Good-quality bottled Key lime juice is also available. If you cannot find fresh Key limes or bottled Key lime juice, you can make this pie with more common Persian limes. You will need about 10 limes.

Caramel Cranberry-Almond Tart

MAKES ONE 9½-INCH (24-CM) TART, OR 8 SERVINGS

CARAMEL SYRUP

For this pie, sugar and water are cooked into a thick, caramelized syrup. The syrup is extremely hot; do not touch or taste it until it has cooled. Use a light-colored saucepan so you can judge the color of the caramel, and do not allow the syrup to turn dark brown. Removed from the heat, the syrup will thicken quickly; use it as soon as possible. Remelt it over low heat if necessary. Adding a squeeze of lemon juice or 1 Tbsp corn syrup in the beginning will prevent the sugar from recrystallizing and help keep the syrup smooth and clear.

Basic Tart Dough (page 373)

1 cup (8 oz/250 g) sugar

2 Tbsp water

1 cup (8 fl oz/250 ml) heavy (double) cream

1½ cups (6 oz/185 g) fresh or frozen cranberries

1 cup (4 oz/125 g) sliced (flaked) almonds, toasted (page 53)

ROLL OUT THE DOUGH DISK into a 12-inch (30-cm) round (see page 385). Transfer the dough round to a 9½-inch (24-cm) tart pan, preferably with a removable bottom. Trim off any excess dough by gently running a rolling pin across the top of the pan. Press the dough into the sides of the pan so that it extends slightly above the rim. Refrigerate or freeze the tart shell until firm, about 30 minutes.

Meanwhile, place an oven rack in the lower third of the oven and preheat to 375°F (190°C). Partially bake the tart shell as directed on page 385. Transfer to a wire rack. Place an oven rack in the middle of the oven; reduce the temperature to 325°F (165°C).

In a heavy-bottomed saucepan, stir together the sugar and water. Bring the mixture to a boil over medium heat and continue cooking, shaking or tilting the pan but not stirring (which would cause the sugar to recrystallize), until the sugar dissolves and the syrup begins to turn golden. Reduce the heat to medium-low and continue cooking until the syrup is golden brown, 6–8 minutes. Remove from the heat.

Place a sieve over the top of the saucepan to prevent splattering and slowly pour in the cream; be careful not to let the hot syrup bubble up and splatter. When the bubbling stops, whisk well. Add the cranberries and almonds and stir to combine. Pour the mixture into the partially baked tart shell.

Bake the tart until the cranberries have collapsed and the mixture is bubbling, 25–30 minutes. Transfer to a wire rack and let cool completely. If using a tart pan with a removable bottom, let the sides fall away, then slide the tart onto a serving plate. Serve at room temperature.

Spiced Apple Pie

MAKES ONE 9-INCH (23-CM) PIE, OR 8 SERVINGS

5 lb (2.5 kg) large, firm baking apples (left)

2 Tbsp fresh lemon juice

6 Tbsp (3 oz/90 g) unsalted butter

⅓ cup (2½ oz/75 g) firmly packed golden brown sugar

⅓ cup (3 oz/90 g) granulated sugar

2 Tbsp all-purpose (plain) flour

1 tsp ground cinnamon

1 tsp ground ginger

¼ tsp ground cloves

Flaky Pie Dough, Double-Crust Variation (page 373)

PEEL AND CORE THE APPLES and cut them into slices ½ inch (12 mm) thick. Transfer the apple slices to a large bowl and toss with the lemon juice.

In a large frying pan over medium-high heat, melt 3 Tbsp of the butter. Add half of the apples and the brown sugar and cook, stirring occasionally, until the apples are just tender and the juices syrupy, about 8 minutes. Spread on a large baking sheet. Repeat with the remaining butter, apples, and granulated sugar. Let the apples cool, then transfer them to a large bowl and toss with the flour, cinnamon, ginger, and cloves.

Roll out the dough disks into two 12-inch rounds (see page 385). Transfer one dough round to a 9-inch (23-cm) pie pan or dish and trim the edge of the dough, leaving ¾ inch (2 cm) of overhang. Pile the apples into the dough-lined pan. Top with the second dough round and trim the edge, leaving 1 inch (2.5 cm) of overhang. Fold the edge of the top round under the edge of the bottom round and pinch together, then flute the edge to seal (see page 386). Cut 5 or 6 slits in the top to allow steam to escape during baking, and refrigerate the pie until the dough is firm, about 30 minutes.

Place an oven rack in the lower third of the oven and preheat to 350°F (180°C). Place the pie on a baking sheet. Bake until the crust is golden and the juices are bubbling, 60–70 minutes. Transfer to a wire rack and let cool for about 1 hour before serving.

APPLES FOR PIE

Some types of apples release excessive juice during baking or cook into an applesauce-like mush instead of retaining their shape. Firm apples with a bit of acidity work best for pie: pippin, Golden Delicious, Fuji, and Granny Smith are good choices, or try a mixture. To prepare the apples for this recipe, peel them and then cut down on each side around the core to make 4 pieces that can easily be sliced lengthwise.

Mock Mincemeat Pie

MAKES ONE 9-INCH (23-CM) PIE, OR 8 SERVINGS

Flaky Pastry Dough, Double Crust Variation (page 373)

½ cup (3 oz/90 g) dark raisins or dried currants

½ cup (3 oz/90 g) golden raisins (sultanas)

½ cup (2 oz/60 g) dried cranberries

4 large, firm, baking apples (page 244), peeled, halved lengthwise, cored, and quartered

1 tsp finely grated lemon zest

1 tsp finely grated orange zest

¾ cup (6 oz/185 g) firmly packed light or dark brown sugar

1 Tbsp cornstarch (cornflour)

¼ tsp ground allspice

¼ tsp ground cinnamon

¼ tsp ground cloves

¼ tsp ground ginger

¼ tsp freshly grated nutmeg

¼ cup (2 fl oz/60 ml) dark rum

ROLL OUT THE DOUGH DISKS into two 12-inch (30-cm) rounds (see page 385). Transfer 1 dough round to a 9-inch (23-cm) pie pan or dish. Trim the edge of the dough round, leaving ¾ inch (2 cm) of overhang. Refrigerate or freeze the pie shell and the second dough round until firm, about 30 minutes.

In a food processor, combine the dark raisins, golden raisins, and cranberries and pulse to chop and combine, about 1 minute. Add the apples and pulse to chop into small pieces. Add the lemon and orange zests. Scrape the mixture into a bowl. Add the brown sugar, cornstarch, allspice, cinnamon, cloves, ginger, nutmeg, and rum and mix well. Immediately transfer the mixture to the dough-lined pan.

Position the second dough round over the filled pie and trim the edge to leave 1 inch (2.5 cm) of overhang. Fold the edge of the top round under the edge of the bottom round and crimp or flute the edges to seal (page 386). Gather the dough scraps and roll out about ⅛ inch (3 mm) thick. Using a very small cookie cutter, cut out shapes of dough. Brush the undersides of the dough shapes with cold water and arrange on the top crust. Using a small, sharp knife, cut 5 or 6 holes or slits in the top crust to allow steam to escape. Refrigerate the pie until the dough is firm, 20–30 minutes.

Meanwhile, place an oven rack in the lower third of the oven and preheat to 375°F (190°C). Bake the pie until the crust is golden and the filling is thick and bubbling, 50–60 minutes. Transfer to a wire rack and let cool completely to set. Serve at room temperature or rewarm in a 350°F (180°C) oven for 10–15 minutes just before serving.

MINCEMEAT

In the past, making mincemeat, a mixture of apples, dried fruits, spices, lean meat such as beef or venison, and brandy, rum, or Madeira, was a way to preserve the harvest. It was canned in late summer or early autumn and left to age and mellow until winter, when it would be opened and enjoyed, especially as a filling for Christmas pies. Nowadays, mincemeat is usually made without meat, although some traditionalists in Britain and the United States add suet (beef fat), and/or meat. It also is sometimes made and used right away, rather than aged.

Strawberry Tart with Orange Cream

MAKES ONE 9½-INCH (24-CM) TART, OR 8 SERVINGS

COINTREAU

Cointreau is a well-known liqueur from western France, where it was first made more than a century and a half ago in the city of Angers. Colorless and with a strong, pleasing aroma, it has an exotic flavor that is a marriage of sweet orange peels from Spain and bitter orange peels from the Caribbean island of Curaçao. Although similar to Triple Sec, Cointreau is drier. You will find it sold in a distinctive square bottle with a bright red ribbon. A popular after-dinner liqueur, Cointreau is also often used as a flavoring ingredient, as in this tart recipe.

Basic Tart Dough (page 373)

8 oz (250 g) cream cheese (see Note), at room temperature

¼ cup (2 oz/60 g) sugar

1 tsp finely grated orange zest

2 tsp Cointreau or other orange liqueur

2 cups (8 oz/250 g) fresh strawberries, hulled and halved lengthwise

½ cup (5 oz/155 g) apricot jam

ROLL OUT THE DOUGH DISK into a 12-inch (30-cm) round (see page 385). Transfer the dough round to a 9½-inch (24-cm) tart pan, preferably with a removable bottom. Trim off any excess dough by gently running a rolling pin across the top of the pan. Press the dough into the sides of the pan so that it extends slightly above the rim. Refrigerate or freeze the tart shell until firm, about 30 minutes.

Meanwhile, place an oven rack in the lower third of the oven and preheat to 375°F (190°C). Fully bake the tart shell as directed on page 385. Transfer to a wire rack and let cool completely.

In a bowl, using an electric mixer on medium speed, beat together the cream cheese and sugar until smooth. Mix in the orange zest and Cointreau. Spread the cream cheese mixture evenly over the bottom of the fully baked tart shell. Arrange the strawberry halves, overlapping them, in concentric circles on top of the cream cheese, completely covering the surface of the tart.

In a small saucepan over low heat, heat the apricot jam until it liquefies. Pour through a fine-mesh sieve set over a small bowl to strain out any fruit chunks. Using a small pastry brush, gently brush the strawberries with a thin coating of the jam to glaze the fruit. Refrigerate until ready to serve, then let stand at room temperature for about 20 minutes before serving. If using a tart pan with a removable bottom, let the sides fall away, then slide the tart onto a serving plate.

NOTE: Do not use nonfat cream cheese for this recipe. Cream cheese with one-third less fat will work, but traditional full-fat cream cheese will yield the best results.

Chocolate Pudding Pie

MAKES ONE 9-INCH (23-CM) PIE, OR 8 SERVINGS

FOR THE FILLING:

2½ cups (20 fl oz/625 ml) whole milk

5 oz (155 g) semisweet (plain) chocolate, chopped into slivers

4 large egg yolks

¾ cup (6 oz/185 g) sugar

3 Tbsp cornstarch (cornflour)

¼ tsp salt

1½ tsp pure vanilla extract

1 Cookie Crumb Crust (page 374), made with chocolate wafers

FOR THE TOPPING:

1 cup (8 fl oz/250 ml) heavy (double) cream

1 Tbsp sugar

1 tsp pure vanilla extract

Chocolate curls for serving (left)

TO MAKE THE FILLING, in a heavy nonaluminum saucepan over low heat, combine the milk and chocolate and heat, whisking, until the chocolate is melted.

In a bowl, whisk together the egg yolks and sugar until pale yellow. Add the cornstarch and salt, then the vanilla, and beat well. Slowly pour the warm chocolate mixture into the yolk mixture, mixing well. Return the mixture to the saucepan and cook over medium heat until it thickens and begins to bubble slowly, 6–8 minutes. Remove from the heat and stir until smooth, about 1 minute.

Pour the filling into the crumb crust and smooth the top. Cover with plastic wrap, pressing it directly onto the surface, and refrigerate until cold and set, 2–3 hours.

To make the topping, using an electric mixer on medium-high speed or a whisk, beat together the cream, sugar, and vanilla until stiff peaks form. Spread the cream on top of the pie. Decorate with chocolate curls. Refrigerate until ready to serve, but let sit at room temperature for 20 minutes before serving to take the chill off.

CHOCOLATE CURLS

To make chocolate curls, wrap a block of semisweet (plain) chocolate in plastic wrap. Rub the wrapped chocolate between your hands for a minute to warm it. For large chunks, microwave on low for about 5 seconds. Unwrap the chocolate and, using a vegetable peeler, slowly and evenly scrape the edge of the chunk until curls form. Repeat, warming the chocolate as necessary. Refrigerate the curls until ready to use.

Fresh Mint–Chocolate Truffle Tart

MAKES ONE 13¾-BY-4¼-INCH (35-BY-11-CM) TART, OR 8 SERVINGS

Basic Tart Dough (page 373)

1½ cups (12 fl oz/375 ml) heavy (double) cream

8–10 fresh mint sprigs (about 40 leaves), plus sprigs for garnish

12 oz (375 g) semisweet (plain) chocolate, chopped into small slivers

2 Tbsp light corn syrup

Confectioners' (icing) sugar or unsweetened cocoa powder for dusting

HAVE READY A RECTANGULAR TART PAN that measures 13¾-by-4¼-inch (35-by-11-cm), preferably with a removable bottom. Roll out the dough and trim to make a rectangle about 2 inches bigger on all sides than the tart pan (see page 385). Transfer the dough rectangle to the tart pan and trim off any excess dough by gently running a rolling pin across the top of the pan. Press the dough into the sides to extend it slightly above the rim. Refrigerate or freeze the tart shell until firm, about 30 minutes.

Meanwhile, place an oven rack in the lower third of the oven and preheat to 375°F (190°C). Fully bake the tart shell as directed on page 385. Transfer the tart shell to a wire rack and let cool completely.

In a small saucepan over medium heat, warm the cream until small bubbles appear on the surface. Remove from the heat and add the mint sprigs. Let stand for 20–30 minutes.

Put the chocolate in the top of a double boiler and melt, stirring occasionally, over barely simmering water (see page 173). Alternatively, in a heatproof bowl, melt the chocolate in the microwave in 30-second intervals. Pour the cream through a fine-mesh sieve into the melted chocolate, discarding the mint sprigs. Add the corn syrup and stir until smooth. Pour the filling into the fully baked tart shell. Refrigerate until well chilled, about 1 hour.

If using a tart pan with a removable bottom, let the sides fall away, then slide the tart onto a serving plate. Let stand at room temperature for about 20 minutes before serving. Just before serving, lay strips of waxed paper over the top of the tart and dust lightly with confectioners' sugar (right). Carefully remove the waxed paper strips and garnish with fresh mint sprigs.

DECORATING WITH STENCILS

Using strips of waxed paper or a stencil when dusting a pie or tart with confectioners' sugar or cocoa powder is a simple and elegant way to add a decorative finish. For rectangular tarts, cut strips of waxed paper. For round pies or tarts, use a precut cake stencil, or cut your own design out of card stock. Lay the strips or stencil over the pie or tart. Put about 1 Tbsp confectioners' (icing) sugar or cocoa powder in a fine-mesh sieve, then tap to sprinkle evenly. Lift off the strips or stencil, leaving the sugar or cocoa pattern behind.

Banana Cream Pie

MAKES ONE 9-INCH (23-CM) PIE, OR 8 SERVINGS

Flaky Pastry Dough (page 373)

FOR THE FILLING:

¼ cup (2 fl oz/60 ml) cold water

2¼ tsp (1 package) unflavored powdered gelatin (page 226)

2 cups (16 fl oz/500 ml) whole milk

4 large egg yolks

½ cup (4 oz/125 g) sugar

¼ cup (1 oz/30 g) cornstarch (cornflour)

¼ tsp salt

1 tsp pure vanilla extract

3 bananas, peeled and cut into slices ½ inch (12 mm) thick

FOR THE TOPPING:

1 cup (8 fl oz/250 ml) heavy (double) cream

1 Tbsp dark rum (optional)

1 tsp pure vanilla extract

1 Tbsp sugar

ROLL OUT THE DOUGH DISK into a 12-inch (30-cm) round (see page 385). Transfer the dough round to a 9-inch (23-cm) pie pan or dish. Trim the edge of the dough round, leaving ¾ inch (2 cm) of overhang. Fold the overhang under itself and pinch it together to create a high edge on the pan's rim. Flute the edge decoratively (see page 386). Refrigerate or freeze the pie shell until firm, about 30 minutes.

Meanwhile, place an oven rack in the lower third of the oven and preheat to 375°F (190°C). Fully bake the pie shell as directed on page 385. Transfer to a wire rack and let cool completely.

To make the filling, pour the cold water into a small bowl and sprinkle with the gelatin. Let sit until the gelatin softens and swells, 5–10 minutes. In a saucepan over medium heat, warm the milk until hot to the touch, about 8 minutes. Remove from the heat. In a bowl, whisk together the egg yolks and sugar until pale yellow. Add the cornstarch and salt, beating until smooth. Add the hot milk to the yolk mixture 1 cup (8 fl oz/250 ml) at a time, mixing well after each addition. Add the softened gelatin and mix well. Return to the saucepan over medium heat and cook, stirring constantly, until the mixture thickens and begins to bubble, 8–9 minutes. Remove from the heat and whisk in the vanilla.

Lay two-thirds of the banana slices in a single layer in the bottom of the fully baked pie shell. Stir the remaining banana slices into the custard and spoon it evenly over the bananas in the shell. Cover with plastic wrap. Prick a few holes in the plastic. Refrigerate for about 4 hours.

To make the topping, in a large bowl, combine the cream, rum (if using), vanilla, and sugar. Using an electric mixer on medium-high speed, beat until soft peaks form. Spread the whipped cream on top of the pie. Refrigerate until ready to serve, then let stand at room temperature for about 20 minutes before serving.

WORKING WITH PIE DOUGH

One way to transfer dough to a pie pan or dish is to fold and unfold the dough into the pan: First, trim the dough about 1 inch (2.5 cm) larger than the pan you are using. Then, fold the dough in half and transfer to the pan. Gently ease the folded dough into the pan, unfold it, and, being careful not to stretch the dough, pat it firmly into the bottom and sides, letting any excess fall over the rim. Trim off the excess dough by using kitchen shears for a pie or by gently running a rolling pin across the top of the pan for a tart. Create a decorative edge as called for in the recipe. You can also use a rolling pin to transfer dough to a pie pan or dish (see page 385).

Coconut Custard Pie

MAKES ONE 9-INCH (23-CM) PIE, OR 8 SERVINGS

Flaky Pastry Dough (page 373)

1½ cups (6 oz/185 g) sweetened shredded or flaked dried coconut

3 large eggs

1 cup (8 oz/250 g) sugar

¼ tsp salt

2 Tbsp all-purpose (plain) flour

1 cup (8 fl oz/250 ml) whole milk

1 Tbsp unsalted butter, melted

2 tsp fresh lemon juice, strained

1 tsp finely grated lemon zest

ROLL OUT THE DOUGH DISK into a 12-inch (30-cm) round (see page 385). Transfer the dough round to a 9-inch (23-cm) pie pan or dish. Trim the edge of the dough round, leaving ¾ inch (2 cm) of overhang. Fold the overhang under itself and pinch it together to create a high edge on the pan's rim. Flute the edge decoratively (see page 386). Refrigerate or freeze the pie shell until firm, about 30 minutes.

Meanwhile, place an oven rack in the lower third of the oven and preheat to 375°F (190°C). Partially bake the pie shell as directed on page 385. Transfer to a wire rack. Place an oven rack in the middle of the oven and reduce the oven temperature to 350°F (180°C).

Spread the coconut evenly on a baking sheet and bake until lightly golden, about 12 minutes. Pour onto a plate to cool.

In a bowl, whisk together the eggs, sugar, and salt until blended. Add the flour, milk, melted butter, lemon juice, and lemon zest and mix well. Stir in the toasted coconut and mix to combine. Pour the mixture into the partially baked crust.

Bake the pie until the top is golden and the filling is firm in the center, 45–55 minutes. Transfer to a wire rack and let cool completely. Serve at room temperature.

DRIED COCONUT

Dried coconut is sold in two styles, shredded and flaked. Either variety may be used here. Both are often sold sweetened, as called for in this recipe, although it is possible to buy unsweetened dried coconut in specialty-foods stores. Look for dried coconut in plastic bags or cans on market shelves. Once the container has been opened, refrigerate the coconut. Toasting the coconut will bring out its naturally nutty flavor.

Blueberry Pie

MAKES ONE 9-INCH (23-CM) PIE, OR 8 SERVINGS

Flaky Pastry Dough, Double Crust Variation (page 373)

4 cups (1 lb/500 g) blueberries

1 Tbsp fresh lemon juice, strained

¾ cup (6 oz/185 g) sugar

3 Tbsp cornstarch (cornflour)

½ tsp finely grated lemon zest

¼ tsp salt

¼ tsp ground cinnamon

1 Tbsp cold unsalted butter, cut into small pieces

ROLL OUT THE DOUGH DISKS into two 12-inch (30-cm) rounds (see page 385). Transfer 1 dough round to a 9-inch (23-cm) pie pan or dish. Trim the edge, leaving ¾ inch (2 cm) of overhang. Refrigerate or freeze the pie shell and the second dough round until firm, about 30 minutes.

Place the berries in a large bowl, sprinkle with the lemon juice, and toss to coat evenly. In a small bowl, stir together the sugar, cornstarch, lemon zest, salt, and cinnamon. Sprinkle the sugar mixture over the berries and toss to distribute evenly. Immediately transfer to the dough-lined pan and dot with the butter.

Position the second dough round over the filled pie and trim the edge to leave 1 inch (2.5 cm) of overhang. Fold the edge of the top round under the edge of the bottom round and crimp or flute the edges to seal (see page 386). Using a small, sharp knife, cut an asterisk 4–5 inches (10–13 cm) across in the center of the top to allow steam to escape during baking. Refrigerate the pie until the dough is firm, 20–30 minutes.

Meanwhile, place an oven rack in the lower third of the oven and preheat to 375°F (190°C). Bake the pie until the crust is golden and the filling is bubbling, 50–60 minutes. Transfer to a wire rack and let cool completely to set, 1–2 hours. Serve at room temperature or rewarm in a 350°F (180°C) oven for 10–15 minutes just before serving.

FRESH VS. FROZEN BLUEBERRIES

Like all berries, blueberries freeze beautifully, so if you cannot find fresh ones, use frozen. Tiny, sweet Maine blueberries are especially good. These low-bush berries, famous for growing wild in Maine and similar cool climates, do not travel well, although nowadays a fairly good-sized crop is cultivated and sold frozen or made into preserves. If using frozen blueberries, do not thaw first, and increase the baking time by 10–15 minutes.

Ricotta-Rice Tart

MAKES ONE 9-INCH (23-CM) TART, OR 8 SERVINGS

FOR THE PASTRY:

1½ cups (7½ oz/235 g) all-purpose (plain) flour

1 tsp finely grated lemon zest

¼ tsp salt

½ cup (4 oz/125 g) cold unsalted butter, cut into Tbsp-sized pieces

4–5 Tbsp (2–3 fl oz/60–80 ml) ice water

FOR THE FILLING:

4 cups (32 fl oz/1 l) milk

11 Tbsp (5 oz/155 g) sugar

1 cup (7 oz/220 g) Vialone Nano or Arborio rice

3 egg yolks

1¼ cups (10 oz/315 g) whole-milk ricotta cheese

1 tsp finely grated lemon zest

Pinch of salt

TO MAKE THE PASTRY, combine the flour, lemon zest, and salt in a food processor. With the machine running, drop in 1 piece of butter at a time, processing until evenly distributed. Pulse, gradually adding the water, just until the dough comes together. Do not overprocess, or the dough will be tough. On a lightly floured work surface, form the dough into a ball. Divide in half, then flatten each half into a disk. Place the disks in a zippered plastic bag and refrigerate for at least 1 hour or up to overnight.

Preheat the oven to 350°F (180°C). On a lightly floured work surface, roll out 1 dough disk into a round about 11 inches (28 cm) in diameter. Fit the round into a 9-inch (23-cm) tart pan, preferably with a removable bottom. Trim off any excess dough by gently rolling a rolling pin across the top of the pan. Line with a round of parchment (baking) paper and fill with pie weights or short-grain rice. Partially bake until firm and slightly colored, about 15 minutes. Remove the weights and parchment paper. Transfer the tart shell to a wire rack and let cool completely. Reduce the oven temperature to 325°F (165°C).

Meanwhile, make the filling. In a saucepan over medium heat, combine the milk and 2 Tbsp of the sugar. Add the rice and cook, stirring frequently, until tender to the bite but slightly firm in the center, about 20 minutes. Remove from the heat. Spread the rice on a baking sheet and let cool.

In a bowl, beat the egg yolks with the remaining sugar. Stir in the ricotta, lemon zest, and salt. Transfer the cooled rice to a bowl and add the ricotta mixture. Stir to blend. Pour the filling into the partially baked tart shell. Roll out the remaining dough disk thinly and drape it over the filled tart. Press it against the bottom tart shell edges in places but do not worry about sealing it completely. Using a small, sharp knife, cut 2 or 3 slits in the top.

Bake the tart until the crust is golden and a knife inserted into one of the vents comes out clean, about 1 hour. Serve warm or let cool to room temperature. If using a tart pan with a removable bottom, let the sides fall away, then slide the tart onto a serving plate.

ABOUT RICOTTA

In Italy, ricotta is a secondary product in cheese making. When rennet (a curdling agent) is added to milk, it causes the milk solids to curdle. The curds are then drained, shaped, and aged. The liquid that remains after the curds are removed is known as the whey. When the whey is further processed, or "recooked" (*ricotta*, in Italian), ricotta cheese is created. Whole-milk ricotta is preferred for this recipe, as the skimmed-milk cheese tends to be more watery.

Classic Pumpkin Pie

MAKES ONE 9-INCH (23-CM) PIE, OR 8 SERVINGS

Flaky Pastry Dough (page 373)

½ cup (3½ oz/105 g) firmly packed light or dark brown sugar

2 large eggs

1 tsp ground cinnamon

1 tsp ground ginger

½ tsp salt

¼ tsp ground cloves

¼ tsp freshly grated nutmeg

1 cup (8 oz/250 g) canned or fresh pumpkin purée (right)

1½ cups (12 fl oz/375 ml) heavy (double) cream

Sweetened Whipped Cream (page 377) for serving

ROLL OUT THE DOUGH DISK into a 12-inch (30-cm) round (see page 385). Transfer the dough round to a 9-inch (23-cm) pie pan or dish. Trim the edge of the dough round, leaving ¾ inch (2 cm) of overhang. Fold the overhang under itself and pinch it together to create a high edge on the pan's rim. Flute the edge decoratively (see page 386). Refrigerate or freeze the pie shell until firm, about 30 minutes.

Meanwhile, place an oven rack in the lower third of the oven and preheat to 375°F (190°C). Partially bake the pie shell as directed on page 385. Transfer the pie shell to a wire rack. Place an oven rack in the middle of the oven and reduce the oven temperature to 350°F (180°C).

In a large bowl, whisk together the brown sugar and eggs until well blended. Add the cinnamon, ginger, salt, cloves, and nutmeg and mix well. Add the pumpkin purée and cream and whisk until smooth. Pour into the partially baked pie shell.

Bake the pie until the filling is slightly risen and firm in the middle, 35–45 minutes. Transfer to a wire rack and let cool until just slightly warm or at room temperature. Slice into wedges and serve with whipped cream.

FRESH PUMPKIN PURÉE

Start with a baking pumpkin, such as Sugar Pie, Baby Bear, or Cheese. Split the pumpkin in half and put the halves, cut sides down, in a baking dish. Add ½ inch (12 mm) of water. Bake at 350°F (180°C) until a knife easily pierces the pumpkin, about 45 minutes, adding water as needed to maintain the water level. Cool the pumpkin. Scoop out and discard the seeds. Scoop the flesh into a food processor or blender and purée until smooth. Or, freeze for up to 3 months.

Mississippi Mud Pie

MAKES ONE 9-INCH (23-CM) PIE, OR 8 SERVINGS

1 cup (6 oz/185 g) semisweet (plain) chocolate chips

4 Tbsp (2 oz/60 g) unsalted butter

¼ cup (2 fl oz/60 ml) heavy (double) cream

2 Tbsp light corn syrup

1 cup (4 oz/125 g) confectioners' (icing) sugar, sifted

1 tsp pure vanilla extract

1 Cookie Crumb Crust (page 374), made with chocolate wafers

½ cup (2½ oz/75 g) toffee bits or coarsely chopped toasted almonds (page 53, see Note)

1 qt (1 l) premium coffee ice cream, softened

IN THE TOP OF A DOUBLE BOILER, combine the chocolate chips, butter, cream, and corn syrup and melt, stirring occasionally, over barely simmering water (see page 173). (Alternatively, in a microwaveproof bowl, combine the chocolate, butter, cream, and corn syrup and melt in the microwave for 30-second intervals. Remove from the microwave and stir until smooth.)

Add the confectioners' sugar and vanilla to the chocolate mixture and mix well. Reserve ½ cup (4 fl oz/125 ml) of the chocolate mixture for the top of the pie. Spread the remaining mixture evenly in the bottom of the cookie crust. Sprinkle with half of the toffee bits. Refrigerate until well chilled, about 1 hour.

In a large bowl, using an electric mixer on medium speed, beat the ice cream until it is spreadable but not runny. Immediately mound into the pie shell and spread it evenly. Freeze until the ice cream is firm, at least 2 hours or up to overnight.

Reheat the reserved chocolate mixture in the top of the double boiler over barely simmering water, or in the microwave for 30-second intervals, until it is spreadable but not hot. Using a silicone spatula, spread it over the ice cream. Sprinkle with the remaining toffee bits and return the pie to the freezer until it is completely firm before serving, 3–4 hours. To slice, run a knife under hot water, then dry it off. If frozen overnight, the pie may need to sit out for a few minutes to soften.

NOTE: You can find packaged toffee bits in the baking section of well-stocked markets, or chop up a toffee candy bar. The toffee bits make this pie a special treat, especially for children. For a more sophisticated version, use toasted almonds.

IMPROVISING A DOUBLE BOILER

A double boiler is used for cooking foods gently on the stove top. Made up of two nesting saucepans, double boilers are available in cookware stores, but a makeshift one is easy to assemble. Choose a saucepan and a heatproof bowl that rests securely in the top of the pan. Fill the saucepan with water to a depth of 1–2 inches (2.5–5 cm). Once the bowl is placed atop the pan, the water must not touch the bowl; allow at least 2 inches (5 cm) of clearance. Bring the water to a boil, set the bowl in place, and reduce the heat so that the water simmers gently.

Key Lime Meringue Tart

MAKES ONE 9-INCH (23-CM) TART, OR 8 SERVINGS

Basic Tart Dough (page 373)

FOR THE FILLING:

1 can (14 fl oz/430 ml) condensed milk

1 tsp finely grated lime zest, preferably Key lime

½ cup (4 fl oz/125 ml) fresh lime juice, preferably Key lime, strained

4 large egg yolks

FOR THE MERINGUE:

4 large egg whites

¼ tsp cream of tartar

½ cup (4 oz/125 g) sugar

ROLL OUT THE DOUGH DISK into a 12-inch (30-cm) round (see page 385). Transfer the dough round to a 9½-inch (24-cm) tart pan, preferably with a removable bottom. Trim off any excess dough by gently running a rolling pin across the top of the pan. Press the dough into the sides of the pan so that it extends slightly above the rim. Refrigerate or freeze the tart shell until firm, about 30 minutes.

Meanwhile, place an oven rack in the lower third of the oven and preheat to 375°F (190°C). Partially bake the tart shell as directed on page 385. Transfer to a wire rack.

To make the filling, in a bowl, whisk together the condensed milk, lime zest, lime juice, and egg yolks until well combined. Pour into the hot partially baked tart shell. Place the filled tart on a baking sheet. Bake until the edges of the filling are beginning to puff, 15–20 minutes. Transfer to a wire rack and let cool completely. Leave the oven on and move the rack to the upper third of the oven.

To make the meringue, in a clean bowl, using an electric mixer on low speed, beat together the egg whites and cream of tartar until foamy. Increase the speed to high and beat just until the whites form soft peaks. Beat in the sugar 1 Tbsp at a time, and continue beating until the whites are stiff and glossy (see page 155).

Pipe rosettes (left) or use the back of a spoon to spread and swirl the meringue over the filling, making sure it touches the crust all around the edge. Bake until the tips of the peaks are a light golden brown, 5 minutes. Transfer to a wire rack and let stand until the meringue is cool, at least 30 minutes, then refrigerate until cold and completely set, 1–2 hours. If using a tart pan with a removable bottom, let the sides fall away, then slide the tart onto a large serving plate. Cut into wedges and serve.

NOTES: This meringue contains egg whites that are only partially cooked. For more information, see page 392. Meringue is best served the day it is made.

PIPING ROSETTES

With a pastry bag and pastry tip, you can apply a simple but beautiful decorative topping to pies, tarts, and other desserts. Fit a pastry bag with a ½-inch (12-mm) star tip and fold down the top edges of the bag. Spoon the meringue into the bag, unfold the bag, and twist the bag closed. To make rosettes, hold the bag in your nondominant hand with the tip about 1 inch (2.5 cm) above the surface of the tart. Moving the bag in a small, tight circle, use even pressure with your other hand to pipe out the meringue into mounds. To discontinue piping, stop applying pressure and lift up the tip. For more information, see page 383.

Lemon Cream Tart

MAKES ONE 9½-INCH (24-CM) TART, OR 8 SERVINGS

Basic Tart Dough (page 373)

4 large egg yolks

4 tsps finely grated lemon zest

1 can (14 fl oz/430 ml) sweetened condensed milk

½ cup (4 fl oz/125 ml) fresh lemon juice, strained

Pinch of salt

Sweetened Whipped Cream (page 377) for serving (optional)

ROLL OUT THE DOUGH DISK into a 12-inch (30-cm) round (see page 385). Transfer the dough round to a 9½-inch (24-cm) tart pan, preferably with a removable bottom. Trim off any excess dough by gently running a rolling pin across the top of the pan. Press the dough into the sides of the pan so that it extends slightly above the rim. Refrigerate or freeze the tart shell until firm, about 30 minutes.

Meanwhile, place an oven rack in the lower third of the oven and preheat the oven to 375°F (190°C). Fully bake the tart shell as directed on page 385. Transfer the tart shell to a wire rack and let cool completely. Reduce the oven temperature to 350°F (180°C).

In a bowl, using an electric mixer on medium speed, beat together the egg yolks and lemon zest until well blended, about 1 minute. Add the condensed milk, lemon juice, and salt, beating well after each addition. Pour into the fully baked tart shell.

Bake the tart until the filling is just firm in the center, 12–14 minutes. Transfer the tart to a wire rack and let cool until completely set, 1–2 hours. If using a tart pan with a removable bottom, let the sides fall away, then slide the tart onto a large serving plate. Cut the tart into wedges and serve with a dollop of whipped cream, if using.

SERVING TIP: For an elegant garnish, cut a thin slice off of a whole lemon, then cut a slit in the lemon slice, twist, and gently place on the tart.

CONDENSED MILK

Condensed milk is evaporated milk with a high proportion (40 percent) of cane sugar. Also known as sweetened condensed milk, condensed milk was developed in 1856 as a way of preserving whole milk without refrigeration. It is ivory in color and has a syrupy consistency and glossy surface. Sold in cans, condensed milk is used mainly in confections and desserts. It will thicken when combined with acidic fruit juice. Do not substitute evaporated milk.

Georgia Peach Pie

MAKES ONE 9-INCH (23-CM) PIE, OR 8 SERVINGS

Flaky Pastry Dough, Double Crust Variation (page 373)

¾ cup (6 oz/185 g) sugar

2 Tbsp cornstarch (cornflour)

2 Tbsp quick-cooking tapioca

1 tsp ground cinnamon

Pinch of salt

6 or 7 ripe but firm peaches, peeled (page 178), pitted, and sliced ½ inch (12 mm) thick (about 5 cups)

1 Tbsp cold unsalted butter, cut into small pieces

ROLL OUT THE DOUGH DISKS into two 12-inch (30-cm) rounds (see page 385). Transfer 1 dough round to a 9-inch (23-cm) pie pan or dish. Trim the edge, leaving ¾ inch (2 cm) of overhang. Refrigerate or freeze the pie shell and the second dough round until firm, about 30 minutes.

In a small bowl, stir together the sugar, cornstarch, tapioca, cinnamon, and salt. Place the peaches in a large bowl, sprinkle with the sugar mixture, and toss to distribute evenly. Immediately transfer to the dough-lined pan and dot with the butter.

Position the second dough round over the filled pie and trim the edge to leave 1 inch (2.5 cm) of overhang. Fold the edge of the top round under the edge of the bottom round. Using a small, sharp knife, cut slices around the edge of the crust, leaving about 1 inch (2.5 cm) between each slice. Fold every other slice up toward the center of the pie to create a decorative edge. Use the knife to cut 5 or 6 slits in the top crust to allow steam to escape during baking. Refrigerate the pie until the dough is firm, 20–30 minutes.

Meanwhile, place an oven rack in the lower third of the oven and preheat to 375°F (190°C). Bake the pie until the crust is golden and the filling is thick and bubbling, 50–60 minutes. Transfer to a wire rack and let cool completely to set. Serve at room temperature or rewarm in a 350°F (180°C) oven for 10–15 minutes just before serving.

SERVING TIP: Serve with a drizzle of heavy (double) cream or a dollop of Crème Fraîche (page 377) or Sweetened Whipped Cream (page 377).

TAPIOCA

A starchy substance derived from the root of the cassava plant, tapioca can be used to thicken fruit fillings for pies. Tapioca comes in three basic forms, pearl (small dried balls of tapioca starch), granulated (coarsely broken-up pearl tapioca), or quick-cooking, also called instant (very finely granulated pearl tapioca).

Tossed Fresh Fruit Tart

MAKES ONE 9½-INCH (24-CM) TART, OR 8 SERVINGS

Basic Tart Dough (page 373)

FOR THE PASTRY CREAM:

2 cups (16 fl oz/500 ml) whole milk

6 large egg yolks

½ cup (4 oz/125 g) sugar

¼ cup (1 oz/30 g) cornstarch (cornflour)

⅛ tsp salt

1 tsp pure vanilla extract

FOR THE TOPPING:

1 cup (4 oz/125 g) strawberries, hulled and cut into ½-inch (12-mm) chunks

1 cup (6 oz/185 g) red seedless grapes, halved lengthwise

1 cup (6 oz/185 g) green seedless grapes, halved lengthwise

1 cup (4 oz/125 g) fresh or thawed frozen blueberries

¼ cup (2½ oz/75 g) apricot jam

ROLL OUT THE DOUGH DISK into a 12-inch (30-cm) round (see page 385). Transfer the dough round to a 9½-inch (24-cm) tart pan, preferably with a removable bottom. Trim off any excess dough by gently running a rolling pin across the top of the pan. Press the dough into the sides of the pan so that it extends slightly above the rim. Refrigerate or freeze the tart shell until firm, about 30 minutes.

Meanwhile, place an oven rack in the lower third of the oven and preheat to 375°F (190°C). Fully bake the tart shell as directed on page 385. Transfer to a wire rack and let the tart shell cool completely.

To make the pastry cream, in a nonaluminum saucepan over medium heat, warm the milk until tiny bubbles appear on the surface, 6–8 minutes. In a bowl, whisk together the egg yolks and sugar. Add the cornstarch and salt. Pour in half of the hot milk while whisking constantly. Whisk in the remaining milk and return to the saucepan. Cook over medium heat, whisking constantly, until the mixture thickens to a firm consistency, 5–8 minutes. Scrape into a bowl. Whisk in the vanilla. Cover with plastic wrap, pressing it directly onto the surface of the pastry cream. Refrigerate for 2–3 hours.

To assemble the tart, stir the pastry cream with a silicone spatula until smooth. Spoon into the bottom of the fully baked tart shell and spread evenly.

In a large bowl, combine the strawberries, red and green grapes, and blueberries. In a small saucepan over low heat, heat the apricot jam until it liquefies. Pour through a fine-mesh sieve set over a small bowl. Pour the warm jam over the fruit and toss gently until the fruit is well coated. Pile the fruit on top of the pastry cream and arrange into a dome. If using a tart pan with a removable bottom, let the sides fall away, then slide the tart onto a serving plate. Cut into wedges and serve right away.

FRUIT TART VARIATIONS

The beauty of this tart is that you can use a combination of fruits according to the seasons or your taste. For a late summer tart, try tossing blackberries or raspberries with juicy, ripe peaches. For a springtime dessert, toss apricots with strawberries and mint. For a fresh winter finale, try sliced kiwi fruit tossed with orange slices.

Summer Berry Pie

MAKES ONE 9-INCH (23-CM) PIE, OR 8 SERVINGS

Flaky Pastry Dough (page 373)

1 cup (8 oz/250 g) sugar

2 Tbsp cornstarch (cornflour)

2 Tbsp quick-cooking tapioca

½ tsp ground cinnamon

Pinch of salt

6 cups (1½ lb/750 g) mixed fresh berries, such as blackberries, blueberries, raspberries, and/or boysenberries

1 Tbsp cold unsalted butter, cut into small pieces

ROLL OUT THE DOUGH DISKS into two 12-inch (30-cm) rounds (see page 385). Transfer 1 dough round to a 9-inch (23-cm) pie pan or dish. Trim the edge, leaving ¾ inch (2 cm) of overhang. Refrigerate or freeze the pie shell and the second dough round until firm, about 30 minutes.

In a small bowl, stir together the sugar, cornstarch, tapioca, cinnamon, and salt. Place the berries in a large bowl, sprinkle with the sugar mixture, and toss to distribute evenly. Immediately transfer to the dough-lined pan and dot with the butter.

Position the second dough round over the filled pie and trim the edge to leave 1 inch (2.5 cm) of overhang. Fold the edge of the top round under the edge of the bottom round and crimp or flute the edges to seal (page 386). Using a small, round cookie cutter or a small, sharp knife, cut 5 or 6 holes or slits in the top crust to allow steam to escape during baking. Refrigerate the pie until the dough is firm, 20–30 minutes.

Meanwhile, place an oven rack in the lower third of the oven and preheat to 350°F (180°C). Bake the pie until the crust is golden and the filling is thick and bubbling up through the slits, 50–60 minutes. Transfer the pie to a wire rack and let cool completely to set. Serve at room temperature or rewarm in a 350°F (180°C) oven for 10–15 minutes just before serving.

HANDLING BERRIES

While some berries can be found in the market year-round, most will taste best in the spring and summer, their natural season. Select plump berries with deep color. Just before using, sort through them carefully and remove and discard any that are blemished or moldy. Gently rinse the berries under cold running water, but do not allow them to soak for any length of time, as they quickly absorb moisture and will turn mushy. Lay the rinsed berries in a single layer on paper towels to dry.

Italian Almond Tart

MAKES ONE 9½-INCH (24-CM) TART, OR 8 SERVINGS

Basic Tart Dough (page 373)

½ cup (4 oz/125 g) unsalted butter, at room temperature

½ lb (250 g) almond paste (right), cut into 1-inch (2.5-cm) cubes

¼ cup (2 oz/60 g) sugar

2 large eggs

⅓ cup (2 oz/60 g) all-purpose (plain) flour

⅓ cup (3½ oz/105 g) raspberry, plum, or cherry jam

⅓ cup (1½ oz/45 g) sliced (flaked) almonds

ROLL OUT THE DOUGH DISK into a 12-inch (30-cm) round (see page 385). Transfer the dough round to a 9½-inch (24-cm) tart pan, preferably with a removable bottom. Trim off any excess dough by gently running a rolling pin across the top of the pan. Press the dough into the sides of the pan so that it extends slightly above the rim. Refrigerate or freeze the tart shell until firm, about 30 minutes.

Meanwhile, place an oven rack in the lower third of the oven and preheat to 375°F (190°C). Partially blind bake the tart shell as directed on page 385. Transfer the tart shell to a wire rack. Place an oven rack in the middle of the oven, and reduce the oven temperature to 350°F (180°C).

In a bowl, using an electric mixer on medium speed or a whisk, beat the butter until smooth. Add the almond paste, one piece at a time, beating until smooth after each addition. While continuing to beat, sprinkle in the sugar. Add the eggs one at a time, mixing well after each addition. Stir in the flour.

Spread the jam evenly in the bottom of the partially baked tart shell. Spoon in the almond paste mixture and spread evenly over the jam. Sprinkle the surface evenly with the sliced almonds.

Bake until the filling is golden and the middle is firm, 35–45 minutes. Transfer the tart to a wire rack and let cool completely. If using a tart pan with a removable bottom, let the sides fall away, then slide the tart onto a serving plate. Serve at room temperature.

ALMOND PASTE

Almond paste is a mixture of finely ground blanched almonds, sugar, and water that has been cooked until smooth. During the grinding process, the almonds release oils that enhance the flavor of the paste. Used in the making of many baked goods, almond paste can be found in cans or plastic tubes in most well-stocked food stores. The canned variety tends to be moister, which makes working with it easier. Do not substitute marzipan for almond paste, as it could alter the flavor and texture of your dessert.

Cinnamon Apple Crumb Pie

MAKES ONE 9-INCH (23-CM) PIE, OR 8 SERVINGS

Flaky Pastry Dough (page 373)

FOR THE TOPPING:

½ cup (2½ oz/75 g) all-purpose (plain) flour

⅓ cup (2½ oz/75 g) firmly packed light or dark brown sugar

1 tsp ground cinnamon

¼ tsp salt

5 Tbsp (2½ oz/75 g) cold unsalted butter, cut into ¼-inch (6-mm) cubes

FOR THE FILLING:

7 large, firm baking apples (page 244)

1 Tbsp fresh lemon juice, strained

⅓ cup (3 oz/90 g) granulated sugar

2 Tbsp cornstarch (cornflour)

1 tsp ground cinnamon

½ tsp freshly grated nutmeg

¼ tsp ground cloves

Pinch of salt

ROLL OUT THE DOUGH DISK into a 12-inch (30-cm) round (see page 385). Transfer the dough round to a 9-inch (23-cm) pie pan or dish. Trim the edge of the dough round, leaving ¾ inch (2 cm) of overhang. Fold the overhang under itself and pinch it together to create a high edge on the pan's rim. Flute the edge decoratively (see page 386). Refrigerate or freeze the pie shell until firm, about 30 minutes.

To make the topping, in a small bowl, stir together the flour, brown sugar, cinnamon, and salt. Using a pastry blender or 2 knives, cut in the butter until the mixture is crumbly. Cover and chill in the refrigerator until ready to use.

To make the filling, peel, halve, and core the apples, then cut them into ½-inch (12-mm) dice; you should have about 6 cups. Place the apples in a large bowl, sprinkle with the lemon juice, and toss to coat evenly. In a small bowl, stir together the granulated sugar, cornstarch, cinnamon, nutmeg, cloves, and salt. Sprinkle the sugar mixture over the apples and toss to distribute evenly. Immediately transfer to the dough-lined pan. Sprinkle evenly with the crumb topping. Refrigerate the pie until the dough is firm, 20–30 minutes.

Meanwhile, place an oven rack in the lower third of the oven and preheat to 375°F (190°C). Bake the pie until the crust is golden and the filling is thick and bubbling, 50–60 minutes. Transfer to a wire rack and let cool completely to set. Serve at room temperature or rewarm in a 350°F (180°C) oven for 10–15 minutes just before serving.

PIE PANS VS. PIE DISHES

Pies are usually baked in pans or dishes with sloping sides. For pies with a top and bottom crust, known as double-crust pies, a metal pie pan, preferably aluminum is best. Metal is an excellent heat conductor, and using a metal pan will produce a crisp, golden crust. Glass pie dishes are also a good choice. However, because they don't conduct heat as well as metal pans, it may take up to 10 or 15 minutes longer for the bottom crust to bake. Deep-dish ceramic or porcelain dishes are attractive choices for serving pies, but keep in mind that they are often deeper and wider than the standard 9-inch (23-cm) pie pans and dishes called for throughout this book; you may need to use more filling.

Rustic Apple Galette

MAKES ONE 9-INCH (23-CM) GALETTE, OR 8 SERVINGS

Flaky Pastry Dough (page 373)

4 large, firm baking apples (page 244), peeled, halved, and cored (right)

1 Tbsp cold unsalted butter, cut into small pieces

2 Tbsp sugar

ROLL OUT THE DOUGH DISK into a 12-inch (30-cm) round. Place the dough round on a baking sheet lined with parchment (baking) paper.

Thinly slice the apple halves crosswise, keeping each half together. Gently nudge one of the apple halves to flatten it slightly, and lay it rounded (skinned) side up in the middle of the dough round. Repeat with the remaining apple halves, arranging them around the center apple half and leaving a 1- to 2-inch (2.5- to 5-cm) border of dough uncovered along the edge. Fold the edge of the dough up and over the apples, pleating the dough loosely all around the edge and leaving the galette uncovered in the center. Dot the apples with the butter and sprinkle with the sugar.

Measure the circumference of the galette and cut a strip of aluminum foil about 2 inches (5 cm) longer and 3–4 inches (7.5–10 cm) wide. Wrap the foil strip around the edge of the galette and secure the ends by folding them together. (The foil helps keep the dough from unfolding.) Refrigerate the galette on the baking sheet until the dough is firm, 20–30 minutes.

Meanwhile, place an oven rack in the lower third of the oven and preheat to 425°F (220°C). Bake the galette for 15 minutes. Reduce the oven temperature to 375°F (190°C) and continue baking until the crust is golden brown and the apples are tender when pierced with a knife, 30–40 minutes longer. Transfer the baking sheet to a wire rack and let the galette cool until slightly warm or room temperature before serving.

PEELING & CORING APPLES

A small, sharp knife is all you need for peeling an apple, although a vegetable peeler may be easier for novice cooks. A melon baller is a handy tool for coring. First, cut the peeled apple in half from the top to the bottom. Press the melon baller into the center of one of the halves and twist it to cut out and remove the core.

Strawberry-Rhubarb Pie

MAKES ONE 9-INCH (23-CM) PIE, OR 8 SERVINGS

Flaky Pastry Dough, Double-Crust Variation (page 373)

1 cup (8 oz/250 g) sugar

2 Tbsp cornstarch (cornflour)

2 Tbsp quick-cooking tapioca

Pinch of salt

4 or 5 stalks rhubarb, trimmed and cut into ½-inch (12-mm) slices (about 3 cups/12 oz/375 g)

3 cups (12 oz/375 g) strawberries, hulled and quartered lengthwise

1 Tbsp cold unsalted butter, cut into small pieces

ROLL OUT THE DOUGH DISKS into two 12-inch (30-cm) rounds (see page 385). Transfer 1 dough round to a 9-inch (23-cm) pie pan or dish. Trim the edge, leaving ¾ inch (2 cm) of overhang. Refrigerate or freeze the pie shell and the second dough round until firm, about 30 minutes.

In a small bowl, stir together the sugar, cornstarch, tapioca, and salt. Place the rhubarb and strawberries in a large bowl, sprinkle with the sugar mixture, and toss to coat the fruit with the sugar mixture. Immediately transfer to the dough-lined pan and dot with the butter.

Position the second dough round over the filled pie and trim the edge to leave 1 inch (2.5 cm) of overhang. Fold the edge of the top round under the edge of the bottom round and crimp the edges to seal (see page 386). Gather all of the dough scraps and roll out about ⅛ inch (3 mm) thick. Using a very small cookie cutter, cut out scalloped circles or other shapes of dough. Brush the edge of the crust and the undersides of the dough shapes with cold water and overlap the shapes around the edge of the pie. Using a small, sharp knife, cut 5 or 6 holes or slits in the top crust to allow steam to escape during baking. Refrigerate the pie until the dough is firm, 20–30 minutes.

Meanwhile, place an oven rack in the lower third of the oven and preheat to 350°F (180°C). Bake the pie until the crust is golden and the filling is thick and bubbling, 50–60 minutes. Transfer to a wire rack and let cool completely to set. Serve at room temperature or rewarm in a 350°F (180°C) oven for 10–15 minutes just before serving.

RHUBARB

Technically a vegetable, rhubarb is treated like a fruit and is traditionally paired with strawberries, which complement its tart, fruity flavor. Rhubarb comes in two types. Field rhubarb, most often available in late spring, is cherry-red and has a more pronounced flavor than its hothouse kin. Hothouse rhubarb is bright pink and is usually in the market year-round. To avoid a stringy filling, slice the rhubarb no wider than ½ inch (12 mm) thick. If the outside of the stalks are stringy, remove the strings with a vegetable peeler.

Cranberry Chess Pie

MAKES ONE 9-INCH (23-CM) PIE, OR 8 SERVINGS

ABOUT CHESS PIE

With its simple custardlike filling of eggs, sugar, butter, and a little flour, chess pie is a classic dessert of the American South. A number of theories exist on the origin of the name. One considers it a variation on the word cheese, which came about because early cookbooks referred to pies with custard fillings as cheesecakes. Another insists that it comes from the fact that the pie kept well in the traditional storage cabinet known as a pie chest.

Flaky Pastry Dough (page 373)

1⅓ cups (11 oz/345 g) sugar

½ cup (4 oz/125 g) unsalted butter, melted

⅛ tsp salt

3 large eggs

¼ cup (1½ oz/45 g) all-purpose (plain) flour

⅓ cup (3 fl oz/80 ml) buttermilk

1 tsp cider vinegar

2 tsps finely grated orange zest

2 cups (8 oz/250 g) fresh or frozen cranberries, coarsely chopped

ROLL OUT THE DOUGH DISK into a 12-inch (30-cm) round (see page 385). Transfer the dough round to a 9-inch (23-cm) pie pan or dish. Trim the edge of the dough round, leaving ¾ inch (2 cm) of overhang. Fold the overhang under itself and pinch it together to create a high edge on the pan's rim. Using a small, sharp knife, cut slices around the edge of the crust, leaving about 1 inch (2.5 cm) between each slice. Fold every other slice up toward the center of the pie to create a chessboard edge. Refrigerate or freeze the pie shell until firm, about 30 minutes.

Meanwhile, place an oven rack in the lower third of the oven and preheat to 375°F (190°C). Partially blind bake the pie shell as directed on page 385. Transfer to a wire rack. Leave the oven on.

In a bowl, whisk together the sugar, melted butter, and salt. Add the eggs one at a time, beating until smooth after each addition. Stir in the flour, then the buttermilk, vinegar, and orange zest, mixing well. Stir in the cranberries. Scrape the mixture into the partially baked pie shell.

Bake the pie until the top is lightly golden brown and the filling is firm, 50–60 minutes. Transfer to a wire rack and let cool completely. Cut the pie into wedges and serve at room temperature.

Little Plum Galettes

MAKES EIGHT 4-INCH (10-CM) GALETTES, OR 8 SERVINGS

Flaky Pastry Dough, Double-Crust Variation (page 373)

½ cup (4 oz/125 g) sugar

¼ tsp ground cinnamon

2 Tbsp cornstarch (cornflour)

⅛ tsp salt

2 lb (1 kg) plums, pitted and cut into small chunks (about 4 cups)

ROLL OUT THE DOUGH DISKS into 12-inch (30-cm) rounds. Using a 6-inch (15-cm) cardboard circle and a small, sharp knife, cut out 3 or 4 rounds from each rolled-out dough round. Press the dough scraps together and reroll to cut out additional rounds. You should have a total of 8 dough rounds.

Carefully fit the dough rounds into eight 4-inch (10-cm) metal tartlet pans, preferably with removable bottoms, and arrange on a baking sheet. Do not trim the edges of the dough.

In a small bowl, stir together the sugar, cinnamon, cornstarch, and salt. Place the plums in a large bowl, sprinkle with the sugar mixture, and toss to distribute evenly.

Place ½ cup (3 oz/90 g) of the plum mixture into each dough-lined pan. Fold the edges of the dough up and over the plums, pleating the dough loosely all around the edges and leaving the galettes uncovered in the centers (right). Refrigerate the galettes on the baking sheet until the dough is firm, 15–20 minutes.

Meanwhile, place an oven rack in the lower third of the oven and preheat to 375°F (190°C). Bake the galettes until the crusts are golden and the juice around the plums has thickened, about 40 minutes. Transfer the baking sheet to a wire rack and let the galettes cool slightly before serving. If using tart pans with removable bottoms, let the sides fall away, then slide the galettes onto individual plates.

PLEATING DOUGH

Pleating the edge of a crust over the filling will give a fruit pie or tart a pretty, rustic look. Make sure there is a border of dough hanging over the edge of the pan of at least 1 to 2 inches (2.5 to 5 cm). One inch is enough in the case of these small galettes. Using both hands, lift the edge of the dough up and over the fruit and then fold it underneath itself every inch or two until the entire edge is a series of loose folds. Work quickly so your fingers do not melt the butter in the dough, which will produce a tough crust.

Lemon Meringue Pie

MAKE ONE 9-INCH (23-CM) PIE, OR 8 SERVINGS

MERINGUE TOPPING

In a saucepan, whisk together 1 Tbsp cornstarch (cornflour) and 1/4 cup (2 fl oz/60 ml) water. Cook over medium heat, stirring constantly, until thick, about 2 minutes. Let cool. In a bowl, using an electric mixer on high speed, whip 4 large egg whites and 1/2 tsp cream of tartar until foamy. Reduce the speed to medium and whip while sprinkling in 1/2 cup (4 oz/125 g) sugar. Return to high speed and whip until the whites form a ribbon that folds back on itself when the beater is lifted. Stir in the cornstarch mixture and beat on high speed until shiny and soft peaks form, 2–3 minutes.

Flaky Pastry Dough (page 373)

FOR THE LEMON FILLING:

1 1/4 cups (10 oz/315 g) sugar

3 Tbsp cornstarch (cornflour)

4 large whole eggs, plus 4 large egg yolks

2 Tbsp finely grated lemon zest

1 cup (8 fl oz/250 ml) fresh lemon juice (about 7 large lemons)

4 Tbsp (2 oz/60 g) unsalted butter, thinly sliced

Meringue Topping (left), made just before using

ROLL OUT THE DOUGH DISK into a 12-inch (30-cm) round (see page 385). Transfer the dough round to a 9-inch (23-cm) pie pan or dish. Trim the edge of the dough round, leaving 3/4 inch (2 cm) of overhang. Fold the overhang under itself and pinch it together to create a high edge on the pan's rim. Flute the edge decoratively (see page 386). Refrigerate or freeze the pie shell until firm, about 30 minutes.

Meanwhile, place an oven rack in the lower third of the oven and preheat to 375°F (190°C). Fully bake the pie shell as directed on page 385. Transfer to a wire rack to cool.

To make the filling, in a bowl, whisk together the sugar and cornstarch. Add the whole eggs and egg yolks and whisk until pale yellow. Whisk in the lemon zest and juice, then the butter. Transfer to a saucepan and cook over medium heat, stirring constantly, until the mixture begins to bubble and is very thick, about 10 minutes. Pour the mixture into a bowl through a medium-mesh sieve. Spread the filling evenly in the fully baked pie shell. Cover with plastic wrap, pressing the wrap directly onto the surface. Refrigerate until well chilled and set, 3–4 hours.

Preheat the oven to 375°F (190°C). Make the topping (left). Heap the topping onto the filling and spread it to the edges of the crust, using a silicone spatula or the back of a spoon to make large swirls. Bake the pie until the meringue is an even light gold, 15–18 minutes. Transfer to a wire rack and let stand until cool, at least 20 minutes.

To serve, cut into wedges using a sharp knife dipped in hot water. The pie is best eaten the day it is baked, but it can be stored in the refrigerator, well wrapped, for 2–3 days.

LINZERTORTE CRUST

An eighteenth-century specialty of the Austrian town of Linz, the almond-rich Linzertorte is identifiable by its decorative interlacing top. To make the lattice, roll out the dough and cut into strips as directed in the recipe. Lay a long strip across the center of the torte. Set a shorter strip on each side of the center strip, equidistant from the center strip and the edge of the torte. Place the second long strip diagonally across the first strips, again in the center of the torte. Place the remaining shorter strips on either side, then proceed as directed.

Linzertorte

MAKES ONE 9-INCH (23-CM) TART, OR 8–10 SERVINGS

1½ cups (7 oz/200 g) all-purpose (plain) flour

¼ tsp ground cinnamon

⅛ tsp ground cloves

¼ tsp salt

1 lemon

1 cup (5½ oz/155 g) unblanched whole almonds

1 cup (3½ oz/100 g) confectioners' (icing) sugar

¾ cup (6 oz/170 g) unsalted butter, at room temperature

3 large egg yolks

1½ cups (18 oz/500 g) raspberry jam

1 Tbsp whole milk

IN A BOWL, SIFT TOGETHER the flour, cinnamon, cloves, and salt into a bowl. Using the finest rasps on a handheld grater, grate the zest from the lemon into the bowl. Set aside. In a food processor, process the almonds with the confectioners' sugar until finely ground. Set aside.

Using a stand mixer, beat the butter with the paddle on medium speed until creamy. Beat in the almond mixture, then 2 of the egg yolks. Reduce the speed to low, add the flour mixture, and beat just until combined. Flatten about a third of the dough into a disk, wrap in plastic, and refrigerate. Grease a 9-inch (23-cm) round fluted tart pan with a removable bottom. Using your fingers, press the remaining dough into the bottom and up the sides of the pan, extending it about ½ inch (12 mm) above the rim. If the dough is overly soft and sticky, refrigerate it until firm enough to continue. Spread the dough with the jam.

On a lightly floured surface, roll the chilled dough into a rectangle about 9 inches (23 cm) long and ¼ inch (6 mm) thick. Using a fluted pastry cutter, cut into 6 strips, each 1 inch (2.5 cm) wide; 2 of them should be 9 inches (23 cm) long and the others slightly shorter. Lay the strips on the torte (left), trimming the edges. Fold the dough extending above the pan back over the filling and strips. Crimp to seal the edges. Place the torte in the freezer for 20 minutes. Preheat the oven to 350°F (180°C).

In a small bowl, whisk together the remaining egg yolk and the milk. Brush the dough with the yolk mixture. Bake until the crust is browned and the jam is bubbling, 45–55 minutes. Let cool on a wire rack until the torte is barely warm. Let the pan sides fall away. Run a thin-bladed knife between the torte and the pan bottom. Transfer the torte to a serving plate and let cool completely. Just before serving, using a fine-mesh sieve, dust the torte with confectioners' sugar, if desired.

Crème Brûlée Tartlets

MAKES SIX 4-INCH (10-CM) TARTLETS, OR 6 SERVINGS

Basic Tart Dough (page 373)

2 cups (16 fl oz/500 ml) heavy (double) cream

½ vanilla bean, split lengthwise

2 large whole eggs, plus 2 large egg yolks

⅓ cup (3 oz/90 g) granulated sugar

⅛ tsp salt

ROLL OUT THE DOUGH DISK into a 12-inch (30-cm) round (see page 385). Using a 6-inch (15-cm) cardboard circle and a small, sharp knife, cut out 3 or 4 rounds from the tart dough. Press the dough scraps together and reroll to cut out additional rounds; you should have a total of 6. Transfer the rounds to six 4-inch (10-cm) tartlet pans, preferably with removable bottoms. Ease the dough into the pans and pat firmly into the bottoms and up the sides. Trim off any excess dough by gently running a rolling pin across the tops of the pans. Press the dough into the sides to extend it slightly above the rims. Refrigerate the shells until firm, about 30 minutes.

Meanwhile, place an oven rack in the lower third of the oven and preheat to 375°F (190°C). Place the tartlets on a baking sheet. Fully bake the shells as directed on page 385. Transfer to a wire rack and let cool.

In a saucepan over medium heat, warm the cream until hot to the touch, 6–8 minutes. Scrape the seeds from the vanilla bean into the cream, then add the pods. In a bowl, whisk together the whole eggs, egg yolks, granulated sugar, and salt until pale yellow. Add 1 cup (8 fl oz/250 ml) of the hot cream while stirring constantly. Mix in the remaining hot cream. Return to the saucepan over medium heat and cook, whisking constantly, until the custard is thick enough to heavily coat the back of a wooden spoon, 4–5 minutes. Strain through a medium-mesh sieve placed over a measuring pitcher. Pour into the tart shells, dividing evenly. Refrigerate until chilled, 3–4 hours.

Caramelize the tops of the tartlets (right). If using pans with removable bottoms, let the sides fall away, then slide the tartlets onto individual plates and serve.

CARAMELIZING SUGAR

Just before serving, preheat the broiler (grill). Sprinkle each tart with 2 tsp turbinado sugar that has been ground finely in a food processor. One at a time, slip the tartlets under the broiler 2–3 inches (5–7.5 cm) from the heat source. Broil (grill) until the sugar caramelizes, 1–2 minutes. Alternatively, use a small kitchen blowtorch to caramelize the sugar. Transfer to a wire rack and let cool for 10 minutes.

Upside-Down Apple Tart

MAKES ONE 10-INCH TART, OR 6–8 SERVINGS

Flaky Pastry Dough (page 373)

6 Tbsp (3 oz/90 g) unsalted butter

¾ cup (6 oz/185 g) sugar

5 or 6 firm baking apples (page 244), 2–2½ lb (1–1.25 kg) total weight, peeled, cored, and quartered

Vanilla ice cream or crème fraîche, homemade (page 378) or purchased, for serving

ROLL OUT THE DOUGH DISK into a 12-inch (30-cm) round (see page 385). Place the rolled-out dough round between 2 pieces of waxed paper and refrigerate until well chilled, at least 2 hours.

Preheat the oven to 400°F (200°C). In a nonstick 10-inch (25-cm) ovenproof frying pan over medium heat, melt the butter. Add the sugar and stir until combined, about 2 minutes. It may look a little lumpy. Arrange the apple quarters, round sides down, in the bottom of the pan, using just enough apples so they fit very snugly in a single layer. Reduce the heat to low and cook until the caramel is brown and the apples are slightly tender, about 15 minutes.

Transfer the frying pan to the oven and bake the apples for 5 minutes. Remove with oven mitts, place on a trivet, and let cool for 10 minutes. Raise the oven temperature to 450°F (230°C). Carefully place the pastry round over the apples, using a small knife to tuck the excess pastry inside the rim of the pan. Bake until the pastry is crisp and golden brown, about 20 minutes.

Carefully remove the frying pan from the oven. Run a knife around the edge of the pan to loosen the tart. Place a 12-inch (30-cm) serving platter upside down on top of the pan. Wearing oven mitts, quickly invert the pan and platter together. Be careful, as the pan and juices will be very hot. Lift off the pan. Serve warm or at room temperature with vanilla ice cream.

PASTRY SAVVY

For a tender, flaky pastry, start with well-chilled ingredients and handle the dough as little as possible to avoid developing the gluten in the flour (the culprit in tough or leathery pastry). Every batch of pastry will take a slightly different amount of water, depending on the dryness of the flour and the humidity of the day. Add just enough water to make the dough come together. Letting the dough rest in the refrigerator before baking helps prevent shrinkage.

YEASTED BREADS

Fig & Walnut Bread

MAKES 2 ROUND LOAVES

ABOUT DOUGH SPONGES

A sponge is a "head start" that gives yeasted breads a good flavor, a light texture, and a crackly outer crust. To make a sponge, a small proportion of the basic ingredients of the bread are mixed together with some of the yeast to form a batter that rises slowly before the remaining ingredients are added to complete the bread dough.

FOR THE SPONGE:

¾ cup (6 fl oz/180 ml) lukewarm water (100°F/38°C)

¾ cup (6 fl oz/180 ml) milk, at room temperature

1½ tsp active dry yeast

1 tsp sugar

1½ cups (7½ oz/235 g) bread flour

3 Tbsp whole-wheat (wholemeal) flour

FOR THE DOUGH:

1½ cups (8 oz/250 g) dried figs, stems removed, coarsely chopped, and soaked in hot water for 1 hour

About 2¼ cups (11½ oz/360 g) bread flour, plus extra as needed

1½ tsp active dry yeast

3 Tbsp olive oil, plus extra for greasing

2 Tbsp honey

2 tsp salt

1 cup (4 oz/125 g) broken or coarsely chopped walnut pieces

TO MAKE THE SPONGE, combine the water and milk in a stand mixer fitted with the whisk attachment. Sprinkle the yeast and sugar over the liquid and stir to dissolve. Let stand until foamy, about 10 minutes. Add the bread and whole-wheat flours and beat on medium speed until smooth and thick, about 1 minute. Cover loosely with plastic wrap and let stand for 1 hour.

To make the dough, drain the figs, pat dry, and toss with 1 Tbsp of the bread flour; set aside. Add the yeast, oil, honey, salt, and 1 cup (5 oz/155 g) of the bread flour to the sponge and switch to the paddle attachment. Beat on medium speed for 1 minute. Beat in the remaining bread flour, ½ cup (2½ oz/75 g) at a time, until the dough pulls away from the bowl sides. Switch to the dough hook. Knead on low speed, adding bread flour 1 Tbsp at a time if the dough sticks, until smooth and elastic, about 4 minutes.

Transfer to an oiled deep bowl and turn to coat with the oil. Cover loosely with plastic wrap and let rise at room temperature until doubled in bulk, 1½–2 hours.

Line a baking sheet with parchment (baking) paper. Turn the dough out onto a lightly floured work surface. Pat it into a large oval and sprinkle evenly with half the figs and walnuts. Roll up the dough, pat again into an oval, and sprinkle with the remaining figs and nuts. Roll the dough up again and knead a few times. Divide the dough in half and shape into 2 tight round loaves, gently pulling the surface taut from the bottom. Place on the prepared sheet at least 4 inches (10 cm) apart. Cover loosely with plastic and let rise until doubled in bulk, 45–60 minutes.

Place a baking stone on the bottom oven rack and preheat to 425°F (220°C). Using a thin, sharp knife, gently slash each loaf with a shallow X. Place the pan on the stone and reduce the oven temperature to 400°F (200°C). Bake until the loaves are golden brown, 30–35 minutes. Transfer to a rack and let cool completely.

Dinner Rolls

MAKES 36 ROLLS

3½ tsp active dry yeast

Pinch of sugar

⅓ cup (3 fl oz/80 ml) warm water (105°–115°F/40°–46°C)

1 cup (8 fl oz/250 ml) tepid buttermilk (90°F/32°C)

¼ cup (2 oz/60 g) sugar or ¼ cup (3 oz/90 g) honey

½ cup (4 oz/125 g) unsalted butter, melted

2 large eggs, lightly beaten

1 tsp salt

4½–5 cups (22½–25 oz/705–780 g) all-purpose (plain) flour, plus extra as needed

Canola oil for greasing

IN A BOWL, sprinkle the yeast and sugar over the warm water and stir to dissolve. Let stand until foamy, about 10 minutes.

In a stand mixer fitted with the paddle attachment, combine the buttermilk, sugar, melted butter, eggs, salt, and 1 cup (5 oz/ 155 g) of the flour. Beat on medium-low speed until creamy, about 2 minutes. Add the yeast mixture and 1 cup of the flour, and beat for another minute. Beat in the remaining flour, ½ cup (2½ oz/75 g) at a time, until the dough pulls away from the bowl sides. Switch to the dough hook. Knead on low speed, adding flour 1 Tbsp at a time if the dough sticks, until a very soft dough forms, about 1 minute. The dough should be softer than typical bread dough, yet smooth and springy.

Transfer the dough to an oiled deep bowl and turn the dough once to coat it with the oil. Cover loosely with plastic wrap and let rise at room temperature until doubled in bulk, about 1½ hours.

Grease two 8-inch (20-cm) round cake pans. Turn the dough out onto a lightly floured work surface. Divide the dough in half and roll each half between your palms into a rope 18 inches (45 cm) long. Cut each rope into eighteen 1-inch (2.5-cm) pieces. Shape each piece into a ball, and place the balls, sides just touching, in the prepared pans. Cover loosely with plastic and let rise at room temperature until puffy, 30–45 minutes.

Preheat the oven to 375°F (190°C). Bake the rolls until light golden brown, 18–23 minutes. Let cool slightly in the pans or transfer to a rack. Serve warm.

SHAPING VARIATION

To make these rolls in the shape of knots, after the first rise, divide the dough into 3 portions. Roll each portion into a rope 10 inches (25 cm) long; cut each rope into 8 equal pieces. Roll each piece into a rope 7 inches (18 cm) long. Tie each rope loosely in a knot, leaving 2 long ends. Cover and let rise until puffy, 30–45 minutes, then place 1½ inches (4 cm) apart on a baking sheet lined with parchment (baking) paper. Bake as directed for 12–14 minutes. Makes 24 rolls.

Baguettes

MAKES 4 BAGUETTES

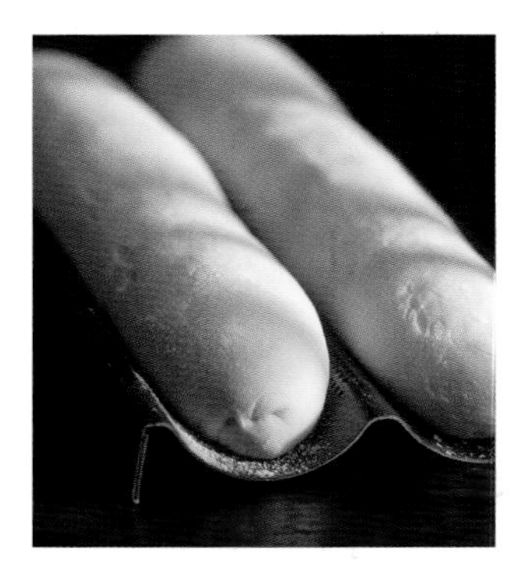

BAGUETTE PANS

You will need 2 dark metal baguette pans to make this recipe. The baguette pans each have 2 curved loaf cradles measuring 2⅜ inches (6 cm) across. The center ridge is perforated to allow for good heat circulation. These pans ensure that you will have perfect, crusty loaves every time you make this recipe.

2½ tsp (1 package) active dry yeast

2½ cups (20 fl oz/625 ml) tepid water (90°F/32°C)

5¾ cups (29 oz/910 g) all-purpose (plain) flour, plus extra for sprinkling

2½ tsp fine sea salt

1½ Tbsp vital wheat gluten (see Note)

Canola oil for greasing

Yellow cornmeal for sprinkling

IN THE BOWL OF A STAND MIXER fitted with the whisk attachment, sprinkle the yeast over the water. Add 2½ cups (12½ oz/390 g) of the flour and beat on medium speed until smooth, about 1 minute. Cover the bowl loosely with plastic wrap and let stand at room temperature until bubbly, 2–3 hours.

Fit the mixer with the dough hook. Sprinkle in the salt, 1½ cups (7½ oz/235 g) of the flour, and the gluten. Beat for 2 minutes on low speed, then increase the speed to medium. Beat in the remaining flour, ½ cup (2½ oz/75 g) at a time, until the dough is smooth, yet sticky enough not to pull away from the bowl sides, about 2 minutes. Knead for 8 minutes longer on low speed to form a moist dough ball. Do not add more flour.

Using a plastic dough scraper, scrape the mass of dough into an oiled deep bowl and turn the dough once to coat it with the oil. Cover loosely with plastic wrap and let rise at room temperature until tripled in bulk, 3–3½ hours. (Alternatively, you may cover the bowl with a double layer of plastic and refrigerate it overnight to let it rise slowly. The second rise, however, will take twice as long.)

Punch down the dough (see page 388), turn it to coat again with oil, cover loosely with plastic wrap, and let rise again until tripled, about 2½ hours.

Grease 2 baguette pans, each with 2 loaf cradles, 17¾ inches (45 cm) long by 5½ inches (14 cm) wide, and sprinkle with cornmeal. Use the plastic dough scraper to scrape the dough out onto a floured work surface. Knead a few times with the scraper to incorporate just enough flour (no more than ¼ cup/1½ oz/45 g) to be able to shape the loaves. Divide the dough into 4 equal portions.

Sprinkle the surface with more flour and shape each dough portion into a 12-by-6-inch (30-by-15-cm) rectangle. Beginning at a long side, roll up each rectangle, using your thumbs to help roll it tightly. Press each roll to flatten it slightly. With the side of your hand, define a depression lengthwise down the center of the dough log. Fold the dough over again lengthwise to make a tight log and pinch the long seam to seal. Stretch each log by using your palms to roll it back and forth on the board a few times until it is about 15 inches (38 cm) long and 2½ inches (6 cm) wide. Tuck the ends under. Quickly and gently transfer each log to a prepared pan, laying it, seam side down, in the cradle and adjusting the dough to fit into the pan. No dough should hang over the ends of the pan. Sprinkle the tops with flour. Cover loosely with plastic and let rise at room temperature until 2½ times its original size, about 1½ hours.

Place a baking stone on the center oven rack and preheat to 450°F (230°C). Using a thin, sharp knife, make 4 or 5 shallow diagonal slashes along the length of each loaf. This must be done gently, as the delicate dough will deflate slightly. Lightly brush the tops of the loaves with cold water. Place the pans on the stone and reduce the oven temperature to 400°F (200°C). Bake until the loaves are crusty and brown and sound hollow when tapped, 30–35 minutes. Transfer the loaves from the pans to wire racks to let cool slightly. Serve warm or at room temperature the same day they are baked.

NOTE: Vital wheat gluten, a substance naturally occurring in wheat, adds body and volume to yeast breads, especially those made with whole-grain flours. Sold in powdered and concentrated form, vital wheat gluten ensures a high-rising, light-textured loaf. The general rule is to add 1 tsp to 1 Tbsp of vital wheat gluten per cup (5 oz/155 g) of flour, depending on the flour's gluten content (bread flour needs less; heavier whole-wheat and nongluten flours need more). Vital wheat gluten is available in the baking section of well-stocked supermarkets and by mail order.

Ciabatta

MAKES 2 LARGE LOAVES

FOR THE STARTER:

1⅓ cups (11 fl oz/340 ml) water, at room temperature

2⅓ cups (12 oz/375 g) all-purpose (plain) or bread flour

¾ tsp active dry yeast

3 Tbsp warm water (105°–115°F/40°–46°C)

¾ cup (6 fl oz/180 ml) warm milk (105°–115°F/40°–46°C)

2 tsp active dry yeast

2–2⅓ cups (10–12 oz/315–375 g) bread flour, plus extra as needed

1½ tsp salt

2 Tbsp olive oil, plus extra for greasing

TO MAKE THE STARTER, in a stand mixer fitted with the paddle attachment, combine the water, 1 cup (5 oz/155 g) of the all-purpose flour, and the yeast. Mix on low speed for 1 minute. Add the remaining all-purpose flour and mix until smooth and soft, about 1 minute. Cover the bowl with plastic wrap and let sit at room temperature until almost tripled in bulk, 4–6 hours. The starter will smell yeasty. Refrigerate for 8–12 hours or for up to 3 days. When ready to make the dough, remove the starter from the refrigerator and let stand for 1–2 hours.

Fit the mixer with the paddle attachment. Add the warm water, milk, and yeast to the starter and mix on low speed until combined. Add 1½ cups (7½ oz/ 235 g) of the bread flour, the salt, and the oil. Mix on low speed, until smooth, about 3 minutes. Add only as much of the remaining bread flour as needed to form a soft, moist dough, and mix on low speed for 5 minutes, occasionally scraping the dough off the bowl sides. The finished dough should pull away from the sides of the bowl but stick to the bottom.

Cover the bowl with oiled plastic wrap and let rise at room temperature until doubled or tripled in bulk, about 2 hours.

Line a heavy baking sheet with aluminum foil and sprinkle generously with bread flour. Turn the dough out onto a lightly floured board, sprinkle lightly with flour, and pat with your fingers into a 14-by-5-inch (35-by-13-cm) rectangle. Fold the rectangle like a letter, overlapping the 2 short sides in the middle to make 3 layers. Turn the dough 90 degrees and repeat the sprinkling and folding, letting the dough rest for 10 minutes if too springy to fold. Cut the dough crosswise into 2 equal rectangles and place each half on the prepared sheet. Cover loosely with plastic wrap and let rest for 20 minutes.

Sprinkle the tops of the dough halves generously with flour. Holding your fingers in an open, splayed position, press and stretch each dough half, making an irregular rectangle about 11 inches (25 cm) long and 5 inches wide. Cover again loosely with plastic and let rest until tripled in bulk, about 1½ hours. Press the dough to accentuate the dimpling 2 more times during the rise. The loaves will remain flat.

Place a baking stone on the lower oven rack and preheat to 425°F (220°C). Sprinkle the tops of the loaves with flour and place the baking sheet on the stone. Bake until deep golden brown, 20–25 minutes. Let cool on the baking sheet. Serve warm or at room temperature.

BAKING STONES

Also known as pizza stones or baking tiles, baking stones are available in large rounds and rectangles. Made of high-fired unglazed clay stoneware, they retain and distribute heat evenly, for a more uniformly baked loaf and nicely browned crusts. To be effective, the stone must be preheated in the oven for at least 30 minutes before the bread is placed on it. Wipe the cooled stone clean after use; do not use soap and water.

Brown Sugar–Raisin Bread

MAKES TWO 9-BY-5-INCH (23-BY-13-CM) LOAVES

ABOUT BROWN SUGAR

Brown sugar is granulated sugar combined with molasses to make a rich and flavorful sweetener. Light, or golden, brown sugar contains a relatively small amount of molasses, giving baked goods a delicate flavor and light color. Dark brown sugar, which has more molasses, has a stronger flavor. To measure brown sugar, pack it into a measuring cup as firmly as possible. It should keep the shape of the cup when tapped out.

1 Tbsp active dry yeast

3 Tbsp granulated sugar

1¼ cups (10 fl oz/310 ml) warm water (105°–115°F/40°–46°C)

1 cup (8 fl oz/250 ml) warm milk (105°–115°F/40°–46°C)

3 Tbsp unsalted butter, melted, plus extra for greasing

1 Tbsp salt

1 large egg, lightly beaten

6–6¼ cups (30–31 oz/940–970 g) bread flour, plus extra as needed

¾ cup (4½ oz/140 g) golden raisins (sultanas)

¾ cup (4½ oz/140 g) dark raisins

FOR THE FILLING:

⅔ cup (5 oz/155 g) firmly packed light brown sugar mixed with 4½ tsp ground cinnamon

IN A BOWL, sprinkle the yeast and a pinch of the granulated sugar over ½ cup (4 fl oz/125 ml) of the water and stir to dissolve. Let stand until foamy, about 10 minutes.

In a stand mixer fitted with the paddle attachment, combine the remaining water, the milk, melted butter, remaining granulated sugar, salt, egg, and 2 cups (10 oz/315 g) of the flour. Beat on medium speed until creamy, about 1 minute. Add the yeast mixture and ½ cup (2½ oz/75 g) of the flour and beat for 1 minute. Add the raisins, then beat in the remaining flour, ½ cup at a time, until the dough pulls away from the bowl sides. Switch to the dough hook. Knead on medium-low speed, adding flour 1 Tbsp at a time if the dough sticks, until smooth and elastic, about 4 minutes.

Transfer the dough to a greased deep bowl and turn to coat it with the oil. Cover loosely with plastic wrap and let rise at room temperature until doubled in bulk, 1–1½ hours.

Lightly grease the bottom and sides of two 9-by-5-inch (23-by-13-cm) loaf pans. Turn the dough out onto a lightly floured work surface. Divide the dough in half and roll or pat each half into an 8-by-12-inch (20-by-30-cm) rectangle. Lightly sprinkle each rectangle with half of the filling, leaving a 1-inch (2.5-cm) border on all sides. Beginning at a narrow end, tightly roll up each rectangle into a compact log. Pinch the ends and the long seam to seal in the filling. Place each log, seam side down, in a prepared pan. Cover loosely with plastic wrap and let rise at room temperature until about 1 inch (2.5 cm) above the rim of each pan, 1–1½ hours.

Preheat the oven to 350°F (180°C). Bake until the loaves are golden brown and pull away from the pan sides, 35–40 minutes. Turn out onto racks and let cool completely.

Whole-Wheat Bread

MAKES TWO 9-BY-5-INCH (23-BY-13-CM) LOAVES

SHAPING THE LOAF

Place the dough on a floured board and pat into a long, even rectangle. Fold a short side over to cover about two-thirds of the rectangle. Fold the other short side to overlap the first side, much like folding a letter. Flatten the dough with your hands. Beginning at a short end, tightly roll up the dough. Using your palms, roll the dough log back and forth until it is the length of the pan. Pinch together the center seam and the spiral seams on both ends to seal the loaf.

1½ Tbsp active dry yeast

Pinch of brown sugar

1 cup (8 fl oz/250 ml) warm water (105°–115°F/40°–46°C)

1½ cups (12 fl oz/375 ml) tepid buttermilk (90°F/32°C)

¼ cup (2½ oz/75 g) maple syrup

¼ cup (2 fl oz/60 ml) canola oil, plus extra for greasing

1 Tbsp salt

3 cups (15 oz/470 g) whole-wheat (wholemeal) flour

3½–4 cups (17½–20 oz/545–625 g) bread flour, plus extra as needed

IN A BOWL, sprinkle the yeast and brown sugar over the water and stir to dissolve. Let stand until foamy, about 10 minutes.

In a stand mixer fitted with the paddle attachment, combine the buttermilk, maple syrup, oil, salt, and 2 cups (10 oz/315 g) of the whole-wheat flour. Beat on medium-low speed until creamy, about 1 minute. Beat in the yeast mixture and the remaining whole-wheat flour and beat for 1 minute. Beat in the bread flour, ½ cup (2½ oz/75 g) at a time, until the dough pulls away from the bowl sides. Switch to the dough hook. Knead on low speed, adding bread flour 1 Tbsp at a time if the dough sticks, until smooth but slightly sticky when pressed, about 5 minutes. Transfer the dough to an oiled deep bowl and turn the dough once to coat it with oil. Cover loosely with plastic wrap and let rise at room temperature until doubled in bulk, 1–1½ hours.

Lightly grease two 9-by-5-inch (23-by-13-cm) loaf pans and form the loaves (left). Place the loaves, seam side down, in the pans. Cover loosely with plastic wrap and let rise until about 1 inch (2.5 cm) above the pan rims, about 1 hour.

Preheat the oven to 350°F (180°C). Bake until the loaves are golden brown and pull away from the pan sides, 35–40 minutes. Turn out onto racks and let cool completely.

Sourdough Bread

MAKES 3 SMALL ROUND LOAVES

1½ cups (12 fl oz/375 ml) lukewarm water (100°F/38°C)

4 tsp active dry yeast

1 cup (8 oz/250 g) Classic Sourdough Starter or Easy Sourdough Starter (page 379)

1 Tbsp honey

6 cups (30 oz/940 g) bread flour, plus extra as needed

1 Tbsp unsalted butter, melted, plus extra for brushing

2 large eggs

2½ tsp salt

2 Tbsp yellow cornmeal mixed with 2 Tbsp bread flour

IN A STAND MIXER fitted with the whisk attachment, combine the water, yeast, sourdough starter, and honey. Beat on low speed just until smooth, about 1 minute. Cover the bowl with plastic wrap and let the starter mixture stand at room temperature until doubled in bulk, about 1 hour. Switch to the paddle attachment and stir the mixture together on low speed. Add 3 cups (15 oz/470 g) of the flour, the butter, eggs, and salt. Beat on medium-low speed until smooth, about 1 minute. Add 2 more cups (10 oz/315 g) of the flour and beat for 2 minutes. Switch to the dough hook. Beating on low speed, add the remaining bread flour, ½ cup (2½ oz/75 g) at a time, until a very soft dough forms that pulls away from the bowl sides. Knead on low speed, adding flour 1 Tbsp at a time if the dough sticks, until smooth, springy, and moist, about 6 minutes. Scrape down the sides of the bowl.

Brush the bowl with a thin film of melted butter and turn the dough to coat it with butter. Cover loosely with plastic wrap and let rise at room temperature until slightly more than doubled in bulk, 1½–2 hours.

Line a baking sheet with parchment (baking) paper and sprinkle with the cornmeal mixture. Turn the dough out onto a lightly floured work surface. Divide the dough into 3 equal portions and shape each into a tight, round loaf. Place the loaves, seam side down and at least 4 inches (10 cm) apart, on the prepared sheet. Sprinkle the tops with flour and rub in. Cover loosely with a double layer of plastic wrap and let rise in the refrigerator for 8–12 hours.

Place a baking stone on the bottom oven rack and preheat to 450°F (230°C). Using a thin, sharp knife, make 3 gentle slashes across the top of each loaf. Place the pan on the stone and bake for about 10 minutes, then reduce the heat to 400°F (200°C) and bake until the loaves are golden brown, 20–25 minutes longer. Let cool completely on racks before slicing and serving.

ABOUT SOURDOUGH

Using a sourdough starter is an ancient method of beginning to make a leavened bread. The starter consists of small amounts of some of the basic bread ingredients such as flour, water, milk, and, in this recipe, yogurt. This mixture is left out to attract wild yeasts from the air. The yeasts feed on the starch in the flour, resulting in the fermentation and souring of the mixture and creating a base to which additional ingredients can be added to make a dough. The starter may be left to develop for many days, depending on the desired degree of sourness.

Potato Focaccia with Olives & Figs

MAKES 1 LARGE FOCACCIA

POTATO VARIETIES

Russet potatoes, which are high in starch, are best reserved for making French fries, mashing, or baking, as in this recipe. Yukon gold potatoes have a buttery taste and firm texture that holds up well to boiling or layering in casseroles. Classified as all-purpose potatoes, they are lower in starch than russets. Other lower-starch, or waxy, potatoes that would substitute well are red or white potatoes.

3 cups (24 fl oz/750 ml) water

1 large russet potato, about 10 oz (315 g), peeled and cut into ½-inch (12-mm) cubes

1 Tbsp honey

2½ tsp (1 package) active dry yeast

2 Tbsp extra-virgin olive oil, plus extra for drizzling (optional)

Kosher salt

About 3¾ cups (19 oz/590 g) all-purpose (plain) flour

¼ lb (125 g) Kalamata olives, pitted and coarsely chopped (about ¾ cup)

¼ lb (125 g) dried Calimyrna figs, stemmed and coarsely chopped (about ¾ cup)

2 Tbsp whole coriander seeds, toasted (see Note)

IN A SMALL, HEAVY SAUCEPAN, bring the water to a boil over high heat. Add the potato and cook until tender, about 12 minutes. Using a slotted spoon, transfer the potato to a shallow bowl, reserving the potato-cooking water. Pour 1 cup (8 fl oz/250 ml) of the potato water into a food processor and add the honey. Let stand just until warm (115°F/46°C), about 20 minutes. Discard the remaining potato water. Sprinkle the yeast over the water in the processor. Let stand until foamy, about 8 minutes.

Mash the potato with a potato masher and measure out ⅔ cup (5 oz/155 g). Add the measured mashed potato, 1 Tbsp of the olive oil, and 1½ tsp kosher salt to the food processor. Process until blended, about 5 seconds. Add 3 cups (15 oz/470 g) of the flour and process until moist clumps form. Add the olives and figs and pulse 6 times. Stir the dough with a spatula to help distribute the olives and figs and pulse 6 more times.

Sprinkle ¼ cup (1½ oz/45 g) of the flour on a work surface. Turn the dough out onto the surface and turn to coat with the flour. Knead gently until smooth, adding more flour as needed, about 3 minutes. Shape into a ball, cover, and let rest for 30 minutes.

Sprinkle a heavy 18-by-12-inch (45-by-30-cm) baking sheet with 3 Tbsp flour. Transfer the dough to the prepared sheet. Press and stretch the dough until almost the size of the sheet and brush with the remaining 1 Tbsp oil. Press the dough all over with your fingertips to dimple it. Sprinkle with the coriander seeds and ¾ tsp kosher salt. Cover loosely with a kitchen towel and let rise until light and puffy, about 1 hour.

Preheat the oven to 400°F (200°C). Bake until browned, about 20 minutes. Transfer to a rack and let cool for 15 minutes. Drizzle with olive oil if desired and serve warm or at room temperature.

NOTE: To toast coriander or other seeds, place in a dry frying pan over medium-low heat, and toast, stirring frequently, until fragrant and beginning to color, 2–5 minutes. Immediately transfer to a plate to cool.

Poppy-Seed Cloverleaf Rolls

MAKES 12 ROLLS

1 cup (8 fl oz/250 ml) milk

2 Tbsp unsalted butter, plus extra for greasing

1 Tbsp sugar

2½ tsp (1 package) active dry yeast

¾ tsp salt

2¾ cups (14 oz/440 g) all-purpose (plain) flour, plus extra as needed

1 tsp corn oil

1 egg, well beaten

1¼ tsp poppy seeds

IN A SMALL SAUCEPAN, combine the milk, the 2 Tbsp butter, and the sugar. Warm over low heat just until the butter melts. Transfer to a bowl and let cool to 105°–115°F (40°–46°C). Sprinkle the yeast over the milk mixture. Whisk in the yeast and let stand until foamy, about 5 minutes. Whisk again and then stir in the salt and the flour, ½ cup (2½ oz/75 g) at a time, until a soft, sticky dough forms.

Turn the dough out onto a well-floured work surface and knead it, adding flour 1 Tbsp at a time as necessary, until it is smooth, elastic, and no longer sticky, about 5 minutes. Coat a bowl with the oil, add the dough, turn to coat it with the oil, and cover with plastic wrap or a damp kitchen towel. Let the dough rise in a warm place until doubled in bulk, about 1½ hours.

Generously grease 12 standard muffin cups. Turn the dough out onto a floured work surface and flatten it into a round. Divide the round into 12 equal portions. Divide each portion into thirds. Shape the pieces into balls and place 3 balls in each cup of the prepared pan. Cover with a kitchen towel and let rise in a warm place until doubled in bulk, about 1 hour.

Preheat the oven to 375°F (190°C). Brush the tops of the rolls with the egg. Sprinkle the poppy seeds over the rolls, dividing them evenly. Bake until the rolls are puffed and golden and the bottoms and sides are crisp, about 15 minutes. Remove from the pan right away. Serve hot or warm.

MAKE-AHEAD TIP: The rolls can be baked 1 day in advance. Let cool completely, then wrap them airtight and store at room temperature. Wrap tightly in aluminum foil and rewarm in a 350°F (180°C) oven for 15 minutes.

PROOFING YEAST

Yeast is proofed, or tested, by letting the granules stand in warm water for 5 minutes, until they turn foamy. Yeast was not always as reliable as it is now, and proofing was an essential step that saved the cook from rolls or loaves that failed to rise. Now, yeast is more consistent, but because it gradually weakens the longer it sits on a pantry shelf, it's a good idea to be sure that yeast is alive and active, and to give it a head start, before it is incorporated into the flour.

Classic Cinnamon Rolls

MAKES 14 ROLLS

ABOUT CINNAMON

This spice was once rare and valuable—the main reason for the Portuguese occupation of Ceylon (now Sri Lanka) in 1505 was for its superior and extensive cinnamon crop. The dried bark of a tree, cinnamon comes from two sources. The commonly available cassia cinnamon is a dark red-brown color and has a strong, sweet taste. Pale tan, delicate-tasting Ceylon cinnamon is grown only in Sri Lanka and is considered by many to be true cinnamon. To grind your own, first break or crush the stick into pieces.

¼ cup (2 fl oz/60 ml) warm water (110°–115°F/43°–46°C)

½ cup (4 oz/125 g) plus 1 tsp granulated sugar

2½ tsp (1 package) active dry yeast

1 Tbsp unsalted butter, at room temperature

3½–4 cups (17½–20 oz/545–625 g) all-purpose (plain) flour

½ tsp fine sea salt

2 large egg yolks

1 cup (8 fl oz/250 ml) warm whole milk (110°–115°F/43°–46°C)

1½ cups (10½ oz/330 g) firmly packed light brown sugar

6 Tbsp (3 oz/90 g) unsalted butter, melted

½ cup (5 oz/155 g) light corn syrup

2 tsp ground cinnamon

½ cup (3 oz/90 g) raisins, soaked in warm water for 15 minutes, drained, and squeezed dry

IN A BOWL, combine the warm water and 1 tsp granulated sugar. Sprinkle with the yeast and let stand for 2 minutes, then swirl and let stand until foamy, about 5 minutes.

Spread the butter over the bottom and halfway up the sides of a large bowl. In another large bowl, combine 3½ cups (17½ oz/545 g) of the flour, the ½ cup (4 oz/125 g) granulated sugar, and the salt. Make a well in the center and pour in the yeast mixture, egg yolks, and warm milk. Slowly mix together until the dough can be formed into a large ball. Transfer the dough to a floured work surface. Knead, sprinkling with the remaining flour as needed to keep the dough from sticking, until smooth and elastic, about 10 minutes.

Gather the dough into a ball, place in the buttered bowl, and turn to coat all sides with butter. Cover with a kitchen towel. Set in a warm, draft-free place and let rise until doubled in size, about 1½ hours.

In a bowl, mix ¾ cup (6 oz/185 g) of the brown sugar, 2 Tbsp of the melted butter, and the corn syrup to a smooth paste. Scoop half into each of two 9-inch (23-cm) round cake pans and spread over the bottoms. In a small bowl, mix together the remaining brown sugar and the cinnamon.

Punch down the dough (see page 388). Turn the dough out onto a lightly floured work surface and roll into a 10-by-18-inch (25-by-45-cm) rectangle. Brush with 2 Tbsp of the melted butter. Scatter with the raisins, pressing them in lightly. Sprinkle the dough with the cinnamon-sugar mixture. Starting at one long edge, roll the dough tightly into a cylinder. Cut off and discard the rough ends. Cut the cylinder crosswise into 14 rounds. Place 1 round in the center of each pan. Arrange the remaining rounds around it. Cover and let the dough rounds rise until doubled, 45–60 minutes.

Preheat the oven to 350°F (180°C). Brush the rolls with the remaining melted butter. Bake until golden brown, about 30 minutes. Place a wire rack over each pan and invert the rolls. Let cool and break apart to serve.

Panettone

MAKES 2 ROUND LOAVES

PANETTONE ORIGINS

A sweet, egg-yellow yeast bread, panettone is a specialty of Milan, Italy, where it has been a traditional holiday bread for centuries. There, family cookbooks always contain a recipe for panettone that has been handed down from generation to generation. Liberally dotted with raisins and candied fruits, the bread is baked in a tall cylindrical mold and is served at Christmas. The literal translation of *panettone* is "big bread," a reference to its quality—an enriched loaf—not to its high domed crown.

FOR THE SPONGE:

¼ cup (2 fl oz/60 ml) warm water (105°–115°F/40°–46°C)

⅔ cup (5 fl oz/160 ml) warm whole milk (105°–115°F/40°–46°C)

4 tsp active dry yeast

Pinch of granulated sugar

½ cup (2½ oz/75 g) bread flour

FOR THE DOUGH:

¾ cup (6 oz/185 g) unsalted butter, melted, plus extra for greasing

½ cup (4 oz/125 g) granulated sugar

Grated zest of 1 orange or lemon

1½ tsp salt

2 large eggs, plus 3 large egg yolks

3½–4 cups (17½–20 oz/545–625 g) bread flour, plus extra as needed

1 cup (6 oz/185 g) golden raisins (sultanas)

Double recipe Candied Citrus Zest (page 378), diced

2 Tbsp raw or coarse sugar

TO MAKE THE SPONGE, combine the water and milk in a stand mixer fitted with the whisk attachment. Sprinkle the yeast and granulated sugar over the liquid and stir to dissolve. Let stand until foamy, about 10 minutes. Add the flour and beat on medium speed until smooth. Cover loosely with plastic wrap and let stand at room temperature for 30 minutes.

Add the melted butter, granulated sugar, zest, salt, eggs, egg yolks, and 1 cup (5 oz/155 g) of the flour to the sponge and switch to the paddle attachment. Beat on medium speed for 1 minute. Beat in the remaining flour, ½ cup (2½ oz/75 g) at a time, until the dough pulls away from the bowl sides. Switch to the dough hook. Knead on low speed, adding flour 1 Tbsp at a time if the dough sticks, until the dough is soft, smooth, and springy, about 5 minutes. Brush a deep bowl with a thin film of melted butter. Transfer the dough to the bowl and turn the dough once to coat it with butter. Cover loosely with plastic wrap and let rise at room temperature until doubled in bulk, 1½–2 hours.

Turn the dough out onto a lightly floured work surface and knead gently for a minute. Return to the bowl, re-cover, and let the dough rise again at room temperature until doubled in bulk, about 1 hour.

Line 2 round cake pans or springform pans, 6 inches (15 cm) in diameter and 3 inches (7.5 cm) deep, with parchment (baking) paper. Brush the paper and the sides with butter. Cut a strip of aluminum foil about 8 inches (20 cm) wide and 2 inches (5 cm) longer than the circumference of the pan. Fold the foil in half lengthwise, and butter one side of the strip. Using kitchen string, tie the strip of buttered aluminum foil, buttered side facing in, around the outside of each pan, making a collar that extends 2–3 inches (5–7.5 cm) above the rim of the pan.

Turn the dough out onto a lightly floured work surface. In a small bowl, stir together the raisins and candied lemon and orange zest. Pat the dough into a large oval and sprinkle evenly with half of the fruit mixture. Press into the dough to adhere and roll the dough up. Pat again into an oval, sprinkle evenly with the remaining fruit, and press to adhere. Roll the dough up again. Knead a few times to smooth out the

Divide the dough into 2 equal portions and shape into 2 tight round loaves, gently pulling the surface taut from the bottom. Place each dough ball in a prepared pan. Cover loosely with plastic wrap and let rise at room temperature until the dough domes up to the rim of the foil collar, about 1½ hours.

Place a baking stone on the center oven rack and preheat the oven to 400°F (200°C). Sprinkle the top of each loaf with half of the raw sugar. Place the pans on the stone and bake for 10 minutes. Reduce the oven temperature to 350°F (180°C) and bake until the loaves are golden brown and a cake tester inserted into the center of each loaf comes out clean, 25–30 minutes longer. Let the breads cool in the pans for 5 minutes, then remove the foil collars. Gently turn the breads out onto wire racks. Turn right side up and let cool completely.

NOTE: Panettone is traditionally made as a tall columnar loaf. In lieu of the cake pans with collar extensions, you can use two 5-inch (13-cm) diameter and 5½-inch (14-cm) deep tinned-steel charlotte molds with collars, or simply shape the loaves into rounds and bake them on a baking sheet lined with parchment (baking) paper.

Swedish Rye Bread

MAKES TWO 8½-BY-4½-INCH (21.5-BY-11.5-CM) LOAVES

FOR THE SPONGE:

2 cups (16 fl oz/500 ml) lukewarm water (100°F/38°C)

1 Tbsp active dry yeast

1½ cups (6 oz/185 g) medium-grind rye flour (right)

¼ cup (2¾ oz/80 g) unsulfured light molasses

3 Tbsp firmly packed dark brown sugar

1½ tsp fennel seeds, crushed

FOR THE DOUGH:

1½ Tbsp canola oil, plus extra for greasing

2 tsp salt

3½–4 cups (17½–20 oz/545–625 g) bread flour, plus extra as needed

Rye flour or brown rice flour for dusting

TO MAKE THE SPONGE, combine the water and yeast in a stand mixer fitted with the whisk attachment. Stir to dissolve. Add the rye flour, molasses, brown sugar, and fennel seeds. Beat on medium speed until smooth, about 1 minute. Cover loosely with plastic wrap and let stand until bubbly, about 1 hour.

To make the dough, add the oil, salt, and 1 cup (5 oz/155 g) of the bread flour to the sponge and switch to the paddle attachment. Beat on medium speed for 1 minute. Beat in the remaining bread flour, ½ cup (2½ oz/75 g) at a time, until the dough pulls away from the bowl. Switch to the dough hook. Knead on low speed, adding bread flour 1 Tbsp at a time if the dough sticks, until smooth and elastic but slightly tacky, about 5 minutes.

Transfer to an oiled deep bowl and turn to coat it with oil. Cover loosely with plastic wrap and let rise at room temperature until doubled in bulk, 1½–2 hours.

Lightly grease two 8½-by-4½-inch (21.5-by-11.5-cm) loaf pans. Turn the dough out onto a lightly floured work surface and divide into 2 equal portions. Knead lightly a few times, then pat each portion into a long rectangle. Fold each rectangle like a letter, overlapping the short sides in the middle; press to flatten. Beginning at a narrow end, tightly roll up the dough into a thick log, then roll back and forth with your palms until it is the same length as the pan. Pinch the ends and the long seam to seal, dust lightly all over with a little rye flour, and place in the pans, tucking the ends under to make a neat, snug fit. Cover loosely with plastic wrap and let rise at room temperature until about 1 inch (2.5 cm) above each pan rim, about 1 hour.

Preheat the oven to 350°F (180°C). Using a thin, sharp knife, gently make 3 shallow diagonal slashes across the top of each loaf. Bake until the loaves are golden brown and crusty, 50–55 minutes. Turn out onto wire racks and let cool completely.

RYE FLOUR

Whole-grain rye is made by grinding rye berries into a variety of textures and colors, categorized according to the amount of bran and germ left in after milling. These grinds include light, medium, and dark flours and pumpernickel rye, which is a coarse meal rather than a flour. The coarser the flour grind, the more robust the flavor, the darker the color, and the denser your bread. The rye flour most commonly available in stores is medium-grind, good for general bread making when combined with wheat flour.

Pita Bread

MAKES TEN 6-INCH (15-CM) FLATBREADS

ABOUT FLATBREADS

The most basic of all breads are flatbreads, typically patted out by hand and baked on a grill over an open fire. Every culture that makes bread has some type of flatbread in its repertoire. The Middle Eastern pita, also known as pocket bread, the nan from Central and South Asia, the Mexican tortilla, the Indian *chapati*, and the Scandinavian *rieska* are all part of the flatbread tradition. Pita differs from some of the others by puffing dramatically during baking, making a nice hollow to be filled. Alternatively, the pita round can be cut or torn into wedges for scooping up food like a spoon.

1 Tbsp active dry yeast

Pinch of sugar

1½ cups (12 fl oz/375 ml) warm water (105°–115°F/40°–46°C)

2 Tbsp olive oil, plus extra for greasing

1½ tsp salt

3½–4 cups (17½–20 oz/545–625 g) all-purpose (plain) flour, plus extra as needed

IN A BOWL, sprinkle the yeast and sugar over ½ cup (4 fl oz/125 ml) of the water. Stir gently to dissolve and let stand at room temperature until foamy, about 10 minutes.

In a stand mixer fitted with the paddle attachment, combine the remaining water, the oil, salt, and 1 cup (5 oz/155 g) of the flour. Beat on medium speed until creamy, about 1 minute. Stir in the yeast mixture. Beat in the remaining flour, ½ cup (2½ oz/75 g) at a time, until the dough pulls away from the bowl sides. Switch to the dough hook. Knead on low speed, adding flour 1 Tbsp at a time if the dough sticks, until stiff and sticky, about 3 minutes.

Transfer the dough to an oiled deep bowl and turn once to coat it with oil. Cover loosely with plastic wrap and let the dough rise at room temperature until doubled in bulk, 1–1½ hours.

Place a baking stone on the bottom oven rack and preheat to 450°F (230°C). Turn the dough out onto a lightly floured work surface and divide it in half. Cover half with plastic wrap. Divide the remaining half into 5 equal pieces and form each piece into a ball. Let rest for 10 minutes while dividing the other dough half. Roll out the balls into rounds about 6 inches (15 cm) in diameter and ¼ inch (6 mm) thick. If the dough does not roll out easily, let it rest, covered, for 10 minutes. Drape each round over a flour-dusted rolling pin and transfer it to a floured kitchen towel. Cover with another towel and let rest until puffy, about 15 minutes.

Preheat a baking sheet in the oven for 6 minutes. Quickly brush the sheet with oil. Transfer 3 or 4 dough rounds to the hot sheet and place it on the baking stone. Do not open the oven door for 3 minutes. Bake until puffed and light brown, 6–7 minutes. Stack the pitas on a plate and cover with a kitchen towel. Bake the remaining pitas, then serve warm.

Onion Focaccia

MAKES 1 LARGE OVAL FOCACCIA

1 Tbsp active dry yeast

1 Tbsp sugar

1½ cups (12 fl oz/375 ml) warm water (105°–115°F/40°–46°C)

½ cup (4 fl oz/125 ml) olive oil

1½ tsp table salt

4–4¼ cups (20–21½ oz/625–670 g) bread flour, plus extra as needed

½ cup (2 oz/60 g) chopped yellow onion

Coarse sea salt for sprinkling

IN A STAND MIXER fitted with the paddle attachment, sprinkle the yeast and a pinch of the sugar over ½ cup (4 fl oz/125 ml) of the water and stir to dissolve. Let stand until foamy, about 10 minutes. Add the remaining water and sugar, ¼ cup (2 fl oz/60 ml) of the olive oil, the table salt, and 1 cup (5 oz/155 g) of the flour. Beat on medium speed for about 1 minute. Add 1 cup of the flour and beat on medium-low speed for 2 minutes. Stir in the onion. Switch to the dough hook. On low speed, beat in the remaining flour, ½ cup (2½ oz/75 g) at a time, until a shaggy dough forms. Knead on low speed, adding flour 1 Tbsp at a time if the dough sticks, until soft and slightly sticky, about 6 minutes. Cover loosely with plastic wrap and let rest for 20 minutes.

Line a heavy rimmed baking sheet with parchment (baking) paper and brush lightly with oil. Turn the dough out onto the prepared sheet. With oiled fingers, press and flatten the dough into an oval 1 inch (2.5 cm) thick. Cover loosely with oiled plastic wrap and let rise at room temperature until doubled in bulk, about 1 hour.

With your fingertips, make deep indentations 1 inch (2.5 cm) apart all over the surface of the dough. Drizzle with the remaining olive oil. Cover loosely with plastic and let rise at room temperature for 30 minutes. Place a baking stone on the bottom oven rack and preheat to 425°F (220°C). Sprinkle the bread lightly with the salt. Slide the pan onto the stone and bake until the bread is lightly browned, 20–25 minutes. Check the bottom and bake for 2–3 minutes longer if it is pale. Serve warm or at room temperature.

FOCACCIA VARIATIONS

To make herb focaccia, sprinkle 1½ Tbsp finely chopped fresh rosemary, oregano, sage, or basil over the dough before topping with oil and salt. For olive and sun-dried tomato focaccia, sprinkle ½ cup (2½ oz/75 g) pitted black olives and ¼ cup (2 oz/60 g) chopped oil-packed sun-dried tomatoes over the dough before topping with oil and salt. For cheese focaccia, sprinkle 1 cup (4 oz/125 g) grated Parmesan over the dough after drizzling with oil. Omit the salt.

Old-Fashioned White Bread

MAKES TWO 9-BY-5-INCH (23-BY-13-CM) LOAVES

¼ cup (2 fl oz/60 ml) warm water (105°–115°F/40°–46°C)

2 cups (16 fl oz/500 ml) warm whole milk (105°–115°F/40°–46°C)

4 tsp active dry yeast

2 Tbsp sugar or honey plus 1 pinch of sugar

2 Tbsp unsalted butter, melted

1 Tbsp salt

6–6¼ cups (30–31½ oz/940–985 g) bread flour, plus extra as needed

Canola oil for greasing

IN A BOWL, combine the water and ¼ cup (2 fl oz/60 ml) of the milk. Sprinkle the yeast and the pinch of sugar over the liquid and stir to dissolve. Let stand until foamy, about 10 minutes.

In a stand mixer fitted with the paddle attachment, combine the remaining milk, the butter, the 2 Tbsp sugar, salt, and 2 cups (10 oz/315 g) of the flour. Beat on medium-low speed just until creamy, about 1 minute. Add the yeast mixture and 1 cup (5 oz/155 g) of the flour and beat for 1 minute. Beat in the remaining flour, ½ cup (2½ oz/75 g) at a time, until the dough pulls away from the bowl sides. Switch to the dough hook. Knead on low speed, adding flour 1 Tbsp at a time if the dough sticks, until smooth and elastic, about 5 minutes.

Transfer the dough to an oiled deep bowl and turn the dough once to coat it with oil. Cover loosely with plastic wrap and let rise at room temperature until doubled in bulk, about 1½ hours.

Lightly grease two 9-by-5-inch (23-by-13-cm) loaf pans. Turn the dough out onto a lightly floured work surface. Divide in half and pat each half into a long rectangle. Fold 1 rectangle like a letter, overlapping the short sides in the middle; press to flatten. Beginning at a narrow end, tightly roll up the dough into a thick log. Roll the log back and forth with your palms until it is the same length as the pan. Pinch the ends and the long seam to seal. Place the loaf, seam side down, in a prepared pan, tucking the ends under to make a neat, snug fit. Repeat with the second portion. Cover the dough loosely with plastic wrap and let rise until about 1 inch (2.5 cm) above the rim of each pan, about 1 hour.

Preheat the oven to 375°F (190°C). Bake until the loaves are golden brown and pull away from the pan sides, about 40 minutes. Turn out onto racks and let cool completely.

RISING DOUGH

Most bread recipes call for two risings. Although a time frame is given for each one, it cannot be precise, for how long any rising takes depends on a variety of factors such as the temperature of the room, the amount of yeast used, and even the weather. To test if a dough has risen adequately for the first rising, press 2 fingers into it. If the indentations remain, the dough is ready to be shaped and left to rise a second time. To test its readiness after the second rising, press against it with a fingertip. If an imprint remains and the dough holds its shape, it is time to bake.

Grissini

MAKES 32 GRISSINI

ABOUT GRISSINI

Grissini is the Italian word for "breadsticks," long, thin dough strips that are baked until crisp all the way through. They are shaped by hand, either by rolling or by stretching out a thin piece of dough to a desired length. Expect some irregularities: handmade *grissini* look very different from their uniform machine-made counterparts. Store in an airtight container for up to 3 days.

2½ tsp (1 package) active dry yeast

½ tsp sugar

1½ cups (12 fl oz/375 ml) warm water (105°–115°F/40°–46°C)

3 Tbsp olive oil, plus extra for greasing

1½ tsp salt

1½ tsp dried rosemary

½ cup (2½ oz/75 g) semolina flour, plus extra for sprinkling

3–3½ cups (15–17½ oz/470–545 g) all-purpose (plain) flour, plus extra as needed

IN A SMALL BOWL, sprinkle the yeast and sugar over ½ cup (4 fl oz/ 125 ml) of the water and stir to dissolve. Let stand until foamy, about 10 minutes.

In a stand mixer fitted with the paddle attachment, combine the remaining water, the oil, salt, rosemary, semolina flour, and 1 cup (5 oz/155 g) of the all-purpose flour. Beat on medium speed until creamy, about 1 minute. Add the yeast mixture and 1 cup (5 oz/155 g) of the all-purpose flour and beat for another minute. Beat in the remaining all-purpose flour, ½ cup (2½ oz/75 g) at a time, until the dough pulls away from the bowl sides. Switch to the dough hook. Knead on low speed, adding all-purpose flour 1 Tbsp at a time if the dough sticks, until smooth and elastic, about 4 minutes.

Sprinkle a work surface with semolina flour. Pat the dough into a 14-by-8-inch (35-by-20-cm) rectangle. Brush the surface with oil. Cover loosely with plastic wrap and let rise on the work surface at room temperature until doubled in bulk, 1–1½ hours.

Place a baking stone on the center oven rack and preheat to 375°F (190°C). Line three 15-by-12-inch (38-by-30-cm) baking sheets with parchment (baking) paper and brush the paper with oil. Rub the surface of the dough with 2–3 Tbsp of semolina flour. With a sharp knife, cut the dough crosswise into 4 equal portions. One at a time, cut each portion lengthwise into 8 strips. Pick up the end of each strip and stretch and roll to the width of a prepared sheet. Place the strips ½ inch (12 mm) apart on the sheets.

One at a time, place the sheets on the stone and bake until the breadsticks are lightly browned and crisp, 16–22 minutes. Transfer to wire racks to cool completely.

Brioche

MAKES 6 BRIOCHES

1 cup (8 oz/250 g) unsalted butter

1½ Tbsp warm whole milk (110°–115°F/ 43°–46°C), or more as needed

1 tsp active dry yeast

3 tsp sugar

3 large eggs, lightly beaten

1¾ cups (9 oz/280 g) all-purpose (plain) flour, plus extra for dusting

1 tsp fine sea salt

FOR THE GLAZE:

1 large egg

2 Tbsp whole milk

CUT THE BUTTER into 24 small cubes and place on a plate in the freezer for 20 minutes.

Place the warm milk in a large measuring cup, sprinkle the yeast and 1 tsp of the sugar over the top, and let stand for 2 minutes. Swirl to combine and let stand until foamy, about 5 minutes longer. Whisk the eggs into the yeast mixture.

In a large food processor, preferably fitted with the plastic dough blade, combine the flour, salt, and remaining 2 tsp sugar. Add the butter and pulse 15–20 times to break the butter up into flour-covered "pebbles." With the machine running, add the liquid ingredients through the feed tube and keep processing until the dough comes together into a rough mass, about 15 seconds. Add milk a few drops at a time until the dough is wet enough to form a soft, slightly sticky mass. The dough will resemble a paste. Let the dough stand in the processor for 5 minutes, then process for 30 seconds longer. Using a plastic dough scraper, scrape the dough out onto a lightly floured work surface and let rest for 2 minutes. Using the dough scraper, knead the dough 25 times, then transfer to a lightly oiled bowl. Cover with plastic wrap and refrigerate overnight.

Thoroughly grease and flour 6 fluted brioche molds 3–4 inches (7.5–10 cm) in diameter. Remove the dough from the refrigerator and shape right away: With floured hands and on a floured work surface, divide the dough into 6 equal pieces. Shape each into a ball. Working with 1 ball at a time, use the side of your hand to pinch apart about one-third of the dough without going all the way through. Roll back and forth against the "neck" of the dough to create a small "head." Place the dough piece, head side up, into a prepared mold. Press the base of the neck down into the larger ball in 2 or 3 places to anchor it. Repeat to shape the remaining brioches.

Place the filled molds on a baking sheet and cover loosely with a tent of aluminum foil; do not let the foil touch the dough. Let rise again for about 1 hour. The dough will increase in size slightly but will not double.

Preheat the oven to 375°F (190°C) and place 2 racks in the lowest 2 oven positions. Five minutes before you put the brioches into the oven, place a small roasting pan containing ½ inch (12 mm) boiling water on the lowest rack.

To make the glaze, beat the egg and milk together. Brush the brioches gently with the glaze and place on the upper rack. Immediately increase the oven temperature to 400°F (200°C) and bake until golden brown and firm, about 18 minutes. Let stand for 1 minute, then remove from the molds and let cool briefly on a wire rack. Serve warm.

BRIOCHE DOUGH

Brioche is one of the most venerable breads in France's rich culinary heritage. This butter-laden bread is light, airy, and so rich that it seems more like a cake than a bread. Making brioche requires a cool and confident hand: cool because if your hands are too hot, the butter can seep out of the dough, and confident because the dough may appear at first as if it is too soft to work. Using a floured dough scraper solves both problems, although you may have to scrape the scraper to return any errant scraps of wet dough to the main mass.

Bagels

MAKES 1 DOZEN LARGE BAGELS

SHAPING BAGELS

Classic bagels are first boiled, then baked. Shape them as described in this recipe, or use an alternative method: Divide the dough in half, then form into a rope 18 inches (45 cm) long by rolling the dough between your palms. Divide each rope into 6 equal portions, then roll each into a rope 8 inches (20 cm) long. Connect the ends and roll the dough back and forth to seal, making a ring. Place on the baking sheet and proceed as directed.

4 tsp active dry yeast

2 Tbsp sugar

2 cups (16 fl oz/500 ml) warm water (105°–115°F/40°–46°C)

2 Tbsp canola oil, plus extra for greasing

1 Tbsp salt

5½ cups (27½ oz/860 g) bread flour, plus extra as needed

2 Tbsp vital wheat gluten (page 285)

Vegetable-oil cooking spray

1 Tbsp baking soda (bicarbonate of soda)

1 egg white beaten with 1 Tbsp water until foamy

IN A BOWL, sprinkle the yeast and a pinch of the sugar over ½ cup (4 fl oz/125 ml) of the warm water and stir to dissolve. Let stand until foamy, about 10 minutes.

In a stand mixer fitted with the paddle attachment, combine the remaining water, the oil, the remaining sugar, the salt, 2 cups (10 oz/315 g) of the flour, and the gluten. Beat on medium speed until creamy, about 1 minute. Add the yeast mixture and 1 cup (5 oz/155 g) of the flour and beat for 1 minute. Beat in the remaining flour, ½ cup (2½ oz/75 g) at a time, until the dough pulls away from the bowl sides. Switch to the dough hook. Knead on low speed, adding flour 1 Tbsp at a time if the dough sticks, until smooth and elastic, about 6 minutes.

Leave the dough in the mixing bowl and cover loosely with plastic wrap. Let rise at room temperature until doubled in bulk, about 1 hour.

Line 2 heavy baking sheets with parchment (baking) paper and brush the paper with oil. Turn the dough out onto a lightly floured work surface and divide into 4 portions. Divide each portion into 3 pieces. Shape each piece of dough into a smooth, round ball and flatten with your palm. Poke a floured finger through the middle of a ball. Stretch the hole, rolling your finger around the inside of the hole, to make it about 1 inch (2.5 cm) in diameter. Continue to roll your finger or thumb around inside the dough to enlarge the hole; it will shrink slightly when you stop.

Place the bagel on a prepared baking sheet and repeat with the remaining dough, spacing the bagels about 2 inches (5 cm) apart. Spray the bagels with the cooking spray. Cover with plastic and let rise at room temperature until puffy, 15–20 minutes. (Alternatively, before this second rise, cover tightly with plastic wrap and refrigerate for up to 24 hours. Remove from the refrigerator 30 minutes before proceeding.)

While the bagels are rising, prepare the water bath. In a large, wide pot, bring 4–6 quarts (4–6 l) water to a boil over high heat. Add the baking soda and reduce the heat to medium to maintain a gentle boil. Preheat the oven to 425°F (220°C).

Using a skimmer (see page 396), carefully lower 3 or 4 bagels into the water. They will drop to the bottom of the pot and then rise to the surface quickly. As the bagels rise to the surface, turn each one over and boil on the second side for 2 minutes. Using the skimmer, transfer the bagels to a dry kitchen towel to drain for a moment, then return

to the prepared baking sheets, placing them 1 inch (2.5 cm) apart. When all the bagels are boiled, brush them with the egg white mixture and sprinkle with the desired toppings (below). Bake until deep golden brown, 16–20 minutes. Remove from the oven and transfer to wire racks to cool completely.

BAGEL TOPPINGS: A classic plain bagel, with its smooth, shiny crust, is simple and delicious all on its own. But many bagel lovers have favorite toppings that can be used in this recipe as well. Among the most familiar are sesame and poppy seeds. Other toppings include caraway seeds or coarse sea salt. For a savory variation, try dehydrated onion flakes or minced garlic or a mixture of any of the suggestions listed above.

BAGEL ACCOMPANIMENTS: For a satisfying and elegant brunch dish, offer sliced and toasted freshly-made bagels alongside accompaniments such as cream cheese, smoked salmon, cucumbers, thinly sliced red onion, and fresh dill.

Jelly Gem Breakfast Rolls

MAKES 18 ROLLS

FOR THE ROLLS:

2½–3 cups (12½–15 oz/390–470 g) all-purpose (plain) flour, plus extra for sprinkling

½ cup (2 oz/60 g) cake flour or white pastry flour

1 Tbsp active dry yeast

⅓ cup (2 oz/60 g) granulated sugar

¼ cup (1 oz/30 g) dry buttermilk powder

1 tsp salt

1 cup (8 fl oz/250 ml) hot water (125°F/52°C)

5 Tbsp (2½ oz/75 g) unsalted butter, cut into pieces and at room temperature

Canola oil for greasing

¾ cup (7½ oz/235 g) jam, such as apricot, blackberry, cherry, or raspberry

FOR THE GLAZE:

1 cup (4 oz/125 g) confectioners' (icing) sugar, sifted

1 Tbsp unsalted butter, at room temperature

¼ tsp pure vanilla or lemon extract

1½ Tbsp warm milk, or as needed

RISING DOUGH IN THE REFRIGERATOR

Letting the dough rise in the refrigerator is an especially handy technique for these morning rolls. The cold of the refrigerator slows but does not stop the rising; in fact, the slower rise creates a more delicate, even texture in the finished rolls. Other doughs, such as bread and pizza doughs, may also be allowed to rise slowly in the refrigerator.

IN A STAND MIXER fitted with the paddle attachment, combine 1 cup (5 oz/155 g) of the all-purpose flour, all of the cake flour, the yeast, granulated sugar, buttermilk powder, and salt. Add the hot water and beat on medium speed for 1 minute. Add the butter and 1 cup of the all-purpose flour and beat on medium speed for 1 minute. Switch to the dough hook. Beat in the remaining all-purpose flour, ½ cup (2½ oz/75 g) at a time, until the dough pulls away from the bowl sides. Knead on low speed until the dough is very soft, smooth, and springy, about 2 minutes.

Transfer to an oiled deep bowl and turn once to coat with oil. Cover loosely with plastic wrap and let rise at room temperature until puffy, 45–60 minutes.

Grease two 8-inch (20-cm) round cake pans. Turn the dough out onto a lightly floured work surface. Divide in half. Gently roll each section into a log 9 inches (23 cm) long and pat the rolled ends to make them neat. Using a serrated knife, cut each log crosswise into slices 1 inch (2.5 cm) thick. Arrange in the prepared pans, cut sides down; the rolls should barely touch. With your thumb, make a depression in the center of each roll. Cover with a double layer of plastic wrap and refrigerate overnight to let the rolls rise slowly. Remove from the refrigerator 30 minutes before baking.

Gently press each depression, taking care not to deflate it, and put 1 rounded teaspoonful of jam in each one. Place the pans in the cold oven and immediately turn the heat to 350°F (180°C). Bake until golden brown, 25–30 minutes. Transfer the rolls to racks.

To make the glaze, in a small bowl, whisk together the confectioners' sugar, butter, vanilla, and milk until smooth. Adjust the consistency with more milk, if needed; it should be thick and pourable. With a large spoon, drizzle the warm glaze in a zigzag pattern over each hot roll. Let cool slightly. Pull apart to serve.

Black Olive Bread

MAKES 1 OBLONG LOAF

FOR THE SPONGE:

½ cup (4 fl oz/125 ml) lukewarm water (100°F/38°C)

1 cup (8 fl oz/250 ml) milk, at room temperature

1 Tbsp honey

1 Tbsp active dry yeast

½ cup (2½ oz/75 g) whole-wheat (wholemeal) flour

½ cup (2 oz/60 g) medium-grind rye flour

FOR THE DOUGH:

1 tsp salt (use ½ tsp salt if olives are very salty)

2 Tbsp olive oil, plus extra for greasing

2–2⅓ cups (10–12 oz/315–375 g) bread flour, plus extra as needed

1½ cups (7½ oz/235 g) pitted black olives, whole or chopped, patted dry

TO MAKE THE SPONGE, combine the water, milk, and honey in a stand mixer fitted with the whisk attachment. Sprinkle the yeast over the liquid and stir to dissolve. Let stand until foamy, about 10 minutes. Add the whole-wheat and rye flours and beat on medium speed until smooth, about 1 minute. Cover loosely with plastic wrap and let stand until bubbly, 1–2 hours.

Add the salt, oil, and 1 cup (5 oz/155 g) of the bread flour to the sponge and switch to the paddle attachment. Beat on medium speed for 1 minute. Beat in the remaining bread flour, ½ cup (2½ oz/75 g) at a time, until the dough pulls away from the bowl sides. Switch to the dough hook. Knead on low speed, adding bread flour 1 Tbsp at a time if the dough sticks, until smooth but slightly tacky when pressed, about 6 minutes.

Transfer the dough to an oiled deep bowl and turn the dough once to coat it with oil. Cover the bowl loosely with plastic wrap and let rise at room temperature until doubled in bulk, 1½–2 hours.

Line a heavy baking sheet with parchment (baking) paper and brush the paper with oil. Turn the dough out onto a lightly floured work surface. Pat it into a large oval and sprinkle evenly with the olives. Fold the dough over and knead it lightly to distribute the olives evenly. Shape into an oblong loaf, gently pulling the surface taut from the bottom. Place on the prepared sheet and cover loosely with plastic wrap. Let rise until doubled in bulk, about 1 hour.

Place a baking stone on the bottom oven rack and preheat to 425°F (220°C). Using a thin, sharp knife, make a few shallow slashes on the diagonal down the length of the loaf. Place the pan on the stone and reduce the oven temperature to 375°F (190°C). Bake until the loaf is golden brown, 45–50 minutes. Transfer to a rack and let cool completely.

OLIVES IN BREAD

Dozens of domestic and imported cured olives exist from which to choose, all varying in size, flavor, color, and degree of saltiness. Many of them make delicious additions to a yeast bread. Black olives are tree ripened and cured in a vinegar brine or dry-cured with salt, which makes them wrinkled instead of plump. Seek out imported Greek Kalamata or French Niçoise olives for this hearty loaf.

Challah

MAKES 1 BRAIDED LOAF

4¼–4½ cups (21½–22½ oz/670–705 g) all-purpose (plain) flour

1¼ cups (10 fl oz/310 ml) warm water (105°–115°F/40°–46°C)

1 Tbsp active dry yeast

4 Tbsp (2 oz/60 g) sugar

2 large eggs, lightly beaten

¼ cup (2 fl oz/60 ml) canola oil, plus extra for greasing

1½ tsp salt

1 egg beaten with 1 tsp water

Sesame or poppy seeds for sprinkling

PUT 3 CUPS (15 OZ/470 G) of the flour in a stand mixer fitted with the paddle attachment. Make a well in the center and pour in the water. Sprinkle the yeast and 1 Tbsp of the sugar over the water. Stir, then let stand until foamy, about 10 minutes.

Add the remaining 3 Tbsp sugar, the eggs, oil, and salt to the well. Beat on medium-low speed until a shaggy mass forms, about 2 minutes. Beat in the remaining flour, ½ cup (2½ oz/75 g) at a time, until the dough pulls away from the bowl sides. Switch to the dough hook. Knead on low speed, adding flour 1 Tbsp at a time if the dough sticks, until smooth and elastic, about 5 minutes. Transfer the dough to an oiled deep bowl and turn once to coat it with oil. Cover loosely with plastic wrap and let rise at room temperature just until doubled in bulk, 1½–2 hours. Gently punch down the dough with your fist, turn it over, re-cover, and let rise again until doubled, about 1 hour.

Line a baking sheet with parchment (baking) paper. Turn the dough out onto a lightly floured work surface, divide into 3 equal portions, and braid (right). Place the braided loaf on the prepared pan. Brush the top with half of the egg mixture. Cover loosely with lightly oiled plastic wrap and let rise until almost doubled, about 40 minutes.

Preheat the oven to 350°F (180°C). Brush the loaf with the remaining egg mixture and sprinkle with the seeds. Bake until deep golden brown, 40–45 minutes. Transfer to a wire rack to cool. Serve warm or at room temperature.

BRAIDING

Roll each dough portion into 3 ropes each 14 inches (35 cm) long. Place the 3 dough ropes parallel to one another on a floured work surface. Lift up the center rope and bring the right-hand rope under it, laying the right rope between the center and left-hand ropes. Now lift up the new center rope and bring the left-hand rope under it, laying the left rope between the center and right-hand ropes. Continue alternately bringing the right and left outside ropes under the center rope. Pinch the ends into tapered points and tuck them under.

Oatmeal-Molasses Bread

MAKES TWO 8½-BY-4½-INCH (21.5-BY-11.5-CM) LOAVES

4 tsp active dry yeast

Pinch of sugar

½ cup (4 fl oz/125 ml) warm water (105°–115°F/40°–46°C)

2 cups (16 fl oz/500 ml) tepid buttermilk (90°F/32°C)

4 Tbsp (2 oz/60 g) unsalted butter, melted

½ cup (5½ oz/170 g) light or dark molasses

1 cup (5 oz/155 g) whole-wheat (wholemeal) flour or graham flour

¾ cup (2 oz/60 g) old-fashioned or quick-cooking rolled oats

½ cup (2½ oz/75 g) fine yellow cornmeal

¼ cup (½ oz/15 g) instant mashed potato flakes

¼ cup (¾ oz/20 g) toasted wheat germ

2½ tsp salt

3–3¼ cups (15–16½ oz/470–515 g) bread flour, plus extra as needed

Canola oil for greasing

IN A BOWL, sprinkle the yeast and sugar over the water and stir to dissolve. Let stand until foamy, about 10 minutes.

In a stand mixer fitted with the paddle attachment, combine the buttermilk, butter, molasses, and whole-wheat flour. Beat on medium speed until creamy, about 1 minute. Add the yeast mixture, oats, cornmeal, potato flakes, wheat germ, and salt, and beat for 1 minute. Beat in the bread flour, ½ cup (2½ oz/75 g) at a time, until the dough pulls away from the bowl sides. Switch to the dough hook. Knead on low speed, adding bread flour 1 Tbsp at a time if the dough sticks, until smooth, about 5 minutes. Let the dough rest for 10 minutes, then knead for 1 minute longer. The dough should be smooth but slightly tacky and nubby when pressed.

Transfer the dough to an oiled deep bowl and turn the dough once to coat it with oil. Cover loosely with plastic wrap and let rise at room temperature until doubled in bulk, 1½–2 hours.

Lightly grease two 8½-by-4½-inch (21.5-by-11.5-cm) loaf pans. Turn the dough out onto a lightly floured work surface and divide in half. Pat each half into an 8-by-12-inch (20-by-30-cm) rectangle. Beginning at a narrow end, roll up each rectangle to make a loaf the length of the pan. Pinch the ends and long seam to seal. Place the loaves, seam side down, in the prepared pans. Cover loosely with plastic wrap and let rise until about 1 inch (2.5 cm) above the rim of each pan, 1–1½ hours.

Preheat the oven to 350°F (180°C). Bake until the loaves are golden brown and pull away from the pan sides, 35–40 minutes. Turn out onto racks and let cool completely.

ABOUT OATS

Rolled oats are found in the cereal section of almost every supermarket. Rich in antioxidant fats, rolled oats can be kept for 1 year at room temperature. Old-fashioned rolled oats are hulled and steamed whole-grain oats that are pressed into flakes. Quick-cooking rolled oats are toasted slightly during the rolling process, making them faster to cook. You may use either quick-cooking or old-fashioned rolled oats in bread recipes.

FRUIT DESSERTS

Ginger-Pear Torte

MAKES 6–8 SERVINGS

FRUIT BRANDIES

Fruit brandies, or *eaux-de-vie*, are distilled liquors made from a variety of fruits. While the most common brandy is made with grapes, framboise is derived from raspberries, kirsch from cherries, poire Williams from pears, and Calvados, a specialty of the French region of Normandy, from apples. These brandies are not sweet, but instead reveal an intense fragrance and flavor of the fruit from which they are made. Fruit brandies are available at most liquor stores.

6 Tbsp (3 oz/90 g) unsalted butter

5 eggs, at room temperature

⅔ cup (5 oz/155 g) granulated sugar

½ cup (2 oz/60 g) sifted all-purpose (plain) flour

1 tsp ground ginger

½ cup (2 oz/60 g) finely ground blanched almonds

1 cup (8 fl oz/250 ml) heavy (double) cream

1 tsp freshly grated nutmeg

2 ripe but firm Bartlett (Williams') pears, about 1 lb (500 g) total weight

1 Tbsp finely chopped candied (crystallized) ginger, page 322, or purchased

3 Tbsp firmly packed golden brown sugar

1 Tbsp fruit brandy, such as poire Williams or Calvados (left)

Confectioners' (icing) sugar for dusting

PREHEAT THE OVEN TO 350°F (180°C). Grease two 8-inch (20-cm) round cake pans. Line the bottom of each pan with parchment (baking) paper. Butter the parchment.

In a small saucepan over medium heat, melt 4 Tbsp (2 oz/60 g) of the butter. Set aside to cool slightly. Meanwhile, using an electric mixer, beat the eggs until blended. Gradually beat in the granulated sugar. Continue to beat until the mixture is pale yellow and a slowly dissolving ribbon forms when the beaters are lifted, 6–8 minutes. Combine the flour and ground ginger. Sift half of the flour mixture over the egg mixture and fold it in with a silicone spatula. Fold in half of the butter. Repeat with the remaining flour mixture and butter. Fold in the almonds.

Divide the batter between the prepared pans. Bake until the edges of the layers are golden and just beginning to pull away from the sides of the pans, 15–20 minutes. Remove from the oven, place on wire racks, and let cool for 10 minutes. Turn the layers out onto the racks, peel off the paper, and let cool completely.

Just before serving, in a deep bowl, beat the cream to soft peaks. Sprinkle the nutmeg over the cream and continue to beat to stiff peaks. Cover and refrigerate.

Place 1 cake layer, bottom side up, on a serving plate. Peel and core the pears and cut into ½-inch (12-mm) chunks. In a large frying pan over medium heat, melt the remaining 2 Tbsp butter. Add the pears and crystallized ginger and cook, stirring once or twice, for 2 minutes. Raise the heat to high, add the brown sugar and brandy, and cook, stirring often, until the liquid is reduced to a thick glaze, about 4 minutes. Spoon the pears over the cake layer on the plate. Top with the second layer. Dust the top with confectioners' sugar. Serve warm with the whipped cream.

Plums with Candied Ginger Crumble

MAKES 6–8 SERVINGS

CANDIED GINGER

You can buy candied, or crystallized, ginger at the supermarket—or make it yourself at home. Making it at home allows you to use the freshest ginger you can find. You can double the recipe and store the remaining candied ginger in a tightly covered jar for up to 3 weeks. Use in other fruit dessert fillings and baked goods for an added sweet-spicy flavor.

FOR THE CANDIED GINGER:

1 cup (8 oz/250 g) sugar

1 cup thinly sliced (1/8 inch/3 mm) peeled fresh ginger

FOR THE PLUMS AND CRUMBLE:

2 lb (1 kg) ripe dark purple plums, pitted and quartered

1/2 cup (1 1/2 oz/45 g) old-fashioned rolled oats

1/2 cup (4 oz/125 g) sugar

6 Tbsp (3 oz/90 g) unsalted butter, at room temperature

1/4 cup (1 1/2 oz/45 g) all-purpose (plain) flour

Vanilla ice cream for serving

TO MAKE THE CANDIED GINGER, bring 1 1/2 cups (12 fl oz/375 ml) water to a boil. Stir in 1/2 cup (4 oz/25 g) of the sugar until it is dissolved. Cook over medium heat for 5 minutes, then add the ginger slices. Reduce the heat to a simmer and cook until tender, about 10 minutes. Drain, then put the ginger in a bowl with the remaining 1/2 cup sugar and toss to coat. Spread the candied ginger out in a single layer and let cool.

Preheat the oven to 400°F (200°C). Put the plums in a greased shallow 8-inch (20-cm) square baking pan just large enough to hold them comfortably. Toss the plums with the candied ginger. Set aside.

In a food processor, combine the oats, sugar, butter, and flour. Pulse for a few seconds until the mixture is coarsely chopped. The mixture will clump together. Sprinkle the oat mixture evenly over the plums. Roast until the plums are bubbling and the top is browned, about 30 minutes.

Scoop the ice cream into dessert bowls and spoon the warm plums on top.

Steamed Cranberry Pudding

MAKES 6–8 SERVINGS

3 Tbsp granulated sugar, plus sugar for sprinkling

1½ cups (6 oz/185 g) coarsely chopped fresh cranberries

1½ cups (7½ oz/235 g) all-purpose (plain) flour

1¼ tsp baking powder

½ tsp baking soda (bicarbonate of soda)

¼ tsp salt

¼ cup (2 oz/60 g) unsalted butter, at room temperature

½ cup (3½ oz/105 g) firmly packed golden brown sugar

¼ cup (3 oz/90 g) unsulfured light molasses

2 tsp minced orange zest

⅓ cup (3 fl oz/80 ml) buttermilk

Boiling water, as needed

Vanilla ice cream, softened slightly if necessary, for serving

GENEROUSLY GREASE THE INSIDE of a decorative 2-qt (2-l) steamed-pudding mold (right), including the lid, with butter. Make sure the bottom of the mold is especially well greased. Dust the mold and its lid with granulated sugar, shaking out the excess.

In a medium bowl, combine the cranberries and the 3 Tbsp granulated sugar and let stand while preparing the batter.

Sift together the flour, baking powder, baking soda, and salt onto a piece of waxed paper.

In a large bowl, whisk together the ¼ cup butter, the brown sugar, molasses, and orange zest. Stir in the flour mixture and the buttermilk and mix well. Fold in the cranberries and any juices from the bowl. Spoon the mixture into the prepared pudding mold and top with the lid.

Place the mold on a wire rack inside a large, heavy pot and add boiling water to come halfway up the sides of the mold, creating a hot-water bath. Place over medium-low heat, cover the pot, and cook, adding more boiling water as needed to maintain the original level, until the pudding pulls away from the sides of the mold and a knife inserted into the center comes out clean, about 1½ hours.

Transfer the pudding mold to a wire rack. Uncover and let the pudding rest in the mold for 15 minutes. Invert onto a plate. Serve warm, cut into wedges and accompanied with the ice cream.

MAKE-AHEAD TIP: The pudding can be prepared 1 day in advance. Wrap in plastic wrap and refrigerate. Bring to room temperature, wrap in aluminum foil, and rewarm in a preheated 300°F (150°C) oven for 20 minutes before serving.

STEAMED-PUDDING MOLDS

Steamed-pudding molds are available at most kitchen specialty stores. They look similar to Bundt pans, with decorative ribbed sides and bottoms, and center tubes for even heat distribution. The pan comes with a lid, sometimes a clamp-on lid, which facilitates the steaming of the pudding.

Blackberry Cobbler

MAKES 8–10 SERVINGS

FOR THE FILLING:

6 cups (1½ lb/750 g) blackberries

⅓ cup (2⅓ oz/70 g) sugar

1 Tbsp all-purpose (plain) flour

1 tsp finely grated lemon zest

Pinch of salt

FOR THE TOPPING:

1¼ cups (5¾ oz/175 g) all-purpose (plain) flour

⅓ cup (2⅓ oz/70 g) sugar

2 tsp baking powder

½ tsp ground cinnamon

¼ tsp salt

1 large egg, at room temperature

½ cup (4 fl oz/125 ml) buttermilk

6 Tbsp (3 oz/90 g) unsalted butter, melted and cooled slightly

½ tsp pure vanilla extract

PREHEAT THE OVEN TO 375°F (190°C). Lightly grease a 2-qt (2-l) round baking dish.

To make the filling, gently toss the blackberries with the sugar, flour, zest, and salt in a large bowl until blended. Pour into the prepared baking dish and set aside.

To make the topping, in a bowl, stir together the flour, sugar, baking powder, cinnamon, and salt. In another bowl, whisk together the egg, buttermilk, melted butter, and vanilla until well blended. Pour the buttermilk mixture into the flour mixture and, using a silicone spatula, fold gently until the flour is moistened and the mixture forms a soft dough.

Drop heaping spoonfuls of the mixture onto the fruit, spacing them evenly over the surface. The topping will not completely cover the fruit. Bake until the fruit filling is bubbling, the topping is browned, and a toothpick inserted into the topping comes out clean, about 45 minutes. Serve warm or at room temperature.

COBBLER VARIATIONS

For another version of this cobbler, try mixing some raspberries and blueberries in with the blackberries. Or, replace the blackberries altogether with sliced peaches or nectarines and a handful of dried sour cherries or cranberries. A combination of 3 or 4 plum varieties, all pitted and quartered, is also wonderful. Add a pinch of freshly ground nutmeg or a dash of pure vanilla extract to the fruit. Or, sprinkle a small handful of sliced (flaked) almonds or chopped pecans over the topping before baking.

Blackberry Pockets

MAKES SIX 4-INCH (10-CM) POCKETS, OR 6 SERVINGS

Flaky Pastry Dough, Double-Crust Variation (page 373)

2 cups (8 oz/250 g) blackberries

2 Tbsp cornstarch (cornflour)

3 Tbsp sugar

Pinch of salt

ROLL OUT THE DOUGH DISKS into 12-inch (30-cm) rounds (see page 385). Using a 4-inch (10-cm) round or scalloped cookie cutter, a 4-inch tart pan turned upside down, or a cardboard circle and a small, sharp knife, cut out 3 or 4 rounds from each rolled-out dough round. Press the dough scraps together and reroll to cut out additional rounds. You should have a total of twelve 4-inch dough rounds.

In a bowl, toss together the blackberries, cornstarch, sugar, and salt. Lay 6 dough rounds on a baking sheet lined with parchment (baking) paper. Divide the blackberries evenly among the dough rounds. Using a small pastry brush, dampen the edge of each round with cold water. Lay the remaining dough rounds over the blackberries. Gently press the top of each dough round down over the berries; the edges of the rounds will not line up. With the tines of a fork, press the edges of the dough rounds together. Refrigerate the pockets on the baking sheet until the dough is firm, 15–20 minutes.

Meanwhile, place an oven rack in the lower third of the oven and preheat to 375°F (190°C). Bake the pockets until golden brown, 35–40 minutes. Transfer the baking sheet to a wire rack to cool slightly. Serve warm.

SERVING TIP: Serve these pockets for breakfast or as a delicious afternoon snack.

PARCHMENT PAPER

Parchment paper, also known as baking paper, is a heavy, moisture-resistant paper used to line baking pans and sheets. It is sold in sheets, rolls, and precut pieces to fit cake pans and can withstand temperatures up to 450°F (230°C). It helps make cleanup easy, as the paper is simply slipped from the pan after use. Other uses include creating packets for cooking fish and vegetables, rolling into cones for piping icing, and placing over a pan of simmering vegetables to keep them immersed in the water. Do not substitute waxed paper for parchment paper.

Prune & Armagnac Clafoutis

MAKES 4 SERVINGS

2 cups (12 oz/375 g) pitted prunes (dried plums), halved

3 Tbsp Armagnac or Cognac

3 Tbsp very hot water (120°F/49°C)

1 large whole egg plus 1 large egg yolk

⅓ cup (3 oz/90 g) granulated sugar

3 Tbsp all-purpose (plain) flour

1 cup (8 fl oz/250 ml) heavy (double) cream

3 Tbsp unsalted butter, melted

Confectioners' (icing) sugar for dusting

IN A BOWL, COMBINE THE PRUNES, Armagnac, and hot water. Toss to combine. Let stand at room temperature, tossing occasionally, until the prunes are plump, about 30 minutes.

Preheat the oven to 400°F (200°C). Grease the bottom and sides of a 9-inch (23-cm) oval or similar-sized baking dish and flour the inside, shaking out the excess.

In a bowl, whisk together the whole egg and egg yolk, then whisk in the granulated sugar. Add the flour and stir to combine. Whisk in the cream and melted butter. With a slotted spoon, transfer the prunes to the base of the prepared dish. Whisk the remaining soaking liquid into the egg batter and pour the batter evenly over the prunes.

Bake the clafoutis until puffy and golden, about 30 minutes. Serve directly from the dish, or let cool slightly, invert onto a rack, and turn right side up onto a serving platter. Serve warm, dusted with a little confectioners' sugar.

ARMAGNAC

Produced and bottled in the Gascony region of southwest France, this brandy is made from white grapes that have been aged in black oak barrels. The combination of prunes and Armagnac is a classic one in traditional French cuisine. The pairing is often featured in ice creams, but is also common in sauces for poultry and pork.

Autumn Fruit Strudel

MAKES 8 SERVINGS

12 sheets filo dough, thawed if frozen

½ cup (4 oz/125 g) unsalted butter, melted and cooled

7 tsp granulated sugar

3 or 4 tart apples (page 331), peeled, halved, cored, and diced (about 3 cups/ 12 oz/375 g)

½ cup (3½ oz/105 g) firmly packed brown sugar

¼ tsp ground cinnamon

⅛ tsp freshly grated nutmeg

1 cup (7 oz/220 g) mixed chopped dried fruits such as sour cherries, apricots, cranberries, currants, golden raisins (sultanas), or nectarines

PLACE AN OVEN RACK in the lower third of the oven and preheat to 375°F (190°C). Line a baking sheet with parchment (baking) paper.

Working with 1 filo sheet at a time and keeping the others covered with a barely damp kitchen towel to prevent them from drying out, place the first sheet on the parchment paper. Using a pastry brush, brush well with some of the melted butter. Lay a second filo sheet on top of the first and brush again with butter. Sprinkle with 1 tsp of the granulated sugar. Repeat, brushing every sheet with butter and sprinkling every other sheet with 1 tsp granulated sugar, until all of the filo is used.

In a large bowl, toss together the apples, brown sugar, cinnamon, nutmeg, and dried fruits. Arrange the apple filling along one long side of the filo stack, positioning it about 1 inch (2.5) from the edge. Fold the edge of the stack over the filling, then carefully roll up the filo into a log with the seam side down. Brush the log with additional melted butter and sprinkle with the remaining 1 tsp granulated sugar.

Bake the strudel until the filo is golden and the apples are tender when pierced with the tip of a knife, 45–55 minutes. Let cool on the pan on a wire rack for 30 minutes. Transfer to a long serving platter, cut crosswise, and serve warm.

WORKING WITH FILO

Filo (or phyllo) dough, best known for its use in Greek and Turkish pastries like baklava, is sold in the freezer section of large grocery stores. It is an elastic dough pulled into very thin sheets and cut into large rectangles. Follow the instructions on the box for thawing. When working with filo, keep the unused dough sheets stacked under a piece of plastic wrap or a barely damp kitchen towel until you are ready to use them; otherwise, they may become brittle and tear easily. Frozen filo dough keeps well, but not indefinitely; it becomes dry or sticky if stored for too long.

Peach & Pistachio Cobbler

MAKES 8 SERVINGS

FOR THE FILLING:

½ cup (4 oz/125 g) sugar

2 Tbsp cornstarch (cornflour)

½ tsp ground cinnamon

¼ tsp ground nutmeg

¼ tsp salt

8–10 peaches, peeled if desired (page 178), pitted, and sliced 1 inch (2.5 cm) thick

FOR THE TOPPING:

2 cups (10 oz/315 g) all-purpose (plain) flour

½ cup (2 oz/60 g) unsalted pistachios, finely chopped

¼ cup (2 oz/60 g) sugar

½ tsp salt

2 tsp baking powder

¾ cup (6 oz/185 g) cold unsalted butter, cut into ½-inch (12-mm) cubes

¾ cup (6 fl oz/180 ml) whole milk

Ground cinnamon and sugar for sprinkling

PLACE AN OVEN RACK in the lower third of the oven and preheat to 350°F (180°C). Grease a 12-inch (30-cm) oval or 9-by-13-inch (23-by-33-cm) rectangular baking dish with a 2-qt (2-l) capacity.

To make the filling, in a small bowl, stir together the sugar, cornstarch, cinnamon, nutmeg, and salt. Place the peaches in a large bowl, sprinkle with the sugar mixture, and toss to distribute evenly. Spread the peach mixture in the prepared baking dish and set aside while you prepare the topping.

To make the topping, in a large bowl, mix together the flour, pistachios, sugar, salt, and baking powder. Using a pastry blender or 2 knives, cut the butter into the flour mixture until the texture resembles coarse meal, leaving some pieces of butter about the size of small peas. Add the milk and stir just until the mixture pulls together. (This process can also be done in a stand mixer fitted with the paddle attachment.)

Pinch off chunks of the dough and place them on top of the peach mixture, covering it nearly completely. Alternatively, on a lightly floured work surface, roll out the dough to the same dimensions as the baking dish and carefully lay it over the filling.

In a small bowl, mix together ¼ tsp cinnamon and 1 Tbsp sugar and sprinkle the cinnamon sugar on top of the dough. Bake until the topping is firm and golden brown and the filling bubbles slowly, 45–60 minutes.

Remove from the oven and let cool for 30 minutes before serving.

SERVING TIP: Accompany the cobbler with a small scoop of vanilla ice cream or a splash of heavy (double) cream.

PISTACHIOS

Unsalted raw pistachios can be found in well-stocked supermarkets and in most Middle Eastern markets and health-food stores. These bright green nuts have a mild flavor that complements the peaches without overpowering them. Pistachios and other nuts are rich in oil, which means they can develop a rancid flavor if stored too long or improperly. Purchase nuts in small quantities as needed, and store them in a cool, dark cupboard or in the freezer.

Apple Crisp

MAKES 8 SERVINGS

FOR THE TOPPING:

½ cup (2½ oz/75 g) all-purpose (plain) flour

1 cup (3 oz/90 g) old-fashioned or quick-cooking rolled oats

½ cup (3½ oz/105 g) firmly packed brown sugar

¼ tsp salt

½ tsp ground cinnamon

½ cup (4 oz/125 g) cold unsalted butter, cut into ¼-inch (6-mm) cubes

½ cup (2 oz/60 g) walnuts, finely chopped

FOR THE FILLING:

¾ cup (6 oz/185 g) sugar

Pinch of salt

¼ tsp freshly grated nutmeg

½ tsp ground cinnamon

6 tart apples (right), peeled, halved, cored, and sliced ¼ inch (6 mm) thick (about 6 cups/1½ lb/750 g)

Sweetened Whipped Cream (page 377)

PLACE AN OVEN RACK in the lower third of the oven and preheat to 350°F (180°C). Lightly grease a 12-inch (30-cm) oval or 9-by-13- inch (23-by-33-cm) rectangular baking dish with a 2-qt (2-l) capacity.

To make the topping, in a bowl, stir together the flour, oats, brown sugar, salt, and cinnamon. Using a pastry blender or 2 knives, quickly cut or rub the butter into the flour mixture until it is crumbly. Add the walnuts and toss to mix. Cover and refrigerate while you prepare the filling.

To make the filling, in a small bowl, stir together the sugar, salt, nutmeg, and cinnamon. Place the apple slices in a large bowl, sprinkle with the sugar mixture, and toss to distribute evenly. Spread the apple mixture in the prepared baking dish. Sprinkle the topping evenly over the apples.

Bake until the topping is golden brown and the apples are tender when pierced with the tip of a knife, about 50 minutes. Serve warm with a dollop of whipped cream, if desired.

TART APPLES

The sweet and tart flavor of apples is a delicious counterpoint to the rich, buttery flavor of the crisp topping in this recipe. Tart varieties such as Granny Smith, pippin, or Fuji work best for baking.

Steamed Persimmon Pudding

MAKES 8 SERVINGS

¾ cup (3–4 oz/90–125 g) mixed dried fruits such as chopped apricots and whole golden raisins (sultanas) and cranberries

¼ cup (2 fl oz/60 ml) brandy

¾ cup (3¼ oz/95 g) all-purpose (plain) flour

¾ tsp ground cinnamon

½ tsp ground ginger

¼ tsp salt

Pinch of ground cloves

1 egg, at room temperature

⅔ cup (5⅓ oz/165 g) firmly packed light brown sugar

⅔ cup (5 fl oz/160 ml) Hachiya persimmon purée, at room temperature (right)

½ cup (4 oz/125 g) unsalted butter, melted and cooled

1½ tsp pure vanilla extract

1 tsp finely grated orange zest

2 Tbsp hot water

1 tsp baking soda (bicarbonate of soda)

Boiling water, as needed

Sweetened Whipped Cream (page 377) for serving

IN A SMALL SAUCEPAN, stir together the dried fruits and brandy. Bring to a boil over medium heat, cover, and remove from the heat. Let stand, stirring occasionally, until the fruit is plumped, about 20 minutes.

Generously grease a 5- or 6-cup (40– or 48–fl oz/1.25- or 1.5-l) steamed-pudding mold (page 323) with a lid and a piece of aluminum foil large enough to cover the top of the mold. Choose a saucepan with a tight-fitting lid deep enough to contain the mold and a wire cooling rack. Place the rack in the bottom of the pan and add water to just cover the rack. The water should be about 1 inch (2.5 cm) deep. Set aside.

In a bowl, whisk together the flour, cinnamon, ginger, salt, and cloves. In a large bowl, beat together the egg and brown sugar until well blended. Add the persimmon purée, melted butter, vanilla, and orange zest and beat until well blended. In a small bowl, stir together the hot water and baking soda. Add to the persimmon mixture and stir until well blended. Sprinkle the flour-spice mixture over the persimmon mixture and stir just until blended. Fold in the plumped dried fruits and any remaining brandy.

Pour the mixture into the prepared mold, smoothing the surface. Cover with the buttered foil, buttered side down, and snap on the mold lid. Set the mold on the rack in the pan, cover the pan, and bring the water to a boil. Reduce the heat to low or medium-low and simmer vigorously until the pudding is firm when the top is pressed, about 1¼ hours. Check the water level every 30 minutes or so and add boiling water as needed to maintain the level.

Carefully transfer the mold to a wire rack and let cool until it can be handled, about 15 minutes. Remove the lid and foil. Invert the mold onto a flat serving plate and carefully lift off the mold. Using a serrated knife, cut into slices while still warm. Let cool to room temperature if desired, and serve with the whipped cream.

ABOUT PERSIMMONS

Fuyu and Hachiya are the two most common varieties of persimmon. The Fuyu is firm and crunchy when ripe, while the Hachiya, shaped like a large acorn with a dry, brown leafy top, is quite soft when ripe. Eaten too early, it has a harsh and astringent flavor. For this recipe, choose 2 or 3 Hachiya persimmons that are bright orange with stem leaves attached and that yield easily when pressed with your fingertip. Cut away the top and scoop out the pulp. Process briefly in a food processor, then press through a sieve to remove any stringy fibers.

ABOUT CLOVES

The dried flower buds of a tropical evergreen tree, cloves impart their deep, almost hot flavor to a variety of dishes, both sweet and savory. Used whole, they're a favorite for steeping in cider and other festive warm drinks, while the ground spice is used to flavor baked goods. The name of these little nail-shaped spices comes from the Latin word *clavus*, for "nail."

Spiced Blueberry Cobbler

MAKES 8 SERVINGS

FOR THE FILLING:

Finely grated zest and juice of 1 lemon

4 cups (1 lb/500 g) fresh or thawed frozen blueberries

½ cup (4 oz/125 g) sugar

¼ cup (3 oz/90 g) unsulphured light molasses

¼ tsp freshly grated nutmeg

¼ tsp ground cloves

2 Tbsp cornstarch (cornflour)

FOR THE TOPPING:

1 cup (5 oz/155 g) all-purpose (plain) flour

¼ cup (2 oz/60 g) sugar

1 tsp baking powder

¼ tsp salt

⅓ cup (3 oz/90 g) cold unsalted butter, cut into ½-inch (12-mm) cubes

1 large egg

⅓ cup (3 fl oz/80 ml) heavy (double) cream

Vanilla ice cream for serving (optional)

PLACE AN OVEN RACK in the lower third of the oven and preheat to 350°F (180°C). Grease a 12-inch (30-cm) oval or 9-by-13-inch (23-by-33-cm) rectangular baking dish with a 2-qt (2-l) capacity.

To make the filling, in a bowl, combine the lemon zest, lemon juice, blueberries, sugar, molasses, nutmeg, cloves, and cornstarch. Stir gently to mix, then spread in the prepared baking dish.

To make the topping, in a large bowl, mix together the flour, sugar, baking powder, and salt. Using a pastry blender or 2 knives, cut the butter into the flour mixture until the texture resembles coarse meal, leaving some pieces of butter about the size of small peas. In a small bowl, beat the egg and cream together, add to the flour mixture a little at a time and stir just until the mixture pulls together. (Alternatively, this process can be done in a stand mixer fitted with the paddle attachment.)

Pinch off chunks of the dough and place them on top of the prepared blueberry mixture, covering it nearly completely.

Bake the cobbler until the topping is firm and golden brown and the filling bubbles slowly, 45–55 minutes.

Let cool for about 45 minutes. Serve with a scoop of vanilla ice cream, if desired.

Roasted Apple Brown Betty with Hard Sauce

MAKES 6–8 SERVINGS

2½ lb (1.25 kg) Golden Delicious or Granny Smith apples, peeled, cored, and cut into slices ¼ inch (6 mm) thick

¾ cup (6 oz/185 g) sugar

1 tsp ground cinnamon

¼ tsp freshly grated nutmeg

2 cups (8 oz/250 g) dried white bread crumbs (page 364) or graham cracker crumbs

4 Tbsp (2 oz/60 g) unsalted butter, melted

Hard sauce (right), vanilla ice cream, or Sweetened Whipped Cream (page 377) for serving

PREHEAT THE OVEN TO 400°F (200°C). Toss the apples with the sugar, cinnamon, and nutmeg. Mound the apples in a roasting pan just large enough to hold them.

Roast, turning twice, until fork-tender, about 1 hour. Drain the apples, reserving the liquid. Let cool. In a food processor, purée the apples, adding the reserved liquid as needed to make a thick applesauce.

Reduce the oven temperature to 375°F (190°C). Toss the bread crumbs with the melted butter. Sprinkle half of the crumbs over the bottom of an 8-inch (20-cm) round or square baking pan. Pour the applesauce over the crumbs and sprinkle the remaining crumbs on top. Bake for 20 minutes.

To serve, spoon the brown betty into shallow bowls and top with the hard sauce, vanilla ice cream, or whipped cream.

HARD SAUCE

The traditional accompaniment to plum pudding, hard sauce pairs well with any hearty autumn or winter dessert. To make hard sauce, combine ½ cup (4 oz/125 g) unsalted butter at room temperature, 1 cup (2 oz/60 g) sifted confectioners' (icing) sugar, 1 Tbsp dark rum or brandy or 1 tsp pure vanilla extract, and ⅛ tsp freshly grated nutmeg. Mix well to blend. If desired, chill before serving.

Apricot-Almond Crisp

MAKES 8 SERVINGS

FOR THE TOPPING:

½ cup (2½ oz/75 g) all-purpose (plain) flour

1 cup (3 oz/90 g) old-fashioned or quick-cooking rolled oats

½ cup (3½ oz/105 g) firmly packed brown sugar

¼ tsp salt

1 tsp ground ginger

½ tsp ground cinnamon

½ cup (4 oz/125 g) cold unsalted butter, cut into 6 pieces

1 cup (4 oz/125 g) sliced almonds

FOR THE FILLING:

¾ cup (6 oz/185 g) sugar

2 Tbsp quick-cooking tapioca or cornstarch (cornflour)

1 tsp peeled and grated fresh ginger

Pinch of salt

2½ lb (1.25 kg) apricots, pitted and diced

PLACE AN OVEN RACK in the lower third of the oven and preheat to 350°F (180°C). Grease a 12-inch (30-cm) oval or 9-by-13-inch (23-by-33-cm) rectangular baking dish with a 2-qt (2-l) capacity.

To make the topping, in a bowl, stir together the flour, oats, brown sugar, salt, ground ginger, and cinnamon. Using a pastry blender or 2 knives, cut the butter into the flour mixture until it is crumbly. Add the sliced almonds and toss to mix. Cover and refrigerate while you prepare the filling.

To make the filling, in a small bowl, stir together the sugar, tapioca, ginger, and salt. Place the apricots in a large bowl, sprinkle with the sugar mixture, and toss to distribute evenly. Spread the apricot mixture in the prepared baking dish. Sprinkle the topping evenly over the apricots.

Bake until the topping is crisp and golden brown and the apricot filling bubbles slowly, about 50 minutes. Serve warm.

FRESH GINGER

Fresh ginger brings a lively, warm spicy flavor to this apricot crisp. In the market, look for ginger that is hard and heavy, with an unbroken peel that is thin, pale, and smooth. To prepare fresh ginger, peel it with a vegetable peeler or paring knife. After it is peeled, it is often grated to capture its flavor without its fibrous texture. Porcelain ginger graters, specially designed to let you use the aromatic juice and flesh without the tough fibers, are sold in Asian markets and specialty cookware stores. You can also use the smallest rasps on a metal grater.

Plum Pavlova

MAKES 6 SERVINGS

FOR THE MERINGUES:

½ cup (4 fl oz/125 ml) egg whites (3–4 large eggs)

Pinch of salt

1 tsp fresh lemon juice

1 cup (8 oz/250 g) sugar

FOR THE PLUMS:

⅔ cup (5 oz/155 g) sugar

3 or 4 firm Simka or Santa Rosa plums, halved, pitted, and each half sliced into 8 slices

Pinch of salt

6 Tbsp (3 oz/90 g) unsalted butter, at room temperature, cut into ¼-inch (6-mm) cubes

PREHEAT THE OVEN TO 250°F (120°C). Line a rimmed baking sheet with parchment (baking) paper.

To make the meringues, in a stand mixer fitted with the whisk attachment, combine the egg whites, salt, and lemon juice. Beat on high speed until the large, foamy bubbles become small, about 2 minutes. Reduce the speed to low and gradually add the 1 cup sugar while continuing to beat. Return the mixer to high speed and beat until the whites are firm and glossy (see page 155), about 8 minutes.

With a spring-loaded ice cream scoop or a large spoon, mound the meringue in 6 well-spaced mounds on the prepared baking sheet. With the back of a spoon, form a depression in the center of each mound. Bake the meringues for 1 hour, turn off the oven, and let the meringues remain in the oven for another hour. Remove the meringues from the oven and let cool to room temperature before serving. (The meringues may be stored in an airtight container at room temperature for up to 1 week.)

In a large, nonreactive sauté pan over medium heat, bring ½ cup (4 fl oz/125 ml) water and the ⅔ cup sugar to a boil, stirring to dissolve the sugar. Boil for 2 minutes to make a thin syrup. Add the plum slices and salt and return to a boil. Reduce the heat to a simmer and cook until the plums are tender, 3–4 minutes. Add the butter and swirl the mixture in the pan until the butter is melted.

Arrange the meringues on individual plates. Spoon the plums along with some of the juice on top of the meringues. Serve the Pavlovas right away.

BAKED MERINGUES

The original Pavlova dessert, a baked meringue topped with fruit and whipped cream, was named for the famous Russian ballerina Anna Pavlova. Making crisp meringues requires a high ratio of sugar to egg whites and a slow oven that will dry them out without giving them color. A gas oven with a pilot light is ideal for drying them out. Bakers seeking hard and completely dry baked meringues will leave them in the oven overnight to dry out. This recipe, however, calls for a softer meringue—crisp on the outside and slightly sticky on the inside.

Cranberry & Pear Crumble

MAKES 8 SERVINGS

FOR THE TOPPING:

1½ cups (7½ oz/235 g) all-purpose (plain) flour

½ cup (4 oz/125 g) sugar

½ tsp ground cinnamon

¼ tsp salt

½ cup (4 oz/125 g) cold unsalted butter, cut into ¼-inch (6-mm) cubes

FOR THE FILLING:

⅔ cup (5 oz/155 g) sugar

Pinch of salt

2 Tbsp cornstarch (cornflour)

6 firm but ripe Anjou pears, peeled, halved, cored, and diced (about 6 cups/ 1½ lb/750 g)

1 cup (4 oz/125 g) fresh or unthawed frozen cranberries, coarsely chopped

Vanilla ice cream or Sweetened Whipped Cream (page 377) for serving

PLACE AN OVEN RACK in the lower third of the oven and preheat to 350°F (180°C). Grease a 12-inch (30-cm) oval or 9-by-13-inch (23-by-33-cm) rectangular baking dish with a 2-qt (2-l) capacity.

To make the topping, in a bowl, mix together the flour, sugar, cinnamon, and salt. Using a pastry blender or 2 knives, cut the butter into the flour mixture until it is crumbly. Cover and refrigerate while you prepare the filling.

To make the filling, in a small bowl, stir together the sugar, salt, and cornstarch. In another large bowl, combine the pears and the cranberries. Sprinkle with the sugar mixture and toss to distribute evenly. Spoon the fruit mixture into the prepared baking dish. Sprinkle the topping evenly over the fruit.

Bake the crumble until the topping is crisp and golden brown and the fruit filling bubbles slowly around the edges, 40–50 minutes. Serve warm with a scoop of ice cream or a dollop of whipped cream.

CHOOSING PEARS

Anjou and Bartlett pears are the best for baking because they remain firm and smooth when cooked. When choosing pears for baking, select those that are firm but not rock hard, have a good fragrance, and are smooth and unblemished with stems still attached. Autumn is the best season for Anjou and Bartlett pears, but they are available almost all year long.

Blueberry Turnovers

MAKES 8 SERVINGS

1¼ cups (5 oz/155 g) blueberries
2 Tbsp firmly packed light brown sugar
1 Tbsp all-purpose (plain) flour
1 tsp fresh lemon juice
½ tsp pure vanilla extract
¼ tsp finely grated lemon zest
Pinch of salt
1 large egg, at room temperature
Flaky Pastry Dough, Double-Crust Variation (page 373)
2 Tbsp sliced (flaked) almonds (optional)
2 tsp granulated sugar (optional)

PREHEAT THE OVEN TO 400°F (200°C). Line the bottom of a rimmed baking sheet with parchment (baking) paper.

In a bowl, toss the blueberries with the brown sugar, flour, lemon juice, vanilla, lemon zest, and salt, crushing the berries slightly with the back of a spoon, until the dry ingredients are evenly moist. Set the mixture aside.

In a small bowl, using a fork, make an egg wash by stirring together the egg and 2 tsp water until well blended. Set aside.

On a lightly floured work surface, roll out one dough disk into a 10½-inch (27-cm) square about ⅛ inch (3 mm) thick. Use a dough scraper or an icing spatula to loosen the pastry if it sticks. Trim away the ragged edges, removing about ¼ inch (6 mm) from each side. Repeat with the second disk. Cut each square into four 5-inch (13-cm) squares.

Spoon some of the blueberry filling onto the center of each square, dividing the filling evenly. Lightly brush the edges of the squares with some of the egg wash, then fold the dough over the filling to form triangles. Crimp the edges with the tines of a fork to seal. Place on the prepared baking sheet about 1½ inches (4 cm) apart. Brush the turnovers with the remaining egg wash and sprinkle evenly with the almonds and granulated sugar, if desired. Cut 2 or 3 small slits in the top of each turnover to allow steam to escape during baking.

Bake the turnovers until golden brown, 20–25 minutes. Let cool on a rack. Serve warm or at room temperature.

EGG WASH

These turnovers, like many double-crust pies, are brushed with an egg wash before baking. The wash, a mixture of egg or egg yolk and water, milk, or cream beaten together just until blended, gives the baked crust a lovely golden color. Use a pastry brush to swab the dough lightly but evenly. The egg wash also helps to hold on toppings like the sugar or almonds used here.

Plum Buckle

MAKES 8 SERVINGS

PITTING STONE FRUIT

Using a paring knife, cut the fruit in half lengthwise, cutting carefully around the pit at the center. Rotate the halves in opposite directions to separate them. Use the tip of the knife to gently dig under the pit and ease it out. You may have to try from a couple of different angles, depending on the ripeness of the fruit and whether you are using clingstone fruit (when the flesh adheres to the pit, making it more difficult to remove).

Vegetable-oil cooking spray

1½ cups (7½ oz/235 g) all-purpose (plain) flour

1 tsp baking powder

¼ tsp salt

1 cup (8 oz/250 g) unsalted butter, at room temperature

1 cup (8 oz/250 g) plus 1 Tbsp sugar

2 large eggs, at room temperature

6–8 plums (about 1 lb/500 g), halved, pitted (left), and each half cut into 4 slices

Ground cinnamon and sugar for sprinkling

PLACE AN OVEN RACK in the lower third of the oven and preheat to 350°F (180°C). Coat a 9-inch (23-cm) round or 8-inch (20-cm) square cake pan with cooking spray. Line the bottom with parchment (baking) paper and coat the paper with more spray.

In a bowl, whisk together the flour, baking powder, and salt. In a stand mixer fitted with the paddle attachment, beat together the butter and the 1 cup sugar until pale and fluffy. Add the eggs one at a time, beating well after each addition. Add the flour mixture and mix well.

Scrape the batter into the prepared pan and spread evenly. Poke the plum slices into the batter, placing them close together. In a small bowl, combine ¼ tsp cinnamon and 1 Tbsp sugar, and sprinkle over the surface.

Bake until the top is golden, the edges pull away from the pan, and a skewer or cake tester inserted into the center comes out clean, 50–60 minutes.

Let cool for about 30 minutes before serving.

NOTE: A homey, old-fashioned dessert, a buckle is a dish in which cake batter is mixed with fruit, often blueberries, and then baked. It is often topped with a cinnamon streusel.

GRINDING ALMONDS

Almonds and stone fruits such as cherries, whose pits have an almondlike flavor, have a natural affinity. Look for finely ground almonds, or almond flour, at specialty markets, or grind whole nuts yourself. Choose raw or blanched untoasted almonds. About ¾ cup (3½ oz/105 g) whole almonds will be needed to yield ½ cup (2 oz/60 g) ground nuts. Almonds are best ground in a nut grinder, although a food processor will also work. Use short pulses and be sure not to grind the almonds for too long, or you'll end up extracting the nut oils and producing almond butter.

Cherry Clafoutis

MAKES 6–8 SERVINGS

1–2 Tbsp unsalted butter, at room temperature

½ cup (4 oz/125 g) plus 2 Tbsp granulated sugar

3 cups (1 lb/500 g) fresh or frozen cherries, pitted (see Note)

4 large eggs

1½ cups (12 fl oz/375 ml) whole milk

2 Tbsp kirsch or other cherry brandy

2 tsp pure vanilla extract

½ tsp finely grated lemon zest

¼ tsp salt

¾ cup (4 oz/125 g) all-purpose (plain) flour

½ cup (2 oz/60 g) finely ground almonds (left)

Confectioners' (icing) sugar for dusting

PREHEAT THE OVEN TO 425°F (220°C). Generously grease a 12-inch (30-cm) oval or 9-by-13 inch (23-by-33-cm) rectangular baking dish with a 2 qt (2-l) capacity with the butter. Dust with the 2 Tbsp granulated sugar. Spread the cherries in an even layer in the dish.

In a blender, combine the ½ cup granulated sugar, eggs, milk, kirsch, vanilla, lemon zest, and salt. Blend until smooth, about 1 minute. Add the flour and ground almonds and blend until smooth, about 1 minute. Scrape down the sides of the blender and blend for 30 seconds more. Pour the mixture over the cherries and spread evenly in the pan.

Bake the clafoutis until the edges are puffed and golden, the center is firm, and a skewer or cake tester inserted into the center comes out clean, 40–45 minutes. Let cool on a wire rack for about 30 minutes.

Using a fine-mesh sieve, dust the surface with confectioners' sugar. Serve warm or at room temperature.

NOTE: In the French countryside, this summertime favorite is typically made with whole unpitted cherries, which prevents the cherry juice from bleeding into the batter as it bakes. You may choose to use whole cherries here, but be sure to alert diners to the presence of the pits.

Peaches & Cream Cobbler

MAKES 8 SERVINGS

1 cup (8 fl oz/250 ml) heavy (double) cream

⅔ cup (5 oz/155 g) plus 2 Tbsp sugar

1 tsp cornstarch (cornflour)

5 lb (2.5 kg) ripe peaches, peeled (page 178), pitted, and cut into wedges ½ inch (12 mm) thick

2 cups (10 oz/315 g) all-purpose (plain) flour

1 Tbsp baking powder

½ tsp ground cinnamon

½ tsp salt

6 Tbsp (3 oz/90 g) cold unsalted butter, cut into ½-inch cubes

⅔ cup (5 fl oz/160 ml) milk, or as needed

1 large egg

1 tsp pure vanilla extract

Vanilla ice cream for serving (optional)

PREHEAT THE OVEN TO 375°F (190°C). Lightly grease a 15-by-10-inch (38-by-25-cm) baking dish. In the baking dish, whisk together the cream, the ⅔ cup sugar, and cornstarch. Add the peaches and mix gently.

To make the cobbler dough, sift together the flour, the 2 Tbsp sugar, baking powder, cinnamon, and salt into a bowl. Cut in the butter (right) until the mixture resembles coarse meal. In a large glass measuring cup, whisk together the milk, egg, and vanilla. Using a wooden spoon, stir enough of the milk mixture into the flour mixture to make a moist dough. You may not need all of the milk mixture.

Divide the dough into 8 pieces and pat each into a ½-inch (12-mm) disk. Place the dough on top of the peaches, covering them nearly completely. Bake until the filling is bubbling and the topping is golden brown, about 50 minutes. Let the cobbler cool for 10 minutes, then spoon it into individual bowls. Top with vanilla ice cream, if desired.

CUTTING IN BUTTER

Cobbler dough calls for cutting cold fat into flour to create a crumbly mixture. The pieces of butter or shortening melt in the oven, forming tiny pockets of steam that contribute to a flaky texture. You can use a pastry blender, 2 knives, or a food processor, but transfer the crumbly mixture to a bowl before stirring in the liquids. Place the cubed butter in the freezer for about 15 minutes before cutting it into the flour.

Strawberry Shortcakes

MAKES 6 SERVINGS

1⅔ cups (7½ oz/235 g) all-purpose (plain) flour

¼ cup (1¾ oz/50 g) plus 2 Tbsp sugar

1 Tbsp baking powder

1 tsp finely grated lemon zest

¾ tsp salt

½ cup (4 oz/125 g) cold unsalted butter, cut into small pieces

¾ cup (6 fl oz/180 ml) buttermilk

½ tsp pure vanilla extract

4 cups (1 lb/500 g) strawberries, hulled and cut into slices ¼ inch (6 mm) thick

Sweetened Whipped Cream (page 377)

PREHEAT THE OVEN TO 400°F (200°C). Have ready an ungreased baking sheet.

In a bowl, whisk together the flour, the 2 Tbsp sugar, baking powder, lemon zest, and salt until well blended. Using a pastry blender or 2 knives, cut in the butter until the pieces are no larger than peas. Add the buttermilk and vanilla and gently toss with a fork or silicone spatula until the flour is just moistened and the ingredients are blended.

Turn the shaggy dough out onto a lightly floured work surface. Gently press the dough into a thick rectangle about 6 by 4 inches (15 by 10 cm). Trim the edges even with a large sharp knife, then cut the dough into 6 equal squares. Place the squares on the baking sheet, spacing them well apart, and bake until puffed and golden, 15–18 minutes. Transfer to a wire rack to cool slightly.

Meanwhile, in a bowl, toss together the strawberries and the ¼ cup sugar with a fork, lightly crushing some of the berries. Cover and refrigerate the berries until chilled.

To serve, split the shortcakes in half horizontally and place the bottom halves, cut side up, on serving plates. Spoon some of the strawberries, including the juices, over each half and top with a dollop of the whipped cream. Top with the shortcake halves, cut side down. Serve right away.

SHORTCAKE DOUGH

When properly mixed, shortcake dough should be rough, even shaggy. You might be tempted to mix it more, but resist, or you won't end up with a flaky biscuit. Work the dough on a lightly floured work surface, gently pressing and patting it into a thick rectangle. Incorporating too much flour will make the dough tough. Cutting the dough into squares is preferable to rounds. Rounds leave scraps, which must be patted back together to form more cakes. The result is overworked dough and a few tough shortcakes. Shortcake squares will all turn out equally tender and delicious.

CUSTARDS & EGG DISHES

Vanilla Bean Crème Brûlée

MAKES 6 SERVINGS

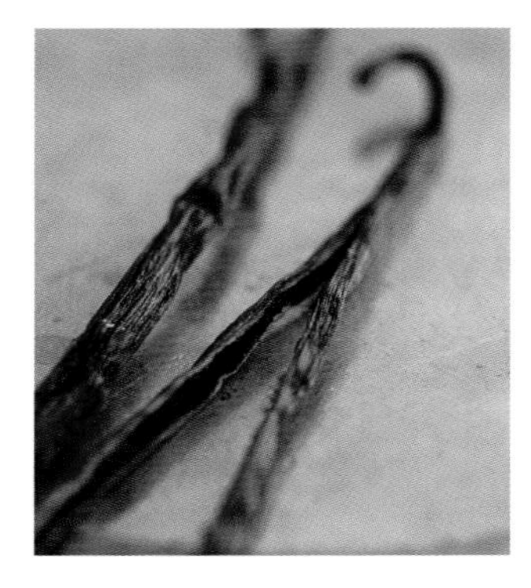

VANILLA BEANS

A vanilla bean is the cured pod of a type of climbing orchid. For the best flavor, choose plump, dark pods showing no signs of shriveling. Most recipes call for a whole or half bean split lengthwise. Splitting the pod allows the tiny seeds to escape and their flavor to permeate a dish. If infusing liquids with vanilla, steep the split bean in the liquid, then remove the pod and scrape the seeds into the liquid. The pod can be used again, although its flavor will be less intense. Once dry, a leftover bean may be buried in a jar of sugar to give the sugar a subtle vanilla flavor.

3 cups (24 fl oz/750 ml) heavy (double) cream

½ vanilla bean, split lengthwise (left)

8 large egg yolks, at room temperature

½ cup (3½ oz/105 g) plus ⅓ cup (2⅓ oz/70 g) sugar

PREHEAT THE OVEN TO 300°F (150°C). Have ready six ¾-cup (6–fl oz/180-ml) ramekins and a shallow roasting pan.

In a saucepan over medium heat, combine the cream and vanilla bean. Bring to a gentle boil, remove from the heat, cover, and set aside for 15–30 minutes to blend the flavors. Remove the vanilla bean from the cream and, using the tip of a knife, scrape the seeds into the cream. Discard the bean or save for another use (left).

Return the cream to medium heat and bring almost to a boil. Remove from the heat. In a bowl, whisk together the egg yolks and the ⅓ cup sugar just until blended. Slowly whisk in the hot cream. Return the mixture to the saucepan over medium-low heat. Cook, stirring constantly, until the custard is thick enough to coat the back of a spoon, about 3 minutes. Do not let it boil. Pour the custard through a strainer into the ramekins, dividing it evenly among them.

Arrange the ramekins in the roasting pan. Pour very hot tap water into the pan to come halfway up the sides of the ramekins. Cover the pan with aluminum foil. Bake until the custards are set but the centers still jiggle slightly when the ramekins are gently shaken, about 40 minutes. Remove from the oven but leave in the water bath until cool enough to handle, then lift out the ramekins. Cover and refrigerate until well chilled, up to overnight.

Just before serving, preheat the broiler (grill). Sift the remaining ½ cup sugar over the tops of the chilled custards to form a thin, even layer and place the ramekins on a baking sheet. Slip the baking sheet under the broiler 2–3 inches (5–7.5 cm) from the heat source and broil (grill) until the sugar melts and caramelizes, 1–2 minutes. Turn the ramekins as needed to cook the sugar evenly. Alternatively, use a small kitchen blowtorch to caramelize the sugar. Serve right away.

Bread Pudding

MAKES 8 SERVINGS

Unsalted butter for greasing

12 slices day-old baguette, cut into ¾-inch (2-cm) cubes (about 6 cups/ 12 oz/375 g)

4 large eggs, at room temperature

½ cup (4 oz/125 g) firmly packed light brown sugar

¾ tsp pure vanilla extract

½ tsp ground cinnamon

Pinch of freshly grated nutmeg

Pinch of salt

4 cups (32 fl oz/1 l) whole milk

¼ cup (1½ oz/45 g) dried cranberries or raisins

Confectioners' (icing) sugar for garnish

LIGHTLY GREASE an 8-inch (20-cm) square baking dish. Spread the bread cubes in it.

In a bowl, whisk together the eggs, brown sugar, vanilla, cinnamon, nutmeg, and salt until well blended. Pour in the milk and whisk until combined. Pour the mixture over the bread cubes. Let sit, pressing down on the bread occasionally, until the bread is evenly soaked, about 20 minutes.

Meanwhile, preheat the oven to 350°F (180°C). Have ready a large, shallow roasting pan.

Scatter the cranberries evenly over the surface of the soaked bread and press to submerge the fruit. Set the baking dish in the roasting pan. Add very hot tap water to the roasting pan to come halfway up the sides of the baking dish.

Bake the pudding until a knife inserted near the center comes out almost clean, 45–55 minutes. Serve warm or at room temperature, with a generous dusting of confectioners' sugar over the top of each slice.

BREAD FOR PUDDING

A simple bread pudding is the perfect use for a day-old baguette or coarse country loaf. These breads have a similar texture and both have a rather bland flavor when stale—the perfect foil for a flavorful custard. Cut the bread into ¾-inch (2-cm) slices, then cut again into ¾-inch (2-cm) cubes. These bite-sized pieces are perfect for soaking up all the custard, yet still hold together well enough to give the dessert some texture.

Grand Marnier Soufflé

MAKES 6–8 SERVINGS

1 cup (8 fl oz/250 ml) whole milk

6 large eggs, separated, at room temperature

⅔ cup (4⅔ oz/145 g) sugar, plus extra for dusting

3 Tbsp all-purpose (plain) flour

2 tsp finely grated orange zest

Pinch of salt

¼ cup (2 fl oz/60 ml) Grand Marnier or other orange liqueur

1 tsp pure vanilla extract

Unsalted butter for greasing

Crème Anglaise (page 377) for serving

SOUFFLÉ SAVVY

A soufflé is made from a light batter leavened by whipped egg whites. In the heat of the oven, the air in the egg white foam expands to make the soufflé rise. Soufflés should be served directly from the oven, before they have a chance to deflate. Soufflé dishes, made of ceramic to help hold in the heat, have tall, straight sides that are usually greased and then dusted with sugar (or, for savory soufflés, bread crumbs) to help the batter climb the sides of the dish.

IN A SAUCEPAN OVER MEDIUM HEAT, warm the milk until small bubbles appear along the edge of the pan. Remove from the heat. In a bowl, whisk together the egg yolks, ⅓ cup (2⅓ oz/70 g) of the sugar, the flour, the zest, and the salt until pale and well blended. Slowly add the hot milk while whisking. Pour the mixture back into the saucepan and place over medium-low heat. Cook, whisking constantly, until the mixture comes to a boil. Continue to cook, whisking constantly, for 1 minute. Remove from the heat and whisk in the liqueur and vanilla. Pour this custard mixture into a large bowl and gently press a piece of plastic wrap directly onto the surface to prevent a skin from forming. Let cool to room temperature or refrigerate until ready to bake.

Preheat the oven to 375°F (190°C). Lightly grease a 6-cup (48–fl oz/1.5-l) soufflé dish and dust with sugar.

Remove the plastic wrap from the custard mixture and whisk until smooth. In a deep, spotlessly clean bowl, using an electric mixer on medium-high speed, beat the egg whites until they are foamy and soft peaks form when the beaters are lifted. Gradually add the remaining ⅓ cup sugar while beating, and continue to beat until stiff peaks form (see page 155).

Scoop one-fourth of the egg whites onto the custard mixture and, using a silicone spatula, gently fold the egg whites in to lighten the mixture. Fold in the remaining egg whites just until no white streaks remain. Scoop the mixutre into the prepared dish. Run a thumb around the exposed part of the inside rim of the dish to keep the batter from sticking and help the soufflé rise.

Bake until the soufflé is puffed and the top is browned, but the soufflé still jiggles slightly when the dish is gently shaken, about 30 minutes. Serve right away with the crème anglaise.

Apple Soufflé with Crème Anglaise

MAKES 4–6 SERVINGS

3 "eating" apples such as Fuji or Golden Delicious, peeled, cored, and cut into eighths

1 Tbsp dry white wine

1 tsp unsalted butter

2 tsp sugar plus 1/3 cup (3 oz/90 g)

6 large egg whites

Pinch of salt

1/4 tsp fresh lemon juice

Crème Anglaise (page 377) for serving

IN A SMALL SAUCEPAN over low heat, combine the apples, wine, and 1 Tbsp water. Cook, covered, until the apples are soft, about 20 minutes. Uncover and continue cooking until the liquid evaporates, 5 minutes longer. Let the mixture cool for 5 minutes, then purée in a food processor until smooth.

Preheat the oven to 400°F (200°C). Grease a 6-cup (48–fl oz/1.5-l) soufflé dish with the butter and dust with the 2 tsp sugar.

In a large metal bowl, using an electric mixer, beat the egg whites until foamy. Add the salt and lemon juice and beat until soft peaks form. Slowly add the 1/3 cup sugar, beating until stiff peaks form. Using a silicone spatula, fold in the apple purée. Scoop the mixture into the dish, mounding a bit above the rim and flattening the top.

Bake until puffed and firm, 25–30 minutes. Serve at once on dessert plates with a spoonful of crème anglaise alongside.

CRÈME ANGLAISE

When making this sauce, it is crucial to keep the egg yolks from getting too hot too quickly. To judge when the custard is done, use the "trail test": Lift the spoon from the saucepan and draw your fingertip across it. If no sauce drips across the trail, it has reached the correct consistency.

Chocolate Pots de Crème

MAKES 6 SERVINGS

USING A WATER BATH

Delicate foods like custards, puddings, and mousses are protected from harsh oven heat by a water bath, also known as a *bain-marie*. Specialty water-bath pans are available, but it is easy to fashion one from your cupboard. All you need is a large, shallow pan to hold the dish or dishes containing the food. Once the dish(es) are in the pan, add hot water to the pan to reach halfway up their sides or as specified in a recipe. Sometimes the recipe will call for covering the pan. The food will cook gently and uniformly in a water bath without overheating.

1⅓ cups (11 fl oz/340 ml) heavy (double) cream

1⅓ cups (11 fl oz/340 ml) whole milk

6 oz (185 g) bittersweet chocolate, finely chopped

1 Tbsp instant espresso powder or instant coffee powder

6 large egg yolks

¼ cup (1¾ oz/50 g) sugar

PREHEAT THE OVEN TO 300°F (150°C). Have ready six ¾-cup (6–fl oz/ 180-ml) ramekins and a shallow roasting pan.

In a saucepan over medium-low heat, combine the cream, milk, chopped chocolate, and espresso powder and cook, whisking frequently, until the chocolate is melted and the liquid is hot. Do not let boil. Remove from the heat.

In a bowl, whisk together the egg yolks and sugar until well blended. While whisking constantly, gradually pour the hot chocolate mixture into the yolk mixture. Pour the custard through a sieve placed over a 4-cup (32–fl oz/1-l) glass measuring pitcher. Using a large spoon, skim off any foam and bubbles from the top.

Divide the custard evenly among the ramekins. Place the ramekins in the roasting pan and pour very hot tap water into the pan to come halfway up the sides of the cups. Cover the pan with aluminum foil.

Bake the custards until they are set but the centers still jiggle slightly when a cup is gently shaken, 55–60 minutes. Remove the pan from the oven and leave the ramekins in the water until cool enough to handle. Cover and refrigerate until well chilled, at least 2 hours or up to overnight. Serve chilled.

German Apple Pancake

MAKES 3 OR 4 SERVINGS

5 large eggs

2 tsp pure vanilla extract

½ cup (4 oz/125 g) plus 1 Tbsp granulated sugar

⅓ cup (2 oz/60 g) all-purpose (plain) flour

1 tsp baking powder

⅛ tsp fine sea salt

1½ Tbsp unsalted butter

2 large, tart apples, peeled, cored, and cut into wedges ½ inch (12 mm) thick

1 tsp ground cinnamon

1 Tbsp confectioners' (icing) sugar (optional)

¾ cup (3 oz/90 g) fresh raspberries (optional)

¼ cup (2 oz/60 g) crème fraîche, homemade (page 378), or purchased

IN A BLENDER, combine the eggs, the vanilla, and the ½ cup granulated sugar and blend until combined, about 5 seconds. Add the flour, baking powder, and salt and mix until smooth, about 10 seconds longer.

Preheat the oven to 375°F (190°C). Place a 10-inch (25-cm) ovenproof, nonstick frying pan over medium heat and add the butter. When the butter has foamed and the foam has subsided, add the apples and sauté, stirring occasionally, until softened, 4–5 minutes. Sprinkle the apples with the cinnamon and the remaining 1 Tbsp granulated sugar. Stir together and sauté until the apples are nicely glazed and the edges are slightly translucent, about 2 minutes longer.

Spread the apples evenly in the frying pan and pour the batter slowly over the top, so the apples stay in place. Reduce the heat to medium-low and cook until the bottom is firm, about 8 minutes. Transfer the pan to the oven and cook until the top of the pancake is firm, about 10 minutes longer.

Remove from the oven, invert a flat serving plate over the frying pan, and then, holding the pan and plate together, invert them together and lift off the pan. Cut the pancake into 3 or 4 wedges and transfer to individual plates. If desired, sprinkle each portion with confectioners' sugar and scatter with a few raspberries. Place a dollop of crème fraîche on top and serve at once.

GERMAN APPLE PANCAKES

The traditional way to make this beloved German dish, known as *Apfelpfannkuchen*, is to flip the pancake in the pan while it is on the stove top to cook the second side. This can be a tricky maneuver since you don't want to displace the apples. Here, the pancake is finished in the oven, which is an easier option. Most other European pancakes are also cooked at least partially in the oven (see Swedish Pancake, page 362). European pancakes often contain pieces of fruit or meat, such as the apples used here or the ham called for in Swedish pancakes.

Coffee & Kahlúa Flan

MAKES 8–10 SERVINGS

MAKING A CARAMEL

Always use caution when making caramel, as the mixture is dangerously hot. Use a heavy, light-colored saucepan, preferably copper, so you can judge the color of the syrup. The addition of a little corn syrup helps prevent the sugar from recrystallizing on the sides of the pan. Once all the ingredients are in the pan, the sugar has dissolved, and the liquid has begun to turn amber, do not stir it. Also, never leave the stove once the syrup starts to color. The caramelizing process is quick, and the syrup can burn easily.

⅔ cup (5 oz/155 g) sugar

1 Tbsp corn syrup

1 can (14 fl oz/430 ml) sweetened condensed milk

¾ cup (6 fl oz/180 ml) half-and-half (half cream)

1 cup (8 fl oz/250 ml) whole milk

2-inch (5-cm) piece Ceylon cinnamon bark or 1-inch (2.5-cm) piece cassia cinnamon bark (page 296)

1 Tbsp Kahlúa or other coffee-flavored liqueur

2 tsp instant coffee powder dissolved in 1 tsp boiling water

5 large eggs

¾ tsp pure vanilla extract

IN A SMALL, HEAVY SAUCEPAN over medium high-heat, combine the sugar, ¼ cup (2 fl oz/60 ml) water, and the corn syrup and bring to a boil, stirring 1–2 times, until the syrup is clear. Reduce the heat to medium and simmer, without stirring, until the syrup begins to darken, 10–15 minutes. Swirl the pan until the syrup is a deep amber, about 1 minute. Immediately pour the resulting caramel into a 9-by-2-inch (23-by-5-cm) round cake pan or into 8–10 individual molds and tilt to distribute evenly over the bottom and a little up the sides. Set aside.

Preheat the oven to 325°F (165°C). In a large saucepan over medium-low heat, combine the condensed milk, half-and-half, whole milk, and cinnamon and bring to a simmer. Remove from the heat and let steep for 10 minutes. Remove the cinnamon and stir in the Kahlúa and the diluted coffee. In a bowl, lightly whisk the eggs until blended. Gradually whisk in the warm milk mixture and then the vanilla. Strain the mixture through a fine-mesh sieve into the prepared mold(s). Place the mold(s) in a large roasting pan and put on the center rack of the oven. Pour boiling water to a depth of 1 inch (2.5 cm) into the roasting pan. Bake, uncovered, just until set and a knife inserted near the center comes out clean, 1–1½ hours for the large flan, and 40–60 minutes for the individual molds. Remove the roasting pan from the oven, remove the flan(s), and transfer to a wire rack. Let cool, cover with plastic wrap, and refrigerate for at least 6 hours or up to 2 days.

To unmold, run a thin knife around the inside edge of the mold(s). Place a serving plate with a rim over the top and invert the plate and flan together. Lift off the mold(s) carefully, scraping out any of the remaining caramel to run over the flan and around the plate. If you have made a large flan, cut into thin wedges to serve.

Swedish Pancake

MAKES 3 OR 4 SERVINGS

LINGONBERRIES

These small, red fruits, grown on bushes that are less than a foot tall, are made into jams, jellies, and preserves, and are popular in Scandinavian cooking. The berries are delicious as a filling for crêpes and as a garnish for other sweet breads and cakes. The name lingonberry originated in Sweden, but the Pacific Northwest now grows more lingonberries than any other region in the world.

¾ cup (4 oz/125 g) all-purpose (plain) flour

¾ cup (6 fl oz/180 ml) whole milk

3 large eggs

1½ Tbsp unsalted butter, melted

1 tsp sugar

⅛ tsp freshly grated nutmeg

Pinch of fine sea salt

2 tsp canola oil

¼ lb (125 g) flavorful cooked ham such as country ham or Black Forest ham, diced

Lingonberry preserves or Dijon mustard for serving

IN A LARGE BOWL, beat together the flour, milk, eggs, butter, sugar, nutmeg, and salt. Cover the bowl and let the batter stand for at least 1 hour to allow the flour to expand. (The batter can be refrigerated for up to 12 hours before cooking, if desired.)

Preheat the oven to 425°F (220°C). Place a 9- or 10-inch (23- or 25-cm) cast-iron frying pan over medium-high heat and add the oil. Swirl around or brush to coat about halfway up the sides of the pan. When the oil is hot, add the ham and stir until crisp and golden, about 4 minutes.

Spread the ham evenly in the frying pan, leaving a 1-inch (2.5-cm) border around the edges. Pour the batter slowly over the top, so the ham stays in place. Transfer the pan to the oven and bake until the pancake is deep, golden brown and very puffy around the edges, 10–15 minutes.

Cut the pancake into 3 or 4 wedges and serve at once, topped with a spoonful of lingonberry preserves or a dollop of mustard.

Potato, Ham & Gruyère Tart

MAKES 4–6 SERVINGS

Flaky Pastry Dough (page 373)

FOR THE FILLING:

1 russet potato, about ½ lb (250 g), scrubbed

1 Tbsp unsalted butter

2 shallots, minced

½ tsp minced fresh thyme

3½ oz (105 g) trimmed Black Forest ham, cut into ⅓-inch (9-mm) dice (about ¾ cup)

½ cup (4 fl oz/125 ml) plus 2 Tbsp heavy (double) cream

1 large egg

Kosher salt and freshly ground pepper

Large pinch of freshly grated nutmeg

⅔ cup (2½ oz/75 g) firmly packed shredded Gruyère cheese

ROLL OUT THE DOUGH DISK into a 12-inch (30-cm) round. Transfer the round to a 9-inch (23-cm) tart pan with removable bottom (see page 385). Trim off any excess dough by gently running a rolling pin across the top of the pan. Press the dough into the sides to extend it slightly above the rim. Refrigerate or freeze the tart shell until firm, about 30 minutes.

Place an oven rack in the lower third of the oven and preheat to 375°F (190°C). Partially blind-bake the shell (right), then transfer the shell to a wire rack to cool. Leaving the oven temperature at 375°F (190°C), place an oven rack in the middle of the oven.

To make the filling, in a pot of salted boiling water, cook the unpeeled whole potato until tender when pierced with a small knife, about 30 minutes. Drain and let cool. Peel and cut into ⅓-inch (9-mm) cubes.

In a heavy frying pan, melt the butter over medium-high heat. Add the shallots and thyme and sauté until the shallots are translucent, about 2 minutes. Add 1 cup (5 oz/155 g) of the potato cubes (reserve any extra for another use). Stir the potato cubes into the shallot mixture and cook for 1 minute. Remove from the heat and stir in the ham.

In a bowl, whisk together the cream, egg, ¼ tsp kosher salt, ¼ tsp pepper, and nutmeg.

Spread the potato mixture evenly in the crust. Sprinkle with the cheese and pour the cream mixture evenly over the top. Bake the tart until the top begins to brown and the center is set, about 15 minutes. Remove from the oven and let cool on a wire rack for 15 minutes. Gently push the bottom of the pan up to loosen the tart from the pan sides. Place the tart, with the pan bottom still adhering to the bottom of the tart, on a serving plate. Serve warm or at room temperature.

BLIND BAKING

Also called prebaking, blind baking means partially or completely baking a pie or tart shell before filling it. To bake partially (as in this recipe), preheat the oven to 375°F (190°C). Lay a sheet of foil over the chilled pastry in the pan. Fit the foil into the pan, completely covering the pastry, and fill with pie weights or raw short-grain rice. Bake until the sides are set but not colored, 15–20 minutes. Remove the pastry shell from the oven and lift off the weights and foil. Return to the oven and continue to bake until pale golden, pricking any bubbles with a fork, about 5 minutes longer.

Cheese Soufflé

MAKES 4 SERVINGS

BREAD CRUMBS

To make fresh bread crumbs, lay slices of fresh French bread flat on a countertop and leave overnight to dry out. Or, use French bread a few days past its peak of freshness. Cut off the crusts, tear the bread into bite-sized pieces, and process in a food processor to the desired texture. For dried bread crumbs, let the bread slices dry out in a 200°F (95°C) oven for about 1 hour. Break the bread into pieces and place in a food processor. Pulse to process into fine crumbs. Sourdough and country-style loaves also make good crumbs.

1 cup (4 oz/125 g) plus 2 Tbsp shredded Gruyère or Comté cheese

2½ Tbsp unsalted butter

3 Tbsp all-purpose (plain) flour

1 cup (8 fl oz/250 ml) whole milk

4 large egg yolks

1 tsp Dijon mustard

Salt and freshly ground white pepper

Pinch of freshly grated nutmeg

5 large egg whites

Pinch of cream of tartar

1 Tbsp fine fresh or dried bread crumbs (left), or purchased bread crumbs

PREHEAT THE OVEN TO 375°F (190°C). Grease a 6-cup (48–fl oz/1.5 l) soufflé dish and then coat the bottom and sides evenly with 1 Tbsp of the cheese.

In a saucepan over medium heat, melt the butter. Add the flour and mix with a wooden spoon for 1 minute. Cook until the mixture is bubbling but still white, about 2 minutes longer. While whisking constantly, add the milk. Bring to a simmer and continue to whisk until the sauce is thick and smooth, about 2 minutes longer. Remove from the heat and let cool for 10 minutes.

Add the egg yolks to the cooled milk mixture and whisk until smooth. Add the mustard, ½ tsp salt, a pinch of white pepper, and the nutmeg and whisk to combine.

In a large, spotlessly clean bowl, using a large balloon whisk or an electric mixer on medium speed, whip the egg whites with a pinch of salt and the cream of tartar until stiff peaks form (see page 155). The peaks should stand upright on the whisk or beaters when lifted. Do not overbeat, or the whites will become rough and lumpy.

Using a silicone spatula, gently fold half of the egg whites into the milk mixture to lighten it. Gently stir in 1 cup of the remaining grated cheese and then fold in the remaining egg whites just until no white streaks remain. Scoop into the prepared dish and sprinkle with the remaining 1 Tbsp cheese and the bread crumbs.

Bake until the soufflé is puffed and the top is browned, 30–35 minutes. Serve at once.

Pepper Jack & Jalapeño Spoon Bread

MAKES 4–6 SERVINGS

1 cup (5 oz/155 g) yellow cornmeal, preferably stone-ground

3 cups (24 fl oz/750 ml) whole milk

1 or 2 large jalapeño chiles, seeded and minced

1 Tbsp finely chopped fresh cilantro (fresh coriander)

½ lb (250 g) pepper jack, Sonoma jack, Monterey jack, or Havarti cheese, cut into ½ inch (12-mm) cubes

4 large eggs, separated, at room temperature

Pinch of sugar

1 tsp fine sea salt

2 Tbsp thinly sliced green onion, tender green parts only

Hot-pepper sauce for serving (optional)

PREHEAT THE OVEN TO 350°F (180°C). Generously grease a 10-inch (25-cm) round or 8-by-10-inch (20-by-25-cm) oval baking dish or cast-iron frying pan.

In a bowl, whisk together the cornmeal and 1 cup (8 fl oz/250 ml) of the milk.

In a large saucepan over medium-high heat, heat the remaining 2 cups (16 fl oz/500 ml) milk until small bubbles appear along the edges of the pan. Pour the cornmeal-milk mixture into the pan and bring to a simmer, stirring constantly. Cook until the cornmeal has thickened enough to see the bottom of the pan when you stir, about 5 minutes. Remove the pan from the heat and stir in the jalapeño(s), cilantro, cheese, egg yolks, sugar, and salt.

In a spotlessly clean bowl, using an electric mixer on high speed, beat the egg whites until stiff peaks form when the beaters are lifted (see page 155). Stir one-fourth of the egg whites thoroughly into the cornmeal mixture to lighten it, then fold in the remaining whites, being careful not to overmix. Pour into the prepared dish.

Bake the spoon bread until puffed and golden, and a toothpick inserted into the center comes out clean, about 45 minutes. Serve at once, sprinkling the green onion and a little hot sauce, if using, over each serving.

ABOUT SPOON BREAD

Despite its name, spoon bread is more like a hearty pudding than a bread. Much like a quiche without the crust, its egg-rich base is the perfect vehicle for featuring endless combinations savory ingredients. Whether you choose fresh spring herbs, rich cheeses, or red bell peppers (capsicums) ripened in the summer sun, it's worth seeking out the highest quality ingredients you can find to feature in this delightfully simple dish.

Rosemary Spoon Bread

MAKES 6 SIDE-DISH SERVINGS

3 cups (24 fl oz/750 ml) whole milk

1 tsp salt

1 cup (5 oz/155 g) yellow cornmeal, preferably stone-ground

4 Tbsp (2 oz/60 g) unsalted butter

3 eggs, separated, at room temperature

2 tsp finely chopped fresh rosemary or 1 tsp crumbled dried rosemary

PREHEAT THE OVEN TO 375°F (190°C). Grease an 8-inch (20-cm) square baking dish (or another baking dish with a 6-cup/48–fl oz/1.5-l liter volume).

In a saucepan, combine 2 cups (16 fl oz/500 ml) of the milk and the salt and bring to a boil over medium-high heat, being careful that the milk does not boil over. Gradually whisk in the cornmeal and return to a boil. Reduce the heat to medium-low and cook, whisking often, until the mixture is quite thick, about 2 minutes.

Remove from the heat. Add the butter and whisk until melted. In a small bowl, whisk together the remaining 1 cup (8 fl oz/250 ml) milk, the egg yolks, and rosemary, then whisk into the cornmeal mixture. Set aside.

In a clean bowl, using clean beaters, beat the egg whites on low speed until foamy. Increase the speed to high and beat just until soft peaks form (see page 155). Using a silicone spatula, stir about one-fourth of the whites into the cornmeal mixture to lighten it, then fold in the remaining whites. Spread the egg white–cornmeal mixture evenly into the prepared dish.

Bake the spoon bread until puffed and golden brown, about 25 minutes. Serve hot.

ABOUT ROSEMARY

A Mediterranean herb, rosemary looks like pine needles on a woody stick. This herb has an assertive flavor that pairs well with lamb, many vegetables, and seafood, but it should be used in moderation. Dried rosemary is very bland compared to fresh, but if used, the hard dry needles should be finely crumbled.

Wild Mushroom Quiche

MAKES 6–8 SERVINGS

Cheese Pastry (right)

1¾ cups (14 fl oz/430 ml) whole milk

1 oz (30 g) dried porcini mushrooms

3 Tbsp unsalted butter

3 Tbsp olive oil

3 shallots, finely chopped

¾ lb (375 g) mixed fresh wild and cultivated mushrooms such as chanterelle, shiitake, and cremini, stems trimmed, brushed clean, and sliced

3 large leeks, white parts only, thinly sliced

1½ Tbsp chopped fresh tarragon

Fine sea salt and freshly ground pepper

1 Tbsp Dijon mustard

¾ cup (6 fl oz/180 ml) heavy (double) cream

3 large whole eggs plus 2 large egg yolks, at room temperature

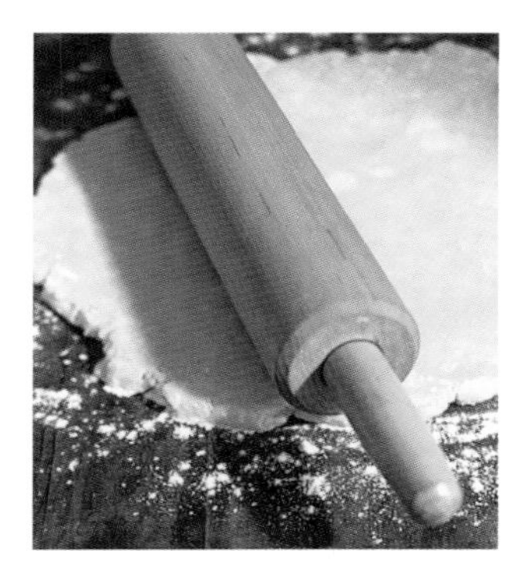

ROLL OUT THE DOUGH DISK into a 10-by-14-inch (25-by-35-cm) rectangle or a 13-inch (33-cm) round. Transfer the pastry to a 9-by-13-inch (23-by-33-cm) tart pan with 2-inch (5-cm) removable sides or a 12-inch (30-cm) round tart pan with removable sides. Ease the pastry into the pan and fold any overhanging pastry back over itself, pressing it into the sides to extend slightly above the rim. Prick with a fork and refrigerate for 30 minutes. Preheat the oven to 400°F (200°C). Line the shell with parchment (baking) paper and fill with pie weights. Bake until the edges begin to shrink away from the pan, about 15 minutes. Remove the paper and weights and bake until the bottom appears dry, about 4 minutes longer. Let cool on a wire rack.

Reduce the oven temperature to 375°F (190°C). In a saucepan over medium heat, heat the milk to just below the boiling point. Remove from the heat, add the dried porcini, and swirl to cover. Let stand until softened, 20–30 minutes. Squeeze the mushrooms, draining the milk back into the pan. Chop the porcini and strain the milk through a fine-mesh sieve. Set both aside separately.

Meanwhile, in a sauté pan over medium-high heat, melt 2 Tbsp each of the butter and olive oil. Reduce the heat to medium and sauté the shallots, stirring, until softened, about 3 minutes. Add all the mushrooms and sauté, stirring, until tender and no liquid remains, about 8 minutes. Transfer to a bowl. In the same pan over low heat, melt the remaining butter and olive oil. Add the leeks and cook, covered, until tender, about 12 minutes. Add the tarragon, season with salt and pepper, and cook for 1 minute.

Spread the base of the pastry shell evenly with the mustard and then the mushroom and leek mixtures. In a bowl, whisk together the reserved milk, cream, eggs, egg yolks, ½ tsp salt, and ¼ tsp pepper. Pour over the vegetables. Bake the quiche until all but the very center is set and lightly browned, 25–30 minutes. Let cool on a wire rack for 15 minutes. Cut into squares and serve.

CHEESE PASTRY

In a food processor, pulse ¼ lb (125 g) diced Gruyère cheese. Add 1½ cups (7½ oz/235 g) all-purpose (plain) flour and ¼ tsp salt and pulse until finely crumbled. Add ½ cup (4 oz/125 g) chilled unsalted butter cut into pieces and pulse until it resembles fluffy bread crumbs. Lightly beat 1 egg, drizzle over the mixture, and pulse twice. Scrape down the bowl sides. Sprinkle 2 Tbsp cold water over the mixture and pulse until a rough mass forms, adding another tablespoon of water if needed. Form the dough into a disk, wrap it tightly with pastic wrap, and refrigerate for at least 2 hours. Let stand at room temperature for 20 minutes before using.

Leek & Goat Cheese Tart

MAKES 4–6 SERVINGS

Flaky Pastry Dough, Quiche Dough Variation (page 373)

2 Tbsp unsalted butter

1 lb (500 g) leeks, including tender green parts, sliced crosswise 1/8 inch (3 mm) thick

Salt and freshly ground pepper

2 whole eggs, plus 1 egg yolk

1 cup (8 fl oz/250 ml) heavy (double) cream or half-and-half (half cream)

Pinch of freshly grated nutmeg

1 cup (4 oz/125 g) shredded Gruyère, Emmentaler, or Jarlsberg cheese

3 Tbsp chopped fresh chives

1/4 lb (125 g) fresh goat cheese, crumbled

ROLL OUT THE DOUGH DISK into a 14-inch (35-cm) round (see page 385). Transfer the dough round to a 9- or 9½-inch (24-cm) tart pan with 2-inch (5-cm) fluted sides, preferably with a removable bottom. Trim off any excess dough by gently running a rolling pin across the top of the pan. Press the dough into the sides of the pan so that it extends slightly above the rim. Refrigerate the tart shell until firm, about 30 minutes.

Meanwhile, place an oven rack in the lower third of the oven and preheat to 375°F (190°C). Partially bake the tart shell as directed on page 385. Transfer the shell to a wire rack. Reduce the oven temperature to 350°F (180°C).

In a large, heavy frying pan, melt the butter over medium-low heat. When it foams, add the leeks, reduce the heat to low, and cook until the leeks are soft and golden, about 15 minutes. Season with salt and pepper and set aside. In a bowl, whisk together the eggs, egg yolk, and cream until blended. Season with the nutmeg, salt, and pepper.

Sprinkle half of the shredded cheese evenly over the bottom of the crust. Top with the leeks, chives, and goat cheese. Pour in the egg mixture, stopping within ½ inch (12 mm) of the rim. Sprinkle with the remaining shredded cheese evenly over the top. Bake until the top is puffed and golden and the filling jiggles slightly, about 25 minutes. Remove from the oven and let stand for 10–20 minutes.

CLEANING LEEKS

Leeks are grown in sandy soil, so they need to be cleaned carefully. Using a sharp knife, trim off the roots and the tough green tops. Peel away the outer layer. Cut a slit lengthwise down the middle of the leek, extending it about three-fourths of the way through the heart of the leek and stopping where the white changes to green. Rinse the slit leek well under cold running water, gently pulling apart the leaf layers to rinse away all of the grit.

Goat Cheese & Ham Soufflé

MAKES 4 SERVINGS

1½ Tbsp unsalted butter

1½ Tbsp all-purpose (plain) flour

1 cup (8 fl oz/250 ml) whole milk

Fine sea salt and freshly ground pepper

5 large eggs, separated

5 oz (155 g) very cold fresh goat cheese

¾ cup (3 oz/90 g) finely diced serrano ham (see Note) or prosciutto

1 Tbsp chopped fresh flat-leaf (Italian) parsley

PREHEAT THE OVEN TO 400°F (200°C). Place a baking sheet on the bottom rack. Generously grease a sturdy 9-inch (23-cm) round or 7-by-10-inch (18-by-25-cm) oval gratin dish or a 6-cup (48–fl oz/1.5-l) soufflé dish and place in the freezer.

In a small saucepan over medium heat, melt the butter. When the foam has subsided, whisk in the flour. Cook, stirring constantly, until the mixture is bubbling and has only just begun to brown, about 2 minutes. Slowly drizzle in the milk, whisking constantly to prevent lumps from forming. Simmer, stirring occasionally, until the mixture thickens, about 5 minutes. Remove from the heat. Stir in ¼ tsp salt and a generous grinding of pepper. Quickly whisk in the egg yolks until completely blended.

In a large, spotlessly clean bowl, combine the egg whites and a large pinch of salt. Using an electric mixer on high speed, beat almost until stiff peaks form when the beaters are lifted (see page 155). Thoroughly stir about one-third of the yolk mixture into the egg whites, then using a large silicone spatula, fold in the remaining yolk mixture, taking care not to crush too much air out of the egg whites. Crumble the goat cheese over the mixture in pea-sized pieces, and scatter the ham and parsley over the top. Fold the mixture once or twice to distribute the ingredients; do not overmix. Scoop the mixture into the prepared dish, smooth the top gently, and place in the oven.

Bake until puffed and golden and still a bit wobbly in the center, about 25 minutes.

NOTE: Spanish serrano ham is salted and hung in dedicated drying halls to air-cure. It is similar to its more famous Italian cousin, prosciutto, but is traditionally cut thicker and has a more earthy flavor.

SEPARATING EGGS

When separating eggs for a soufflé, never allow even a speck of egg yolk to fall into the egg whites. Just a little bit of yolk will prevent the whites from whipping up properly. Crack each egg over a small bowl and pass the yolk back and forth between the shell halves, letting the whites fall into the bowl. Slip the yolk into a separate bowl, and transfer the whites to a third bowl. Separate each additional egg over the original empty bowl to ensure that the whites in the third bowl remain untainted.

Basic Recipes

Flaky crusts, light cakes, fluffy frostings, and tender doughs are essential for delicious desserts, pastries, and breads. Learn these basic recipes, and you can even improvise the rest, creating delicious fillings and toppings to suit your taste.

Flaky Pastry Dough

MAKES DOUGH FOR ONE 9-INCH (23-CM) SINGLE-CRUST PIE OR ONE 10-INCH (25-CM) GALETTE

1¼ cups (6½ oz/200 g) all-purpose (plain) flour

1 Tbsp sugar

¼ tsp salt

½ cup (4 oz/125 g) cold unsalted butter, cut into ¼-inch (6-mm) cubes

3 Tbsp ice water, plus more if needed

Hand Method

In a large bowl, stir together the flour, sugar, and salt. Using a pastry blender or 2 knives, cut the butter into the flour mixture until the texture resembles coarse meal, with butter pieces no larger than small peas. Add the 3 Tbsp water and mix with a fork just until the dough pulls together. If the dough is dry, mix in more water 1 Tbsp at a time.

Stand Mixer Method

Fit the mixer with the paddle attachment. In the bowl of the mixer, combine the flour, sugar, and salt, and with the mixer on low speed, stir together the ingredients. Add the butter and toss with a fork to coat with the flour mixture. Mix on medium-low speed until the texture resembles coarse meal, with butter pieces no larger than small peas. Add the 3 Tbsp water and mix on low speed just until the dough pulls together. If the dough is dry, mix in more water 1 Tbsp at a time.

Food Processor Method

In the bowl of a food processor, combine the flour, sugar, and salt and pulse to blend. Add the butter and pulse 5 or 6 times, until the mixture is the texture of coarse meal with butter pieces no larger than small peas. Add the 3 Tbsp water through the feed tube, pulsing once after each addition and adding just enough to make a crumbly dough; it will not hold together on its own but will when gathered into a ball with your hands. If the dough is dry, mix in more water 1 Tbsp at a time.

To Shape the Dough

Transfer the dough to a work surface, pat into a ball, and flatten into a disk. (Although many dough recipes call for chilling the dough at this point, this dough should be rolled out right away for the best results.) Lightly flour the work surface, then flatten the disk with 6–8 gentle taps of the rolling pin. Lift the dough and give it a quarter turn. Lightly dust the top of the dough or the rolling pin with flour as needed, then roll out as described on page 385 into a round at least 12 inches (30 cm) in diameter and about ⅛ inch (3 mm) thick, or according to the recipe.

MAKE-AHEAD TIP: Pastry dough can be made ahead and frozen for up to 2 months. To freeze, pat the dough into a disk and wrap well with plastic wrap.

VARIATION: DOUBLE-CRUST DOUGH
Make Flaky Pastry Dough using double the amount of ingredients. Cut the dough in half, and then pat each half into a round, flat disk. Roll out one disk into a 12-inch (30-cm) round as directed and line the pan or dish (see page 385). Press any scraps trimmed from the first round into the bottom of the second disk. Roll out the second dough disk into a round at least 12 inches (30 cm) in diameter and about ⅛ inch (3 mm) thick and refrigerate until ready to use.

VARIATION: LATTICE-TOP DOUGH
Make Flaky Pastry Dough using double the amount of ingredients. Cut the dough in half, and pat one half into a round, flat disk. Roll out the disk into a 12-inch (30-cm) round as directed and line the pan or dish (see page 385). Press any scraps trimmed from the first round into the bottom of the remaining dough half. Pat the dough into a rectangle and roll out into a rectangular shape about ⅛ inch (3 mm) thick. Trim to cut out a 14-by-11-inch (35-by-28-cm) rectangle and refrigerate until ready to use.

VARIATION: QUICHE DOUGH
Make Flaky Pastry Dough, but increase the flour to 1½ cups (7½ oz/235 g). Omit the sugar, increase the salt to ½ tsp, and increase the butter to 10 Tbsp. You will also need to use 1–2 Tbsp more water.

Basic Tart Dough

MAKES DOUGH FOR ONE 9½-INCH (24-CM) TART, TWELVE 2-INCH (5-CM) TARTLETS, OR ONE 13¾-BY-4¼-INCH (35-BY-11-CM) TART

1 large egg yolk

2 Tbsp ice water, plus more if needed

1 tsp pure vanilla extract

1¼ cups (6½ oz/200 g) all-purpose (plain) flour

⅓ cup (3 oz/90 g) sugar

¼ tsp salt

½ cup (4 oz/125 g) cold unsalted butter, cut into ¼-inch (6-mm) cubes

Hand Method

In a small bowl, stir together the egg yolk, the 2 Tbsp water, and vanilla. In a large bowl, stir together the flour, sugar, and salt. Using a pastry blender or 2 knives, cut the butter into the flour mixture until the texture resembles coarse meal, with butter pieces no larger than small peas. Add the egg mixture and mix with a fork just until the dough pulls together. If the dough is dry, mix in more water 1 Tbsp at a time.

Stand Mixer Method

In a small bowl, stir together the egg yolk, the 2 Tbsp water, and vanilla. Fit the mixer with the paddle attachment. In the bowl of the mixer, combine the flour, sugar, and salt, and with the mixer on low speed, stir together the ingredients. Add the butter and mix on medium-low speed until the texture resembles coarse meal, with butter pieces no larger than small peas. Add the egg mixture and mix just until the dough pulls together. If the dough is dry, mix in more water 1 Tbsp at a time.

Food Processor Method

In a small bowl, stir together the egg yolk, the 2 Tbsp water, and vanilla. In the bowl of a food processor, combine the flour, sugar, and salt and pulse to blend. Add the butter and pulse until the mixture resembles coarse meal with butter pieces no larger than small peas. Add the egg mixture and pulse just until the dough pulls together. If the dough is dry, mix in more water 1 Tbsp at a time.

To Shape the Dough

Transfer the dough to a work surface, pat into a ball, and flatten into a disk. The dough can be used right away or wrapped in plastic wrap and refrigerated until well chilled, about 30 minutes.

Lightly flour the work surface, then flatten the disk with 6–8 gentle taps of the rolling pin. Lift the dough and give it a quarter turn. Lightly dust the top of the dough or the rolling pin with flour as needed, then roll out as described on page 385 until the dough is about 1/8 inch (3 mm) thick. If making a tart or standard-sized tartlet, use a small, sharp knife to cut out a round or rounds 2–3 inches (5–8 cm) larger in diameter than the pans. If making miniature tartlets, use a small, sharp knife or a cookie cutter to cut out rounds 1/2–1 inch (12 mm–2.5 cm) larger in diameter than the pans. If using a rectangular tart pan, pat the dough into a rectangular shape about 1/8 inch (3 mm) thick. Trim to cut out a rectangle about 2 inches (5 cm) larger on all sides of the pan.

MAKE-AHEAD TIP: This tart dough can be made ahead and frozen for up to 2 months.

Graham Cracker Crust

MAKES ENOUGH FOR ONE 8-INCH (20-CM) CAKE

Nonstick vegetable-oil cooking spray

1½ cups (4½ oz/140 g) graham cracker crumbs

2 Tbsp sugar

½ tsp ground cinnamon

4 Tbsp (2 oz/60 g) unsalted butter, melted

Place an oven rack in the lower third of the oven and preheat to 325°F (165°C). Grease an 8-inch (20-cm) springform pan with the cooking spray.

In a bowl, combine the graham cracker crumbs, sugar, and cinnamon. Stir in the melted butter until the crumbs are evenly moistened. Press the mixture firmly and evenly into the pan, bringing it 2–3 inches (5–7.5 cm) up the sides. Bake until the crust is a light golden brown and is set, about 10 minutes.

VARIATION: 9-INCH CRUST For the Vanilla Cheesecake recipe on page 167, use a 9-inch (23-cm) springform pan. Increase the amount of sugar in the crust to 3 Tbsp, and bake the cheesecake at 400°F (200°C).

Cookie Crumb Crust

MAKES ONE 9-INCH (23-CM) CRUST

1¼ cups (4 oz/125 g) cookie crumbs such as graham crackers, chocolate wafers, or gingersnaps

5 Tbsp unsalted butter, melted

3 Tbsp sugar

Place an oven rack in the middle of the oven and preheat to 350°F (180°C). In a bowl, combine the cookie crumbs, melted butter, and sugar and stir until the crumbs are evenly moistened. Press the mixture firmly and evenly into the bottom and all the way up the sides of a 9-inch (23-cm) pie pan or dish.

Bake until firm, about 5 minutes. For a firmer, crunchier crust, bake for an additional 5 minutes.

Yellow Sponge Cake

MAKES ONE 8-INCH (20-CM) ROUND CAKE OR ONE 12-BY-9-INCH (30-BY-23-CM) SHEET CAKE

Nonstick vegetable-oil cooking spray

½ cup (2 oz/60 g) cake (soft-wheat) flour

3 large eggs, separated

2 Tbsp unsalted butter, melted and slightly cooled

1 tsp pure vanilla extract

½ cup (4 oz/125 g) sugar

Preheat the oven to 350°F (180°C). Grease an 8-inch (20-cm) round cake pan or 12-by-9-inch (30-by-23-cm) jelly-roll pan (also called a quarter-sheet pan) with the cooking spray and line with parchment (baking) paper. Measure the cake flour into a sifter and set aside.

In a small bowl, mix together the egg yolks, melted butter, and vanilla; set aside. In a large bowl, using an electric mixer on high speed, whip the egg whites until foamy. Slowly add the sugar and continue whipping until the egg whites are stiff and shiny.

Pour the yolk and butter mixture into the egg whites and sift half of the flour on top. Using a silicone spatula, fold the ingredients together. Sift the remaining flour over the batter and fold in.

Pour the batter into the prepared pan and spread it evenly. Bake until the cake is golden, the center springs back when lightly touched, and the edges are beginning to pull away from the pan sides, 20–25 minutes for the 8-inch round, and 7–9 minutes for the sheet pan.

Let the cake cool completely on a wire rack. To unmold, run a table knife around the inside edges of the pan and invert the cake onto a work surface.

Génoise

MAKES ONE 9-INCH (23-CM) ROUND CAKE

4 large eggs

½ cup (3½ oz/100 g) sugar

¾ cup (3 oz/85 g) cake (soft-wheat) flour, sifted

3 Tbsp unsalted butter, melted

Preheat the oven to 375°F (190°C). Line the bottom of a 9-by-3-inch (23-by-7.5-cm) round cake pan with parchment (baking) paper.

In the bowl of a stand mixer, whisk together the eggs and sugar by hand until combined. Place the bowl over a saucepan of simmering water. Gently whisk until the mixture registers 140°F (60°C) on an instant-read thermometer, about 3 minutes. Put the bowl on the mixer and fit the mixer with the whisk attachment. Beat on high speed until the mixture is pale, fluffy, and has almost tripled in volume, 5–8 minutes.

Remove the bowl from the mixer. Sift the flour over the egg mixture in 2 additions and carefully fold in the flour with a large silicone spatula. Fold a large dollop of the egg-flour mixture into the melted butter, then fold the butter mixture back into the egg-flour mixture.

Pour the cake batter into the prepared pan and smooth the top. Bake until the top is browned, about 20 minutes.

Chocolate Ladyfingers

MAKES ABOUT 20 LADYFINGERS

3 large eggs, separated

½ cup (3½ oz/100 g) sugar

½ cup (3½ oz/100 g) all-purpose (plain) flour

2 Tbsp Dutch-process cocoa powder

Preheat the oven to 400°F (200°C). Cut a piece of parchment paper to fit a 12-by-18-by-1-inch (30-by-45-by-2.5-cm) baking sheet. Using a pencil, draw 2 pairs of lines, spacing each pair 3 inches (7.5 cm) apart, down the length of the piece of parchment (baking) paper. You should have 4 lines. Put the paper, marked side down, on the baking sheet.

Using a stand mixer fitted with the whick attachment, beat the egg whites on medium speed until they start to foam. Add a third of the sugar and beat until the whites are opaque, then beat in another third of the sugar. When the whites start to increase in volume and become firm, add the remaining sugar and increase the speed to high. Beat until the whites form soft peaks but still look wet (see page 155).

In a bowl, whisk the egg yolks by hand until blended. Using a large silicone spatula, carefully fold the yolks into the beaten whites. Sift half of the flour and the cocoa powder over the egg mixture and carefully fold in. Fold in the remaining flour.

Fill a pastry bag fitted with a ¾-inch (2-cm) plain tip with the batter (see page 383). Pipe 3-inch (7.5-cm) strips of batter, with the edges just barely touching, between each set of lines on the piece of parchment paper. You should have about 20 ladyfingers. The ladyfingers will spread as they bake and adhere together, but still retain their individual shapes.

Bake until the batter is puffed, lightly browned, and slightly cracked, 10–12 minutes. Transfer the pans to wire racks and let the ladyfingers cool.

VARIATION: CLASSIC LADYFINGERS

To make classic ladyfingers, follow the instructions for chocolate ladyfingers, omitting the cocoa powder. You will need one baking sheet and one piece of parchment paper marked as described at left with 2 sets of lines, each set of lines spaced 3 inches (7.5 cm) apart. Before baking, using a fine-mesh sieve, dust the strips of dough with a fine layer of confectioners' sugar.

Chocolate Frosting

MAKES ENOUGH FROSTING FOR ONE 9-INCH (23-CM) CAKE

4 oz (125 g) bittersweet chocolate, finely chopped

2 oz (60 g) unsweetened chocolate, finely chopped

1 cup (8 oz/250 g) unsalted butter, at room temperature

2 cups (8 oz/250 g) confectioners' (icing) sugar, sifted

3 Tbsp light corn syrup

1 tsp pure vanilla extract

Pinch of salt

In the top of a double boiler, or in a heatproof bowl, combine both types of chocolate. Set over barely simmering water and stir occasionally until melted (see page 173). Let the melted chocolate cool slightly.

In a large bowl, using an electric mixer on medium speed, beat together the butter and confectioners' sugar until smooth and fluffy. Beat in the corn syrup, vanilla, and salt. Continue to beat while gradually pouring the melted chocolate into the butter-sugar mixture. Beat until smooth.

Royal Icing

MAKES ABOUT 2 CUPS (16 FL OZ/500 ML)

3 large egg whites, at room temperature

¼ tsp cream of tartar

4 cups (1 lb/500 g) confectioners' (icing) sugar, sifted

In a large bowl, using an electric mixer on medium speed, beat the egg whites with the cream of tartar until foamy. Reduce the speed to low and gradually beat in the confectioners' sugar until blended, then beat on high speed until thick and glossy, about 2 minutes.

VARIATION: EGG-FREE ROYAL ICING

In a large bowl, using an electric mixer on medium speed, combine 3 Tbsp meringue powder and 6 Tbsp (3 fl oz/ 90 ml) warm water. Reduce the speed to low and gradually beat in 4 cups (1 lb/ 500 g) confectioners' sugar until blended, then beat on high speed until thick and smooth, about 5 minutes. Beat in more warm water, 1 Tbsp at a time, if the icing is too thick to spread or pipe.

Vanilla Buttercream

MAKES 3 CUPS (24 FL OZ/670 ML)

1½ cups (12 oz/335 g) unsalted butter, at room temperature

½ cup (4 fl oz/110 ml) whole milk

¾ cup (6 oz/160 g) sugar

5 large egg yolks

2 tsp pure vanilla extract

Using a stand mixer fitted with the paddle attachment, beat the butter on medium speed until it is the consistency of mayonnaise. It should not be melted. Transfer to another bowl and thoroughly wash and dry the mixer bowl.

In a saucepan over medium heat, heat the milk and ¼ cup (2 oz/60 g) of the sugar, stirring occasionally, until small bubbles appear along the edges of the pan.

Meanwhile, in the stand mixer fitted with the whisk attachment, beat the egg yolks and the remaining ½ cup (4 oz/ 100 g) sugar on medium-high speed until the mixture is pale and thick, about 3 minutes. Reduce the speed to low and pour in the hot milk mixture in a thin stream. Return the mixture to the saucepan. Thoroughly wash and dry the mixer bowl and whisk attachment.

Cook the mixture over medium heat, whisking constantly, until it registers 170°F (77°C) on an instant-read thermometer, 5–7 minutes.

Pour the mixture back into the mixer bowl fitted with the whisk attachment and beat on medium speed until cool, 5–10 minutes. Beat in the vanilla. Add the butter in 4 additions, incorporating each addition before adding more butter.

Use right away, or refrigerate until ready to use or for up to 3 days. If the buttercream has been refrigerated, whisk it by hand over a saucepan of barely simmering water until it reaches spreading or piping consistency.

VARIATION: LEMON BUTTERCREAM

Substitute 1 Tbsp pure lemon extract for the vanilla extract.

Coffee Meringue Buttercream

MAKES 2½ CUPS (20 FL OZ/560 ML)

¾ cup (6 oz/170 g) unsalted butter, at room temperature

3 large egg whites, at room temperature

¾ cup (5½ oz/155 g) plus 3 Tbsp sugar

4 tsp instant espresso powder, dissolved in 1 tsp boiling water

In a bowl, whisk the butter by hand until creamy.

Using a stand mixer fitted with the whisk attachment, beat the egg whites on medium speed until they start to foam. Add 2 Tbsp of the sugar and beat until the whites become opaque and increase in volume.

Meanwhile, make a sugar syrup: In a saucepan over medium heat, bring the ¾ cup sugar and 3 Tbsp water to a boil, stirring until the sugar dissolves. Using a damp pastry brush, brush down any crystals that form on the pan sides. Cook the syrup, undisturbed, over medium-high heat until it registers 240°F (115°C) on a candy thermometer. While the syrup boils, increase the mixer speed to high and add the remaining 1 Tbsp sugar to the egg whites.

When the syrup registers 250°F (120°C), remove it from the heat. With the mixer speed on high, pour the syrup into the whites in a thin stream, aiming for the side of the bowl. Reduce the speed to medium and beat until the meringue cools to room temperature and is stiff, about 5 minutes.

Beat in the dissolved espresso, then add the butter in 3 additions, beating well after each addition. When all the butter has been added, reduce the speed to medium-high and beat until thick and smooth, about 1 minute.

Use right away, or refrigerate for up to 3 days. If the buttercream has been refrigerated, whisk it by hand over simmering water until it reaches spreading consistency.

Cream Cheese Frosting

MAKES ENOUGH FROSTING FOR ONE 9-INCH (23-CM) CAKE

4 oz (110 g) cream cheese, at room temperature

2 Tbsp unsalted butter, at room temperature

¾ cup (3 oz/85 g) confectioners' (icing) sugar

¾ tsp pure vanilla extract

Using a stand mixer fitted with the paddle attachment, beat the cream cheese, butter, confectioners' sugar, and vanilla on medium speed until the mixture is completely smooth and well combined. Use right away or store in the refrigerator for up to 3 days.

Crème Anglaise

MAKES ABOUT 1¾ CUPS (14 FL OZ/430 ML)

1 cup (8 fl oz/250 ml) whole milk

¾ cup (6 fl oz/180 ml) heavy (double) cream

1 vanilla bean, split lengthwise, or ½ tsp pure vanilla extract

⅓ cup (3 oz/90 g) sugar

4 large egg yolks

In a heavy saucepan, combine the milk and cream. Scrape the seeds from the vanilla bean into the pan, then add the pod. Set the pan over medium heat and bring just to a simmer. Remove from the heat, add the sugar, and stir to dissolve. Let cool for 30 minutes; discard the vanilla pod.

In a small bowl, whisk the egg yolks until blended. Return the milk mixture just to a boil over medium-high heat, then remove from the heat. Slowly whisk one-fourth of the milk mixture into the yolks. Pour the egg mixture into the pan, whisking until blended.

Return to medium-low heat and cook, stirring constantly, until the sauce is thick enough to coat the spoon, 3–4 minutes; do not let it boil. Transfer to a heatproof bowl and stir frequently until cooled to room temperature. If using vanilla extract, stir it in. Cover and refrigerate until ready to use or for up to 2 days.

Pastry Cream

MAKES ABOUT 1 CUP (8 FL OZ/225 ML)

1 cup (8 fl oz/225 ml) whole milk

5 Tbsp (2½ oz/70 g) sugar

3 large egg yolks

2 Tbsp cornstarch (cornflour)

1 tsp pure vanilla extract

In a small saucepan over medium heat, heat ¾ cup (6 fl oz/170 ml) of the milk and 2 Tbsp of the sugar, stirring to dissolve the sugar, until small bubbles appear along the edges of the pan. Meanwhile, in a bowl, whisk together the egg yolks and the remaining 3 Tbsp sugar until well combined. In a small bowl, whisk together the remaining ¼ cup (2 fl oz/55 ml) milk and the cornstarch; whisk into the yolk mixture.

Pour the hot milk mixture into the yolk mixture in a slow, steady stream, whisking constantly, then return the mixture to the pan. Bring to a boil over medium heat, whisking constantly. Whisk in the vanilla. Pour the pastry cream into a bowl, cover with plastic wrap, and refrigerate until needed or for up to 4 days.

Strawberry Topping

MAKES ABOUT 2 CUPS (16 OZ/454 G)

4 cups (1 lb/500 g) strawberries, hulled and thickly sliced

¼ cup (1¾ oz/50 g) sugar

2 Tbsp fresh lemon juice

In a saucepan over high heat, combine the berries, sugar, and lemon juice. Bring to a boil, stirring often. Boil until the liquid is clear and somewhat thick, about 2 minutes. Pour into a clean bowl and refrigerate until cold.

Caramel Sauce

MAKES 1 CUP (8 FL OZ/225 ML)

1 cup (7 oz/200 g) sugar

1 cup (8 fl oz/225 ml) heavy (double) cream

In a large, heavy saucepan over medium heat, bring ¼ cup (2 fl oz/60 ml) water and the sugar to a boil, stirring until the sugar dissolves. Using a damp pastry brush, brush down any crystals that form on the sides of the pan. Cook the syrup, undisturbed, over medium-high heat until it is a light caramel color, 5–10 minutes. Turn off the heat.

Meanwhile, in a saucepan over medium heat, bring ½ cup (4 fl oz/110 ml) water to a boil. In another saucepan over medium heat, heat the cream just until it comes to a boil, then immediately remove from the heat. Wearing oven mitts, carefully whisk the cream into the syrup in 3 additions; it will bubble up dramatically. Whisk in the boiling water in 3 additions. Let the sauce cool, then cover and refrigerate until needed or for up to 1 week.

Raspberry Coulis

MAKES ABOUT 1 CUP (8 FL OZ/250 ML)

3 cups (12 oz/375 g) raspberries

¼ cup (1 oz/30 g) confectioners' (icing) sugar, plus more as needed

1 tsp fresh lemon juice

In a food processor, combine the raspberries and confectioners' sugar. Pulse until the berries are puréed. Pass the purée through a fine-mesh sieve placed over a small bowl, pressing on the contents of the sieve with the back of a large spoon to extract all the juice. Stir in the lemon juice. Taste and add more sugar, if desired.

Sweetened Whipped Cream

MAKES 1½ CUPS (12 FL OZ/375 ML)

¾ cup (6 fl oz/180 ml) heavy (double) cream, well chilled

2 Tbsp sugar

½ tsp pure vanilla extract

In a deep bowl, combine the cream, sugar, and vanilla. Using a wire whisk or an electric mixer on medium-high speed, beat until soft peaks form and the cream is billowy, about 2 minutes. Cover the bowl and refrigerate until ready to use or for up to 2 hours.

Fluffy Whipped Cream Topping

MAKES ENOUGH TOPPING FOR ONE 8-INCH (20-CM) CAKE

2 cups (16 fl oz/500 ml) heavy (double) cream, well chilled

2 tsp pure vanilla extract

2 Tbsp confectioners' (icing) sugar

In a deep bowl, combine the cream, sugar, and vanilla. Using a wire whisk or an electric mixer on medium-high speed, beat until soft peaks form and the cream is billowy, 6–8 minutes. Cover the bowl and refrigerate until ready to use or for up to 2 hours.

Ancho Whipped Cream

MAKES ABOUT ⅔ CUP (6 FL OZ/180 ML)

⅓ cup (3 fl oz/80 ml) plus 1¼ cups (10 fl oz/310 ml) heavy (double) cream, well chilled

1 tsp ground ancho chile powder

1 Tbsp pure vanilla extract

3 Tbsp sifted confectioners' (icing) sugar

In a bowl, whisk together the ⅓ cup cream and the chile powder. Let stand for up to 5 minutes.

Whisk the confectioners' sugar into the cream-chile mixture and pour the mixture into a deep bowl. Add the 1¼ cups cream and vanilla and, using an electric mixer fitted with the whisk attachment, beat on medium-high speed until soft peaks form and the cream is billowy, about 2 minutes. Cover the bowl and refrigerate until ready to use or for up to 2 hours.

Bourbon Whipped Cream

MAKES ABOUT 1 CUP (8 FL OZ/250 ML)

½ cup (4 fl oz/125 ml) heavy (double) cream, well chilled

1 tsp confectioners' (icing) sugar

2 tsp bourbon

1 tsp pure vanilla extract

In a deep bowl, combine the cream, confectioners' sugar, bourbon, and vanilla. Using a wire whisk or an electric mixer fitted with the whisk attachment on medium-high speed, beat until the soft peaks form and the cream is billowy. Cover the bowl and refrigerate until ready to use or for up to 2 hours.

Maple Whipped Cream

MAKES ABOUT 4 CUPS (32 FL OZ/1 L)

2 cups (16 fl oz/500 ml) heavy (double) cream, well chilled

⅓ cup (4 fl oz/125 ml) pure maple syrup

In a deep bowl, using an electric mixer fitted with the whisk attachment on medium-high speed, beat the cream just until it begins to thicken. Add the maple syrup and continue beating until soft peaks form and the cream is billowy. Cover the bowl and refrigerate until ready to use or for up to 2 hours.

Maple Butter

MAKES ABOUT ½ CUP (4 OZ/125 G)

½ cup (4 oz/125 g) unsalted butter, at room temperature

3 Tbsp pure maple syrup

In a small bowl, with a silicone spatula, beat together the butter and maple syrup until well combined and completely smooth. Store, covered, in the refrigerator for up to 3 days. Bring to room temperature before serving.

Applesauce

MAKES ABOUT 2½ CUPS (22 OZ/690 G)

2½ lb (1.25 kg) apples such as Granny Smith, Newtown pippin, or McIntosh, peeled, cored, and chopped

Sugar

Place the apples in a heavy saucepan with ⅓ cup (3 fl oz/80 ml) water. Bring to a boil, reduce the heat to a simmer, and cook, partially covered, stirring occasionally, until very soft, 20–30 minutes. Remove from the heat. Mash the apples with a fork or pass through a food mill. Taste and add sugar if needed. The applesauce can be stored for up to 2 weeks in the refrigerator. Serve at room temperature or cold.

Crème Fraîche

MAKES ABOUT 1 CUP (8 FL OZ/250 ML)

1 cup (8 fl oz/250 ml) heavy (double) cream, not ultrapasteurized

1 Tbsp buttermilk

In a small nonreactive saucepan over medium-low heat, combine the heavy cream and buttermilk and heat to lukewarm. Do not let simmer.

Remove the saucepan from the heat, cover, and let the mixture stand at room temperature until it has thickened, 8–48 hours. The longer the mixture sits, the thicker and tangier it will become. Chill for 3–4 hours before using.

Candied Citrus Zest

MAKES ABOUT ½ CUP (3 OZ/90 G)

2 oranges, preferably organic

2 lemons, preferably organic

1½ cups (10½ oz/300 g) plus ⅓ cup (6 fl oz/170 ml) sugar

1 Tbsp fresh lemon juice

Thoroughly scrub the oranges and lemons. Cut a slice from the blossom end of each fruit so it stands upright on a work surface. Working from top to bottom, use a vegetable peeler or a paring knife to cut strips of zest, leaving the white pith behind. Stack the strips and cut them lengthwise into narrow strips 1/4 inch (6 mm) wide.

Bring a saucepan of water to a boil. Add the zest strips and cook for 5 minutes. Drain the zest, refill the pan with water, and repeat.

In another saucepan over medium heat, combine the 1 1/2 cups sugar with the lemon juice and 3/4 cup water (6 fl oz/170 ml) and bring to a boil, stirring occasionally. Add the zest strips, reduce the heat to very low (barely a simmer), and cook until the strips are translucent and tender, about 30 minutes. With a fork, lift the strips from the syrup and place on a wire rack set over waxed paper, making sure that the strips are not touching. Let dry overnight at room temperature.

Put the remaining 1/3 cup sugar in a small, wide bowl. Toss the zest, about 10 strips at a time, in the sugar. If not using the candied zest right away, store in an airtight container. It will keep for up to 1 month at room temperature.

NOTE: To make less candied zest, simply cut the recipe in half, thirds, or fourths. Depending on the size of the fruit, each piece of fruit yields about 1/8 cup (3/4 oz/22 1/2 g) candied zest.

Candied Flowers

MAKES 20–30 CANDIED FLOWERS

1 large egg white, at room temperature, or 1 Tbsp meringue powder

20–50 pesticide-free fresh flowers, such as violets, pansies, small roses, or Peruvian lillies

Sugar as needed

Line a baking sheet with parchment (baking paper). In a bowl, beat the egg white until it is covered with a light foam. (If using the meringue powder, whisk it with 2 Tbsp warm water until dissolved.)

Using a clean, small paintbrush, lightly and evenly coat the flowers with the egg white or meringue powder mixture, then sprinkle them with sugar. If the sugar is absorbed in a few minutes, sprinkle the flowers again.

Put the coated flowers on the parchment paper and let dry at room temperature for 24 hours. The candied flowers will keep for up to 3 days, stored between layers of waxed paper in an airtight container at room temperature. Use to decorate cakes and pastries.

Classic Sourdough Starter

MAKES 3 CUPS (24 OZ/750 G)

2 cups (16 fl oz/500 ml) lukewarm water (90°–100°F/32°–38°C)

1/3 cup (2 1/2 oz/75 g) plain yogurt

2 cups (10 oz/315 g) bread flour

1/4 cup (1/2 oz/15 g) nonfat dry milk powder or 1/4 cup (1 oz/30 g) dry buttermilk powder

In a bowl, whisk together the water and yogurt. Add the flour and dry milk powder; beat until well blended and smooth. Transfer the mixture to a 1-qt (1-l) glass jar, ceramic crock, or plastic container.

Cover the jar loosely with plastic wrap or a double thickness of cheesecloth (muslin) and let stand at room temperature for 48 hours, stirring the mixture with a whisk twice each day. It will be bubbly, with a fresh sour smell and have the consistency of pancake batter. A clear or pale yellow liquid will form on the top; just stir it back in. If the liquid is any other color, discard the starter and make a new batch. Cover the starter loosely with plastic wrap and store in the refrigerator.

To use the starter, measure out the amount called for in a recipe and let stand at room temperature until it starts to bubble, about 1 hour. To feed the remaining starter, add 1 cup (5 oz/155 g) flour and 1 cup (8 fl oz/ 250 ml) water, stir to incorporate, and let stand at room temperature for 24–48 hours to begin fermenting again. Store in the refrigerator, covered loosely. The flavor of a sourdough starter improves with age and keeps indefinitely.

Easy Sourdough Starter

MAKES 1 1/2 CUPS (12 OZ/375 G)

1 package (1/2 oz/15 g) commercial dry sourdough starter, about 1 1/2 Tbsp

1 cup (5 oz/155 g) bread flour

3/4 cup (6 fl oz/180 ml) lukewarm water (90°–100°F/32°–38°C)

2 Tbsp plain yogurt

In a bowl, combine the dry starter and the flour. Whisk in the water and yogurt until smooth. Transfer the mixture to a 1-qt (1-l) glass jar, ceramic crock, or plastic container.

Cover loosely with plastic wrap or a double thickness of cheesecloth (muslin) and let stand at room temperature for 48 hours, stirring the mixture with a whisk twice each day. It will be bubbly, with a sour smell. Store the starter in the refrigerator, loosely covered. Follow the storage and feeding instructions for the Classic Sourdough Starter.

NOTE: For a starter with a more sour flavor, after the first 48 hours, add 1/4 cup (1 1/2 oz/45 g) flour and 1/4 cup (2 fl oz/ 60 ml) water, whisk until smooth, and let stand 24–48 hours longer.

Baking Tips & Techniques

Learn just a few fundamental baking principles and techniques and you are well on your way to making delicious baked goods. In the following pages, you will find some basic tips as well as photographed step-by-step how-tos for a variety of baking tasks.

PREPARING TO BAKE

Choosing a recipe, preparing a clean work space, getting your equipment off the shelf, and assembling all your ingredients are important first steps to making any baking recipe. Once you have selected the recipe, read through it carefully to see what ingredients or even equipment (such as a special pan) you might need to purchase, or borrow, before getting started. It is also a good idea to calculate the total preparation time and fit it into your schedule, so that you do not begin the baking ritual only to be interrupted.

BAKING EQUIPMENT

Whether baking cookies, muffins, cakes, pies, or breads, it is important to use the right equipment and bakeware to ensure optimal results. Many of the recipes in this book call for using a stand mixer for such tasks as creaming butter and sugar, whipping egg whites, or kneading dough. While these tasks can also be done with a handheld electric mixer or by hand, a stand mixer will significantly reduce the prep time required for the recipes.

Using the correct sized-pan as called for in the recipe is also essential. An overfull pan will cause muffin, quick bread, or cake batter to spill over the sides of the pan. A underfilled pan will alter the cooking time and produce unattractive results. For pie and tart recipes, using the right sized pan is especially important so that the crust will accommodate the filling, and the pie or tart will bake to the appropriate doneness.

MEASURING & READYING INGREDIENTS

The French phrase *mise en place*, literally "putting in place," is a governing rule for baking that calls for measuring all ingredients before beginning a recipe. Successful baking depends on accuracy, so having the correct amount of each ingredient is crucial. If you bake often, a scale is a good investment, as weighing ingredients is the most accurate way to measure them. If you use cup measures, however, keep these points in mind: Measuring cups for dry ingredients and liquid ingredients are not interchangeable. Dry measuring cups are made of metal or heavy-duty plastic and have straight sides, while liquid measuring cups are formed from clear glass or plastic, resemble pitchers, and have horizontal markings indicating volumes on their sides.

When measuring a dry ingredient, such as flour or sugar, scoop up the ingredient with a large spoon and place it in a dry measuring cup without tamping it down, then level the top with the blunt edge of a knife. Brown sugar should be tightly packed into a measuring cup or spoon. Measuring spoons can also be dipped into the container, then leveled. To measure liquid, pour it into a liquid measuring cup, then peer at it at eye level for the most accurate reading.

Dry ingredients are sometimes sifted to aerate them or to combine them. A sifter or a fine-mesh sieve will do the job. Sifting onto waxed paper or parchment paper eliminates the need to clean a bowl.

The temperature of ingredients is also key for good results. Many recipes call for butter—and sometimes eggs, milk, or other liquids—to be at room temperature before using them in a recipe. This is crucial so that the ingredients can be successfully beaten together. For example, if the butter is too cold, it can cause a batter to separate when eggs are added to it. If the recipe calls for room-temperature butter, make sure to take the butter out of the refrigerator right away; depending on the temperature of your kitchen, it can take quite a while for the butter to soften.

Bring egg whites for whipping to room temperature so that they will whip to their optimal volume. Cold eggs are easier to separate, though, so you can opt to separate the eggs while they are cold and then bring them to room temperature before using.

When a recipe calls for ingredients to be cold, it is equally important to keep them refrigerated until you are ready to use them. If necessary, measure or prepare the ingredients as specified in the recipe and then store them in the refriegerator until ready to use.

OVEN SAVVY

The temperature inside an oven often does not agree with the thermostat setting. Put an oven thermometer on the rack on which you are baking to determine your oven's accuracy, then adjust the thermostat accordingly. Also, no oven bakes evenly. Rotate pans 180 degrees halfway through baking, whether or not a recipe instructs you to do so, to ensure even baking and browning.

About Cakes

A few basic techniques are used when making nearly any cake; master them and it will ensure beautiful and delicious results.

PREPARING PANS

With the exception of tube pans used to bake chiffon or angel food cakes, which need fat-free surfaces to help them rise, most cake pans in this book are lined with parchment (baking) paper, buttered, or buttered and floured to aid unmolding. If the pan has straight sides, such as round or rectangular pans, line the bottom with a round of parchment paper cut to fit precisely. Generously coat pans with sculptured sides, such as Bundt pans, with soft, not melted butter to prevent pools of butter collecting in the pan. Unmolding most cakes is as simple as running a table knife around the sides of the cooled cake and inverting it onto a plate.

BAKING & TRIMMING A CAKE

For cake-baking tips, see page 202. After cakes cool completely, you can cut them into layers (see page 205), if desired. If the cakes are uneven or domed, you might need to trim off the very tops of the cakes so that they fit together and create a flat surface for frosting. To trim the cake, use a serrated knife and a gentle sawing motion to cut a thin, even layer around the circumference of the cake, being careful not to trim away too much.

FROSTING A LAYER CAKE

Place one cake layer on a large plate or decorating turntable. If placing the cake on a plate, slide 4 waxed paper strips under and along the edges of the bottom layer. Then, arrange the layers and filling as directed in the recipe. Use a straight frosting spatula that is as long as the diameter of the cake.

Follow the steps described below and shown at left for frosting a cake:

1 **Apply a crumb coat:** Using a dry pastry brush, gently brush away any loose crumbs from the top and sides of the cake layer. Using the spatula, mound no more than a third of the frosting on the top of the cake. Smooth the frosting over the top and down the sides to cover the entire surface. This thin coating of frosting will adhere the excess crumbs to the surface.

2 **Frost the top:** If some of the frosting will be used to decorate the finished cake, set aside the amount indicated in the recipe. Mound the remaining frosting in the center of the top of the cake and smooth it evenly. The frosting will cover the top in a thick layer.

3 **Cover the sides:** Evenly smooth the frosting from the top of the cake down the sides, turning the cake as you work. As you cover the sides, hold the spatula almost perpendicular to the top of the cake.

4 **Smooth the frosting:** Holding the spatula almost horizontal to the cake's top, smooth the top with long strokes. Then run the spatula around the sides, spreading the frosting as smooth as possible. Using short strokes, remove excess frosting from the top edge. Discard the waxed paper strips.

SERVING CAKES

Serve cakes at room temperature to fully appreciate their flavor. Exceptions are cakes with gelatin, such as mousse cakes, which should be refrigerated until serving so that they remain firm, and cakes frosted with whipped cream.

Use a sharp, serrated knife or a sharp, thin-bladed knife to cut cakes. Delicate, airy cakes, such as chiffon and angel food, are difficult to cut; a serrated knife and a gentle sawing motion work best.

If a cake is frosted or filled, or if it is a cheesecake, dip the knife blade in water and wipe it clean after each cut.

PASTRY BAGS & TIPS

Also known as decorating bags or piping bags, funnel-shaped pastry bags are made of plastic-lined canvas, plain canvas, polyester, nylon, or disposable plastic. You can also make your own by cutting off a corner of a resealable plastic bag. The most useful bags are 8 to 12 inches (20 to 30 cm) long and have a wide opening for filling them at one end and a narrow opening at the other.

Pastry tips, conical-shaped decorating tools designed to fit snugly into the narrow ends of pastry bags, are usually made of tinned or chromed steel and make it possible to achieve a wide variety of decorative effects when piping frosting or icing, or shaping soft pastry or cookie doughs. Popular tips include *plain tips*, or tips with small circular openings for writing messages or piping detailed designs; *star tips*, used to pipe ridged bands or rosettes; *fluted tips*, used to pipe shells and decorative borders; and *flat tips*, tips with narrow to wide slits to shape ribbons. Some pastry tip sets are sold with a device called a *coupler*, which allows the tips to be screwed onto the pastry bag. The coupler makes it easier to change tips without emptying the frosting out of the bag.

FILLING A PASTRY BAG

To fill a pastry bag, firmly push the desired decorating tip down into the small hole in the pastry bag. If your bag comes with a coupler, follow the manufacturer's instructions for attaching it to the pastry bag. Next, fold down the top of the bag to form a cuff. The cuff should be about one-third the length of the bag. To make it easier to fill, you can also fold the cuff over a tall glass, with the tip inside the glass.

Then, place one hand under the cuff of the pastry bag. Using a silicone spatula, scoop the filling or frosting mixture into the large opening in the bag, filling it no more than half full. Unfold the cuff. Push the filling or frosting down toward the tip, forcing out any air at the same time. Trapped air bubbles can cause problems while piping. To further ensure against air bubbles, and to keep the mixture flowing steadily, twist the bag several times at the location where the filling ends.

Finally, with your dominant hand, hold the bag where you just made the twist. With your nondominant hand, hold the bag near the tip and proceed to pipe, following the instructions below.

PIPING WITH A PASTRY BAG

After you have frosted the cake, you can use a pastry bag and tips to create decorative designs. Follow the steps described below and shown at right for decorating a cake:

1 Hold the bag at an angle: Use your upper hand to apply pressure, and your lower hand to guide the tip. Hold the bag with the tip 1 inch (2.5 cm) above the cake and at a 60-degree angle.

2 To pipe rosettes: Using the star tip, apply gentle pressure to pipe a mound ½ inch (12 mm) wide. Pull the bag up, lessening the pressure and reducing the angle. Repeat to form a row of rosettes.

3 To pipe shells: Using the fluted tip, pipe a mound about ½ inch long. Pull the bag up, lessening the pressure and reducing the angle slightly. Repeat to form a row of shells.

4 To pipe dots: Using a small plain tip, pipe a small mound of frosting, lifting up the bag to make a point on the top. Repeat to form the desired pattern of dots.

When you are finished piping, expell any remaining frosting and reserve for another use. Wash the pastry bag with warm, soapy water and turn it inside-out to dry completely.

About Pies & Tarts

Whether filled with fresh berries or a rich custard, a light, flaky crust is one of the most important elements in a pie or tart. Pies are usually baked in a pie pan or pie dish with sloping sides and may include both a bottom and top crust. In contrast, tarts are baked in a straight-sided tart pan and almost always have only a bottom crust. For the crust recipes in this book, butter is used instead of lard or shortening to make crusts that are both flavorful and tender. Select unsalted butter, all-purpose (plain) flour, and fine-grained (table) salt when making doughs. Recipes for Flaky Pastry Dough and Basic Tart Dough appear on pages 373–74 and can be used for the pie and tart recipes throughout this book.

HAND METHOD

Described below and shown at left are the basic steps in mixing pie or tart dough by hand:

1 Combine the dry ingredients: In a large mixing bowl, combine the recipe's flour, sugar, if called for, and salt and stir with a fork to mix the ingredients evenly.

2 Cut in the butter: Cut the cold butter into ¼-inch (6-mm) cubes. Scatter the cubes over the flour mixture and toss with a fork to coat evenly with the flour. Using a pastry blender or 2 knives, cut the butter into the flour mixture until the mixture is crumbly and the largest pieces of butter are the size of small peas.

3 Mix in the liquid: Drizzle the liquid component, typically ice water, over the flour mixture and toss with a fork until the dough is evenly moist. If the dough seems too crumbly, add more cold liquid, 1 tablespoon at a time, and toss to mix just until the dough pulls together.

4 Form the dough into a disk: When the dough is done, it should come together in a rough mass. Do not overmix or the crust will be tough. Gently gather the dough together. Transfer the dough to a work surface, pat into a ball, and flatten into a disk. Flaky Pastry Dough (page 373) should be rolled out right away. Basic Tart Dough (page 373) can be rolled out right away or wrapped in plastic wrap and refrigerated for up to overnight.

FOOD-PROCESSOR METHOD

To make pie and tart doughs in a food processor, be careful not to overprocess the dough or it will be tough instead of flaky and tender. Add the dry ingredients to the bowl of a food processor and pulse 2 or 3 times to mix. Add the butter and pulse 8–10 times, until the mixture is crumbly, but there are still pieces of butter the size of peas. Add the ice water and pulse 10–12 times. To test the dough, stop the food processor and squeeze a piece of dough. If the dough crumbles, add more ice water, 1 tablespoon at a time and pulse just until the dough holds together when pinched. When done, the dough should come together in a rough mass but not form a ball. Follow step 4 of the hand method to finish the dough.

TROUBLESHOOTING: DOUGH MIXING

Whether making pie or tart dough by hand or in a food processor, cutting butter into flour is an important first step in making the dough. To ensure success, start with butter cold from the refrigerator and work quickly. The butter-flour mixture should resemble coarse meal before the liquid is added. Test the butter by giving it a quick pinch. If the small butter chunks are cold, your fingers will be grease free; if they are too soft, your fingers will be greasy, and if you work it too much, the dough could get tough. If the butter seems too soft, chill the mixture for 20–30 minutes before proceeding.

ROLLING OUT THE DOUGH

Place the dough disk on a lightly floured work surface and tap it with the rolling pin to flatten and spread it out a bit. Lightly flour the rolling pin. Sprinkle flour beneath the dough and on the rolling pin as you work to help prevent sticking. Described below and shown at right are the basic steps for rolling out pie or tart dough. As you work, continue to sprinkle the work surface and the rolling pin with flour to prevent sticking:

1 Roll out the dough: Starting with the pin in the center of the disk, roll it away from you toward the far edge, stopping just shy of the edge. Bring the pin back to the center of the disk and roll it toward you. Give the dough a quarter turn and repeat. Use steady pressure as you roll, and work quickly. Continue turning and rolling until the dough is about 1/8 inch (3 mm) thick and 2–3 inches (5–8 cm) wider than the pan's circumference.

2 Trim the dough: Place your pie pan or dish in the center of the dough round and, using a small knife, trim the dough into a neat circle, leaving extra dough as called for in the recipe. Tart dough is easily trimmed after it is transferred to the pan(s) (see below).

3 Transfer the dough: Roll the round(s) of dough loosely around the rolling pin and unroll over the pie or tart pan(s). Press the tart dough into the sides of the pan(s), and then trim the tart dough by running a rolling a pin across the top of the pan(s).

4 Fit the pie dough into the pan: If using pie dough, lift up the edges of the dough circle as you gently ease it into the contours of the pan, being careful not to stretch the dough. Trim the dough, leaving an overhang as called for in the recipe.

TROUBLESHOOTING: DOUGH TEARS

If the dough tears while shaping it, you can repair it with some of the dough you trimmed off. Simply press a scrap of dough slightly larger than the tear over it, pushing gently around the edges to seal. The dough scraps will bake into the crust and prevent fillings from leaking.

BLIND BAKING

Some pie and tart recipes call for fully or partially baking the crust before filling it. This is especially true for recipes with fillings that need limited or no further cooking or those with juicy fillings that could make the crust soggy.

Place an oven rack in the lower third of the oven and preheat to 375°F (190°C). Remove the pastry shell or shells from the refrigerator or freezer. Line with a sheet of aluminum foil or parchment (baking) paper large enough to overhang the sides, patting the foil into the bottom and up over the sides. Cover the bottom of the shell with a generous layer of pie weights (page 395) or raw short-grain rice on top of the foil. The weights help prevent the pastry from shrinking during baking.

For a partially baked pie or tart shell, bake for 20 minutes, then lift an edge of the foil to check the dough. If it looks wet, continue to bake, checking it every 5 minutes, until it is pale gold. The total baking time will be 25–30 minutes.

For a fully baked pie or tart shell, remove the weights and foil. Return the shell to the oven and continue to bake until golden, 7–10 minutes longer, for a total baking time of 30–40 minutes. (For fully baked tartlet shells, bake as directed for the pie or tart shell, but reduce the initial baking time to 15 minutes. Remove the weights and foil and continue to bake until golden, 5 minutes longer, for a total baking time of 20–25 minutes.)

If bubbles form in the crust during baking, press them down with a fork. Do not prick them, or you may create holes in the bottom of the crust.

Working with Piecrust

Fluting the edge of a single-crust pie adds a pretty edge, while fluting or crimping a double-crust pie embellishes, but also seals the bottom and top crusts together, which prevents the filling from oozing out as the pie bakes. Applying pastry cutouts or weaving a lattice top are two other ways of decorating pies.

FLUTING SINGLE-CRUST PIES

To form a scalloped edge on the dough, pinch the folded edge between the index finger of your nondominant hand and the index finger and thumb of your dominant hand every 2–3 inches (5–7.5 cm) around the edge. Or, with a thumb on top of the rim and a forefinger underneath, pinch together the dough edges, pressing the thumb down into the dough.

CRIMPING & FLUTING DOUBLE-CRUST PIES

Begin by tucking about 1 inch (2.5 cm) of the top dough round under the bottom dough round. To crimp the edge, use a fork to press down and make an imprint on the edge of the dough. Or, to flute the pastry edge, follow the directions for fluting a single-crust pie (above).

MAKING PASTRY CUTOUTS

Pastry cutouts also add a pretty touch. Reserve any scraps from the rolled-out dough. Roll out the scraps, then cut out decorative shapes with a small knife or cookie cutters.

For single-crust pies, sprinkle the cutouts with sugar and bake in a 350°F (180°C) oven until golden brown, 10–12 minutes. Let cool, then arrange on the filling of the cooled baked pie.

For double-crust pies, use a pastry brush or your finger to moisten the undersides of the cutouts with cold water and arrange them in an attractive pattern on the top crust. Or, instead of creating steam vents, use small cookie cutters to make a pattern of pretty shapes in the top crust before you place it over the filling.

MAKING A LATTICE-TOP PIE

Weaving pastry strips together into a lattice on top of a filled pie is a dramatic way to create a decorative, golden crust. Described below and shown at left are the steps for making a lattice top. Follow the Lattice-Top Variation in the Flaky Pastry Dough recipe for rolling out a rectangle for a lattice top (page 373). Leave the overhang of the bottom crust untrimmed until the lattice is finished.

1 Arrange 8 dough strips: Starting at the short end of the dough rectangle, and using a pastry wheel or small knife, cut the dough into 16 strips, each about 3/4 inch (2 cm) wide. Lay about 8 of the strips across the filled pie shell horizontally. Think of the top strip as number 1 and the bottom strip as number 8.

2 Begin to weave: Fold strips 2, 4, 6, and 8 back onto themselves to your left. Lay a strip vertically down the center at a slight angle. Unfold the strips.

3 Alternate the strips: Fold strips 1, 3, 5, and 7 onto themselves to your left. Lay a vertical strip to the right of the center strip. Unfold the strips.

4 Weave the remaining strips: Fold strips 1, 3, 5, and 7 onto themselves to your right. Lay a vertical strip to the left of the center strip. Unfold the strips. Add the remaining strips to both sides of the pie in the same manner.

To finish the pie, using a paring knife, trim the edges of the strips even with the rim of the pan. Fold the overhang from the bottom dough round up and over the edges of the lattice and crimp to seal. Alternatively, fold the lattice and overhang underneath themselves to form a rim and press gently to seal.

About Yeast Breads

When baking yeast breads, a defined sequence of steps is followed in a set order. No matter what type of loaf you are preparing, the basic progression for assembly remains the same.

Most basic yeast breads contain three ingredients: flour, yeast, and water. Flour contains the protein known as gluten. When flour is mixed with water, the gluten takes on an elasticity. Once you have combined all the ingredients for the dough and begin kneading, the gluten forms an elastic web that ensnares the gas released by the yeast. This reaction is what causes bread to rise and form a honeycombed texture, or crumb. The amount of gluten in any flour varies depending on the type of wheat milled. The primary flours used in this book are bread flour, all-purpose (plain) flour, and whole-wheat (wholemeal) flour (see page 393 for more information on these three flours).

Yeast is the living substance that animates dough, consuming its sugar and giving off carbon dioxide and ethyl alcohol to expand the gluten in the flour and cause the bread the rise. All of the recipes in this book call for active dry yeast because it is easy to use but still imparts great flavor to the bread. It comes in 4-ounce jars or foil-lined envelopes and needs to be dissolved in warm water to be activated. One envelope of active dry yeast measures about 2¼ teaspoons.

The third ingredient, water, we take for granted, since all we need to do is turn on the faucet. But if your tap water tastes strongly of other chemicals, or is of otherwise poor quality, its unpleasant flavor will be transferred to your bread. Use filtered water or bottled spring water if your tap water is less than satisfactory.

ACTIVATING THE YEAST

The first step in making a yeast bread is activating the yeast by mixing it into warm liquid. Within a few minutes, the yeast should begin to bubble and foam. This step is referred to by professional bakers as "proofing" the yeast, or testing it to make sure it is still active. (The test was more important before the advent of active dry yeast, which has a long shelf life.) If no bubbling occurs, discard the yeast and start again with new yeast.

MAKING YEAST DOUGH

Bread dough can be made by hand, in an electric mixer, or in a food processor with similar results. The recipes in this book primarily call for a heavy-duty electric stand mixer. An electric mixer is especially useful for kneading sticky or very soft doughs, such as those for brioche that would otherwise require lots of arm work.

The basic steps in preparing yeast dough with a stand mixer are described below and shown at right:

1 Mix the dough: In a stand mixer, use the paddle attachment to beat the dough ingredients on medium-low speed. The dough may be very sticky at this stage.

2 Knead the dough: Switch to the dough hook to knead the dough on low speed. It will become smooth and elastic and should start to come away from the bowl sides.

3 First rise: After kneading, place the dough in a greased deep bowl, turn the dough to coat it with the fat, and cover loosely with plastic wrap. Let rise at room temperature until doubled in bulk, 1–2 hours.

4 Second rise: After the dough has risen, punch it down (page 388) and shape it as directed in the recipe. If called for, let the dough rise at room temperature until it doubles in bulk again, 30–45 minutes. The dough is ready to bake when it is smooth and springy to the touch.

USING STARTERS

Sponges and other starters originated as a way to give bread dough a "head start" and ensure a good rise. To make a starter, relatively small amounts of the basic ingredients of the bread—flour, yeast, water—are mixed to form a batter that rises for a time before the remaining ingredients are added to make the dough. Starters are popular in today's bread making because they impart a distinctive flavor to the bread and improve its texture. Any salt and fat called for in the recipe are added with the remaining ingredients in the later stages when the dough is formed. Sourdough starters (see page 379) are mixed like other starters, but stand longer to develop a distinctive, tangy flavor.

KNEADING

The process of kneading combines all of the ingredients thoroughly, distributes the yeast, releases the gases produced by the growing yeast, and strengthens the moistened gluten strands to a springy elasticity to ensure a good rise. If you have an electric stand mixer or food processor with a dough hook attachment, this step goes quickly.

If you are kneading bread dough by hand, make sure that your work surface is at a height that allows for easy arm movement at the elbows. Turn out the shaggy mass of dough onto a lightly floured work surface. A plastic or metal dough scraper is invaluable for manipulating the dough if it is still a bit sticky. At first, the dough will be quite soft, needing gentle motions. Using large, fluid movements, slowly push the dough away from your body with the heel of the hand.

Use your fingers to lift the farthest edge of the dough, give it a quarter turn, then fold the dough in half toward you. Then, push the dough away again. The dough will slide across the surface as you knead, absorbing the small amount of flour it requires. Repeat the kneading sequence: push, turn, and fold rhythmically, using a pressure equal to the resistance you feel.

The kneading process can take from from 3 to 5 minutes for machine-mixed doughs and 10 to 15 minutes for hand-mixed doughs. As you work, sprinkle additional flour on the work surface 1 tablespoon at a time, only if needed to prevent sticking. Wait until the flour has been absorbed before adding more. This helps ensure that the bread will end up with the correct consistency.

THE FIRST RISE

Most breads undergo two risings. During rising, the yeast in the dough ferments, giving off carbon dioxide and transforming the dough into a puffy mass. As the gases expand, strands of gluten in the flour expand and stretch into a web that will give the bread its distinctive texture.

Dough tends to rise best in a deep bowl, rather than a wide, shallow container where it will expand horizontally and form a big puddle. Grease the bowl by brushing it with oil or melted butter, or coat it with a film of vegetable-oil cooking spray. Form the dough into a ball and place it in the bowl. Turn it once to coat the top with the oil or butter; this will prevent it from drying out and forming a skin. Cover the bowl loosely with plastic wrap, to help retain the moisture; a damp clean kitchen towel can also be substituted. For later reference, mentally note or mark on the container where the dough should be when it has doubled in bulk.

Predicting exact rising times is difficult because they depend on the temperature of the finished dough, the amount of yeast used, and the general atmospheric conditions. Generally, a dough takes 1 to 2 hours to rise to the classic "doubled in bulk" stage at room temperature, about 75°F (24°C). (Sponges typically rise for 30 minutes to 2 hours.) Any subsequent risings are faster. To test a risen dough, poke it with two fingers. If the indentations remain, the dough is adequately risen. If the marks fill in right away, re-cover the bowl and let the dough sit for 15 minutes longer before testing it again.

SHAPING & THE SECOND RISE

After the first rise, the dough will be doubled in bulk and delicately domed. At this point, the trapped gases need to be released and the dough allowed to rise again. This makes the texture more even and prevents the elastic strands in the bread from overstretching and breaking. Turn the dough out onto a lightly floured work surface. Some recipes call for punching down the dough, which means literally sinking a fist into it to deflate it. Even though the simple act of turning the dough out of the bowl will naturally force out the trapped air, physically punching the dough may be necessary if you are making a very large batch of bread. Kneading is no longer required at this point, as it can overactivate the gluten, making the dough difficult to work with. Shape the dough as directed in individual recipes.

If a recipe calls for forming the dough into a round loaf, begin by pressing the dough flat and then forming it into a ball. Now, using both hands, stretch the sides of the dough downward and under, rotating the ball as you do and pulling the surface taut to form a compact ball. If a recipe calls for shaping dough for a loaf pan, see page 290. The dough should fill the pan one-half to two-thirds full. Less, and you will have a flat loaf; more, and you will have a top-heavy loaf.

Drape the pan with plastic wrap or a damp kitchen towel and let the dough rise again. Typically, the dough is ready when it again doubles in bulk, or rises about 1 inch (2.5 cm) above the pan rim. This takes about half the time of the first rise, usually 30 to 45 minutes. Dough that is ready for baking will be smooth and springy to the touch, not sticky. A fingertip pressed into the dough should leave behind an imprint that does not fill in, and the dough should hold its shape without collapsing.

SLASHING LOAVES

Some recipes, such as Baguettes (page 284), call for slashing the dough, or cutting slits in it before baking. This allows the carbon dioxide and steam that builds up during baking to be released. Do not be timid about slashing. If you go a little deeper and make the slashes slightly longer, the result will be more beautiful than if you just skim the surface of the dough.

To slash the dough, hold a sharp paring knife or a single-edged razor blade at a shallow (45-degree) angle so that you cut just under the surface of the dough. Make 2 to 5 slits, depending on the shape of the dough, or according to the recipe.

For round loaves, you can slash the dough to create different designs on top of the bread. For example, to slash a crescent, hold the blade at a shallow (45-degree) angle. Starting at the side of the loaf farthest away from you, slash a slit along the curve of the loaf on the right or left side, positioning the cut just off-center.

To slash a crisscross, hold the blade straight over the center of the loaf. Starting at the far side of the loaf, slash a straight slit across the center of the round. Turn the pan so the slit is vertical to you, and slash a perpendicular slit from one side of the loaf to the other.

BAKING & COOLING BREADS

About 20 minutes before baking, or 30 minutes if preheating a baking stone at the same time, preheat the oven to the temperature specified in a recipe. If using dark-finish pans or glass baking dishes, lower the oven temperature by 25°F (4°C), as these pans cook food through more quickly.

Using a baking stone gives good results in bread baking. The preheated stone helps replicate the brick floor of a baking oven, radiating heat and creating a very hot surface on which to place a loaf pan or sheet pan. Unless otherwise specified, bread should be baked on an oven rack in the center of the oven for the most even baking and a well-browned bottom crust. Leave at least 2 inches (5 cm) of space between loaves or pans to allow for heat to circulate. Breads on baking sheets are best baked in the center of the oven, one sheet at a time. If you have a large oven, arrange the racks in the lower and upper third positions and bake as directed for half the baking time, then exchange the positions of the baking sheets to finish baking.

Loaves are done baking when they have turned golden brown. Breads baked in loaf pans will start to pull away from the pan sides. They should sound hollow when tapped on the top and bottom with your finger. Many bakers swear by the method of checking a loaf's internal temperature with an instant-read thermometer to determine its doneness. To do this, insert a thermometer into the side of the bread just above (but not touching) the pan rim. Breads are thoroughly baked when a thermometer registers 190°F (88°C). Note that a loaf has not completely finished baking until it is completely cool, at which point all the moisture has evaporated.

Unless otherwise indicated in a recipe, once a loaf has finished its time in the oven, it should be removed immediately from its pan or baking sheet by being turned out onto a rack to cool. The rack is important, as it allows air to circulate, thus preventing steam from softening the bottom of the loaf.

STORING YEAST BREADS

For short-term storage, place cooled loaves in moisture-proof bags at room temperature or in an old-fashioned bread box. Country-type breads made without fat are best eaten the day they are made. In general, refrigeration should be avoided, as it quickly draws out moisture. If, however, breads contain perishable ingredients such as cheese or other dairy products, refrigeration halts rancidity.

The best way to store bread for more than a few days is to let it cool completely and then freeze it. Wrap it airtight in plastic wrap to prevent freezer burn, then in a layer of aluminum foil or a zippered plastic freezer bag. Freeze for up to 3 months. Thaw frozen loaves at room temperature for at least 3 hours in their freezer wrappings, shaking out any accumulated ice crystals. Unwrap the bread and reheat in a 325°F (165°C) oven until the bread is heated through and the crust is crisp, 8 to 10 minutes. Smaller loaf breads and rolls are best reheated wrapped in foil since they tend to dry out quickly. Refresh sliced breads in a toaster and rolls in a microwave at 1-minute intervals.

Glossary

ALMOND PASTE See page 265.

APPLES, BAKING See page 244.

BACON, SMOKED See page 113.

BAKING PANS Used for brownies or other bar cookies, baking pans can be deep glass or ceramic dishes, or metal pans. They come in all shapes and sizes. Foods bake more quickly in glass or ceramic dishes, so if a recipe has been written for a metal pan, you may need to reduce baking times and temperatures if using a baking dish.

BAKING POWDER VS. BAKING SODA Baking powder and baking soda are chemical leaveners. They work by reacting with both liquids and heat to release carbon dioxide gas, which in turn leavens a batter, causing it to rise as it cooks. Baking powder is a mixture of an acid and an alkaline, or base, that is activated when it is exposed to moisture or heat. Double-acting baking powder contains two acids. The first acid reacts while mixing the batter, and the second acid reacts in the oven during the baking process. Baking soda, also called bicarbonate of soda, is an alkaline, or base, that releases carbon dioxide gas only when it comes into contact with an acidic ingredient, such as sour cream, buttermilk, or molasses.

BAKING SHEETS The most commonly used pans for baking cookies, baking sheets are rectangular metal pans with shallow, slightly sloping rims. They come in several forms, including the half-sheet pan and the jelly-roll pan.

BANANAS See page 66.

BIGA Rustic-style breads, such as Ciabatta (page 287), are often made with an Italian-style starter called a *biga*, which is firm like a bread dough rather than soft like a sponge (page 396). The *biga* must rest overnight, so plan to make breads using a *biga* over the course of 2 days.

BOURBON This slightly sweet whiskey takes its name from a county in Kentucky and is made from fermented grain, primarily corn. Straight bourbon must be at least 51 percent corn.

BRAN FLAKES, UNPROCESSED See page 106.

BUTTER, UNSALTED See page 26.

BUTTERMILK See page 136.

CHEESE Made from sheep, goat, or cow's milk in countless varieties, cheese adds unique flavor and texture to biscuits, breads, and other baked goods.

Goat A longtime specialty of French cheese makers, goat cheese is sold in a range of styles, from only a few days old and quite soft to months old and very dry. As the cheese ages, its flavor becomes more pungent and pronounced. Soft fresh goat cheeses are sold in *tommes*—small to medium rounds—or shaped into pyramids, balls, or logs. They may be seasoned with herbs, pepper, or nuts, or they may be rolled in ashes. Hard-aged goat cheese usually comes in the form of a *tomme.*

Roquefort Near the village of Roquefort in southern France are ancient caves where the world-famous Roquefort cheese is aged. A blue mold, *Penicillium roqueforti,* thrives there in the cool, damp atmosphere. The same species of mold is now used all over the world to create blue cheeses such as Stilton in England; Gorgonzola in Italy; and Wisconsin blue, Maytag blue, and others in the United States.

Gruyère See page 149.

Cheddar See page 139.

Monterey jack This soft, white, mild cow's milk cheese originated in California and may be smooth or have tiny "eyes."

Ricotta See page 254.

Jarlsberg Made from partially skimmed cow's milk, this cheese is characterized by its hole-filled interior and mild, slightly nutty flavor.

Parmesan This aged, firm cheese has a pale yellow color and slightly salty flavor. Made from partially skimmed cow's milk, Parmesan is aged for 1 to 3 years in large wheels to achieve a granular texture and rich, complex flavor. The trademarked name Parmigiano-Reggiano refers to true Parmesan, produced in the Emilia-Romagna region of northern Italy.

Mozzarella Originally from Italy, mozarella cheese was traditionally made from the milk of water buffaloes, but now is usually made from cow's milk. It is available in both the familiar supermarket version and in a fresh version—rolled by hand into small or medium balls (the smallest of which are called *bocconcini,* meaning "little mouthfuls), packed in water, and with a distinctive milky taste.

CHERRIES In all forms, cherries add a sweet, sometimes tart accent to muffins, quick breads, cookies, and other baked goods.

Candied, red Also known as glacéed cherries, these cherries are used chiefly in breads, cakes, and puddings. Look for them in gourmet food shops and store in an airtight container in a cool, dry place. Dried cherries can be substituted but will alter the texture and taste of the final product.

Fresh See page 220.

Sour See page 99.

Dried tart Unlike dried sweet Bing cherries, sun-dried tart cherries contribute a sweet-tart flavor as well as color to baked goods. Look for them in specialty-foods shops.

CHESTNUTS, CANDIED Known in French as *marrons glacées*, these chestnuts are packed in a sugar syrup and sold in cans or jars. They can be found at specialty-foods stores.

CHOCOLATE TYPES See pages 29 and 103.

CITRUS ZEST, CANDIED Candied citrus zest is a delcious addition to cookies, cakes, and breads. To make your own, see page 378. Or, you can buy candied zest at most specialty-foods stores.

COCOA POWDER See page 83.

COOKIE CUTTERS The best quality cookie cutters are made of metal, so that the cutting side holds its edge. Cookie cutters come in differerent shapes and sizes, from basic rounds to holiday icons and seasonal motifs. When using cookie cutters, dip them in flour periodically so they won't stick to the dough, and cut as many cookies as you can at one time. Carefully lift away the unshaped edges (scraps), and use a wide spatula to transfer the cutout cookies to the prepared baking sheet.

COOLING RACKS Almost all baked goods benefit from cooling on wire racks, which permit air to circulate on all sides. The racks, which come in squares, rectangles, and rounds and stand on short legs, are made of tinned steel, stainless steel, anondized aluminum, or chrome- or nickel-plated metal. Have on hand enough racks to handle 2 baking sheets of cookies.

COOKIE SHEETS Flat metal pans, cookie sheets usually have a low rim on one or two ends to allow for sliding cookies onto a cooling rack. Avoid very dark sheets, which may cause your cookies to overbrown or burn. Nonstick cookie sheets work well and are easy to clean. Insulated cookie sheets, which have an interior air pocket between two layers of metal, guarantee that no cookie will ever have an overbrowned bottom. They do not, however, work well for thin, crisp cookies, which benefit from intense heat. You will want to have at least 2 cookie sheets on hand when baking big batches of cookies.

CORN SYRUP This syrup, made from cornstarch, is a common commercial sweetener, but it can also be used in home cooking and baking. Available in dark and light versions, it adds moisture and chewiness to cakes and cookies.

CORNMEAL, YELLOW See page 92.

CORNSTARCH Also called cornflour, cornstarch is a highly refined, silky powder ground from the endosperm of corn—the white heart of the kernel. It is used as a neutral-flavored thickening agent in fruit fillings, puddings, and glazes. Fillings and glazes thickened with cornstarch have a glossy sheen, unlike those thickened with flour, which are opaque. Recipes that call for cornstarch require additional cooking to eliminate any starchy taste.

CREAM OF TARTAR This white powder is potassium tartrate, a by-product of wine making. It is used to stabilize egg whites so that they whip up more easily. Cream of tartar also inhibits sugar from crystallizing, adds creaminess to frosting, and contributes to whiter, finer crumbs and greater loft in cakes. It is also mixed with baking soda to create baking powder.

CRÈME FRAÎCHE A soured cultured cream product originally from France, crème fraîche is similar to sour cream but sweeter and milder with a hint of nuttiness. It may be purchased, or to make your own, see page 378.

CURRANTS, DRIED While fresh currants are berrylike fruits grown and used widely in Europe, dried currants are actually Zante grapes, tiny raisins with a distinctively tart-sweet flavor. If they are unavailable, substitute raisins.

DATES See page 75.

DOUBLE BOILER A set of two pans, one nesting atop the other, outfitted with a lid that fits both pans. A small amount of water is barely simmered in the lower pan, while ingredients are placed in the top pan to heat them gently, keep them warm, or melt them. To improvise a double boiler, see page 257.

EGGS, RAW Uncooked eggs carry a risk of being infected with salmonella or other bacteria, which can lead to food poisoning. This risk is of most concern to young children, older people, pregnant women, and anyone with a compromised immune system. If you have health and safety concerns, do not consume raw egg; you can seek out a pasteurized egg product to replace it. Eggs can also be made safe by heating them to 160°F (71°C).

ESPRESSO POWDER, INSTANT See page 43.

EXTRACTS These concentrated flavorings made from plants are often used to flavor sweet recipes. Extracts are made by distilling the essential oils of a plant and then suspending the oils in alcohol. Among the most common extracts used in baking are vanilla, almond, coconut, anise, and mint. When possible, choose pure extracts over imitation flavorings, which rely on synthetic compounds and have a less complex flavor. Store extracts in a cool, dark place for up to 1 year. For more on vanilla extract, see pages 102 and 397.

FIGS, DRIED See page 89.

FLOURS When finely ground, grains, dried vegetables, or nuts may all be flours, which are used to provide the body and substance of breads, cakes, and cookies.

All-purpose This popular general-use flour is made from a mixture of soft and hard wheats, with the bran and germ removed. It is available both bleached and unbleached. Some bakers prefer to use only unbleached flour to avoid an unnecessary chemical and because they believe they can taste the difference in the finished product.

Bread An unbleached, hard-wheat flour, bread flour has a high protein content that creates an elastic dough for higher rise and more structure. Some bread flours include malted barley flour to feed the yeast.

Cake See page 170.

Corn The Mexican corn flour used for making tortillas and tamales, *masa harina* is made by grinding corn kernels that have been simmered in a slaked lime solution and then dried. It is sold in well-stocked food stores and in Latin markets.

Garbanzo See page 96.

Graham A type of whole-wheat flour in which parts of the wheat kernel are ground together separately and then mixed together. It has a pleasant coarse texture.

Pastry With slightly more protein than cake flour, pastry flour has the additional structure needed for puffed and layered pastry dough but is more tender than all-purpose (plain) flour.

Rye See page 301.

Semolina This somewhat coarse flour is milled from durum wheat, a variety that is high in protein. The flour is preferred for use in the manufacture of dried pasta. It is also used in some bread doughs.

Whole-Wheat See page 69.

GANACHE A rich mixture of chocolate melted in heavy cream, ganache is used as a glaze or icing for cakes and pastries.

GELATIN, UNFLAVORED POWDERED See page 226.

HAM, BLACK FOREST Traditionally, this ham is made in Germany according to strict guidelines. It is carefully seasoned, cured, and then smoked. The Black Forest ham that is widely available in the United States is smoked ham with a dark exterior made to look like the traditional version.

HERBS The fragrant leaves and tender stems of green plants, herbs enliven breads, muffins, egg dishes, and more. Most are best when used fresh, although heartier varieties can be used dried. Seek out fresh herbs that look bright and healthy and are fragrant. To store fresh herbs, wrap them in damp paper towels, then store in a tightly sealed plastic bag in the crisper drawer of your refrigerator. Alternatively, keep long-stemmed herbs in a container of water, like a bouquet of flowers. Replace dried herbs after 6 months, as they fade in color, fragrance, and flavor.

Basil Used in kitchens throughout the Mediterranean and in Southeast Asia, basil tastes faintly of anise and cloves. Many different varieties are available, including common green Italian basil and reddish purple Thai basil.

Chives The slender, bright green stems of chives are used to give an onionlike flavor without the bite. The hollow, grasslike leaves can be snipped with a pair of kitchen scissors to any length and scattered over egg dishes or any dish that could benefit from a boost of mild oniony flavor.

Cilantro Also called fresh coriander and Chinese parsley, cilantro is a distinctly flavored herb used extensively in Mexican, Asian, Indian, Latin, and Middle Eastern cuisines. It is best when added at the end of cooking; its flavor disappears during long exposure to heat. When shopping, do not confuse cilantro and flat-leaf (Italian) parsley, which look very similar and can be mistaken for each other.

Marjoram Similar in taste to oregano, but with a milder and sweeter flavor, marjoram is available fresh in many supermarkets and produce stores. It is also easily grown at home.

Mint The mint family includes hundreds of species, but the variety most commonly used in the kitchen is spearmint. Fresh mint is both easily grown and widely available.

Oregano Aromatic, pungent, and spicy, this herb is also known as wild marjoram. It can be used fresh or dried as a seasoning for all kinds of savory dishes and is especially compatible with tomatoes. Mexican oregano has a flavor distinct from the other varieties and is worth seeking out for Mexican recipes.

Parsley Flat-leaf parsley, also called Italian parsley, has a more complex and refreshing flavor than curly leaf parsley. Although curly leaf parsley makes a decorative garnish, it imparts little distinctive flavor to a dish. For best results, always use fresh flat-leaf parsley for cooking.

Rosemary See page 367.

Savory With a taste resembling both thyme and mint, savory can be found in two varieties: summer and winter. Both are quite potent and should be used sparingly to season dishes.

HONEY The natural, sweet, syruplike substance produced by bees from flower nectar, honey subtly reflects the color, taste, and aroma of the blossoms from which it was made. Milder varieties, such as clover and orange blossom, are the best choices for general cooking. For more on honey varieties, see page 145.

KEY LIMES See page 241.

LINGONBERRIES See page 362.

LIQUEURS Often called crèmes, liqueurs are spirits flavored by natural extracts, essential oils, pure fruit syrups, sugar syrups, or in the case of liqueurs of lesser quality, chemical extracts. A liqueur may be sipped in small quantity as an after-dinner drink or used to flavor desserts and sauces. Following are the liqueurs used in this book.

Amaretto See page 118.

Chambord Named for the Loire Valley's largest Renaissance chateau, Chambord is a rich purple-rose blackberry liqueur flavored with honey, vanilla, mace, ginger, and other spices and aged in wooden barrels. Packed in a distinctive clear, round glass bottle with a gold, crown-shaped cap (in acknowledgment of its noble name), Chambord is often served neat as an after-dinner drink and is also a popular ingredient in cocktails. Its flavor marries well with chocolate.

Cognac This double-distilled brandy is made only in the Charente and Charente-Maritime areas in western France. Smooth and potent, Cognac derives its distinctive flavors from the region's chalky soil in which the grapes are grown and from the special oak barrels used for aging. Cognac is labeled according to barreling age: V.S. (Very Special) has been aged for at least two years, while V.O. (Very Old), V.S.O.P. (Very Special Old Pale), and Réserve have been finished in wood for at least four years. Cognacs labeled X.O., Vieille Réserve, or Hors d'Age have been aged for at least six years, although many top-quality Cognacs are aged longer.

Cointreau See page 246.

Grand Marnier The grande dame of orange-flavored liqueurs, which also include Cointreau, curaçao, and Triple Sec, Grand Marnier is made by flavoring brandy with bitter Haitian orange peel, vanilla, and spices. It is typically sipped over ice when not being used—always sparingly—in desserts and sauces.

Kahlúa Produced in Mexico, this liqueur is coffee-flavored with notes of vanilla and chocolate.

Kirsch Also known as kirschwasser, this clear brandy of German origins is made from cherries.

MANGO This highly aromatic fruit was first cultivated in India. Now, mangoes are among the most commonly eaten fresh fruits in the world. When shopping for ripe mangoes, choose fruits that emit a full aroma at their stem end, give slightly to gentle pressure, and have smooth skin. For more on preparing mangoes, see page 158.

MAPLE SYRUP See page 108.

MARZIPAN See page 191.

MERINGUE POWDER This pasteurized egg product, made from egg whites, sugar, cornstarch (cornflour), vanilla flavoring, and other ingredients, allows bakers to avoid the use of raw egg whites, which in rare instances can be a health risk. Once opened, store in an airtight container in the refrigerator.

MILK POWDER Made from dehydrated milk solids, dried milk powders are sometimes used in baking recipes when excess liquid would cause the batter or dough to be thin. You can find it in well-stocked supermarkets.

MILK, UNSWEETENED COCONUT Coconut milk, which is thicker and richer than coconut water, is extracted from grated coconut meat and is a labor of love to make at home. Canned unsweetened coconut milk is a fine convenience product; be sure to shake the can well before using.

MOLASSES A thick, robust-tasting syrup, molasses is a by-product of cane sugar refining. Each step in the molasses-making process produces a different type of molasses. Mixed with pure cane syrup, light molasses has the lightest flavor and color. Dark molasses is thicker, darker, and stronger in flavor and less sweet than light molasses. Both light and dark molasses may be bleached with sulfur dioxide. Processed without sulfur, unsulfured molasses has a milder flavor. Molasses gives a distinctive flavor to many sweet and savory baked foods.

MUSHROOMS Many varieties of exotic mushrooms are in the market these days, some gathered from the wild and others cultivated commercially. Forest-gathered mushrooms, such as chanterelles, porcini (cèpes), morels, and others, can be found seasonally at specialty grocers and farmers' markets. Cultivated varieties, like portobello, cremini, shiitake, oyster, and enoki mushrooms, can be found in most markets year-round. Because they absorb water readily, mushrooms will become soggy and flavorless if immersed in water for too long. To clean them, wipe with a damp towel or brush.

NECTARINES See page 230.

NUTS Below are some nuts commonly used in baking recipes. For more information on toasting nuts, see page 53, and for grinding nuts, see page 58.

Almonds With their delicate flavor and smooth texture, almonds are delicious in baked goods. Sliced, blanched (peeled), slivered, whole, and salted almonds are all easy to find in supermarkets. To blanch almonds at home, place the shelled nuts in a large heatproof bowl and pour boiling water over them. Let stand for about 1 minute, then drain the nuts in a colander and rinse with cold running water to cool. Pinch each nut to slip off its bitter skin.

Brazil nuts Enclosed in a dark, hard, roughly textured shell shaped like a small orange segment, Brazil nuts taste somewhat like the meat of a coconut. The seeds of very tall trees that grow only in tropical regions of South America, they require time and skill to harvest. Brazil nuts are best eaten as snacks or used in desserts.

Hazelnuts See page 70.

Macadamia See page 122.

Pecans See page 21.

Pine nuts The seeds of certain pine species, pine nuts can be found nestled in the scales of pine cones. They are small and rich, with an elongated, slightly tapered shape and a resinous, sweet flavor.

Pistachios See page 330.

Walnuts See page 111.

OATS See page 317.

OLIVE OIL A staple of Mediterranean cooking, olive oil is both delicious and healthful. France, Spain, Italy, Greece, California, and Australia all produce high-quality olive oils. Extra-virgin oils are pressed without the use of heat or chemical solvents. Depending on the location and type of olive, the color of these oils can range from a rich gold to a murky deep green. Show off the rich flavor of extra-virgin olive oil by using it uncooked in vinaigrettes, as a seasoning, or as a condiment. "Pure" olive oil is extracted from a subsequent pressing, usually by means of heat or chemicals, and generally has a less distinctive olive flavor. It is often labeled simply "olive oil" and is good for general cooking, frying, or sautéing. Olive oil will solidify at cold temperatures; store it in a cool dark place rather than in the refrigerator.

OLIVE VARIETIES See page 314.

PARCHMENT PAPER See page 326.

PEACHES, PEELING See page 178.

PIE PANS VS. PIE DISHES See page 266.

PIE WEIGHTS Also known as pastry weights, these small aluminum or ceramic pellets are used, along with parchment (baking) paper or aluminum foil, to weight down pastry dough when it is partially or fully baked (see page 385). Raw short-grain rice will work in their place. If blind baking 2-inch (5-cm) tartlets, paper muffin-cup liners and coins are quick and easy substitutes for parchment paper and pie weights.

POLENTA See page 93.

PUMPKIN PURÉE See page 255.

RICE, ARBORIO Arborio is an Italian rice with a large, plump grain and high starch content, which makes it ideal for risotto. Arborio is characterized as a "superfine" rice.

ROLLING PIN Chief among the most essential tools for pie and tart bakers, rolling pins come in various styles. A heavy, smooth hardwood or marble pin at least 15 inches (38 cm) long is best. Some bakers prefer a French-style pin without handles, either a straight dowel or a dowel with tapered ends, while others prefer pins with handles. If you choose the latter, look for one with handles that move on ball bearings for the smoothest roll.

SALT One of the most important and basic of all seasonings, salt heightens the other flavors in a dish and is used in nearly every recipe, savory or sweet.

Kosher Kosher salt is preferred over table salt by many cooks because it has no additives and because its coarse grains are easy to pick up in the fingers to add to foods when cooking. Don't use kosher salt in baking recipes unless it is specified; it can throw off the results.

Sea Gathered from salt pans on the edge of the sea, this salt contains no additives and has a clean, natural taste. It comes in both fine and coarse grinds; fine sea salt is best for most cooking.

Table The most common of the various kinds of salt available, table salt usually contains added iodine along with additives that prevent it from caking and keep it pouring easily.

SAVARIN MOLD A specialty ring mold oringinally used to make a yeast-risen, syrup-soaked cake of the same name. Unlike classic ring molds, savarin molds have rounded rather than flat bases. Classic ring molds can be substituted in most recipes.

SHALLOTS See page 90.

SHORTENING, VEGETABLE Solid vegetable fat made by hydrogenating a vegetable oil, such as cottonseed or soybean, shortening contains millions of tiny air bubbles and so requires less creaming than butter and makes tender, light-textured baked goods. Because it is virtually flavorless, shortening is sometimes used in place of, or in combination with, butter.

SHREDDED SWEETENED COCONUT See page 251.

SKIMMER With a long handle and a large flat strainer or shallow bowl of wire mesh, a skimmer is designed to remove the scum or foam from the top of simmering stocks. It is also the perfect tool for scooping items like bagels, donuts, eggs, or other small pieces of food from boiling water or hot oil.

SPICES Essential oils are the source of flavor in spices, but they will evaporate over time, so replace your spices periodically. If stored in tightly closed containers in a cool, dark place, ground spices will keep for about 6 months and whole spices for about 1 year. Purchase spices in small amounts from stores with high turnover, and label them with the date of purchase. For the most pronounced flavor, use whole spices and grind them fresh (see page 182).

Allspice See page 72.

Aniseed See page 23.

Cardamom This intense spice is the dried fruit of a plant in the ginger family. Cardamom is highly aromatic and has an exotic flavor. Its small, round seeds, which come enclosed in a husklike pod, may be purchased whole or already ground.

Cayenne pepper Ground dried red cayenne chiles yield a bright orange-red powder that adds spark to many savory dishes. Use just a tiny amount at first and then increase it according to your taste, as it is a powerful ingredient.

Chile powder, ancho Considered to be the best pure chile powder, this spice is made from mild, dark reddish brown, squat-looking dried poblano chiles. The powder packs a bit of heat along with a natural sweetness.

Chili powder Chili powder is a commercial spice blend that combines ground dried chiles with spices such as cumin, garlic, oregano, and coriander. Chili powder is not to be confused with pure chile powder, the lightly toasted ground powder of an individual variety of chile, such as ancho or pasilla.

Cinnamon See page 296.

Cloves See page 334.

Coriander This spice is the dried ripe fruit of fresh coriander, or cilantro. Coriander is a relative of parsley. Its tiny, round ridged "seeds" have an aroma said to be like a combination of lemon, sage, and caraway. The ground seeds add an exotic flavor to both savory and sweet foods, including baked goods.

Fennel seeds These muted green, ridged seeds have a delicate anise flavor. They are commonly used to season both sweet and savory dishes and liqueurs.

Ginger A knobby, brown rhizome, or underground stem, from a tropical plant, ginger has a warm, spicy fragrance and flavor. For cookies and other baked goods, ginger is most often used ground.

Mace When the bright red, lacy membrane that covers the nutmeg seed inside the fruit is removed and dried, it turns orange-yellow and is sold as mace, usually in ground form.

Nutmeg See page 193.

Paprika, Hungarian Made from ground dried red peppers and ranging from orange-red to red, paprika is used both as a garnish and as a flavoring. Hungary makes the finest paprika. Three basic types are available: sweet, half-sweet, and hot. Sweet paprika is the most commonly used.

Pepper, white Made from peppercorns that have had their skins removed and berries dried, white pepper is often less aromatic and more mild in flavor than black pepper. It is favored in the preparation of light-colored sauces when cooks want to avoid flecks of black pepper in the final dish.

SPONGE A portion of dough that is prepared ahead of time and allowed to ferment—developing a spongy consistency—before being mixed with remaining ingredients. It is usually a combination of yeast, water, and flour. For more information about dough sponges, see page 280.

SPRINGFORM PANS See page 198.

SUGAR Processed from sugar cane or sugar beets, sugar imparts sweetness, moisture, and flavor to baked goods. It contributes texture, encourages yeast to grow, helps to aerate ingredients, stabilizes egg whites, and is used for decoration. Following are the several types of sugar most commonly used in baking.

Brown See page 288.

Coarse See page 24.

Confectioners' Also called powdered or icing sugar, confectioners' sugar is granulated sugar that has been crushed to a powder and mixed with a little cornstarch (cornflour).

Granulated The most common sugar is granulated white sugar, which has been extracted from sugarcane or beets and refined by boiling, centrifuging, chemical treatment, and straining. For baking, buy only sugar labeled cane sugar; beet sugar may have an unpredictable effect on many recipes.

Raw Most sugars marketed as "raw" are actually partially refined. Turbinado, a common raw sugar, has light brown, coarse crystals. Demerara and Barbados are also varieties of raw sugar.

Superfine Also known as caster sugar, this finely ground granulated sugar is often called for in drinks and other recipes in which it is important that the sugar dissolve quickly. It is ideal for making candied citrus peel because the sugar will coat the peel evenly. To make your own superfine sugar, whirl granulated sugar in a blender or food processor for a few seconds.

TAPIOCA See page 261.

VANILLA Lending perfume, depth, and nuance to a wide variety of baked goods, vanilla may be used either in its whole-bean form or as vanilla extract. A vanilla bean is the cured pod of a type of climbing orchid. There are three primary types of vanilla beans: Bourbon-Madagascar, Tahitian, and Mexican. Bourbon-Madagascar beans, the most common, make up about three-fourths of the world's supply of vanilla. They have a stronger flavor than the more floral Tahitian beans. Mexican beans carry the boldest flavor of the three. Some Mexican beans are known to contain coumarin, however, a substance that can be toxic, so purchase them only from a reputable source. Most recipes call for a whole or half vanilla bean split lengthwise. Splitting the pod allows the tiny seeds to escape and their flavor to permeate a dish. Vanilla extract is made by chopping the beans and soaking them in a mixture of alcohol and water, then aging the solution. Avoid imitation vanilla, which is made of artificial flavorings and has an inferior taste. Vanilla extract is most often made from Bourbon-Madagascar beans, and the best-quality vanilla extracts should state this on their label.

VINEGAR, CIDER Made from apples, cider vinegar is commonly used in many traditional American recipes and is noted for its distinctive apple flavor. For the best flavor, buy real cider vinegar, not cider-flavored distilled vinegar.

VITAL WHEAT GLUTEN See page 285.

WALNUT OIL See page 104.

WHEAT GERM, TOASTED Rich in many vitamins and minerals, wheat germ is the part of the wheat berry that is responsible for the germination of new wheat plants. It is available in its toasted form at most health food stores.

WHITE CHOCOLATE Despite its name, white chocolate is nothing more than cocoa butter, sugar, and milk solids. It does not contain cocoa or chocolate liquor, which explains its ivory color. Choose the brand you prefer from any number of high-quality chocolate manufacturers such as Lindt, Callebaut, or Valrhona. White chocolate will not melt as easily as dark chocolate; as it is stirred, however, it will smooth out. Do not confuse white chocolate with a similar product called confectionery coating, which is bright white and made with vegetable fat flavored to taste like chocolate.

Measuring liquids by volume

When measuring liquids, use standard measuring spoons for small amounts. For amounts over 3 tablespoons, use a liquid measuring cup. Make sure to place the measuring cup on a flat surface and pour in the liquid. Let the liquid settle, then read the measurement at eye level. The table below can help you when multiplying recipes for larger servings.

TEASPOONS		TABLESPOONS		FLUID OUNCES		CUPS		PINTS		QUARTS		GALLONS
3 teaspoons	=	1 tablespoon	=	½ fluid ounce								
		2 tablespoons	=	1 fluid ounce								
		4 tablespoons	=	2 fluid ounces	=	¼ cup						
		8 tablespoons	=	4 fluid ounces	=	½ cup						
		16 tablespoons	=	8 fluid ounces	=	1 cup						
				16 fluid ounces	=	2 cups	=	1 pint				
				32 fluid ounces	=	4 cups	=	2 pints	=	1 quart		
				128 fluid ounces	=	16 cups	=	8 pints	=	4 quarts	=	1 gallon

Metric Conversions by volume

To convert tablespoons to mililiters, multiply the number of tablespoons by 14.79. To convert ounces to grams (right), multiply the number of ounces by 28.35.

U.S	METRIC
1 teaspoon	5 milliliters
1 tablespoon	15 milliliters
¼ cup	59 milliliters
1 cup	236 milliliters
1 pint	473 milliliters
1 quart	946 milliliters
1 gallon	3.8 liters
METRIC	**U.S.**
10 milliliters	2 teaspoons
30 milliliters	1 fluid ounce
100 milliliters	½ cup minus 1 tablespoon
500 milliliters	2 cups plus 2 tablespoons
1 liter	4¼ cups, or 1 quart plus ¼ cup

Metric Conversions by mass

U.S.	METRIC
1 ounce	28.35 grams
1 pound	454 grams (0.45 kilogram)
METRIC	**U.S.**
100 grams	3.5 ounces
500 grams	1.1 pounds (17.6 ounces)
1 kilogram	2.2 pounds (35.2 ounces)

High-Altitude Baking

Below are some adjustments you can make to ingredient amounts when baking at 3,000 feet and above.

INGREDIENT	ADJUSTMENT
Eggs	Add an additional egg to delicate, airy batters (popovers, sponge cakes)
Egg whites	Do not beat beyond soft peaks for meringues or cake batters
Leavener	Decrease by one-quarter the amount
Sugar	Reduce every 1 cup sugar by 1–2 Tbsp

Volume of Standard Baking Pans

Use this chart to compare the volumes of pan sizes when substituting one pan for another.

PAN	DIMENSIONS	VOLUME
Square	8 x 8 x 1½ inches	6 cups
	8 x 8 x 2 inches	8 cups
	9 x 9 x 2 inches	10 cups
	10 x 10 x 2 inches	12 cups
	12 x 12 x 2 inches	16 cups
Rectangular	11 x 7 x 2 inches	8 cups
	13 x 9 x 2 inches	12 cups
Jelly Roll	10½ x 15½ x 1 inch	10 cups
Loaf	8 x 4 x 2½ inches	4 cups
	8½ x 4½ x 2½ inches	6 cups
	9 x 5 x 3 inches	8 cups
Round	6 x 2 inches	3¾ cups
	8 x 1½ inches	4 cups
	8 x 2 inches	7 cups
	9 x 1½ inches	6 cups
	9 x 2 inches	8½ cups
	10 x 2 inches	10¾ cups
	12 x 2 inches	15½ cups
	14 x 2 inches	21 cups
Springform	9 x 2¾ inches	10 cups
	9 x 3 inches	12 cups
	10 x 2¾ inches	12 cups
Bundt	9 x 3 inches	9 cups
	10 x 3½ inches	12 cups
Tube	9 x 3 inches	10 cups
	10 x 4 inches	16 cups

Common Liqueur Flavors

Liqueurs add unique flavor to baked goods. Listed below are the most commonly used liqueurs for popular flavors.

FLAVOR	LIQUEUR
Almond	amaretto; crème d'amandes; crème de noyaux; Noyau de Poissy
Anise	anisette; ouzo; pastis; Pernod; sambuca
Apricot	crème d'abricot; Abricotine; Apry
Cherry	crème de cerise; maraschino (sweet); Cherry Rocher; Peter Heering; Wishniac
Chocolate	crème de cacao; Chocolat Suisse; Chéri-Suisse (chocolate-cherry); Vandermint (chocolate-mint); Sabra (chocolate-orange)
Coffee	Kahlúa; Kona; Pasha; Tía Maria
Currant, black	crème de cassis
Hazelnut	Frangelico
Herbs & Flowers	Chartreuse (herbs); Chartreuse verte (herbs); Bénédictine (herbs); Liquore Galliano (herbs); crème de rose (rose); crème de violette (violet)
Melon	Midori
Orange	Cointreau; Curaçao; Grand Marnier; mandarine; Triple Sec
Peppermint	crème de menthe; peppermint schnapps
Vanilla	crème de vanille

Frosting Amounts

When filling and covering a cake with light, fluffy frosting, use the larger amount listed below.

CAKE TYPE	AMOUNT
8- or 9-inch cake, 2 layers	2½ to 3 cups
8- or 9-inch cake, 3 layers	3 to 3½ cups
10-inch tube cake	3 to 3½ cups
13 x 9-inch sheet cake	3½ to 4 cups
12 large cupcakes	1½ to 2 cups

Substitutions and equivalents

The following chart lists the equivalent weight or amount for specific measurements of certain foods, as well as acceptable substitutes for certain foods, when available.

FOOD	AMOUNT	EQUIVALENT	SUBSTITUTE
Almonds, whole	1 cup	¾ cup ground	—
Apricots, dried	1 cup	6 ounces	—
Baking powder	1 teaspoon	—	¼ teaspoon baking soda plus ⅝ teaspoon cream of tartar or ½ cup buttermilk or yogurt
Butter	½ stick	4 tablespoons, ¼ cup, 2 ounces	—
	1 stick	8 tablespoons, ½ cup, 4 ounces	—
	2 sticks	1 cup, 8 ounces	⅞ cup vegetable oil or 1 cup lard
	4 sticks	2 cups, 16 ounces (1 pound)	—
Buttermilk	1 cup	8 ounces	1 cup milk plus 1 tablespoon fresh lemon juice, or 1 cup plain yogurt
Cheese	1 cup grated	4 ounces	—
Cherries	1 pound	2 to 2½ cups pitted	—
Chocolate	1 square (1 ounce)	4 tablespoons grated	—
Chocolate chips	6-ounce package	1 cup morsels or bits	—
Coconut, shredded	1 cup	4 ounces	—
Cornstarch	1 tablespoon	—	2 tablespoons flour or 1 tablespoon arrowroot
Cranberries	12-ounce bag	3 cups	—
Cream, heavy	1 cup	2 cups whipped	—
Eggs	1 large	—	¼ cup liquid egg substitute
	1 white, large	2 tablespoons	—
	1 yolk, large	1 tablespoon	—
	5 whole, 7 whites, or 14 yolks, large	1 cup	—
	3 large	—	2 jumbo, 3 extra-large, 3 medium, or 4 small
	4 large	—	3 jumbo, 4 extra-large, 5 medium, or 5 small
	6 large	—	5 jumbo, 5 extra-large, 7 medium, or 8 small

FOOD	AMOUNT	EQUIVALENT	SUBSTITUTE
Flour, cake	1 pound	4½ cups sifted	———
	1 cup	———	1 cup less 2 tablespoons all-purpose flour (with 2 tablespoons cornstarch added if possible)
Flour, self-rising, unsifted	1 cup	5 ounces	1 cup all-purpose flour plus 1½ teaspoons baking powder and ½ teaspoon salt
Gelatin	1 envelope	1 tablespoon	4 sheets gelatin
Hazelnuts, shelled	1 cup	5 ounces	———
Herbs	1 tablespoon (3 teaspoons) fresh	1 teaspoon dried herbs	———
Lemons	1 medium	1 to 3 tablespoons juice, 1½ teaspoons zest	———
Limes	1 medium	1½ to 2 tablespoons juice	———
Milk, whole	1 cup	———	½ cup evaporated milk and ½ cup water; reduce the sugar in the recipe slightly; OR 1 cup skim milk plus 1 tablespoon cream or melted butter
Nuts, whole	4 ounces	¾ to 1 cup chopped; 1 cup ground	———
Oranges	1 medium	⅓ cup juice, 2 to 3 tablespoons zest	———
Prunes	1 pound	2¼ cups pitted	———
Raisins	1 cup	5 ounces	———
Shortening	1 pound	2 cups	2 cups butter (for baking)
Sugar, brown	1 pound	2¼ cups packed	———
	1 cup	———	1 cup granulated sugar combined with 2 tablespoons light or dark molasses
Sugar, confectioners'	1 pound	3½ to 4 cups	———
Sugar, granulated	1 cup	8 ounces	⅞ cup honey
Tapioca, instant	1 tablespoon	———	1 tablespoon flour (for thickening)
Vanilla	1 teaspoon extract	———	1-inch piece vanilla bean, halved and scraped
Yeast, active dry	1 package	2¼ teaspoons	1 cake (.06 ounces) compressed yeast
Yogurt, plain	1 cup	8 ounces	———

CUP
CUP
CUP
CUP

Index

C

G

H

Q

R

U

V

W

Y

Z

ACKNOWLEDGMENTS

Weldon Owen wishes to thank the following people for their generous support in producing this book: Photographers Noel Barnhurst, Bill Bettencourt, Maren Caruso, Sheri Giblin, Jean-Blaise Hall, and Tucker & Hossler; Photographer's Assistants Noriko Akiyama, Faiza Ali, Selena Aument, and Heidi Ledendorf; Food Stylists Sandra Cook, George Dolese, Kim Konecny, and Erin Quon; Cover Food Stylist Kevin Crafts; Assistant Food Stylists Sharon Ardiana, Melinda Barsales, Leslie Busch, Kris Hoogerhyde, Alexa Hyman, Jennifer McConnell, Elisabet der Nederlanden, Lori Nunokawa, and Annie Salisbury; Prop Stylists Carol Hacker and Natalie Hoelen; Decorating Consultant Diane Gsell; Authors Brigit Binns, Abigail Johnson Dodge, Fran Gage, Barbara Grunes, Beth Hensperger, Pamela Sheldon Johns, Farina Wong Kingsley, Carolyn Krebs, Michael McLaughlin, Carolyn Miller, Selma Brown Morrow, Rick Rodgers, Marie Simmons, Marlena Spieler, Marilyn Tausend, Carolyn Beth Weil, and Diane Rossen Worthington; Contributing Writers Kate Chynoweth and Stephanie Rosenbaum; Consulting Editors Carrie Bradley, Judith Dunham, Norman Kolpas, and Sharon Silva; Recipe Consultants Melinda Barsales, Peggy Fallon, Jennifer McConnell, Elisabet der Nederlanden, and Ann Tonai; Copyeditors Kris Balloun, Carrie Bradley, Carolyn Miller, Sharon Silva, Sharron Wood; Proofreaders Desne Ahlers, Linda Bouchard, Carrie Bradley, Kate Chynoweth, and Arin Hailey; Production Assistant Kathy Song; Indexer Elizabeth Parson

PHOTOGRAPHY CREDITS

Noel Barnhurst: pages 1, 2, 12, 13, 14 (recipe), 15, 18–25, 27–29, 32, 33 (recipe), 34–43, 44 (recipe), 45–47, 48 (recipe), 49, 51, 54–61, 64, 65, 66 (recipe), 67–100, 102 (recipe), 103–112, 114–119, 122–124, 126–131, 134–138, 140, 141, 144, 145, 154, 156, 157, 158 (recipe), 162 (sidebar), 164, 165, 168–170, 172, 173, 176–178, 182, 184–189, 193, 196, 197, 202–205, 207–211, 212 (sidebar), 214, 220, 253, 254, 274, 280–291, 294, 295, 298–307, 310–317, 321, 323, 331 (sidebar), 337, 350, 372, 382, 387, 402; Bill Bettencourt: pages 14 (sidebar), 33 (sidebar), 44 (sidebar), 183 (sidebar), 192 (sidebar), 216, 217, 383; Maren Caruso: pages 16, 17, 26, 30, 31, 48 (sidebar), 50, 52, 53, 66 (sidebar), 101, 102 (sidebar), 113, 125, 132, 133, 139, 142, 143, 146–149, 152, 153, 155, 158 (sidebar), 159–161, 163, 166 (recipe), 167, 171, 174, 175, 180, 181, 183 (recipe), 190, 191, 192 (recipe), 194, 195, 198–201, 206, 212 (recipe), 213, 215, 221–252, 255–273, 275–277, 292, 293, 296, 297, 308, 309, 320, 322, 324–330, 331 (recipe), 332–336, 338–347, 351–354, 356–359, 361–371, 380, 384–386, 390; Sheri Giblin: pages 162 (recipe), 355, 360; Jean-Blaise Hall: page 179; Tucker & Hossler: cover; page 166 (sidebar)

OXMOOR HOUSE

Oxmoor House books are distributed by
Time Inc. Home Entertainment
135 West 50th Street, New York, NY 10020

VP and Associate Publisher Jim Childs
Director of Marketing Sydney Webber
Brand Manager Victoria Alfonso

WILLIAMS-SONOMA, INC.

Founder & Vice-Chairman Chuck Williams

WELDON OWEN INC.

Chief Executive Officer & President Terry Newell
Senior Vice President, International Sales Stuart Laurence
Vice President Sales & New Business Development Amy Kaneko
Director of Finance Mark Perrigo

Vice President & Publisher Hannah Rahill
Executive Editor Jennifer Newens
Associate Editor Julia Humes

Vice President & Creative Director Gaye Allen
Associate Creative Director Emma Boys
Designer Lauren Charles

Production Director Chris Hemesath
Production Manager Michelle Duggan
Color Manager Teri Bell

Group Publisher, Bonnier Publishing Group John Owen

Color separations by Embassy Graphics
Printed by Tien Wah Press
Printed in Singapore

THE WILLIAMS-SONOMA BAKING BOOK

Conceived and produced by Weldon Owen Inc.
415 Jackson Street, Suite 200, San Francisco, CA 94111
Telephone: 415 291 0100 Fax: 415 291 8841
www.weldonowen.com

In Collaboration with Williams-Sonoma, Inc.
3250 Van Ness Avenue, San Francisco, CA 94109

A WELDON OWEN PRODUCTION

The recipes in this book have been previously published in individual titles in the Williams-Sonoma Collection series.

First printed in 2009
10 9 8 7 6 5 4 3 2 1

Library of Congress Cataloging-in-Publication
Data is available.
ISBN-13: 978-1-60320-107-0
ISBN-10: 1-60320-107-6

A NOTE ON WEIGHTS AND MEASUREMENTS

All recipes include customary U.S. and metric measurements. Metric conversions are based on a standard developed for this book and have been rounded off. Actual weights may vary.

This book is printed on paper harvested from forests managed with sustainable and environmentally sound practices.